TEA WAR

TEA WAR

A HISTORY OF CAPITALISM IN

CHINA AND INDIA

ANDREW B. LIU

Studies of the Weatherhead East Asian Institute,
Columbia University

The Studies of the Weatherhead East Asian Institute
of Columbia University were inaugurated in 1962 to
bring to a wider public the results of significant new
research on modern and contemporary East Asia.

Yale UNIVERSITY PRESS
New Haven and London

Published with assistance from the Mary Cady Tew Memorial Fund.

Yale University Press books may be purchased in quantity for educational, business, or
promotional use. For information, please e-mail sales.press@yale.edu (U.S. office) or sales@
yaleup.co.uk (U.K. office).

Set in Sabon Roman type by Newgen North America, Austin, Texas.
Printed in the United States of America.

Library of Congress Control Number: 2019947813
ISBN 978-0-300-24373-4 (hardcover : alk. paper)

A catalogue record for this book is available from the British Library.

This paper meets the requirements of ANSI/NISO Z39.48-1992 (Permanence of Paper).

10 9 8 7 6 5 4 3 2

Contents

Acknowledgments

The seeds for this work were planted my sophomore year in college, when I decided on a whim to enroll in the introductory history courses of modern South Asia and China, respectively, in consecutive semesters. Though the details from those courses are blurry now, I distinctly recall being captivated by the appearance of the fateful British-Indian-Chinese triangular trade within both national historiographies, each of which approached it from a distinct angle. Writing this book has been an attempt to explore those global connections further, and it has also presented the stimulating, sometimes overwhelming, challenge of finding a common language to speak to the very different concerns of the two fields.

South Asian history is a fiercely sharp discipline, especially as it was introduced to me by Anupama Rao. As a confused teenager, I found it offered a fresh entry point into the heady theoretical debates swirling around campus and New York City in the 2000s, from postcolonial and subaltern studies to post-Marxist social theory to critical approaches to race and gender. The Chinese history field is steeped in its own rich institutions, of course, and it held a more personal attraction. Though born and raised in the Pacific Northwest, I found the study of modern China immediately familiar yet also an enticing prospect for combining my personal background with the public life (and intellectual rush) of research and argumentation. However, attempting to tackle the entirety of Chinese and Indian history through some abstract comparison seemed not only daunting—encompassing half of humanity, essentially—but also intellectually naive. It has proven far more rewarding to start from a shared concrete process—namely, the opium and then tea trades—and build my categories and units of analysis upward from there, examining how the Chinese, Indian, and British participants were directly interacting across wide expanses of time and space in surprising and fascinating ways. That my research has taken me on a similarly expansive journey was made practicable, even enjoyable, by generous teachers and friends.

I could never have imagined a life of research, writing, and critique without my policy debate family, and I thank them for those early formative experiences. I spent over a decade at Columbia University and formed relationships with faculty in New York that I cherish to this day. I thank Carol Gluck, Yukiko Hanawa, Sudipta Kaviraj, Dorothy Ko, Eugenia Lean, Bill McAllister, and Greg Pflugfelder. Madeleine Zelin was a thoughtful reader of my work, guiding me through the field of Chinese history. Andrew Sartori provided vital, impactful feedback and advice in an informal role. Anupama Rao was my first history professor, and she has never stopped teaching me, surprising me with brilliant insights and making me feel welcome within South Asian studies. Discussions with Harry Harootunian about capitalism and history brought together the many disparate interests in my mind and provided me direction for this project. Rebecca Karl has been my strongest advocate, an exceptional scholar with a clear moral compass and limitless dedication to her students. Finally, I benefited tremendously from my time with my advisor Adam McKeown, who passed away unexpectedly in late 2017. A co-founder of Columbia's International and Global History program, Adam constantly pushed me to think beyond convention, and many of his insights I began to understand only long after he had already left the academy.

Overseas language acquisition and research were made possible by several grants, including Foreign Language and Area Studies grants; a Fulbright-Hays doctoral dissertation grant; a Social Science Research Council (SSRC) International Dissertation Research Fellowship; an American Institute of Indian Studies (AIIS) junior fellowship; a Villanova University Faculty Development Grant; a postdoctoral grant from the Henry Luce Foundation/American Council of Learned Societies Program in China Studies; an SSRC Transregional Research Junior Scholar Fellowship; and a Villanova University subvention of publication.

My studies in East Asia began with a Blakemore Foundation grant, which provided the opportunity to learn from wonderful teachers in the International Chinese Language Program at National Taiwan University. From my experiences in China, I thank, from Xiamen University, Dai Yifeng, Shui Haigang, Zhang Kan, Wang Jun, and Zheng Li; from Anhui Normal University, Kang Jian, Liu Meng, and Wang Shihua; from Fudan University, Wang Zhenzhong and Zou Yi; and from Renmin University, Hu Xiangyu and Wang Pu. I also thank the independent scholar Wang Liping based in Shanghai. I studied Bengali in the New York area with Dwijen Bhattacharjya and Minakshi Datta and then in Kolkata with the AIIS language program, learning from Protima-di and Prasenjit-da. While based at the Centre for Studies in Social Sciences, Calcutta, I learned from historians and students from across India, particularly Rana Behal, Chitra Joshi, Bodhisattva Kar, and Prabhu Mohapatra. I also thank the archivists and librarians who helped me over the years, especially those at the First Historical Archives in China and the Institute of Modern History in Taiwan; the West Bengal State Archives and the National Archives of India; and the British Library and the Cambridge University Library. Research was also made possible by help from the family members of several subjects discussed in this book. I thank the descendants of the Jiang family featured in chapter 2, Jiang Chiyu and Jiang Haoran, as well as Wu Ning, granddaughter of Wu Juenong, featured in chapter 7.

Many friends provided crucial help and sustained my morale throughout the research and writing process. I thank Selda Altan, Ramona Bajema, Aparna Balachandran, Emily Baum, Debjani Bhattacharyya, Joel Bourdeaux, Adam Bronson, Uday Chandra, Becky Chang, James Chappel, Meghna Chaudhuri, BuYun Chen, Chen Wei-chi, Rishad Choudhury, Maggie Clinton, Robert Cole, Stephen Curry and the Golden State Warriors, Rohit De, Anatoly Detwyler, Ariel Fox, Ricky Garner, Aimee Genell, Arunabh Ghosh, Nate Gorelick, Kimberley Hoang, Hsieh I-Yi, Alex Hsu, my friends from INCITE, Paul Johnson, Abhishek Kaicker, Ken Kawashima, Macabe Keliher, S. E. Kile, Yumi Kim, Elizabeth LaCouture, Brian Lander, Liza and Collin Lawrence, James Lin, Wendy Matsumura, Jenny Wang Medina, Owen Miller, Viren Murthy, Golnar Nikpour, Ben Parker, Josh Plumridge, Meha Priyadarshini, Shakeer Rahman, Nate Roberts, Nikil Saval and Shannon Garrison, Chelsea Schieder, Dwaipayan Sen, Jacob Shell, Seiji Shirane, Nate Shockey, Matt Shutzer, Ben Siegel, Rich So, Julie Stephens,

Struggles 5, Simon Taylor, Philip Thai, Brian Tsui, Anand Vaidya, Rupa Viswanath, Stacey Van Vleet, Max Ward, Mari Webel, Benno Weiner, Jake Werner, Albert Wu, Tim Yang, Shirley Ye, and Zhu Qian.

My work also benefited tremendously from feedback provided by senior scholars in various forums. I thank Jeremy Adelman, Jairus Banaji, Ritu Birla, Piya Chatterjee, Alex Day, Prasenjit Duara, Jacob Eyferth, Siyen Fei, Engseng Ho, Chris Isett, Elizabeth Köll, C. K. Lee, Peter Perdue, Kenneth Pomeranz, the late Moishe Postone, Emma Rothschild, William Rowe, and Margherita Zanasi.

I am grateful to the Weatherhead East Asian Institute of Columbia University book series and the tireless efforts of Ross Yelsey; Jaya Chatterjee, Mary Pasti, Eva Skewes, and the entire team at Yale University Press; my copy editor, Eliza Childs; and the anonymous reviewers for both the series and the press.

At Villanova, I have enjoyed the generous support of Albert Lepage and his gift to young historians within the department. My work has been greatly enriched by conversations with colleagues, and I particularly thank Marc Gallicchio, Judith Giesberg, Jeffrey Johnson, Maghan Keita, Catherine Kerrison, Elizabeth Kolsky, Adele Lindenmeyr, Whitney Martinko, Timothy McCall, Paul Rosier, Cristina Soriano, and Paul Steege.

My late grandmother Lee Ting-Shung helped raise me and provoked within me a fateful spark of curiosity about the world she had come from. My parents, Caroline Fong-Chi Yang and Michael Chia-Huei Liu, worked thanklessly long hours to provide for my brother Ken and me, encouraging me to follow my passions and asking for nothing in return. They all have my undying gratitude. Along the way, the entire extended Liu and Yang families nourished me in various stages of life and work across multiple continents. I especially thank Gina, Reid, Lily, and Marie; Elisa, Jonas, Sue-ayi, and Er-yidie; Huimin-gugu, Bahram, and Sina; Shushu and Shenshen; uncle D. Y. and aunt Nini; and uncle B. T. (the resident family historian) and Jenny. Finally, my partner, Reiko, has lived with this project from the start, patiently enduring countless transcontinental flights and sleepless mornings, offering unending love and support at every step. I dedicate this work to her and to our daughter, Mika, to whom the world now belongs.

Note on Spellings, Transliterations, and Translations

Spellings and transliterations are based on contemporary pronunciation, with the exception of place names featuring different conventional or historical spellings, such as Bombay, Calcutta, Canton, Ceylon, Hong Kong, Jorehaut, Madras, and Sibsagar.

Chinese words are spelled in *pinyin* for Mandarin pronunciation unless otherwise noted. Bengali words are spelled based upon a transcription, rather than precise transliteration, of sounds. For instance, the three different "sh" sounds (transcribed as ś, ṣ, s) are represented by only "s" or "sh." Diacritics are used to differentiate between short and long vowels; I spell the inherent vowel with a plain "a." Diacritics are also used for short and long Japanese vowels.

Unless otherwise noted, translations are by the author.

TEA WAR

Introduction

OVER THE COURSE of the twentieth century, Wu Juenong (1897–1989) earned a reputation as the foremost authority on tea in China, writing influential books and spearheading government programs to revive the industry. In his early twenties, as with thousands of his compatriots at the time, he spent several years living in Japan studying foreign languages and sciences. It was in the Makinohara region of Shizuoka prefecture where he first learned the latest techniques for modern tea cultivation. During those years, he recalled, his Japanese classmates at the agricultural college would often pick up pieces of fruit, such as pears or oranges, and ask him, "Are these things in China, too?" Their lack of knowledge was understandable, he explained, for textbooks printed in Japan at the time often proclaimed that different plants and fruits could be found only within the empire's own borders. And tea had been no exception:

> Likewise, ever since England began to operate tea industries in India and Ceylon, and ever since Japan and Taiwan have increased their sales, the question of the birthplace of tea [*yuanchan di*] has become an object of speculation as well. As an extreme illustration of our country's disgraced condition, it has been widely reported that when English and American people see labels for "China Tea," they too will ask skeptically, "is there tea in China, too?"[1]

"Is there tea in China, too?" How could this question even be raised? Tea had long been synonymous with China, down to its two names used across the world's languages, "tea" and "cha": distinct pronunciations of the same Chinese character, 茶. It was in early imperial China where tea was first ritually imbibed as a medicinal and religious drink, and it was eighteenth-century Chinese merchants who helped popularize it as a global commodity, enabling it to become the most consumed commercial beverage in the world today.

And yet: over the course of the next century the Indian tea industry, operated by British colonial planters and based in the northeast territory of Assam, suddenly overtook China as the world's top exporter (figure 1). British and, later, Japanese propagandists seized upon this inversion in the global division of labor. The rise and dominance of Indian tea had been so decisive, they wrote, that it must have been preordained. It was a difference not of degree but of kind, one attributable to the natural properties of the plant itself and its compatibility with

Figure 1. Overall tea exports from China and India, in millions of pounds, 1868–1939. Figures from Hsiao, *Trade Statistics*; Lyons, *Maritime Customs*; ITA Report (1920), 403; (1931), 375; (1940), 201.

the physical landscape. Propagandists dismissed Tang- and Song-era (618–1279) records of tea in China as unreliable, asserting instead that the true "birthplace of tea" must have been in India or Japan.

Among the proponents of this theory was David Crole, an English planter who had managed estates in India for a decade. In a pamphlet printed in 1897, Crole speculated that "the plant must have had its original habitat in the country whose soil, climate, etc., are most suitable to its well-being; and there can be no doubt as to Assam answering these requirements far better than any localities situated within the dominions of the Emperor of China." Elsewhere, he attributed the crisis of Chinese tea to the "obstinate barbarism" of the "Celestials," a "perversely conservative race," in contrast to the "civilization," "intelligence, science, and research" of "the West" (never mind that Assam was a remote frontier between South and Southeast Asia; British planters saw Assam tea as their own creation, and they selectively applied to it the same logic).[2] With his soil theory, Crole was stretching cultural arguments about commercial divergence to an extreme, naturalizing them, literally, into a property of the earth itself. If he believed the Chinese trade had collapsed due to its unchanging native traditions, then he could just as easily blame the Chinese soil and climate as well.

Underlying the ostensibly scientific debate over the birthplace of tea, then, was an overtly political attempt to rationalize the jarring upheavals wrought by the global market across the nineteenth and twentieth centuries. British and Japanese propagandists explained the divergent fates of Chinese and Indian tea as the inevitable product of innate and static civilizational differences, even attributing these economic reversals to the natural properties of the earth itself, distorting the historical record. It was a clear demonstration that the social and economic revolutions that we typically associate with the advent of modern capitalism also brought with them revolutions in perception and ideology. More broadly, while it would sound absurd today to ask whether or not "there is tea in China, too," the same underlying logic of *naturalization* found in Crole's soil theory has continued to be echoed in so many studies on modern Asia since his day. These works have long presumed that the disparate economic fortunes of the world could be explained by "some unique homegrown ingredient of industrial success" found in the "West"—its climate? the soil? civilization and culture?—but nowhere else in the "Rest."[3]

This book both challenges and historicizes such naturalistic explanations of economic change. It does so by presenting the histories of Chinese and colonial Indian tea as a dynamic, unified story of global interaction, one mediated by modern capitalist competition. Across Chinese villages and Indian plantations, I demonstrate, global competition reshaped the rhythms of local social and economic life, and in turn, observers and participants in the tea trade—Chinese, Indian, and British—came to understand this new reality as the natural order of human organization and progress. The global story of tea thus entailed both a history of novel forms of economic life and a history of transformations in economic thought. Their implications shall unsettle many of our conventional assumptions about capitalism in China and India—or its absence thereof—and in so doing, they provocatively contribute to a more global conception of capitalism's history as a whole.

In the following pages, we shall see how although imperial propagandists framed the divergence between Chinese and Indian tea in terms of static civilizational and natural traits, their theories were belied by a far more turbulent history of competition that tied together the agrarian hinterlands of coastal China and eastern India. In a Qing China (1644–1912) liberalized by wars of free trade, merchant financiers traveled from the treaty ports of Canton (Guangzhou), Fuzhou, and Shanghai to rural Anhui and Fujian, where millions of peasant households in the hills and makeshift workshops in the valleys roasted green, oolong, and black teas tailored to the palates of European and American consumers. In the 1830s, British officials established the Indian industry by hiring colonial merchants and botanists to scour Singapore, Canton, and inland China and bring both Chinese tea seedlings and human teamakers back to India. And as commercial pressures reshaped the Asian tea districts at the turn of the century, new generations of Chinese and Indian nationalists forged their own set of political-economic principles to make sense of the laws of global capital. For Wu Juenong in particular, the birthplace of tea controversy—that anyone could even entertain the notion that there was no tea in China—pushed him to devote his life to reviving China's tea trade through "modern capitalist methods," even traveling to India in the 1930s—a mirror image of British colonial adventures one century earlier—to study its new national rivals. The contours of the global tea trade entailed novel horizontal connections across colonial Asia, not only China and India but also

Ceylon, Japan, Taiwan, and the Dutch East Indies. Really, the modern history of tea belonged to the types of "inter-Asian" and "connected" histories foregrounded by scholars in recent years, interactions across the global South long marginalized by analyses rooted in nations, area studies, and center-periphery relations.[4]

Indeed, at the margins of his pamphlet, even Crole himself recognized that the fortunes of each region had been shaped not only by local and natural conditions but primarily by the global and historically contingent "struggle for supremacy between Chinese and British-grown teas." A half century after the first Opium War (1839–1842) had drawn to a close, Crole described the current economic rivalry as "the tea war that has been and is still being waged."[5] At the same moment off the southern coast of China, the famed Qing reformer Zheng Guanying (1842–1922) completed his own magnum opus (1894), unknown then to the English-speaking world, in which he famously described the onslaught of overseas industrial threats facing Chinese tea and silk merchants by conjuring the phrase "commercial warfare" (shangzhan).

If the economic fates of Chinese and Indian tea had diverged at the turn of the century, then they had at the same time been drawn closer together, pitched on opposite sides of a mutual war of competition.

*

Tea War sets out to tell the story of the global tea trade as a history of emergent capitalism in modern China and India. Through a history of economic life and economic thought, it both challenges past depictions of Asian stagnation, as embodied in the birthplace of tea controversy, and also accounts for how such ideas were naturalized in the first place at the turn of the twentieth century. Tea War demonstrates how the producers, merchants, and planters of the Chinese and Indian hinterlands were connected through overlapping circuits of accumulation as well as pressures toward intensive production that they shared in common with the rest of the industrial world. At the same time, these global and dynamic pressures produced, paradoxically, a view of naturalized economic progress that saw Chinese and Indian societies as particular and backwards, a view embraced by nationalist groups across Asia as well. In this book, such ideas shall themselves be read as objects of historical inquiry, for they indexed distinctly modern political-economic views corresponding to novel social patterns found across East and South Asia. Thus, the story of tea ultimately helps us understand both the historical emergence of modern economic concepts *found within* China and India as well as several key ideas *about* modern Asia in its relationship to the rest of the world.

I present this book as an unfolding, back-and-forth dynamic between the two regional tea industries over the course of a century, a global and comparative history grounded in the process of competition. It begins with the end of the English East India Company's monopoly over trade with Canton (1833) and the subsequent Opium War, which produced a massive spike in Chinese tea exports into the 1880s. The colonial Indian industry took off only after planters employed penal labor laws to relocate indentured workers, known as "coolies," from central India to Assam, where they toiled on sprawling plantations described euphemistically as "tea gardens." Indian tea toppled its rivals by the 1890s, but by the new century, merchants and planters from both industries grew preoccupied with adapting to changing global conditions. In India, colonial officers and Indian nationalists clashed over the viability of labor indenture in a modern world that had endorsed the free wage contract. In China, reformers implored the Republican (1912–1949) government to overhaul the tea trade by eliminating archaic commercial institutions they labeled "feudal." I conclude with the outbreak of the Second World War (1937–1945), after which the ideologies of economic nationalism historicized here continued to shape the political-economic frameworks of postcolonial India and Communist China.

As a work of multi-sited inquiry, this book rethinks the story of tea in modern China by emphasizing its connections with the Indian industry, at the same time drawing new conclusions about the latter in light of its entanglements with the former. Scholars have long remarked that the histories of China and India share many comparable features as continent-sized agrarian empires in Asia, but until recently they have rarely been studied in terms of their material historical connections.[6] The competition in tea was one such moment of concrete conjuncture, presenting an opportunity to bring together the distinct historiographical traditions of each region, borrowing their categories to illuminate each other's stories. Namely, whereas historians of South Asia have excelled in their analysis of colonial labor, scholars of China have foregrounded commercial processes of domestic circulation and global markets. In pursuing a combined analysis, I pay particular attention to peasant and seasonal tea production in the Chinese districts while conversely situating the Indian tea garden within global circuits of migration, finance, and accumulation.

Such comparative analysis is grounded within historical connections forged by the process of capitalist competition. For neoclassical economists, "perfect competition" is envisioned as a tranquil marketplace equilibrium; however, the "real" history of competition, as economist Anwar Shaikh recently argued, has been "antagonistic by nature and turbulent in operation," as different from perfect competition "as war is from ballet."[7] Competition points beyond standard histories organized by nations toward a new set of analytical units: discrete industries and producers pitted against one another across the global market, united by abstract movements of price, and undertaking concrete strategies to topple one another, from cutting wages to technical innovation to—as with the birthplace of tea controversy—advertising and propaganda. The tea districts of China and India shared a mutually determinative impact on each other's fates, and neither side of the tea war can be fully understood without studying the other. Transnational competition thus serves not only as this book's framing but also as its argument for how best to understand the historical dynamics of capital accumulation. In turn, these connections also help decenter the privileged role of the North Atlantic in histories of capitalism, drawing attention to the experiences of labor and the movement of capital across China, India, and the rest of Asia—where, after all, the majority of the world's manufacture for the global market now takes place.

Through this geographically expansive approach, I pursue the methodological question of how to write a history of capitalism in the Chinese and Indian tea hinterlands—and marginal sites like them—both as a local story and as part of a broader reconceptualization of the social logics animating the global division of labor. *Tea War* highlights two aspects of change in particular. First, as a social history, it illustrates how the labor-intensive production patterns of Chinese peasant families and indentured Indian coolies played a central role in generating patterns of accumulation that were massively profitable for British and Chinese merchant houses. These findings contradict older approaches that presumed the Chinese merchant and peasant were too traditional, and the Indian coolie too unfree, to belong to the modern world, and they suggest that standard interpretations of capitalism as a system distinguished by free markets and free labor need to be rethought. Second, as an intellectual history of political economy outside the North Atlantic, this book demonstrates how participants in the tea war living in China and India came to articulate increasingly abstract notions of value, production, and labor in order to make sense of the global marketplace. Novel conceptualization, in turn, compelled Asian reformers to envision their own societies through the historicist and evolutionary framework of economic progress, measured in degrees of freedom and innovations of technique. As with the birthplace of tea controversy, these nationalist thinkers abstracted from a dynamic history of competition a set of natural and spatially bound economic laws. In particular, they fixed their attention on the parasitic "comprador" merchant of China and the unfree "coolie worker" in India, respectively, as idiosyncratic markers of Asian backwardness.[8] Paradoxically, this imagery of backwardness, so popular within writings on Asia throughout the twentieth century, in fact reflected how these regions were *already immersed* within the very modern logics of accumulation.

TEA IN WORLD HISTORY

The tea plant (*Camellia sinensis*) had been cultivated and consumed in East Asia for over a millennium before it became a truly global commodity in the seventeenth century. European and American aristocrats grew enamored with tea as part of an early modern, worldwide craze for "drug foods," including coffee, opium, chocolate, tobacco, and sugar: stimulants and depressants incorporated into everyday rituals. For nearly two centuries, British and Dutch merchants purchased Chinese tea from a collection of thirteen houses that controlled the southern port of Canton. On the supply side of this "Canton system" (1700–1842), the British EIC and its army of private "country traders" profited by selling Indian opium, using their returns to buy shiploads of tea, and carrying the leaves back to London in order to cash out their profits. On the demand side, European and American trading companies actively worked to create domestic markets for tea throughout the eighteenth century, with an eye toward enriching governments and paying for wars. Soon, the bourgeois and working classes of western Europe had begun to drink tea with milk, sugar, and sweet pastries several times per day. Tea and sugar formed what Sidney Mintz called a "tea complex," in which sugar served as "both a sweetener of the tea itself and a fundamental ingredient of many of the foods that accompanied the tea." Tea time became a sacred ritual, one ascribed with moral, psychological, even "magical" effects beyond the chemical properties of caffeine and calories. The sugar arrived courtesy of the West Indies, where the British operated slave plantations for cultivating cane. The result was a "very strange thing," in the words of an English contemporary: that the "common people" of Europe should "use, as part of their daily diet, two articles imported from opposite sides of the earth."[9]

The modern history of tea entered a new phase in the 1830s. Dissatisfied British merchants, freed from the constraints of the EIC's charter, believed they could sell more opium to Qing merchants if only they could expand activities beyond the Canton system, which they condemned as a monopoly. A survey of correspondence from that decade reveals two common proposals by merchants and politicians: either open up new ports of trade in China or experiment with tea cultivation in regions controlled by the British Empire. The first solution was accomplished infamously by the Opium War. After a lopsided British victory, the 1842 Treaty of Nanjing opened up five new trading ports, liberalizing the export of Chinese tea. Within a decade, the arteries of commerce had been relocated to Fuzhou in the southeast and Shanghai at the mouth of the Yangzi River. The middle decades of the 1800s were a golden age for the Chinese tea trade, as exports and prices reached unprecedented heights.

At the same time, British officials in India championed tea cultivation in the northeast Brahmaputra Valley by using the same rhetoric of the Opium War hawks, claiming that Indian tea would "destroy" and "annihilate the Chinese monopoly."[10] Colonial experiments with Indian tea in the 1830s constituted the second solution to the Chinese monopoly: it was war by other means. In the 1860s, colonial officials introduced penal contract labor laws that prevented migrant coolies from leaving their employer under the threat of criminal punishment. Labor indenture powered the rise of Indian tea, whose exports to Britain first surpassed the Chinese trade in the 1889 season and thrived for decades afterwards (see figure 1).

By the early twentieth century, the combined annual tea exports from China and India reached over five hundred million pounds: an elevenfold jump from on the eve of the Opium War. The global tea market also featured new entrants from Japan, Taiwan, Ceylon, and Java, and the contrast between a dominant Indian industry and a collapsing Chinese one had become reified in the minds of observers, lending plausibility to Crole's soil theory. If the Opium War had unleashed the powers of the Chinese tea trade, then the tea war would nearly destroy it. The divergence was depicted in exaggerated comic imagery in a 1910 pamphlet put out by the colonial Indian Tea Association (figure 2).

During the period covered by my study, the mid-eighteenth to mid-twentieth centuries, tea was one of, if not *the*, most emblematic commodity in the export economies of China and colonial India. For the Qing Empire, it was not only a basis for the creation of the treaty-port system but also by far the most valuable export in the nineteenth century. For the subcontinent, the plantations of Assam and Bengal became, for Samita Sen, "the most spectacularly successful colonial enterprise." At the turn of the century, tea ranked number one in India among private industries in terms of numbers of companies and total investment. By the 1930s, the first systematic calculations of labor revealed that for both regions, tea employed more workers than any other export-oriented commodity sector in their country, whether cotton, jute, or silk: over five hundred thousand in Assam and three million in China. It would be difficult to tell a history of modern capitalism in either China or India without considering the place of tea.[11]

Yet tea was not unique in its mobilization of labor. Over the course of the eighteenth and nineteenth centuries, greater volumes of goods traveling between Asia, Europe, Africa, and the Americas required wider sources of capital and credit, entailing an expansion of employed labor on a global scale. Merchants, companies, and planters engaged peasants across Asia and transported millions of African slaves to work in plantations across the Americas, supplying cheap drugs, raw materials, and clothing for their home markets. Chinese tea helped keep alive Caribbean slavery at a time when sugar consumption was declining. It was also traded for opium produced on factory-like plantations in India and cotton grown by enslaved Africans in the United States. For centuries, tea was supplied exclusively by peasant farms and seasonal factories, joined later by indentured coolies who operated the sprawling gardens of Assam. The diverse workforces of Chinese and Indian tea represented but two nodes within a broader constellation of forms

COMPARATIVE CONSUMPTION OF INDIAN & CHINA TEA

162,500,000 lbs.

104,500,000 lbs.

9,750,000 lbs.

6,250,000 lbs.

1867   1907

Figure 2. Illustration of Chinese and Indian tea sales in an Indian Tea Association pamphlet, 1910. Buckingham, *A Few Facts*.

of commodified labor—slave, indenture, sharecropping, family, peasant tenantry, and free wage—bound together and mobilized in support of the first truly global division of labor. In the early twentieth century, for instance, W. E. B. Du Bois spoke of a "dark and vast sea of human labor in China and India, the South Seas and all Africa; in the West Indies and Central America and in the United States . . . spawning the world's raw material and luxury—cotton, wool, coffee, tea."[12]

A recognition of the interconnectedness of these global commodities, I believe, prompts us to rethink the history of capitalism as something radically at odds with past paradigms, which emphasized the uniqueness of the North Atlantic world, and instead explore a more truly global conception of capital accumulation and its dynamics. In doing so, this book builds upon recent research that has reexamined economic "divergences" between Asia and Europe as well as the new "histories of capitalism."

GLOBALIZING THE HISTORY OF CAPITALISM

Since the origins of modern political-economic writing, China and India have long been seen as formerly flourishing civilizations that were nevertheless constrained from achieving modern industrial capitalism. They lacked the dynamics of "improvement" outlined by Adam Smith (1723–1790), the bourgeois class relations of Karl Marx (1818–1883), and the capitalist rationality of Max Weber (1864–1920). The logic of this classic literature has had a profound impact on modern social-scientific thought, embodied, for instance, by Crole's contrast between China and the West. It was precisely these types of "Europe-centered stories" that were challenged by Kenneth Pomeranz's now-classic *The Great Divergence* (2000) and a prolific, subsequent "divergence" literature.[13] Pomeranz's masterful synthetic work proposed that in the eighteenth century the Yangzi Delta and England shared similar commercial dynamics and Malthusian constraints, suggesting that the nineteenth-century divergence between western Europe on the one hand and China, India, and Japan on the other was highly contingent on non-market factors, such as geography and politics, rather than on profound social and economic incompatibilities. Likewise, *Tea War* shares the "divergence" scholarship's ambitious goal of challenging purely localistic analyses through a reciprocal comparison between historically constituted regions. Hence, in this book I will examine comparabilities between the tea districts of southern Anhui, northwest Fujian, and upper Assam, rather than the aggregate units of the Qing Empire and colonial India, in addition to material and commercial connections.

But *Tea War* also pushes the eighteenth-century story forward to the turn of the twentieth, and it asks a different question about social transformation. In their explanations of divergence, Pomeranz and others—for example, Prasannan Parthasarathi in his analysis of India and England—controlled for social and economic differences, emphasizing the *continuity* between Asian and European dynamics and between early modern and modern growth: a laudable counterweight to past Orientalist scholarship. In this book, by contrast, I set out to explore the *discontinuity* of the modern world, which brought with it unprecedented levels of material wealth and, as Pomeranz and Parthasarathi readily assert, revolutionary patterns of capital concentration and technological innovation.[14] If, over the past two centuries, the global economy has witnessed a *quantitative* divergence in levels of national income, then it has also at the same time experienced a *qualitative* convergence in terms of shared social practices and intellectual forms. While historians of Asia take for granted that China and India were embedded within such patterns by the last century, what remains conceptually underdeveloped is the *interregnum* between early modern commerce and high modern industry.

My interest in rethinking the economic upheavals of the past two centuries also naturally places this work in conversation with the new "histories of capitalism" literature. Such research has focused mostly on the North Atlantic, providing fresh perspectives on the global cotton trade, plantation slavery, and consumer finance. It draws inspiration from both topical concerns—globalization, historic inequality, and the 2008 subprime mortgage crisis—as well as the scholarly suspicion that specialized studies on labor, business, and growth had hit an impasse. What was needed was a more interdisciplinary and denaturalizing perspective, one offered by the category "capitalism." Notably, a hallmark of these works has been the refusal to explicitly define capitalism itself, fearing the foreclosure of newer approaches. But as sympathetic scholars have observed, this refusal threatens to undermine the project's scholarly coherence and hence any positive research agenda. These concerns can be restated in geographic terms. For historians of the United States and western Europe, their sites of study have been considered the center of the modern capitalist order from the outset of its conceptualization, and suspending those older frameworks may appear highly liberating. But East and South Asia have been excluded from that tradition for just as long, and we have far fewer tools to describe capitalism's history in those regions in positive terms. Rather than underspecification, then, the more useful project for scholars of the world outside the North Atlantic, it seems to me, would be a *more conceptually rigorous specification* of capitalism's historical tendencies, illustrated through a concrete examination of how those regions were being subtly reshaped by, and also actively reshaping, the global activities of production, exchange, and accumulation in which they participated.[15]

Thus, for instance, while this work draws upon Erika Rappaport's admirable world history of tea centered on the experiences of the British Empire, my aim is to understand what capital accumulation meant at the *edges* of European empire, in colonial Asian societies often seen as incapable of modern growth. The existing historical literature on Chinese and Indian tea is replete with works suggesting that, although the world tea trade was highly profitable, neither regional industry could be said to be "capitalist" insofar as neither adhered to the only available historical model, namely, Euro-America. Indeed, within the broader economic historiography of Asia, the de facto approach has been a "technicist" one, focused on the individual *technical* benchmarks associated with twentieth-century Fordism: technological innovation, mass production, and strong state and corporate power. Such conventions remain even within the new history of capitalism literature, for example, Sven Beckert's laudable research on cotton, which, although foregrounding global history, depicts modern productivity gains as the result of sudden and local innovations in England.[16] Within this technicist frame, modern capitalism can only be viewed as something invented in northwest Europe and later disseminated to Asia and the "rest" of the world.

Today, such modular assumptions appear less ironclad. As researchers in recent decades have studied workers in Asia, Africa, and Latin America, they have grown aware of the degree to which the world market relies upon patterns of accumulation that defy the original models. Meantime, interpretations of North Atlantic capitalism have become less certain, as nineteenth-century British mechanization now appears to have been slower, less powerful, and less widespread than initially thought. These studies have occurred against the backdrop of the erosion of Euro-American factories and labor unions, whose employers have for decades now continuously relocated production to low-wage regions overseas: "flexible accumulation" in the words of geographer David Harvey. In Asia, the world's center of export manufacture today, businesses rely upon deregulated, semi-independent, coerced, and paternalistic workforces, patterns that look uncannily similar to the types of employment that animated the earliest eras of capitalist production. Labor-intensive strategies are deployed alongside capital-intensive ones, and the scale of operation ranges from factory to living room. To exclude these diverse social arrangements, Jairus Banaji has argued, would leave "large swathes of capitalism's history unexplained and shrouded in mystery."[17]

A more globally adequate vision for the history of capitalism, then, would need to explain the revolutionary transformations of social and economic life in recent centuries while also retaining the divergence literature's emphasis upon social dynamics shared across the world outside Euro-America. It is with these aims in mind that *Tea War* draws inspiration from a critical reexamination of capitalism's underlying dynamics undertaken since the 1970s—in light of the crises of accumulation known as "stagflation" and consequent reconfigurations of the world economy—centered upon a rereading of Karl Marx's mature critique of political economy. In this view, capitalism is not to be imagined as an inflexible path toward the English model but rather as an abstract dynamic, of which, in Marx's time, Victorian England happened to provide the most cogent illustration. The real object of this analysis is not capital-intensive industry and its breathtaking technical achievements but rather the underlying drive to endlessly accumulate profit for its own sake and the various forms it has assumed historically. For clarity of understanding, I first broadly sketch out Marx's categories before concretizing them historically.[18]

Throughout the many drafts of his critique of political economy, Marx pursued the question of what, fundamentally, distinguished the epoch of the past several centuries from preceding ones. As Rebecca Karl has put it, it was not the earlier eras of direct human organization but rather "capitalism" that was "so odd and indeed irrational that it needs explanation." The answer could not have been the development of world trade, nor, contradicting the earlier *Communist Manifesto* (1848), a special set of class relations founded upon surplus extraction, for both were common to many other types of society. Rather, capitalism was set apart by a peculiar abstract dynamic marked by both constant change, with cyclical bubbles and bursts, and by a relentless, underlying drive to raise productivity through both technique and technology, breaking through Malthusian limits and expanding into new geographies and aspects of everyday life. The result has been the paradox of ever-growing productivity and material wealth paired with the secular cheapening of commodities: in William Sewell's words, a "genuinely weird temporality."[19]

Marx came to explain this dynamic in highly idealized terms. For him, modern capital accumulation originated centuries earlier with capitalist production on a small scale—as early as the fourteenth century—which itself built upon the development of a world market, established currencies, and agricultural and manufacturing skills. What distinguished it was the employment of free waged workers: "free" of property and of personal obligations—that is, neither peasants nor serfs and slaves. This was pivotal for two reasons. First, at a technical level, labor mobility proved superior to other systems for organizing work, an issue I explore below. But Marx's analysis also pointed toward a second, more fundamentally transformative aspect of wage labor: when "generalized," or, predominant across society, waged work ushered in a new, historically determinate form of wealth grounded in productivity. Whereas human labor to produce crops and clothing was "immeasurably old," earlier it would have been distributed primarily through non-market mechanisms such as the *overt* relations of servitude, family, sex and caste, religion and custom, and so on. By contrast, modern waged workers spent their time producing commodities for the marketplace, under the direction of their employers, and such production, in turn, relied upon the prior purchase of the workers' time as a commodity. Products of labor were now distributed through the *covert* mechanisms of the market. Within societies wherein wage-based production had become dominant (initially sixteenth-century Holland and England, Marx speculated), a merchant or artisan seeking to accumulate wealth would need to first employ commodified labor and then, in order to earn a profit, sell that labor's products as a new commodity: commodities were now both the "premise" and "result" of modern accumulation.[20]

The generalization of waged labor and commodities transformed the practical significance of both. On the one hand, human relations were now animated by impersonal yet interdependent acts of buying and selling. The proliferation of acts of exchange reinforced an abstract notion of equality between buyers and sellers, leveling natural and political differences. Workers and kings, so long as they used the same money to pay for the same goods, were equals in the marketplace. This liberal, exchange-premised view of human equality would feature centrally in political movements against both the ancien régime and the institution of African slavery and, as we shall see, in the campaign by Indian nationalists to abolish labor indenture on the Assam tea gardens.[21]

On the other hand, commodities now constituted a new form of wealth. As production and exchange developed, prices settled into regular patterns. Goods as *qualitatively different* as silk and sugar, tea and textiles were being *quantitatively equated* through their sole common denominator: the amount of labor to produce them. As production exploded, merchants and consumers calculated values through an estimated average of how much labor was needed to produce each item, relative to one another. Accordingly, a producer who worked at above-average speeds, using less labor to produce the same amount, would earn even higher profits, and a slower producer, lower. The abstract measurement of working time thereby began to preoccupy merchants and managers of production. For instance, overseers in Chinese tea factories used seemingly archaic technologies, such as slow-burning incense sticks, to measure and reward above-average efficiency. Likewise, colonial planters in India used gongs and an informal piece-wage system to keep their coolie workers on task. Such sentiments were captured by eighteenth-century political economy's notion of "value," described below, as well as by Benjamin Franklin's famous dictum, central to Weber's analysis of capitalism, that "time is money."[22]

Marx put it this way: the defining trait of the capitalist epoch was that the abstract, social, and quantitative aspects of labor came to have a determinative effect over its concrete, private, and qualitative ones— that the value of my own work is constantly being measured, commensurated with, and calculated relative to all the labor performed by the rest of society. Thus, already within the very phenomenon of generalized commodity exchange (as the exchange of products of labor) we can locate capitalism's "immanent drive, and a constant tendency, towards increasing the productivity of labor, in order to cheapen commodities and, by cheapening commodities, to cheapen the worker himself [*sic*]."[23]

LABOR AND POLITICAL-ECONOMIC THOUGHT: CONCRETE HISTORIES OF ABSTRACT DYNAMICS

This reinterpretation of capitalism as a social logic is admittedly abstract, but precisely for that reason it is more flexible and productive for writing global history than standard technicist readings of Marx as an evolutionary theorist of national development. It suggests that capital-intensive industrialization, although often seen as the starting point for the modern world, was in fact one result among many stemming from the pressures of accumulation shared across regions beyond northwest Europe, not only the Asian tea industries but also the trades in silk, cotton, coffee, sugar, and opium. In terms of envisioning this abstract logic more concretely, Marx pointed to the process of competition. "Competition merely *expresses* as real," he wrote, ". . . that which lies within the nature of capital."[24] It is thus valuable to study the histories of Chinese and Indian tea together, rather than through separate national stories, in order to highlight the role played by transnational competition in local histories of change. In this book I pursue the concrete history of these abstract dynamics from two different perspectives: through an exploration of both labor intensification in the tea districts of Asia and, its flipside, through the ascendance of the category "labor" within the political-economic thought of modern China and India.

First, this work is concerned with an analysis of Chinese and Indian tea production, organized along seemingly precapitalist principles yet enmeshed within global circuits of accumulation. Here it is necessary to confront the conventional Marxist view of capitalism and labor, which holds that the former could only take off with truly "free labor," epitomized by England. In this view, only proletarian labor enabled specialization and combination into large-scale concerns, whereas traditional social arrangements, such as serfdom or smallholding, would have inhibited growth. *Pace* this influential body of work, I agree with a new global labor history literature that the "classic" description of proletarianization was only an "ideal type" or "simplifying assumption" within the logic of political economy. In truth, such descriptions did not correspond to any real society, not even Victorian Britain. Although free mobility *did* represent a crucial technical advantage, "freedom" cannot be viewed as the defining feature of capitalism. So what could? Again, when Marx introduced the wage labor concept, he laid emphasis upon its condition of *market dependence*. It was the constant necessity to produce goods for sale in order to survive that transformed commodities into a category mediating society-wide relationships of interdependence. Many other instances of "capitalist labor" in this sense—market-dependent and commodity-producing labor—can also be found across Eurasian history, at least as far back as the eleventh-century foundries of Jiangsu, China, or the putting-out systems for wool and silk in Renaissance Florence.[25]

Tellingly, in the margins of his work Marx offered two primary instances of capitalist production that defied the proletarian ideal type but which have in recent decades gained increased attention from historians. First, in the Americas, the long-established institution of enslaved African labor became drawn into the technologically and financially advanced world markets for sugar and cotton. The brutal extractive activities of slavery thus began to operate on the basis of efficiently calculating labor inputs and output, implicating industrial England and the northern United States with the intensification of slavery, a subject receiving fresh attention in the new histories of American capitalism. Second, across countless commercial agrarian societies, peasant agriculture and home-based domestic industry came to depend on production for, and purchases from, the marketplace to reproduce itself. Today, economic historians refer to these patterns as the "industrious revolutions" of northwest Europe and East Asia, wherein seventeenth-century "market-oriented [household] labor" grew more intensive and continuous. Notably, Jan de Vries has argued that European domestic industry was conducted not along the lines of a subsistence household economy but instead following the principles of individual wages, for the economy had long been characterized by regular labor markets of property-less workers: a suggestion, similar to Marx's, that waged work, once generalized, reshaped preexisting social forms.[26]

These stark historical examples attest to a subtle, vital, and yet often overlooked distinction in Marx's analysis. On the one hand, modern capitalism has been most prominently identified with the "specifically capitalist mode of production," or, economic arrangements "specific" to the past few centuries. For instance, the American automobile factory may have captured the spirit of the twentieth century, but it would have been unthinkable in the fifteenth. On the other hand—and more fruitfully for world history—the earliest instances of modern accumulation rested upon "inherited" forms of "*available, established labour process[es]*," which predated the modern era, were compatible with many other social orders, and yet were appropriated by modern capitalists in search of a pliable workforce.[27]

Taking this history of "inherited," *non*-specifically capitalist processes seriously helps us analyze how and why Chinese farms and Indian plantations became bound up with the social patterns of modern accumulation. In both regions, extant practices were repurposed toward profit-seeking commodity production. In the tea districts of Anhui and Fujian, peasant households were driven to usurious loans in order to grow tea from year to year, selling raw leaves to makeshift factories that pushed workers to their physical limits. The tea gardens of upper Assam may have been built anew by colonial capital, but they drew upon archaic "master and servant" laws to pin down their coolie workforces. In spite of the planters' rhetoric of industrial revolution, they owed their economic gains to a draconian regime of overworked and underpaid men, women, and children. Both regional industries also organized workers along older distinctions of ethnicity and sex, and they employed patriarchal figures of village authority to shoulder the modern tasks of recruitment and management. Indeed, Chinese and Indian tea workers represented both extremes of "independent" and "unfree," supposedly noncapitalist labor found at the margins of modern economic history—and yet they were unmistakably implicated within the expansion of British, Chinese, and Indian capital, prized in the twentieth century for the immense commercial value they generated.

Second, this social process of tea labor intensification was matched by an ideological counterpart, namely, the discovery of the category "labor" by participants in the Chinese and Indian tea trades. For these Asian hinterlands, as with the rest of the global market, nineteenth-century competition signaled more than a continuation of timeless commercial activities. It represented a disorienting, epochal shift in economic behavior that brought with it novel forms of subjectivity and consciousness. In the history of western Europe, these were famously indexed within the tradition of thought known as "classical political economy," spanning the period roughly from Smith to Marx. "It was no mere coincidence," Maxine Berg has observed, "that industrialisation and the emergence of political economy occurred at virtually the same time." Political economy was the first discourse to posit the measure and substance of wealth as neither foreign trade, as the mercantilists had argued, nor nature, as the French Physiocrats averred, but instead a general notion of human labor. In modern Asia, a century after Smith's celebrated *Wealth of Nations* (1776), similar political-economic claims would also come to saturate the writings of Chinese, British, and Bengali observers contemplating the turbulence of the world tea market. Their works shared an uncanny resemblance in presentation, challenging traditional economic ideas revolving around physical substances such as bullion and agriculture in order to delineate an abstract notion of value-producing human labor in the same tradition that Smith had established.[28]

But while it is of course meaningful in itself to document the transmission of these ideas into Asia, "there is also," at a deeper level of explanation, Andrew Sartori has suggested, "a history to be told about the very availability, plausibility, and purchase of political-economic concepts as modalities of claims making." On what social basis could writers in China and India latch onto the principles of human-labor-based wealth, originating in Glasgow and London, in order to explain their immediate circumstances in rural Asia? Any such "analysis of political economy's historical significance in any specific context," Sartori continued, "must first consider . . . the degree to which the real abstractions it names are operative as practices structuring social interdependence."[29] The suggestion offered in this book is that the conditions of possibility for abstract, human-labor-premised theories of value turned upon specific historical limitations and determinative social practices, whether living in Glasgow or Shanghai. Namely, the global competition in tea meant greater employment of seasonal migrant workers, tenant farmers, family labor, and plantation coolies spread out across the Chinese and Indian tea districts. This expansion and intensification of forms of labor that were abstracted through exchange and "generalized" in practice—here, in the sense that they could be hired to perform different tasks on a nonspecific, "general" basis—is what helped observers in Asia, as in Euro-America, find it plausible that in modern society hired labor served as the measure and substance of wealth. For Chinese and Indian economic thinkers, abstract conceptions of labor in thought paralleled the abstraction of labor in social practice, further highlighting a history of capitalist dynamics in the tea districts of rural Asia, in spite of the absence of their traditional technical markers.

Over time, these political-economic categories invited new conclusions about how Chinese and Indian societies should view themselves in relation to the rest of the world. For instance, by the standards of the early nineteenth century, there was little particularly scandalous about merchant capital in China and unfree labor in India; Qing and British colonial officials even praised them as crucial tools for expansion. But by the turn of the century, after decades of intensive activity, Chinese and Indian nationalists castigated both institutions as anachronistic when measured against new global norms. Reformers in Republican China drew upon political economy's notion of productive labor to demonize the non-manufacturing comprador tea merchants as feudal and unproductive parasites. In eastern India, the liberal Bengali intelligentsia contested the penal contract, employing Smithian language to assert that in the wake of global abolitionism, tea coolies deserved legal and political equality with British subjects, free to sell their labor unencumbered, as with any circulating commodity on the market. Thus, both figures of the parasitic Chinese "comprador" and unfree Indian "coolie" became castigated by nationalist thinkers in Asia, embodying the local social tensions generated and exacerbated by global competition.

As with the British and Japanese propagandists' birthplace of tea theory, the economic discourses of Chinese and Indian nationalists emerged from a set of naturalized, evolutionary principles aimed at explaining why some nations prospered while others did not. Indeed, for so many in twentieth-century East and South Asia, liberation from the depredations of imperialism appeared impossible without first mastering the principles of political economy within their own vocabulary, as they launched projects to develop their own "national capital" and stave off a vulturous world market. Rather than a story of dissemination and assimilation, then, this study suggests that modern capital has never been exclusively "Western" in nature but global in character throughout its history, in practice and in thought. If the two tea industries followed patterns resonant with the broad segments of Asia, and the world, that have come to participate in the international division of labor, then they also took on forms peculiar to the remote, mountainous frontiers of China and India, whose land and people were responsible for supplying enough tea to fulfill the rest of the world's insatiable craving for the magical leaf.

NARRATIVE OF THE WORK

In the chapters that follow, I begin with an overview of the history of tea cultivation and consumption in imperial China, its popularity in Euro-American markets, and experimental colonial projects to transplant cultivation to eastern India. For these regions in East and South Asia, participation in the global tea trade entailed a transformation from an early modern luxury trade to a decisively modern competition between capitalist industries. Chapter 2, set in nineteenth-century China, inaugurates the story of competition by examining how market pressures forced tea producers in the provinces of Anhui and Fujian to increase productivity in an industrial manner, despite lacking cutting-edge technology. Drawing on the family archives of the Jiang family in southern Anhui and social-scientific surveys of the Wuyi Mountains in Fujian, I describe how guest merchants became factory managers, employing slow-burning incense sticks and arcane local customs to measure, regulate, and raise labor productivity, all in response to a rising global demand followed by plummeting prices.

In chapters 3 and 4 I turn to contemporaneous attempts by British capitalists to establish a tea industry in colonial Assam, beginning in chapter 3 with the initial failures by colonial officials to profit from tea, from about 1830 to 1860, and a subsequent reexamination of classical political-economic principles. After colonial schemes to lure "free migrant" families from China failed, the bureaucrat W. N. Lees implored the colonial Government of India to dispense with liberal Smithian ideals and instead embrace the "colonization" schemes of Edward G. Wakefield, drawing upon historicist, paternalistic theories that were popular in the late nineteenth century. This debate introduces classical political economy's concept of "value" as a key category for the rest of the book. Chapter 4 describes how these illiberal views buttressed a system of indentured labor recruitment to Assam, starting in the 1860s, that would enable Indian tea to topple its rivals. In this chapter I challenge historiography that has argued capitalist production must, by definition, rely upon free labor and technological innovations. Instead, it resituates the mechanization of Indian tea production within the social dynamics of escalating labor productivity. Along the way, this chapter draws out key similarities between the work regimes of Chinese and Indian tea and, together with chapter 2, suggests that across both regions, the purportedly precapitalist practices of "merchant capital" and "unfree labor" were actually central to the emergence of capitalist development in Asia.

After the rise of Indian tea triggered a collapse of its Chinese rivals, the Chinese trade underwent its own crisis of economic principles in the 1890s, the subject of chapter 5. Here I provide an overview of economic ideas during the high age of the Qing Empire, which entailed a sophisticated grasp of economic growth revolving around the utility of the soil and the importance of trade. In a parallel with the classical economists, late Qing thinkers broke with tradition under pressure from overseas competition. The Qing bureaucrat Chen Chi penned an influential memorial on reviving the tea trade, with much of his analysis tied to a simultaneous engagement with the translated works of English economist Henry Fawcett, ultimately arriving at the same classical tenets of "value" outlined by Lees in India.

In the second part of the book I look ahead to the long-term implications of political-economic categories in modern Chinese and Indian political thought. If the previous four chapters connected the emergence of a theory of value with the corresponding intensification of capitalist production, then these final two examine how thinkers in China and India appropriated and repurposed political economy for their own ends.

From the time penal labor laws were liberalized in the 1880s until they were abolished in 1926, Indian nationalists charged that indenture was unfree and resembled slavery. I analyze this controversy in chapter 6 by focusing on the Bengali writer Ramkumar Vidyaratna and his social novel *Sketches of Coolie Life*. Drawing direct comparisons with the emancipation of enslaved Africans, Vidyaratna's work rested upon the assumption that labor was a commodity that should naturally be free to seek employment wherever it desired, an idea plausible partly because a disposable waged workforce in eastern India had become a general feature of economic life. If chapter 4 challenged the theoretical equation between "capitalism" and "free labor," then this chapter accounts for that equation's historical emergence by grounding it within changing social conditions in India. Whereas free labor was the major controversy that dogged the Indian tea industry, in China, it was the problem of the traditional comprador merchants. I conclude in chapter 7 by analyzing how the Republican economic reformer Wu Juenong, in his attempts to revive the collapsed industry, articulated a criticism of the tea merchants as parasitic. These were the same houses who earlier played a crucial, dynamic role during the nineteenth-century golden years of Chinese tea. What had changed by the 1930s was not the merchants' own behavior but instead the perspectives of Chinese economic thought, now rooted in a division between "productive" labor and "unproductive" finance. As with free labor in India, the oppositional categories of productive and unproductive labor in China signaled an embrace of the industrial capitalist model by nationalists across Asia, in spite of a dearth of the traditional signs of industrialization in either region.

1   The Two Tea Countries
A Brief History of the Global Tea Trade

Truly she is a goddess worthy of the sacrifices the world has made for her.
—*Marshall Sahlins*

All the Singpho territories are overrun with wood jungle, and if only the under wood was cleared, they would make a noble Tea country.
—*Charles A. Bruce, superintendent of tea culture to the Government of India Tea Committee (1838)*

THE BEVERAGE WE call tea comes from the leaf of the plant species *Camellia sinensis*. Aside from water, tea is the most consumed drink around the world today. It has been incorporated into a variety of highly ritualized and well-known customs, from English afternoon tea to Zen Buddhist ceremonies in Japan. But tea is mostly consumed as part of the daily rhythm of work and rest, a source of stimulation or an occasion for socialization. It can be prepared from a powder, cake, loose leaf, or bag, supplemented with sugar, milk, honey, spices, or nothing at all. The almost universal demand for tea has not relied upon a single supply source but rather a variety of producers in tropical and subtropical climates, including Argentina and Kenya, but with the majority located across Asia—China, India, Sri Lanka, Indonesia, Iran, Turkey, Japan, and Taiwan—a historical connection reflected in a map of tea production in the early twentieth century (figure 3).

Scholars today speculate that the tea plant is native to a belt of land spanning upper Assam, eastward across northern Myanmar and Thailand, and into southwest China. This conclusion partly validates proponents of the birthplace of tea theory, but the initial history of tea cultivation was unquestionably tied to the records of early China, which locate tea's first consumption in the modern Sichuan Province sometime before the Han Dynasty (202 BCE–220 CE). Today, *Camellia sinensis* can be found in two varieties, named after its two most important sites

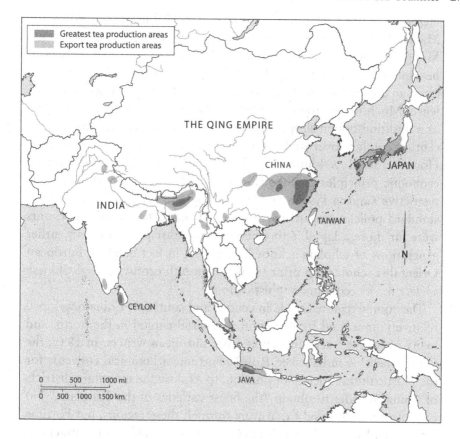

Figure 3. Major tea-producing regions at the turn of the twentieth century. Cartography by Bill Nelson, based on *The Atlas of the World Commerce Maps, Text and Diagrams* by J. G. Bartholomew (London: George Newnes Limited, 1907), 82–83.

of production: China (*var. sinensis*) and India (*var. assamica*).[1] Understanding the global popularity of tea requires starting from these two regional histories.

THE CHINA TEA COUNTRIES

The story of tea's dissemination beyond Asia begins in late imperial China. The Qing Empire (1644–1912) was a multiethnic polity with a sophisticated political administration, a growing economy, and an increasingly open relationship with the rest of Eurasia. Ruled by the Manchus, a northern non-Han ethnic group, it expanded into Tibet, Mongolia, the northwest, and parts of Southeast Asia and Taiwan to become the second largest political entity in the region's history. It featured an unprecedented degree of ethnic integration but also ethnic violence. Much of twentieth-century scholarship characterized the Qing as a tradition-bound sleeping giant, as scholars interpreted nineteenth-century conflicts over trade as a reflection of deep-seated xenophobia. However, we now know that, domestically, imperial officials prized economic principles analogous to free trade and, internationally, the restrictive Canton system (1700–1842) simply followed the empire's standard policies toward its frontiers.[2] Local officials and merchants were far more adaptable to emergent capitalist practices than earlier generations of scholars acknowledged, and in fact much of European Orientalist scholarship prior to the nineteenth century prized Chinese society for its economic sophistication.

The commercial tea trade in central and southeast China developed relatively unnoticed by Beijing, the imperial capital in the north, and many of our best accounts come from European writers. In 1847, the Government of India asked Robert Fortune, a botanical collector for the Horticultural Society of London, to explore the mountain districts of China in order to obtain "the finest varieties of the Tea-plant." No European had traveled extensively through these regions, but Fortune already had in mind two destinations indispensable to his itinerary: "the great green-tea country of Hwuy-chow" (*Huizhou*) in Anhui and "the far-famed Bohea" mountains (*Wuyi* in Mandarin; pronounced *Bu-i* in the southern Fujian dialect) of northwest Fujian Province. These proximate mountainous regions had long enjoyed fame as the chief producers of export teas. Dark teas, known as Bohea, Congou (*gongfu*), and Souchong (*xiaozhong*), primarily came from the Wuyi Mountains, and green teas, sold as Singlo (*songluo*), Twankay (*tunxi*), and Hyson (*xichun*) came from Huizhou. Unfettered by political and provincial boundaries, Fortune conceived of China's great "tea country" as a single, unified chunk of land: "The principal tea districts of China lie between the 25th and 31st degrees of north latitude," he wrote.[3]

Fortune's vision reflected the culmination of a much longer and more complex history of cultivation and consumption across China. At the turn of the first millennium, tea was seen as a medical concoction produced exclusively in the southwest by non-Han groups, such as the Ba and the Shu. By the fourth century, it had made its way to the greater Yangzi Delta, including Anhui, but the true inflection point was not until the Tang Dynasty (618–907), specifically the eighth century, when tea consumption grew ubiquitous throughout the empire, punctuated by the completion of *The Classic of Tea* (*Cha Jing*) by Lu Yu, an encyclopedic reference of all tea-related knowledge up to that point. Tea's spread coincided with the popularization of Buddhism and its proscriptions on alcohol consumption—lest one wish to incur misery, illness, and loss of reputation. Tea was central to a spiritual program of temperance, a pattern to be repeated in northwest Europe one millennium later. During the Tang, tea was also traded to nomadic groups in Central Asia for military horses, and the Song Dynasties (960–1279) institutionalized this practice with the creation of the Tea and Horse agency. By then, tea consumption and production had expanded into new regions, across new routes, and into new levels of economic significance. It gained a foothold in northwest Fujian, where the imperial Northern Park estate produced the emperor's luxurious "wax teas" in an intense, factory-like system that presaged the cliff factories of the Wuyi Mountains (see chapter 2). Tea also spread to Japan and to northern groups, such as the Mongols, who would preside over the Yuan Dynasty (1271–1368), and the Jurchens, who would remake themselves as the ruling Manchus of the Qing.[4]

Up to this time, teas had generally been steamed and molded into cakes or ground into powder. The now-familiar loose-leaf style was an invention of the Ming Dynasty (1368–1644), whose first emperor banned the labor-intensive wax teas. Loose-leaf teas are distinguished by preparation in a pan over heat, a task variously translated as "firing" or "stir-frying," and which I shall refer to as "roasting." By the Ming, teas were crucial to the monastery economy, prepared in special fashion by individual tea masters. The monks of Songluo Mountain in southern Anhui concocted their signature product during the reign of the Longqing Emperor (1567–1572). Soon, the Songluo tea craze traveled southwards to the Wuyi Mountains.[5] A 1710 travelogue summarized the process of dissemination:

One day, someone [in the Wuyi Mountains] tried out the Songluo method, and the color and flavor were pleasing. . . . The teamakers today are still the monks. Recently, there was one who summoned monks from Huangshan [a mountain in Huizhou] who prepared teas with the Songluo method. They were no different from Songluo teas, and in fact the flavor was superior. Sometimes, they are called Wuyi Songluo teas.[6]

In the sixteenth century, both Songluo and Wuyi were singled out as among the best teas from a pool of fifty-plus varieties. Tea was still viewed as a medicine or luxury good, and it was not produced on a large scale. But by the nineteenth century, monasteries were fully engaged in the massive export boom. Qing literatus Jiang Heng contravened any romantic image of the monks as pre-commercial artisans: "The Buddhists and the Daoists on the mountain monopolize and hoard the tea. They emulate the behavior of brokers. The worst are licentious peddlers, and they flee their debts. They smash images of Buddha, melt down bells and gongs, and they sell them and their mountain cottages to the merchants."[7]

At bottom, all loose-leaf teas share the same three steps of preparation: first, a roasting that denaturalizes, or halts, the leaf's enzyme activities; second, rolling the leaves; third, roasting them over heat again. These steps produce a green tea. In the eighteenth-century Wuyi Mountains, producers invented a darker tea by first wilting the leaves in the sun and allowing their enzymes to oxidize into a darker color (a process colloquially known as fermentation). In China, these were known as "oolong" (*wulong*, lit. "dark dragon") and, in Europe, "black teas." The 1790 text *Recipes from the Sui Garden* noted that the Wuyi drink is "heavy and bitter . . . the tea leaves may be infused up to three times, yet their flavor is not depleted." In the 1830s, British colonial officials documented the teamaking process taught to them by Chinese workers brought to Assam, and their descriptions, too, matched the oolong method. Only in the late nineteenth century did a newer, darker black tea emerge, eventually dominating European and imperial markets. It required several more phases of oxidization, producing a stronger, bitter flavor, and it is known in Chinese and Japanese today as "red tea" (*hongcha, kōcha*). The new black teas were not a purely native product, and their invention crystallized the relationships of mediated interdependence between the Chinese tea districts and the world market. These entailed expansive networks of foreign trading companies; itinerant Chinese merchants ferrying between treaty port and hinterland;

village manufactories in rural market towns; and commercial-oriented peasant farms. These patterns varied greatly according to region and period, and in this book, I will analyze their details as they were discovered in Chinese and foreign sources over the course of the late nineteenth and twentieth centuries.[8]

TEA AND EARLY MODERN COMPANY CAPITALISM

Starting in the seventeenth century, tea from Qing China gradually found itself enmeshed in a global circuit of bullion, commodities, and people. Tea first appeared in European sources in the mid-sixteenth century, found in Portuguese and Italian accounts of China. It was first spelled as "chai," "cia," and "chaw," reflecting its northern pronunciation; its subsequent metamorphosis to "tea"—the pronunciation in southern Fujian—reflected that region's growing importance by the 1700s. The Dutch East India Company (VOC) was the first to acquire tea, buying from the port of Hirado in Nagasaki, Japan, in 1609. Tea was "*easily* the most profitable product" that the VOC dabbled in at the time. A large portion was also repackaged and smuggled into England, soon tea's biggest overseas market. Standard histories recall that Catherine of Braganza (1638–1705), the Portuguese wife of Charles II, was "England's first tea-drinking queen." Tea supplanted home-brewed beer, sugary wines, and gin, and it joined coffee and chocolate as novel colonial beverages imported from tropical locations. The English East India Company (EIC), founded in 1600, was able to expand operations mainly due to its monopoly on the tea trade with China. Originally, the Company focused on importing spices and cotton textiles from South and Southeast Asia. After domestic textile manufacturers pushed for protectionist measures in the 1690s, the EIC pivoted to Chinese tea, around the same time the Qing lifted a ban on maritime trade and opened up access to the southern ports of Zhoushan, Xiamen, and Canton. In 1712, it imported 156,000 pounds of tea from China; by 1738, the number jumped to nearly three million. As a historian of tea wrote, the Company "was so powerful that it precipitated a dietetic revolution in England, changing the British people from a nation of potential coffee drinkers to a nation of tea drinkers."[9]

But official numbers only provide a partial sense of the total trade. By mid-century, the Company was joined by a massive network of illicit smugglers. As the British Empire entered into battles in Europe and North America, the state increasingly relied upon raising tea duties to pay for war. The tax rate climbed from 60 percent to a peak of 119 in 1784, creating incentives for a cheaper network of smugglers—unjust taxes on tea, after all, helped spark the Boston Tea Party. Whereas the EIC auctioned off its teas in London, the smugglers, operating through smaller boats, imported cargoes by way of continental Europe—France, Holland, Sweden, and Denmark—and landed off the British coast in such locations as Scotland, Ireland, and the Channel Islands. By one estimate, smuggled tea outnumbered legal tea by a count of seven versus five million pounds per year. In the Company's warehouses, a "mountain" of leaves piled up, as much as seventeen million pounds. To stymie this trend, Parliament passed the Commutation Act of 1784, reducing tea duties from 119 to 12.5 percent and authorizing the purchase of teas from smugglers and merchants who had bought at earlier rates. The goal was to bring the trade back within the purview of the Company's monopoly, and as sales climbed from 5 to 33 million pounds by 1833, the Company's income from tea also rose to £3 million annually.[10]

The English desire for Chinese tea became a major motivation in the eventual military conflicts between the British and Qing Empires, but more broadly what was at stake was the continued expansion of interlocking circuits of accumulation on a global scale, driven forward over several centuries by a handful of major commodities in extreme demand and across far-flung distances. First, starting in the sixteenth century, an early modern world circuit was catalyzed by the high price of silver in Ming and Qing China, where it was valued at twice the rates of the rest of the world. Dutch, Spanish, Portuguese, and English merchants acquired Chinese silks, porcelains, and gold by funneling in more than fifty thousand tons of New World and East Asian silver, approaching up to one-half of world silver production at the time. Second, it was within this context that the profitability of tea emerged as an engine of trade in the 1700s, as it was sold in London at several times its original Chinese price. But as I have just indicated, tea profits experienced their fair share of turbulence, so why did the EIC persist in pushing the trade? The answer comes from a third development, namely, the Company's acquisition of the *diwani*, tax collection duties, from the Mughal Empire in 1765. The Company knew better than to simply strip Bengal of its currency, and it sought to reinvest tax revenue into Asian manufactures that could be sold elsewhere, fixing their attention on Chinese tea as the most profitable candidate. Tea from China, in other words, became a medium of transferring value from India back home to England.[11]

Fourth, Company rule also meant the growth of Bengal opium starting in the 1770s, as the Company arrogated to itself exclusive rights to cultivate and sell the drug. With tea smuggling under control by 1784, the twin monopolies over Indian opium and Chinese tea spawned the well-known, awesomely profitable "triangular trade" between Britain, India, and China. Opium exports grew sixfold in two decades, outpacing Chinese tea sales and producing the once-unthinkable phenomenon of a *drain* of silver out of China. At the same time, historians have speculated that opium profits helped underwrite the creation of the modern city of Bombay in western India, and that the opium trade in Canton, because of its controversial nature, spawned anonymous instruments of exchange that elevated the nineteenth-century British financial system. Finally, one last factor was the role of British textile interests. British cotton had grown formidable by the end of the eighteenth century, the product of protectionist measures, innovations in manufacture, and new practices of labor mobilization in England and the New World. The movement of British cotton cloth to India, as well as raw cotton in the opposite direction, was the third leg of the trade triangle with China and India, and its profits buttressed the other two.[12]

Tea, therefore, was not the sole engine of intercontinental trade but one of many catalysts within expansive and interlocking commodity flows, spanning the silver mines of Potosí to the poppy fields of Malwa. On the other hand, expansive accumulation would not have been possible without skyrocketing demand for tea in northwest Europe. During the century preceding the Opium War, annual tea consumption in the United Kingdom quintupled, from one-third to one and a half pounds per person. "Tea was, in fact," an early historian of the China trade wrote, "the god to which everything else was sacrificed."[13]

Over several centuries, Europeans and Americans grew infatuated with tea, imbuing it with symbolic meanings: a reflection of morality, healthiness, and class and gender respectability. Tea drinking extended beyond the elite to poor and illiterate groups, impacting "the standard of living of a whole swath of the European public." Most important, although tea itself has almost no calories, it was paired with Caribbean-grown sugar at the turn of the eighteenth century, the moment when consumption of both skyrocketed. Sugar and caffeine became inseparable in western European diets. "The success of tea," Mintz pronounced, was "the success of sugar." In the late 1700s, when the centuries-old slave-driven sugar plantations had plateaued, the popularization of tea helped reinvigorate them. Sweetened tea was linked to the redistribution of time and nutritional sources accompanying massive social changes, namely, the greater proletarianization and urbanization of northwest Europe. After the 1784 Commutation Act, tealeaves—lower quality, dense, reusable—became cheaper, making tea more affordable than beer, milk, and other beverages, and its hot temperature complemented cold meals of bread and pastries. Bread and tea were a convenient staple for a market-dependent working class that was denied the luxuries of home cooking and subsistence agriculture. These demographic patterns shared an ideological component. Across the nineteenth-century British Empire, Christian Evangelicals and political economists alike championed replacing alcohol with tea on moral and financial grounds. At "temperance tea parties" held in churches and farmhouses, speakers echoed the same anti-alcohol message of Buddhist writers in Tang China, but in the specific context of industrial revolution, they elaborated that sobriety would help workers fight greedy bosses and the specter of mechanization. These parties also featured extensive feasts of confectionary goods, a social opportunity for working men and women to learn how to behave as modern, rational consumers within the broader imperial emporium. Thus, the Canton tea trade was connected to western European industrialization in multiple senses, both propelled by the export of manufactured goods from Britain and imported to help nourish its new urban working classes.[14]

The triangle trade produced profits that were pivotal to the birth of English industrial capitalism and the British Empire. By 1834, the entirety of the EIC's trade gains stemmed from tea. In India, profits from opium represented 5 to 10 percent of the Company's total revenue. Without the trade, one historian declared, "there probably would have been no British Empire." Even in 1830, during the heyday of Company rule, its auditor-general stated bluntly, "I am prepared to say that India does entirely depend upon the profits of the China trade."[15]

It is thus understandable why so many British interests were alarmed at the prospect of restricting the China trade through limitations placed by the EIC and the Qing Empire. For anti-monopoly critics in Manchester, Glasgow, and Liverpool, the Company's monopoly on the

China trade hurt textile exports, both for the Indian market, which relied upon opium sales to Canton as an outlet, and directly to the Chinese market itself. In 1833, the British Parliament dissolved the Company's monopoly on the China trade, resulting in a flood of English merchants to the shores of Canton. Meanwhile, the Daoguang Emperor (1821–1850) resolved to enforce an idle ban on opium imports. The tension erupted in November 1839, when the Royal Navy opened fire on Qing forces in the Pearl River; three years later, the first Opium War ended with the inauguration of the treaty-port system. "Britain was able to overcome the unfavorable trade balance it contracted from its tea habit," Sahlins has written, "only by inflicting an even greater addiction on the Chinese in the form of opium imported from India: an illegal traffic backed up in 1839 by an infamous war."[16] For Chinese tea producers, the treaty ports were a boon, and profits soared to unprecedented levels in the coming decades. But this golden age came to a dramatic halt by the end of the century, coinciding with the rise of Indian tea (figure 4). To fully understand the boom and busts of

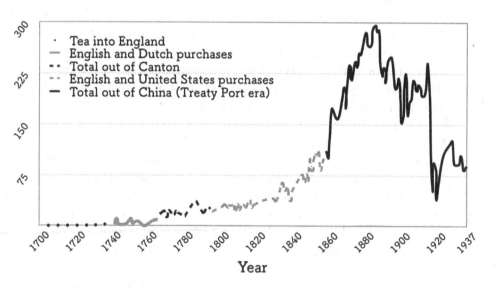

Figure 4. Total tea exports from China, in millions of pounds, 1700–1937. Figures from Lyons, *China Maritime Customs*; Pritchard, *Anglo-Chinese Relations*, 216–217; U.S. Department of the Treasury, Bureau of Labor Statistics, *Imports of Coffee and Tea*, ca. 1896, pp. 18–21; British House of Commons Parliamentary Papers, Reports on "India and China (exports and imports)," 1859 Session 2, p. 38; 1871, p. 347.

Chinese tea, it is necessary to turn our attention to simultaneous developments in colonial India.

THE CREATION OF A "NOBLE TEA COUNTRY": THE COLONIZATION OF ASSAM

Since the sixteenth century, much of what is known today as modern South Asia was ruled by the Islamicate Mughal Empire (1526–1857), a sophisticated yet decentralized political entity not unlike its Qing counterpart. Both, in fact, could trace their lineage to the stunningly vast Mongol Empire (1206–1368) of several centuries earlier. The first rulers traveled from Central Asia and made their capital Delhi in the north. Their hold upon eastern India was never absolute, as local administrators operated semi-independently from the central administration. Their chief role was to extract tax revenues for the capital, and the top official was known as the *diwan*. The EIC successfully captured the grant of *diwani* in 1765 after nearly a decade of battle in Bengal, inaugurating British colonial rule on the subcontinent. As in southern China, merchants in eastern India had long done business with multiple European companies, and at first British rule was chiefly aimed at the commercial enterprise of controlling routes and extracting taxation. By the turn of the century, however, merchants gradually came to see the advantages of capital investments into the production of cash crops such as indigo, opium, and, eventually, tea.[17]

In 1834, as British officials began to drum up support for the Opium War, the colonial Indian government announced plans to experiment with tea cultivation. For years, the British had worried they could not depend solely upon the Qing Empire to satiate growing demand. In the 1830s, these fears were amplified by a greater American presence in China and the specter of competition from the VOC's tea experiments in Java. Indeed, the 1830s colonial experiments in Assam had their origins within a broader impulse by European countries to seek and capture exotic plants and bring them within the orbit of their imperial territories. As early as 1774, the English essayist Samuel Johnson asked, "Why does any nation want what it might have? Why are not spices transplanted to America? Why does tea continue to be brought from China?" Other examples included the spread of coffee from the Middle East to Latin America, the transplantation of American rubber plants to the Malay Peninsula, and countless experiments with American rice, tobacco, and cotton from the United States to colonial India. By the 1830s, British officials had already attempted growing tea in the Americas, the Mediterranean, and Southeast Asia.[18]

Speculation over tea in India began in the eighteenth century when botanist Sir Joseph Banks formally proposed cultivating tea in Bengal, and in 1816, Edward Gardner claimed to spot a tea plant in Kathmandu. Seven years later, Major Robert Bruce and his brother Charles discovered a tea plant being served as an herbal beverage by the Singpho people in the upper reaches of the contested territory Assam, a site called "Suddeya" (Sadiya) within the Lakhimpur district. Less than a year after the start of the colonial experiments, officials announced that the Assam plant was "beyond all doubt" an indigenous "tea shrub." One of the major problems facing the colonial government was that upper Assam, located hundreds of miles from Calcutta, remained a mystery to English traders. When the EIC had won the Bengal *diwani*, Assam was still under jurisdiction of the five-hundred-year-old Ahom kingdom, which had resisted Mughal rule for centuries. Governor-General Lord Charles Cornwallis wrote in 1792, "we know little more of the interior parts of Nepal and Assam than those of the interior parts of China," and not much had changed in the intervening decades.[19]

The valley surrounding the Brahmaputra River is long and narrow, surrounded by mountains on three sides, an arrangement that facilitated greater contact with the Indo-Gangetic plains while limiting interaction with China and Burma. Its history dovetails with Willem van Schendel's and James Scott's description of "Zomia": a region at the interstices of South, East, and Southeast Asia marked by the "dialectic or coevolution of hill and valley, as antagonistic but deeply connected spaces."[20] Known as an exotic wilderness, Assam is rich in natural resources such as natural gas, timber, and tea. But Assamese locals themselves have long been seen as preindustrial in nature, described locally with the phrase "*laahi laahi*," or, "slowly" and "leisurely." The ruling people, known as the Ahoms, were ethnically and linguistically related to the Tai-Shan people of modern-day Myanmar, Thailand, and southern Yunnan. They migrated in the fourteenth century and began to consolidate power through superior agricultural techniques. *Sali* (wet-rice) agriculture was labor intensive but yielded two hundred more pounds per acre than the local dry variety. The Ahoms used their surplus to grab power, and, in their effort to collect, tax, distribute, and protect their wealth, they developed state-like functions. From 1600 to 1750, the Ahoms consolidated lands, organized and mobilized the peasantry (*paiks*) through units of corvée labor (*khels*), and redistributed the surplus through centralized mechanisms.[21]

At their height, the Ahoms represented only 9 percent of the valley's population, but by extracting loyalty from other groups they successfully checked Mughal forces in the seventeenth century. By the middle of the eighteenth, however, the region experienced a brutal civil war triggered by a millenarian heterodox sect. The Ahom king fled the capital under siege, and his Ahom leadership sought help from outside armies, including the EIC. After a temporary peace, the deposed Ahom viceroy enlisted the help of the Burmese military. The region fell into the grips of Burmese forces, and the British, protective of Bengal, declared war in 1817. After victory in 1826, British officials found evidence of a Burmese reign of terror that included bodily mutilation, cannibalism, and rape. The population had been cut down to perhaps one-third of its height a century earlier. Initially, officials were unsure how to integrate the region into the greater Indian economy. The discovery of a wild tea plant in upper Assam provided them the means. Over the next century, they would pursue the creation of a British-owned Indian tea industry with ruthless ambition.[22]

GLOBAL COMMODITIES AND GLOBAL LABOR: MARKET INTEGRATION AND CAPITALIST COMPETITION

The competition between Chinese and Indian tea simply marked the next chapter in an ongoing story of expansive world trade featuring the exchange of tea, opium, sugar, cotton, and silver. As commodities, their exchange also connected countless systems for employing, organizing, and disciplining producers. Indian opium entailed hundreds of thousands of peasant cultivators who received cash advances from local merchants and village lenders, bankers, brokers, and commission agents. These agents set notoriously low prices, and they designated special subcastes, Kachhis and Koiris, as particularly fit for opium production. Sugar grown in the Caribbean islands relied upon a combination of European smallholders, indentured servants, and enslaved African and indigenous peoples. From the eighteenth century onward,

African slavery won out as the preferred method of Dutch, English, and French investors. Cotton, of course, was sourced through two distinct stages of production: first, most raw cotton came from the American South, where slavery had gained new life in the 1790s. Second, manufacturing relied on putting-out systems employing household labor and, later, waged workers employed in factories across the United States, continental and eastern Europe, and Britain. These mills mostly employed single women and children, coerced by their families' dwindling income in the countryside, and paid about half of what adult men earned. Thus, globally traded commodities relied upon a variety of local workforces, from indebted Indian cultivators to African chattel slaves in America to the super-exploited daughters of poor peasant families in Europe.[23]

If world trade and interlocking systems of labor had been flourishing already for centuries, how can we meaningfully distinguish different epochs within global economic history and the history of capitalism? I approach this question by looking at two useful yet methodologically distinct theories of modern globalization.

For economists Kevin O'Rourke and Jeffrey Williamson, truly modern globalization was distinguished by the integration of different markets: the gradual disappearance of differentials between the purchase and sales price of commodities. Only then could world regions be said to belong to *one market*. The centuries of intercontinental trade prior to the nineteenth century may have represented a spike in volume, but it did not markedly affect domestic commodity markets since so much of the trade involved noncompeting luxury goods: spices, silk, and sugar to Europe and silver and woolens to Asia. Only the nineteenth century witnessed a greater flow of competing goods, such as wheat, raw cotton, and textiles, enabled by cheaper transportation costs and the reduction of monopoly rents. As a result, commodity prices began to converge, and domestic economies were forced to respond to the importation of global goods.[24]

The story of Chinese tea to British markets followed the same pattern. At the turn of the eighteenth century, the sales prices for Chinese tea could reach ten times its purchase price; one century later, the figure was about 2.5; and by the turn of the twentieth century, only 1.5.[25] The key development—in addition to the opening of the Suez Canal, faster transportation, and the opening of new Chinese markets—was the advent of Indian tea, the price of which was hardly marked up at all in London. Whereas in the eighteenth century tea was a noncompeting luxury good, one century later it had become a daily necessity, taken for granted by European and American consumers and available from several markets.

Market integration has also been a crucial concept for historical sociologists of capitalism. Working within the traditions of Marx and Weber, they have stressed that capital accumulation over the long run has featured an array of patterns not necessarily tied to industrialization but also that it was the nineteenth-century regime of globalization driven by North Atlantic industry that produced the canonical image of capitalism, uniting producers from across the world into the same rhythms of breakneck expansion. Immanuel Wallerstein has suggested the origins of a true global division of labor was coterminous with the transition from luxury to necessity trades. He, too, highlighted the erosion of price differentials, which, qualitatively speaking, meant that conditions abroad would force a response at home, what he called "hooking." As tea producers in China and India found profits harder to come by, they responded with more efficient methods. Integration entailed an interdependence between China, India, and Britain, in which each region depended upon the others for the products of their labor. Properly speaking, a true global division of labor emerged only when trading partners relied less on exchanging bullion for goods and instead exported valuable commodities integral to their trading partners' economies. Thus, during the late eighteenth century, as British merchants began to substitute China-bound silver exports with opium, similar processes occurred between Europe and India, the Ottoman Empire, Russia, and West Africa.[26]

Admittedly, these narratives of globalization are open to criticisms of Euro-American bias. What is worth retaining, however, is the *analytical* distinction between commerce and competition, which carries a truly global relevance.[27] Certainly the 1800s were preceded by centuries of transoceanic trade, even featuring temporary moments of regional price convergence. Those histories, however, cannot be equated with the more recent patterns of escalating output and social and technological innovation. Rather, it was *upon* those preexisting foundations of world trade that novel, mutually constitutive competitive pressures became generalized across different commodity markets. Falling prices and their attendant pressures toward productivity undergirded not only spectacular industrialization but also the social transformations of older arrangements in rural Asia and elsewhere. In different regions and at different moments, wealth accumulation assumed a more intensive character. In order to expand, the production and consumption of commodities would require the continued discovery, employment, and disciplining of supplies of labor. In the "tea countries" of Huizhou, the Wuyi Mountains, and Assam, it was during the nineteenth century when falling prices and productivity pressures asserted themselves upon local populations. It was these abstract and impersonal demands that constituted the underlying engine pushing forward the intertwined, back-and-forth story of competition laid out in the following chapters.

I COMPETITION AND CONSCIOUSNESS

The Chinese and Indian
Tea Industries, 1834–1896

2 Incense and Industry

Labor-Intensive Capital Accumulation in the Tea Districts of Huizhou and the Wuyi Mountains

THROUGH MUCH OF the nineteenth century, the tea districts of China experienced a massive boom of export sales to Europe and America. During this time, rural tea production in China exhibited social dynamics that belong squarely within the modern history of capitalism. In the commercial regions of Huizhou and the Wuyi Mountains, tea producers, despite exhibiting few signs of technological breakthrough, became enmeshed in the social logic of competitive accumulation, distinguished by an obsessive fixation on productivity. In order to survive in a world market crowded by domestic and overseas competition, inland tea merchants assumed greater control over production, contracting out tasks to factory managers who supervised seasonal workers. Managers in turn chased increased productivity by reshaping the labor process to become more specialized, coordinated, and efficient. The inland factories relied upon a two-pronged strategy of time measurement and labor discipline to map out the movements behind such tasks as plucking, roasting, sifting, and sorting leaves. The emphasis on productivity—squeezing out a greater rate of output (tea) per labor input—constituted a strategy of labor-intensive capital accumulation. The inland tea merchants, in other words, attempted to remain profitable in a world of falling prices by asking seasonal laborers to work harder, faster, and for less reward.

This dynamic history of evolving practices departs radically from past scholarly depictions of the Chinese tea trade. In the 1930s, when Chinese tea had fallen far behind its competitors in Japan and colonial India, a common refrain among young nationalist reformers was that production had remained unchanged for "several thousands of years," "operated by uneducated and poor farmers and merchants who specialized in exploitation for their daily operations." These claims anticipated the view of subsequent generations of China historians who argued that the rural economy had for centuries been stuck in precapitalist patterns known as "involution" and "growth without development."[1] Though peasant production had expanded greatly, and though families had intensified their work schedules in response to Malthusian pressures, they did not exhibit signs of greater efficiency or innovation.

Such claims relied upon the historiographical category of "merchant capital," popular within both Marxist and neoclassical scholarship, which has portrayed merchants as a residue of precapitalist economic life. In this theory, merchant capital, unlike modern "industrial capital," did not intervene into production and hence could not improve it through vertical integration or labor-saving technology. But the opposition between merchant and industrial capital, Jairus Banaji has argued, was a simplifying assumption for understanding the twentieth-century world of mass production, which featured its own specific logic of expansion. To project it backward into time would be anachronistic and Eurocentric. Likewise, Frank Perlin emphasized that "economic development in the period before industrialization was mainly characterized by changes in the size and *organization* of circulating [as opposed to fixed] capital, and in its increasing control over large quantities of labour extensively dispersed through space in households and large workshops." In economic terms, the possibilities for preindustrial development have been fleshed out by Kaoru Sugihara and Jan de Vries, who demonstrated that the intensification of family and rural labor played an expansive rather than moderating role in the emergent capitalist dynamics of Japan, England, and countless other sites.[2]

Labor-intensive accumulation provides a useful framework for articulating how tea merchants of the nineteenth century straddled conventional divisions between early modern merchant capital and modern industrial capital. They accumulated their wealth through guild-based trade with overseas companies, but they also sought to rationalize production in sync with higher productivity levels dictated by competitors. *Pace* extant scholarship, labor intensification in *this* sense was driven not by the natural and physical laws of overpopulation and diminishing land quality but rather by the *social* tendencies of capital accumulation to demand greater output at lower cost. We need to draw a distinction, I believe, between labor intensification as working longer in the absence of innovation—presumed in much of the classic literature—versus labor intensification as a distinctively modern, market-driven strategy to raise the productivity of human activity. In this sense, my approach draws inspiration from a host of scholars who have articulated new concepts for understanding this liminal period of history, including Perlin, Sugihara, R. Bin Wong, and Peng Nansheng, whose work I explore in this chapter's conclusion.[3]

The main strategy pursued by Huizhou and Fujian tea merchants was a conscious effort to regulate the labor time of their seasonal employees in response to competition. Consciousness of time and efficiency has of course been central to any standard account of the industrial revolution. Cutting-edge labor-saving devices like the cotton gin and the steam engine were crucial because they exceeded what extant technologies could accomplish in a given period. Human-labor-intensive gains that *were not* accompanied by capital-intensive innovation, then, required strategies aimed at more efficiently reorganizing the living actors themselves, increasing the ratio of time spent on productive activity relative to the overall working day. Past examples included absorbing idle household labor (women and children) into sideline activities, reallocating labor into more profitable sectors, or, as I show in this chapter, measuring and regulating the time of specialized tasks. The peculiar historical combination of time consciousness without accompanying mechanical innovation was observed long ago by such notable thinkers as Max Weber, writing about eighteenth-century America, and E. P. Thompson, describing early modern England.[4] What united the "industrious" and "industrial" revolutions was a general drive toward greater efficiency generated by the capitalist market. In real historical terms, labor-intensive accumulation has meant nothing less than pushing older arrangements to their limits.

In order to rationalize the roasting, rolling, and sifting of teas, merchants in nineteenth-century China measured the amount of time needed for each task, designed instructions to minimize wasted activity, and used a piece-wage system to provide employees with incentives to work as hard as their bodies allowed. The famed merchants of Huizhou deployed a millennia-old device for keeping time—incense sticks that burned at a regular rate—in order to keep pace with the dynamic world market for tea. In the Wuyi Mountains, overseers regulated tea plucking and firing through a set of arcane local rituals and customs that struck observers as primitive and superstitious, "inherited" from earlier modes of economic life. My argument does not hinge upon the technical sophistication of the incense sticks themselves—which were certainly less accurate than mechanical clocks—or of the rituals in Fujian. Rather, merchants used these available tools to organize a regimen of fixed and abstract "timed labor" resembling the systems of work discipline recognized by Thompson. It was the social context of the tea factory, rather than the incense sticks themselves, then, that endowed these pre-mechanical labor processes with an industrial, distinctively modern character.

THE LONG TRAJECTORY OF NINETEENTH-CENTURY TEA PRODUCTION

From Guest Merchant to Tea Factory

Robert Fortune had singled out Huizhou, Anhui, and the Wuyi Mountains of Fujian as the centers of production for green and black teas, a reflection of their international reputation as the center of China's commercial tea production. In 1907, British cartographers represented these regions as two halves of a single contiguous land mass of specialized tea production (figure 5).

Although local historians in China have traditionally recounted the dramatic story of tea from the perspectives of individual provinces, each tea country really constituted only one part of a general, *trans-provincial* process. During the eighteenth and nineteenth centuries, both Huizhou and the Wuyi Mountain regions underwent similar experiences of integration into the world market, albeit with regional differences. Because of their important roles, they will be treated here as representative, but not exhaustive, of the empire-wide trade. Other regions include Yangloudong in Hubei and the Ningbo tea districts of Zhejiang. According to a Republican-era account, each export tea

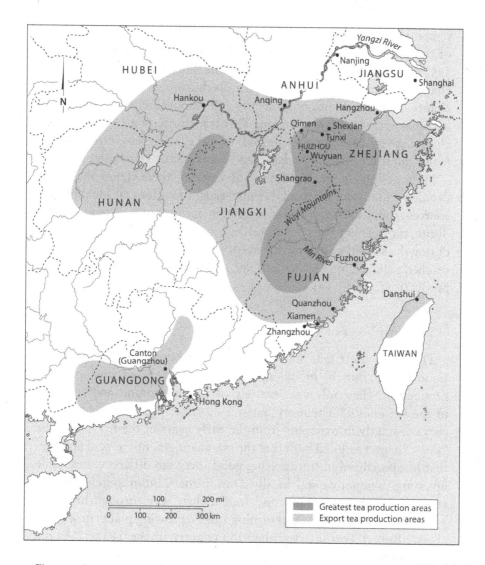

Figure 5. Export tea production regions in China at the turn of the twentieth century. The darkest section stretches across Huizhou in Anhui and the Wuyi Mountains in Fujian. Cartography by Bill Nelson, based on *The Atlas of the World Commerce Maps, Text and Diagrams* by J. G. Bartholomew (London: George Newnes Limited, 1907), 83.

region shared in common three key moments in the transformation of the trade: first, local peasant producers sold their goods to itinerant "guest merchants"; second, during the nineteenth century, the merchants became more involved in tea production; and finally, the merchants themselves undertook nearly full responsibility for the design and management of production. This transformation of inland merchant activity can be characterized, to use the Chinese terms, as that from "guest merchant" (keshang) to "tea factory" (chachang).[5]

In the following sections I give substance to these claims through a detailed exploration of available materials. I first look at local history sources from Anhui and Fujian to give an account of merchant activity during the years of the Canton trade. Second, I describe developments during the second half of the nineteenth century, during which the trade reached new heights of sales and inspired new levels of involvement in production.

The Early Years of Trade

The first export teas sold in Canton were produced by monasteries in Fujian, but the monks did not spearhead the expansion of tea production. Their job was "entirely of turning around and selling it to the tea guests." The term "guest," short for "guest merchant," recurs constantly in materials from the early years of the tea trade. The "guest" aspect implied both that the merchant was not a local and also that he specialized in transporting goods between different sites while investing minimal capital locally. During the Canton system, outsiders "entered the mountains and fought their way through brambles and bushes, moving hills and turning stones, growing plants in weeded areas." Robert Fortune described the country in the 1840s: "As the traveller threads his way amongst the rocky scenery of Woo-e-shan, he is continually coming upon these plantations, which are dotted upon the sides of all the hills."[6]

In Fujian, many of the local manufactories were opened by merchants from neighboring Jiangxi, and the long-distance trade to Canton was coordinated in conjunction with Cantonese and Shanxi merchants, who became known as "western guests" (xike). "Each merchant house had about two to three million yuan of capital," surveys recorded, "and the travel of goods formed an unbroken thread." The tea districts in

Huizhou, by contrast, suffered no shortage of local commercial activity. In fact, the merchants of Huizhou were one of the largest, most successful regional merchant groups in late imperial China. As the famed twentieth-century reformer and Huizhou native Hu Shih (1891–1962) explained, Huizhou merchants came to prominence in the fifteenth century, and almost all literati and gazetteer writings since then have cited the oft-quoted phrase "many mountains, sparse fields" (*shanduo tianshao*) to explain the disproportionate popularity of trade among the region's men. So widespread were the Huizhou merchants that another popular idiom emerged: "It's not a town without Huizhou merchants" (*wu Hui bucheng zhen*). When prices for Songluo teas rose sharply in the eighteenth century, families across Huizhou began to harvest and sell teas modeled after the signature style.[7]

By far the most intact and illuminating body of materials from the Qing tea trade is the personal archive of the Jiang family of Fangkeng Village in Shexian (She county), Huizhou. Although officially a village, Fangkeng is barely more than a shaded row of houses that lies some twenty miles east of the central market town Tunxi. In late 2010, I visited Fangkeng with the help of students from Anhui Normal University. Even then, the village was nearly impossible to find without catching a motorboat across the Xin'an River, which winds across Huizhou. In the 1980s, historians from the university discovered materials from the Jiang descendants on an informal suggestion; they turned out to provide some of the most in-depth records of late imperial economic life yet available to China historians. The Jiang merchants could trace their business activities to the middle of the Wanli era of the Ming Dynasty (1572–1620). The family genealogy describes how Jiang Kejian (1659–1712) "landed in Kengkou village, with red dirt and many hills. He used a license to become a peddler in order to accumulate some capital." The "license" here referred to a "salt license," for the salt trade constituted the "financial backbone" of the Huizhou merchants through the middle of the nineteenth century. Only with Jiang Youke (1792–1854) did the clan enter into the export tea trade at Canton. In the early eighteenth century, Jiang Youke and his son Jiang Wenzuan (1821–1862) opened a tea shop in Shexian. They bought leaves from locals, refined and sifted them in their makeshift workshop, and brought the final product to Canton. Eventually, the two Jiang men settled down and created a relatively permanent life for themselves on the coast. In this respect, theirs were no different from the typical practices of Huizhou merchants who, on average, would allow themselves only one month per year to return home and live with their families.[8]

Whereas the Jiang family pivoted from salt to tea, merchants from the neighboring county of Wuyuan, Huizhou, originally focused on the timber trade. Timber was distinct from salt, which was extracted in Yangzhou, because it was supplied locally. "In the production areas," the historian Shigeta Atsushi wrote, "the merchants would buy up timber, tie it together onto rafts, and sell it to consumers downstream, where they would take a profit from the differences in price." At this early moment in the itinerant domestic trade, "the most representative form" adopted by the merchants of Huizhou remained that of guest trader. Although they added labor to the product, "merchants expended almost all their energy on transport and circulation, and from there they extracted the greatest amount of profit." The tea merchants of Wuyuan borrowed this "representative form" and applied it to tea. During the years of the Canton trade, merchants involved themselves in production, but their intervention was minimal.[9]

If the guest merchants who collected leaves from the inland households focused mainly on circulation, with only a subsidiary interest in production, they also constituted merely one node in a larger network of distribution. The tea trade was segmented, and the coastal merchants were initially separate from the inland merchants, who depended on Canton for advance loans. The thirteen Cohong (*gonghang*) merchants on the coast "simultaneously played the role of dealers as well as creditors to the [inland] Wuyuan merchants." Sometimes the smaller merchants would not be paid for their deliveries until long after the tea season ended. Other times, they simply accrued debts they could not repay. In one example, a merchant went broke due to bad loans, and he sold his wife in order to repay his debts.[10] The powerful coastal merchant who acted as broker and creditor was a figure that would persist under different identities in future generations of the trade, an enduring feature of Chinese economic life that would come under attack in the twentieth century.

The Late Nineteenth-Century Factories

For nearly a decade after the 1842 Treaty of Nanjing opened five new ports of trade, overseas commercial activity remained concentrated in

Canton. Such patterns changed only after the disaster of the uprising of the Taiping Kingdom (1850–1864), a bloody civil war involving the Qing state, local militias, and a millenarian peasant movement that occupied much of eastern and central China. Tea producers in Huizhou and the Wuyi Mountains were forced to redirect their shipments to Shanghai in the east and Fuzhou in the southeast. This redirection was an inflection point in the history of overseas trade, coinciding with a massive spike in the export of silk, cotton, and especially tea.

In 1853, Tao Chengzhang, a magistrate in northern Fujian, encouraged businessmen to reroute their transactions to Fuzhou. One year later, the American firm Russell & Co. was the first foreign firm to buy teas there. In 1850, only five British subjects lived in the port town, and as Fuzhou began to thrive, merchant groups in the neighboring cities of Zhangzhou and Quanzhou took advantage of fortuitous timing and location to occupy the local trade. Before long, "the business of western guests [from Shanxi] gradually fell, and the three business cliques of the 'lower-province' [xiafu, from Zhangzhou and Quanzhou], Canton, and Chaozhou continued to grow. From the end of the Daoguang period [1850], the foreign trade was dominated by these three cliques."[11]

To minimize risk, foreign firms initially contracted with individuals to buy tea in advance of the season. They were known in the letters of American and British employers as "teamen"—with names such as Ahee, Taising, Acum, Chunsing, and Ateong—and their rise and fall provide useful insight into the expansion of the 1850s through seventies. For instance, the Scottish firm Jardine Matheson & Co., the largest foreign opium and tea dealer in China, relied on teamen during the first decades of the treaty-port era. In September 1854, correspondence within their Fuzhou office acknowledged, the Min "River [running through Fujian] is very dangerous in some places, being full of rocks and the Teamen are well aware of this and attach considerable importance to it, that is to say many of them are afraid to bear the risk of bringing the teas here, preferring Shanghae or Canton." At the time, employing individual agents to travel to the Wuyi Mountains was still a high-risk, high-reward proposition, for tea prices were low, and supplies in Fuzhou were scarce. However, in June 1871, the Shanghai office declared, "the system of advances to the Chinese for upcountry purchases must be finally abandoned" for the system "encourage[s] the Chinese middlemen to raise the prices of leaf against us in the Country." By this point, the Min River was a well-worn circuit, saturated with new middlemen who had inserted themselves between the foreign firms and the inland producers. For Euro-American buyers, hiring teamen to offer direct advances was now costly and impractical, a byproduct of the growing institutionalization of the Chinese side of the trade.[12]

Correspondence with the teamen also provides a peek into the dynamics of the upcountry trade. Most often, they simply brought their advances to a preexisting local market in the tea districts. In 1860, the teaman Taising wrote that prices "had gone up in consequence of there being considerable competition among the Teamen and agents of Foreign Houses." In 1866, clerks in Fuzhou received a description of the hectic country marketplace: "Taising has returned from the country. . . . He says the state of affairs was fearful, that the leaf only came to market catties at a time & for which 50 or 60 buyers would directly appear bidding over one another." This correspondence also disclosed the dynamic relationship between price and production. One of Jardine's hired men wrote, "high prices will stimulate production. . . . My conviction is that it is a question of price, and that buyers will be found to pay sufficient to make this season's export the largest on record, and quite equal to the demands of the world." Greater demand drove greater production and, consequently, increased specialization. During this golden era of endless demand, the Chinese tea trade embodied the circulation-driven dynamic of commercial capitalism.[13]

If supplies were indeed elastic, then more land, tea bushes, and workers were being mobilized in response to high prices. How did this demand get transmitted to the interior? It was the inland guest merchants who came to serve as proactive intermediaries between world demand and the inland districts, directly encouraging cultivation and manufacture. If they had formerly concentrated their efforts on transportation, they now shifted their energies onto refinement. Their motivation was simply control over production in order to meet runaway demand. New facilities became a physical necessity as the existing farms and monasteries had reached their limits.

In fact, overseas demand had been slowly reshaping the countryside for almost a century already. As the market overwhelmed domestic supplies, the workshops had begun to cater to foreign tastes. In the 1840s, Fortune noted, in the green tea districts "where the teas are manufactured solely for exportation, the natives are very particular in the rolling process, and hence the teas from these districts are better divided and more *even*." He also grew aware that the scale of the trade had expanded in recent years before his arrival. "Thousands of acres were observed under tea-cultivation," he wrote, "but apparently the greater part of this land had been cleared and planted within the last few years." In Guangze county, just across the Jiangxi border, gazetteers recorded, "Ever since the reigns of Xianfeng and Tongzhi (1850–1875), everywhere people grew tea." Expanded production required more workers, who were recruited from neighboring towns in Jiangxi. When the Taiping Kingdom interrupted transportation in 1850, Ahee, a comprador for Jardine Matheson & Co., reported that because of the rebellion, "no one is plucking the tea. . . . The tea laborers are all from Jiangxi, places like Hekou. Because Jiangxi is in chaos, very few of their workers come over." Hekou was a town located in the county of Shangrao, just across the provincial border. Ever since the trade outgrew the sparse local population of the Wuyi Mountains, merchants had relied upon migrants from Jiangxi each spring, and these workers eventually became associated with tea production in Fujian. For instance, when British officials recruited Chinese teamakers to Assam in the 1830s, those men were probably from Shangrao, as they claimed to come from a place "called 'Kong-see' [Jiangxi] . . . two days from the great Tea country 'Mow-ee-san' [Wuyi Mountains]."[14]

The seasonal tea industry, and the attendant migrant workforce, grew to a massive scale. In the 1850s, the literatus Jiang Heng declared that "in the town of Ouning alone [in the plains near Wuyi], there are over one thousand factories. The big factories employ over one hundred people, and the small ones several dozen. If there are a thousand factories, there must be 10,000 people." In the late eighties, the governor-general Bian Baodi wrote, "During every tea season since the Xianfeng reign (1850 to 1861), hundreds of thousands of tea workers come over from Jiangxi." However, tea cultivation itself seemed to remain within the purview of the small peasantry, as land arrangements remained unaffected. In the twentieth century, researchers confirmed that many of the tea districts looked the same. But although most "tea peasants usually undertake tea as a secondary occupation, and their management is often crude and rough . . . the one exception is Chongan."[15]

Chongan was the market town nearest the Wuyi Mountains. There, merchants in the last half of the nineteenth century began to experiment with the organization of cultivation in unique ways. Such experiments coincided with the appearance of the lower-province clique. As with their Huizhou contemporaries, these Fujianese merchants could monitor their local investments in the Wuyi Mountains once trade had relocated from Canton. Over time, those cliques became the key source of circulating capital for inland tea manufactories and, as in Perlin's description, began to assert greater control over production itself. They established a new system that combined cultivation with precisely monitored processing known as the "cliff tea factory" (*yanchachang*), the descendants of the Song-era Northern Park plantations that produced excessively labor-intensive wax teas for the imperial court: "Merchants from Zhangzhou and Quanzhou arrived, from no farther than one thousand *li* [about three hundred miles], and further developed the trade. They did not hesitate to spend large amounts of capital, and atop the cliffs of the Wuyi Mountains, they established factories, in which they pluck and process tea by themselves." Twentieth-century surveyors hinted that, compared to other varieties, the cliff teas required the most capital: "Because the owners of the mountains saw profitable opportunities, they did not hesitate to pour large amounts of capital and engage in business."[16]

By contrast, the Huizhou merchants never took over control of the cultivation and plucking of tea. Nevertheless, they too developed tea factories of increased scale and complexity. In official gazetteers published in the late century, Shigeta noted, "It would be almost impossible to find someone not involved in the tea trade somehow." During the last third of the century, the phrase "carving out a career through tea" (*yecha qijia*) became "the most ubiquitous phrase in the biography section" of these gazetteers. In short, "the tea trade became the most magical industry of the time."[17]

When the Canton trade diminished in the 1850s, for instance, Jiang Youke and Jiang Wenzuan did not hesitate to transfer their business to Shanghai. Again, the immediate trigger was the Taiping Kingdom. Jiang Wenzuan wrote to his concubine Xiulan in Canton: "This year we planned on going to Canton to sell our tea. This would be best for everyone. But we didn't predict that the long-haired rebels [*changmao*, a reference to members of the Taiping] would cause a disturbance and they would block the roads through Jiangxi. . . . As a result, none of the Wuyuan teas can get to Canton." Shanghai itself was also gaining momentum as the new commercial and financial capital of the Qing. As exports rose, however, prices fell, hitting the Jiang family hard. Less than twelve months after arriving in Shanghai, Jiang Youke died at the age of fifty-two. Jiang Wenzuan continued the business but confided to his concubine, "The family business is in crisis; it is vanishing to nothing. It's hard to get enough to eat. Our family struggles to survive each passing day." In 1861, Jiang Wenzuan died on the road to Shanghai. His eldest son, Jiang Yaohua, was only fifteen at the time. The family was forced to sell their property, and Jiang Yaohua had to look for work elsewhere.[18]

As further testament to the magical pull of the tea trade, the youngest Jiang found little alternative but to try his own hand at tea when he grew older, despite having witnessed the ruin of his father and grandfather. Penniless at first, he saved enough money from odd jobs, including work in a tea factory, to open his own tea shop in Suzhou. There, according to family legend, Jiang Yaohua crossed paths with Qing official Li Hongzhang, an Anhui native, who introduced him to a large tea broker based in Shanghai. He came to an agreement with this broker, a Cantonese man named Tang Yaoqing, who was interested in teas from Huizhou. Jiang served as a middleman for Tang, from which he saved enough capital to open up another shop back in Huizhou, on a scale much larger than the retail store he ran in Suzhou. From the 1860s to the 1920s, Jiang Yaohua set up shop in the market town of Tunxi, Huizhou, and undertook responsibility for manufacture as well, using space in his family shrine, rooms in his house, or a rented building in town.[19]

During the late nineteenth century, the tea factories were said to have employed between a hundred and a thousand people each season. The younger Jiang used at least thirteen different names to run his activities, and he needed to take out loans each season to finance the outlay on raw materials and workers. He employed nearly twenty permanent staff members in management and service positions—accountants, labor overseers, scale managers, and so on—as well as dozens of temporary manual workers for roasting, fanning, sifting, and sorting leaves.[20] Jiang Yaohua's ventures grew along with the Shanghai trade, and eventually he operated an enterprise far more complex than that of his father and grandfather. At its apex, the export tea trade consisted of a network of coastal warehouse merchants, known as "tea warehouses" (chazhan), such as Tang Yaoqing, who engaged with inland merchants, such as Jiang Yaohua, who simultaneously took on the role of operating and managing tea manufactories. The specific details of this intricate chain of commerce and production, whose inner dynamics were systematically uncovered by Chinese surveyors for the first time in the twentieth century, will be examined more closely in chapter 7.

For now, it is worth observing that the basic structure of the tea trade shared parallels with the other circuits for silk and cotton, both raw and manufactured goods. In the case of silk, Chinese merchants established machine filatures in cities such as Shanghai and Wuxi, Jiangsu, and they collected raw silk from the countryside by relying upon personal compradors who resembled the teamen of the Fuzhou trade. The cotton trade was dramatically transformed in the 1880s, when China was pulled into greater world demand for raw silk and the influx of cheaper, machine-spun yarn led to greater weaving activities in Chinese households. Both silk and cotton were organized by a collection of powerful, almost monopolistic cliques of brokers who coordinated production and distribution on behalf of foreign firms. In the silk trade, they were known as *zhangfang* (account houses), and in the cotton trade, *guanzhuang* (merchants north of the Great Wall). As in the tea trade, these merchants played expansive roles by intervening into production, even if by the twentieth century they were demonized as mercantile parasites.[21]

During this nineteenth-century era of expansion, the lines between merchant and industrial capitalism—circulation, finance, and manufacture—were blurred, defying any tidy categorization between premodern and modern patterns of capital. As Shigeta observed, the nineteenth-century tea merchants were no longer "simply tea merchants who specialized in traveling back and forth between the production districts and the trading ports," nor "simply middlemen," but now "also oversaw the production process to the end. They realized features of intensive production."[22] Already by 1967, when Shigeta conducted the first academic case study on Huizhou tea, he could speculate on the modern intensive techniques of production in the tea factories. Subsequently unearthed materials would vindicate him.

A HISTORY OF LABOR-INTENSIVE ACCUMULATION

Inside the Tea Factory and the Division of Labor

In both Huizhou and the Wuyi Mountains, the tea "shops" (*hao*) or "factories" (*chang*) undertook responsibility for processing the leaves, having first purchased raw leaves from households in surrounding territories, but regional differences influenced the degree to which the factories intervened. Although various teas require different finishing processes, as all connoisseurs know, production could always be roughly divided into two stages: an "initial processing" (*chuzhi*), followed by a "*re*-processing" (*zaizhi*), more commonly called "refinement" (*jingzhi*). The initial process turned raw leaves into a semifinished product known as *maocha*, meaning rough and immature tea. The goal was to halt oxidation processes that would brown the leaf within the first twenty-four hours of plucking. Most often, peasants who plucked the tea would stir the leaves inside the same kitchen woks they used to cook dinner. The transfer of *maocha* from peasant cultivators to inland factories served as the practical division between the two stages.[23] In Huizhou, factory managers controlled only the second stage, and merchants relied upon peasant households to provide the raw materials. By contrast, merchants in the Wuyi Mountains oversaw the entire process from cultivation to packaging.

It is useful to situate the tactics employed inside the tea factories within a broader trajectory of labor-intensive practices in Chinese history, namely, an older division of labor across the peasant workforce. Historically, the division of labor has been one of the most basic, earliest, and universal techniques for increasing productivity. Within the Chinese tea trade, the most obvious form was the division of tasks along gendered lines, which grew more pronounced as workforces grew larger. In general, women were hired to pluck leaves on private gardens, and seasonal factories hired both men and women to work together in manufacture (figure 6). In the 1910s—long after the golden age of tea had passed—Japanese researchers in China documented that Huizhou featured about fifty to sixty tea factories, with about two to three hundred workers each. Men fired and packed leaves, women sorted them, and both groups sifted. In the Wuyi Mountains, managers relied on outside male labor combined with local women workers. The largest factories were in central China, in Hubei and Hunan, where up to thirteen hundred people could be seen in one location. On a busy day, observers noted "the strange sight of old, young, men, and women lining up to go to work like ants."[24]

Historian Lu Weijing has described the employment of women alongside men in the tea trade as a pattern that "ran counter" to Confucian gender norms. Such norms were premised upon the separation

Figure 6. Early nineteenth-century gouache painting of tea plucking featuring female labor. This genre of painting was produced in China for the European market, and it portrayed Chinese economic life in far more idyllic terms than late nineteenth-century photographs would reveal. Copyright 2018 by The Kelton Foundation.

of sexes and embodied in the famous phrase "men plow and women weave" (*nangeng nüzhi*). In Lu's interpretation, custom and tradition were pitted against the economic dynamics of the cash crop tea. However, what Lu was pointing to could also be seen as *two different kinds* of gendered division, one moralistic and one rooted in economic accumulation. As a moral discourse, "men plow and women weave" emphasized the physical separation of sexes, and this was certainly being violated by the co-presence of male and female workers. However, the same dictum also took on a new meaning during the seventeenth century, becoming an economic principle grounded in specialization and labor allocation in order to maximize income. "Men plow and women weave" was not an immutable tradition, historians Francesca Bray and Li Bozhong have shown, but rather a rational economic strategy resembling the industrious revolutions recorded in European and Japanese history. Peasant households in the Yangzi Delta region discovered that women's labor could be maximized by spinning and weaving silk and cotton. Thus, what was happening in the tea districts was not unique, as a new division of labor rooted in maximizing revenue had already begun to emerge in other commercialized regions in China, one analytically distinct from its traditional, moralist version.[25]

This is not to say, of course, there was no moral significance projected onto gendered division, nor that economic mobility gave women equal status with men. On the one hand, femininity among tea pickers was romanticized and fetishized from the Song Dynasty onward. Poems drew parallels between the fragrance of young leaves and the fresh smell on young women's hands and breasts. This "naturalization" of gendered labor was historically belied by records of men plucking leaves and women doing "manly" tasks such as roasting them. In the 1810s, for instance, a Huizhou factory manager claimed that he owned one hundred roasting pans and employed three hundred women, for they were cheaper than their male counterparts. On the other hand, Lu was correct that the mixing of sexes incurred moralistic hand-wringing from literati, who viewed female physical labor and the singing of work songs as "unvirtuous."[26] In 1889, the Guangxu Emperor received a memorial urging the prohibition of hiring female workers:

> Every export tea district needs tea factories, and every factory needs a sorting room, and every sorting room can accommodate several hundred people. They invite many girls into the factory to sort tea, with young men overseeing them. Every time the new leaves come onto the market, women from the villages travel in groups to the factories. Some stay in guesthouses, and others sleep outside, inviting violent behavior and causing serious incidents to arise.[27]

Though some scholars have described the introduction of waged work as "liberating" for women, many in the tea industry were unable to simply trade away their familial obligations, as they carried the double burden of wage work plus the womanly duties of the household.[28] As we shall see in chapter 4, women in the Indian tea industry, which was far more feminized, faced the same double burden, along with the fetishization and devaluation of their activities as "naturally" feminine. For now, what is worth emphasizing is that the regimes of labor discipline that arose in the nineteenth-century tea trade were made possible by an older and more general process of specialization, especially along gendered lines, which was reinforced and capitalized on by factory managers.

Huizhou: Incense and Industry

Although the earliest tea merchants in Huizhou could earn a comfortable living based solely on the differential between the cost of leaves at home and the prices paid in Canton, greater competition over time eroded the rate of profit, and margins could be salvaged only by developing more efficient methods of production. The Jiang family's first two generations of tea traders fared reasonably well when the Canton market was limited by the monopoly of Cohong merchants. When they moved to Shanghai, the Jiang men encountered a very different business climate. There, Jiang Wenzuan wrote, "The profits are not great, but business is fast." "Compared to the Canton business," he noted, "it's extremely tough to make money. One tough year just leads to another!"[29] Jiang Youke and Jiang Wenzuan had relied upon relatively loose, makeshift workshops that fit into a few rooms inside their house. When Jiang Yaohua reentered the trade decades later, he increased the scale of production in order to compete on the Shanghai market.

In years both good and bad, efficient production was crucial to the collaboration between Jiang Yaohua and his Shanghai partner Tang Yaoqing. As an instance of a good year, we may take a letter written by Tang, in which he opened by saying, "reserves of green teas for export are low," and his company needed new supplies from inland:

> If we are not quick, then we need you to be decisive and pay attention to manpower [renshou], to act with guts and move quickly to supply us with a thousand dan [about 100,000 pounds] of leaves. Ship them quickly to Shanghai, and we can definitely get thick profits. . . . We hope you can quickly get us tea supplies. Find your men and get to work, and if prices stay strong and your goods are high-quality, then we will ask for eight hundred more dan of tea.

While speed helped Jiang Yaohua respond favorably to high prices in good years, in poor years efficiency reduced production costs and maintained hopes of profit. Many of Tang's letters concluded, "Next year, our soundest strategy is to be more selective about quality, push down mountain [raw material] prices, and cut costs [chengben]."[30]

The word chengben refers to the general outlay of capital and expenses, but historically it came to specifically denote production costs. Chengben was always a concern to merchants, but as tea shops took over production, they paid even closer attention to materials and labor. In a small handbook entitled An Outline for Buying Tea, Jiang Yaohua emphasized the importance of calculating costs prior to buying mao-cha from peasants. Though all factories aspired to adhere firmly to these principles, prices were beyond their control. A quick survey of the Jiang account books demonstrates that during the 1898 season Jiang Yaohua paid an average of 0.192 yuan per jin (just over one pound) of raw leaves, but in 1906 he paid a rate of 0.297 yuan. Just as inland tea factories could not fully tame mountain prices, neither could they fully prepare for Shanghai prices, which had crept down throughout the second half of the century. In the 1903 season, the merchants of Shanghai reported that "with Ceylon now producing so much tea, the foreigners haggle on the pretext that Ceylon tea is high-quality and very flavorful, and Chinese dealers don't know if they're telling the truth. This makes it even harder for Chinese dealers to sell their goods." Surrounded by unpredictability on both sides, inland merchants realized the importance of controlling the only costs they could directly influence: the costs of production in the refinement processes. Thus, production costs moved from the margins of their considerations to the center.[31]

These concerns were apparent in another manual written by Jiang Yaohua, titled An Outline for Making Tea (Zuocha Jielüe), in which he detailed every step in the production process of Huizhou green teas. Whereas earlier texts had merely sketched the steps in teamaking regardless of scale and efficiency, Jiang's handbook described how to produce large amounts in minimal time. Central was a regimen of work organized around timed intervals, the crucial mechanism for which was a peculiar type of nonmechanical timekeeping device: incense sticks that burned at a regular rate (figure 7).

Consider the futility of lighting sticks of incense in a factory for processing raw tea. The woody smell of wilted tealeaves is intense, almost nauseating to novices. This, combined with the steady stream of smoke emanating from burning stoves, impaired the original function of the incense, for workers must have been only vaguely aware of the aroma.

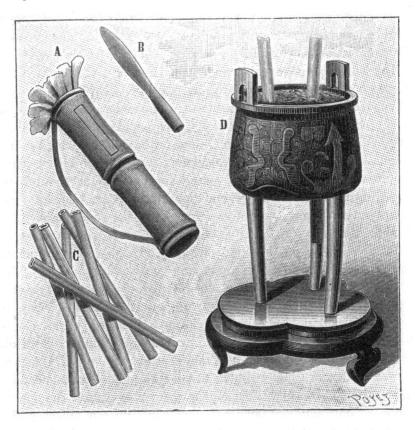

Figure 7. Incense stick timekeepers used in East Asia. From Mathieu Planchon, *L'Horloge: Son Histoire Retrospective, Pittoresque et Artistique* (Paris, 1898), reproduced in Bedini, "Scent of Time," 24.

Nevertheless, for twelve hours each day, when operations were under way, everyone in the factory remained constantly mindful of the slow-burning sticks. These timekeepers were available in various lengths and burning speeds, but they were generally designed to last forty minutes per stick. Incense regulated every operation in the tea-making process: roasting, sifting, weighing, sorting, dyeing, and packaging (figure 8).

Of all the tasks, the most important duty was shouldered by the tea roasters, who were also burdened with the most exacting instructions:

Once the *maocha* are brought into the tea shop, they undergo their first roasting. In Wuyuan county, this is known as "pulling out dampness" [*tuo chaoshen*], and in Xiuning and Shexian counties, this is called "expelling the little ones" [*chu xiaohuo*].

In every pot, 1.85 *jin* [one kilogram] of leaves can be fired in the time it takes to burn two and a half to three sticks of incense. When the leaves are first placed in the pot, instruct the roasters to stir the leaves around in cool air to shake out the sour, musty smell. Do this until about 80 per cent to a full stick of incense has been used, then do not air the leaves any further. The roasters must then concentrate, using a light touch to rotate the pot as they press down the leaves, evenly distributing the heat. Do this for half a stick of incense.

Lay the pot directly over the furnace and roast until two and three-quarters of a stick of incense has been burned, rub them once more, and take them out of the pot. By now, the leaves must be vibrant and green in color, tightly rolled but not crumbling. The *maocha* that first come into the shops cannot be packed tightly. In order to avoid causing the leaves

Figure 8. Tea roasters (detail), with a bundle of sticks resembling an incense timekeeper visible behind the head of the middle figure. Tea Industry Photograph Collection, ca. 1885. Baker Library, Harvard Business School (olvwork710883).

to lose their original green color and become red and yellow, they need to be quickly taken off the flame and packaged immediately.[32]

At first sight, the idea of relying upon incense sticks to regulate industrial production is puzzling. Considering the low level of technology required for these nonmechanical timekeepers, Chinese peasants must have been using incense sticks for centuries before the 1800s. How novel or noteworthy could this labor arrangement really have been?

The first documented record of incense timekeepers in China can be traced to the sixth century, when the poet Yu Jianwu (487–550) wrote:

By burning incense [we] know the o'clock of the night,
With graduated candle [we] confirm the tally of the watches.[33]

Incense sticks were used regularly for timekeeping from at least the Tang Dynasty, and the practice persisted into the twentieth century, when curious foreign sources confirmed their presence in the daily life of China. Samuel Ball, an EIC inspector stationed in Canton during the 1810s, frequently heard from merchants that they used incense sticks in the manufacture of green tea. "The time of roasting," he wrote, was "regulated by means of the instrument denominated a Che Hiang" (*xiang*, "incense"). Rudolf Hommel, a German photographer traveling in the 1920s, noted that coalminers "stay underground continuously for about 3 hours, and to tell the time they carry with them an incense stick which glows for about 3 hours. The Chinese call it 'Timepiece.'"[34] In order to understand what was so historically distinctive about the Jiang handbook, it would be useful to first delve deeper into the relationship between capitalist labor and time.

Concrete and Abstract Time

The phenomenon of labor-intensive accumulation I have proposed here describes a process of efficiency, which in turn hinges on measuring activities within time. It is unsurprising, then, how historians and anthropologists have frequently remarked that the rise of industrial capitalism coincided with qualitative changes in the perception and consciousness of time among workers and farmers. For instance, time in the early modern English countryside appeared to the farmer as something contingent upon external, natural phenomena such as the crow of the rooster or pastoral chores:

> Labor from dawn to dusk [wrote E. P. Thompson] can appear to be "natural" in a farming community, especially in the harvest months: nature demands that the grain be harvested before the thunderstorms set in . . . sheep must be attended . . . cows must be milked; the charcoal fire must be attended.[35]

Thompson described this natural time as "task-orientation." The category also applied to the demanding schedules of rural life in imperial China. Natural events organized the tea trade linearly: tea plucking only began after the Qingming festival in April, raw leaves needed to be dried immediately after plucking, and *maocha* needed to be roasted again within twenty-four hours of preparation. Tea production was always task-oriented. Imperial China, Joseph Needham forcefully argued, was not one of those supposedly primitive, timeless societies. Rather, "linear concepts [of time] were the elements that dominated the thought of Confucian scholars and Taoist peasant-farmers alike."[36]

It has been claimed, however, that a great divergence between West and East emerged with the advent of clock time in Europe. Alongside the rise of industrial capitalism, mechanical timekeeping displaced natural time as the regulator of daily life. Attention to accurate clocks was necessary for the mechanical, calculable work of industry: what Thompson called "timed labor." Until now, the horological history of China—or, the study of the history of time—has been dogged by pessimism and failure. David Landes claimed that daily activities in Tang and Song China were regulated "by the diurnal round of natural events and chores," or patterns of natural time. Imperial China did not graduate to the modern usage of accurate, commensurable time units until the arrival of European technologies. This failure appeared paradoxical since scientific knowledge during the Tang and Song was sophisticated enough to keep independent measurements of time accurately, and yet these devices were not used to regulate daily activities within the populace. The juxtaposition of accurate timekeeping devices with the predominance of task orientation suggested to Needham that technological progress in a vacuum was insufficient without a corresponding cultural desire to popularize it. This paradox became known as the Needham problem: why did Chinese civilization "not spontaneously develop modern natural science as western Europe did, though China had been much more advanced in the fifteen pre-Renaissance centuries"? Building upon Needham's work, Landes wrote that "productivity, in the sense of output per unit of time, was unknown" in imperial China.[37]

The opposition between a time-disciplined Europe and a task-oriented Asia, however, now appears less tenable, as Landes and Needham seem to have exaggerated the difference between premodern and modern forms of timekeeping. Moishe Postone helpfully reinterpreted the relationship between the two by offering the category of "abstract" time, which he described as the inversion, rather than the opposite, of "concrete" time. The operative distinction was "whether time is a dependent or an independent variable." Concrete time was a "function of events" and referred to "particular tasks or processes." Abstract time, by contrast, was "independent of events." While Thompson's pair of categories have been criticized as simplistic and mechanical, such concerns can be allayed with the caveat, emphasized by Postone, that the history of abstract time has been context dependent. Conceptions of independent, abstract time did not emerge ex nihilo; rather, they derived from earlier methods of time measurement, such as those based on sunrise and sunset (the day) or phases of the moon (the month). Such natural events once determined the duration of units of time; eventually, with emergent demands for higher productivity, the units themselves began to determine the expected pace and quantity of work. The passage from concrete to abstract time was subtle. Rather than inventing a new type of time consciousness, the keepers of abstract time inverted the relationship between human activity and time measurement.[38]

Given the logical coexistence of concrete and abstract time, the predominance of the former in the Chinese countryside should not preclude the possibility that there may have emerged specialized realms of life wherein the latter achieved major significance. In particular, although the pace of the tea trade was constrained by the seasonal and physiological limits of the tea plant, merchants attempted to increase productivity during working hours by imposing a disciplined regimen of abstract timed labor.

Such processes can be clearly demonstrated through a closer examination of the practical effects of using incense sticks to regulate tealeaf roasting in Huizhou. The amounts of time Jiang Yaohua specified—for example, cooling the leaves for the time it took to burn one stick—at first appeared to be dictated by the natural properties of the leaves: fanning the leaves for the burning of one incense stick was an ideal period of time because it resulted in the best-tasting tea that fetched good prices. Ball observed in the early century that "great attention is paid to the colour; and, though the roastings are regulated by the measure of time designated a che hiang (the one I tried burnt forty-five minutes), yet that instrument is used more as a guide than a rule; for, as the time of roasting draws to a close, each parcel is frequently compared with a sample kept for that purpose, and the roasting increased or diminished as the colour approximates to that of the sample."[39] These measurements were based upon natural variables and constituted a determination of concrete time. They were a recipe.

Given these physical limits on productivity, Jiang had proceeded to design a work regimen that maximized the amount of time spent roasting leaves in a continuous manner throughout the working day. Strategies of labor-intensive accumulation do not so much raise productivity by overcoming technical limits as they maximize the amount of time spent working within a given period. The tea factories mapped out the precise movements involved in roasting tea because they expected roasters to work all day, finishing as many baskets as possible within those hours. According to Jiang's handbook, the working day lasted as long as eighteen sticks of incense, or six baskets of leaves per roaster. In the 1930s, social surveyors found that tea factory production remained essentially the same, as factories still burned eighteen sticks per day. The surveyors further noted that this period of time took an immense toll on the workers' bodies: "The time it takes to burn all eighteen sticks of incense spans from approximately 5 a.m. to 5 p.m., in total just over twelve hours. During that time, however, one day of roasting labor completely depletes all muscle strength." Roasters needed to complete each basket of leaves within the specified three-incense-stick interval in order for the factory to squeeze in six cycles of roasting. Gone was the flexibility toward roasting time and the priority given to color and taste from Ball's day. It was crucial that factory managers "command" the roasters to perform certain movements at specified intervals. Those intervals, for example, eight-tenths of a stick, had now been transformed from a measurement *of* activity into a "normative measure *for* activity."[40]

The subtle inversion between task and time in the workshops of Huizhou does not merely contravene Landes's assertion that the cultural standard of "busyness" immunized imperial China against Western notions of "productivity." It also turns the Needham problem on its head. Rather than remaining baffled at why Chinese society wasted its opportunities to exploit accurate timekeeping technology, Jiang's handbook demonstrates how the most traditional and purportedly primitive technologies could be, and were, deployed as tools of industrial labor management. The emergence of abstract time was less a matter *of* accuracy than a desire or need *for* accuracy. What was crucial in these burgeoning social forms, then, was not the appearance of new mechanical clocks but the different functions to which technologies, old and new, were put to use.

The radical implications of abstract time in Huizhou would become visible decades later, when field researchers observed the wage system in action. Fan Hejun, a social surveyor in the 1930s, took extensive notes on tea production in Tunxi, Huizhou. He documented how the incense sticks also served as a basis for determining remuneration:

> Eighteen sticks of incense are one working day [*gong*]. Because the supplementary firing requires more time, six sticks of incense count as one shift [*lun*]. The workers who are more skilled can roast four baskets of tea in one shift. Those who are not skilled can only roast two baskets. When they have finished roasting for one shift, the skilled roasters then roast four more baskets, but there are still six sticks of incense remaining, and so they burn four more baskets. Finally, all eighteen sticks of incense are burned up. . . .
>
> Taking four baskets as one shift, the skilled workers can earn four units of wages, with each unit worth one *jiao* four *fen* four *li* [about fifteen cents]. The unskilled workers who can only roast two baskets per shift only earn, in the span of eighteen incense sticks, two units of wages. This is the situation for the supplementary roasters. . . .
>
> Thus, wages are calculated this way: for a given amount of baskets [*ruogan lou*] roasted during each shift, they receive a given amount of wages [*ruogan danwei gongzi*].[41]

The tea factories used a system of piece wages, as opposed to time wages. Again, at first glance, piece wages appeared to escape the element of productivity and time-discipline (the sense of "time is money") which forms the basis for the modern industrial labor process. Whether one roasts a basket of leaves in one hour or two should be immaterial to the basket's price. The idea that piece-rates were a symbol of preindustrial, unhurried work charmed E. P. Thompson, among others. But the distinction between piece and time wages in this sense was a red herring. In practice, it did not matter whether wages were calculated by the hour or by the piece. Rather, what mattered was the underlying basis for how much a "piece" was really worth. The answer, it turned out, remained a time-based determination. The wages for seasonal labor were calculated purely on the basis of the going rate for labor itself, determined both by the availability of workers (never in short supply in Huizhou) and average productivity. Although masquerading as something distinct, piece-rates for seasonal factory workers were simply another version of time wages: money paid to compensate labor time. Furthermore, contra Thompson's expectations, piece-rates were actually more conducive to the intensification of labor. If the tea roasters were paid only a normal day rate based upon working eighteen incense sticks—that is, twelve hours—the clumsy roaster would be paid the same amount as their skilled colleagues, despite producing half the output. But because piece wages were determined by the total number of baskets, the factory paid the skilled worker twice as much as the clumsy one. The wage system rewarded individuals who worked more quickly and efficiently even though all the individuals labored for the same number of hours.[42]

One of the clearest indications that piece wages were more ruthless than time wages was the fact that the tea factories reserved the harsh conditions of the former for the most abject, least valued workers: women and migrants. In general, the majority of factory workers were local men, who gravitated toward the least arduous jobs, such as sifting leaves. These men received a stable daily wage, including food and lodging, and their meals were "high quality, and at every meal they are served some meat." The female sorters and the migrant roasters, by contrast, were employed in a casual labor system (sangong), and neither food nor housing was provided. Both were paid by the piece.[43]

Fan Hejun was most noticeably disturbed by the working conditions of the roasters. Tea roasting was reserved for workers from the impoverished town of Anqing, west of Huizhou. Because employers did not contribute to food and housing costs, the roasters had to pay one yuan out of their own pockets per day to stay at a hostel, about one-third of their wages. For lunch, "because they must actively prepare for the afternoon shifts, they cannot eat much. At about 11 a.m., they bring out some uncooked rice they have brought with them, place it in an enamel container inside an iron can and put it on the fire to cook slowly." And the work itself routinely pushed the roasters to their physical limits. Just reading descriptions of their daily routine is enough to make the reader sweat:

> Of all the work for producing tea for export, roasting is the most bitter. This is because roasters are required to lean into the stove fire, and during the spring and summer the intense sun blazes down mercilessly. Together the sun and the stove gang up on the worker. . . .
>
> The factory we observed had eighteen rows of stoves in total, with six stoves per row, making a total of ninety-eight [sic]. At the busiest time, they could employ forty-nine men working at the same time. A fire is lit between two stoves positioned back to back, with the fire heating the pots from below and the men standing on the outside. But next to this pair of stoves is another pair, and so groups are aligned one behind the other, with only a narrow space separating each row. Two back-to-back stoves are separated by only fifty-three centimeters, and only seventy centimeters separate them from the next row. The workers stand between the rows, facing one another, a whole row of men directly facing the fire. The heat is extreme, but if the stoves could be spaced further apart, then the heat would be slightly reduced. On the basis of studying this one factory, the rows are too packed, and the spaces where the men stand are nothing less than a steam basket [zhenglong]. . . .
>
> Because the labor is so strenuous, the workers sometimes come down with sunstroke, to the point where they fall down dead. There is no shortage of such cases.[44]

Twentieth-century surveys presented a detailed picture of the tea labor process to a general readership for the first time. But insight into the daily life of factory workers could also be found in personal documents from the late nineteenth century. Among the materials in Jiang Yaohua's personal archive was a folk song he had written in thirty-six stanzas, in which he described the tea trade in colloquial rhyming couplets. Four stanzas in the middle focused on the workers in the factories, suggesting that, even during the best years of the trade, the factory managers worked the men and women to the point of exhaustion:

> The work manager must be most dignified, shouting commands and raising his voice.
> Watching the fire intently, in one day he burns many incense sticks.

Industrious, the most pitiable tea roaster, sweat stains his shirt, now
  half red.
Bent back, crooked waist, both hands busy, in a past life he must have
  been a loafer.

The tea sifters line up in order, just like the shakers and fanners.
The overseer wants them to work harder and puts out some cold food.

The roaster works night after night, three shifts and he still hasn't
  gone home.
He agrees to come in early tomorrow morning, wages to chase away the
  sleep demons.[45]

The Cliff Tea Factories of the Wuyi Mountains

In northwest Fujian, some two hundred–plus miles south of Huizhou, managers did not use physical timekeeping devices, but they
still deployed similar tactics of labor-intensive accumulation, extracting greater productivity from seasonal workers by relying upon local
legends and idiosyncratic customs and traditions. As with the incense
timekeepers, these customs appeared primitive and unchanging to the
modern observer. For this reason, so many observers overlooked the
modern quality of efficiency that animated such practices. Furthermore, the history of cliff factories illustrated how industrial labor discipline could be enforced through coercive and paternalistic measures,
contrary to liberal conceptions of capitalism as a system founded on
individual freedom, a theme explored more closely in chapter 4.

The Wuyi Mountain cliff tea factories were a unique institution
that regulated labor starting from the inaugural stages of plucking, for
cliff teas were grown on mountains where few families lived. "The entire Wuyi area is covered with abrupt, hanging cliffs, deep holes, and
large valleys," the twentieth-century surveyor Lin Fuquan reported.
"In terms of tea-growing, it is truly an ideal environment, but it also
has geographical limitations." In order to mitigate coordination problems, merchants funneled capital and labor into both cultivation and
refinement.[46]

Nearly all of the merchants in Chongan, the market town at the foot
of the mountains, maintained factories on the cliffs. The merchants
would contract out production and labor management to overseers

known as "baotou." The term was short for *baogong tou* (where *tou* means "leader"), and the contractor system known as *baogong* (where *bao* means "contract," derived from its original meaning as a "concealed package," and *gong* means "labor") suggested an opaque bond between employee and employer that regulated work struggles. Similar systems of contract work have been documented in other industries as far back as the Ming and continue to be used in Chinese-speaking industrial organizations today. In the tea trade, the baotou's most important occupational requirement was the ability to communicate with both workers and merchants. The Wuyi Mountains lay at the crossroads of the southern Fujian dialects spoken by merchants from Zhangzhou, Quanzhou, and Xiamen; the northern Fujian dialects of Fuzhou, the town from which the teas were shipped overseas; and the regional dialects of Jiangxi, where seasonal workers hailed from. The baotou himself was usually a Jiangxi native who over time had learned to speak the different dialects in order to serve as an agent of Fujian capital. During the nineteenth century, over 130 cliff tea factories were established at the top of the mountains, although this number had fallen to about 55 by the 1940s; similarly, the refineries at the foot of the mountains had diminished from 60 to about 30. The seasonal work staff arrived from Shangrao, Jiangxi, every spring, and over time the Jiangxi workers earned a special reputation for their skill. "The locals of Chongan county all say: 'the ol' Jiangxi folk [*Jiangxi lao*] are the ancestors of the creators of Wuyi Mountain tea, and without the ol' Jiangxi folk, Wuyi cliff tea would not be so beloved.'"[47]

The cliff factories relied upon the overt enforcement of the baotou and a repertoire of mythologies and customs to keep workers on task. Lin Fuquan called it a combination of "material encouragement and emotional stimulation" (*wuzhi guli, jingshen ciji*). Much of the labor process revolved around traditions tied to the mythical founder of Wuyi tea, a man named Yang Taibai, who centuries earlier came over from Jiangxi and prepared the first batch of cliff tea. No written records about Yang Taibai have yet been unearthed, but workers continued to feel his presence in the bundle of rituals organized around his legend. "The rules and modes of labor management," Lin wrote, relied upon "customs" and "mystical power." As a result, "each spring, the amount of power extracted from each worker far surpasses the limits of a normal person." The mythologies of Wuyi tea helped quell any potential disquiet. "No one complains," for the regulations were considered a "sacred law."[48]

These unique features of the Wuyi labor process could be observed from the first day of tea season, when pluckers climbed the mountain to collect leaves. This was called "opening the mountains" (*kaishan*), and it required the workers' utmost obedience:

> On the day of opening the mountain, all the workers wake up at the crack of dawn, and the baotou will light some incense to the mountain god Yang Taibai. . . . During this ritual, one cannot talk. According to legend, they do not talk in order to avoid the god of illness and in order to have a rich, bountiful harvest. Breakfast is eaten standing up, it is forbidden to sit down. After breakfast, the baotou and several leaders bring workers up the mountains to the tea gardens and begin picking, and the baotou leaves. The workers must walk straight to the garden, still silent, and without turning their heads. According to legend, if one turns their head to look back, they will suffer an eye disease. Turning one's head symbolizes not fully committing to the labor, and this would offend the mountain gods, incurring their wrath. . . . After arriving at the garden, the tea picking leaders point out where to pick, and after about an hour the baotou returns and gives each worker some cigarettes. After that, all the taboos are lifted. The workers take a smoke break and begin to chat. About now, the morning fog begins to scatter, and the sun illuminates the beautiful mountains. They sing songs and laugh, and it is at this stage of singing and laughing that the process of tea production truly begins.[49]

Another custom forbade the workers from eating their lunch anywhere else but near the factory at the top of the mountains, where the baotou could monitor them. When Lin Fuquan asked why, he was told "this was a rule set by the tea ancestor Yang Taibai and no one dares violate it." For Lin, these customs appeared as nothing more than cynical tactics for asserting control over the pluckers. Whereas in Huizhou, the tea roasters suffered the worst conditions, in the Wuyi Mountains, it was the pluckers who bore the brunt of discipline. Both were subjected to a day-wage system that in practice functioned as a piece wage, with the goal to measure and maximize labor intensity. "Wages for plucking labor are determined based upon efficiency [*xiaolü*]," Lin wrote, "with meticulous rules and clear rewards and punishments."[50]

In lieu of incense sticks or other timekeepers, the baotou relied on a system of "covertly" weighing leaves at unexpected times of the day. On the so-called big day (dari), the overseers would select a random moment to weigh leaves in order to calculate wages:

> Five or six days [after opening the mountain], when the leaves are fully green and mature, they have what is called the "big day." Every day on the mountain, the tea master brings up the triangular red flag (it is about two feet long, triangular in shape, and it has ling ["command"] written on it to signify it is the banner of command of Yang Taibai) and a small scale in order to covertly measure the labor of the pluckers. . . . At any given moment during any day, when no one expects it, the baotou will suddenly yell "Everybody! Time for a smoke break!" The workers will suddenly stop plucking, and the baotou will weigh the amount of leaves in each basket individually and record the weights. This type of unexpected weighing is known as "covert weighing" [ancheng].[51]

This system functioned similarly to the incense sticks in Huizhou. By halting tea plucking at the same time, the tea masters established a baseline for measuring each worker's output and efficiency. The tea masters made no attempt to keep time accurately, yet because they managed time independently of the tasks themselves, they practiced, in Postone's argument, a form of calculation premised on "abstract time."

The overseers also paired the basic material incentives of wages with disciplinary tactics founded on customs and shame. The worker who had picked the least amount of leaves was forced to carry the red flag down the mountain at night. "Having received this type of humiliation," the theory went, "that worker will definitely exert great effort on the following day." Lin designated this a form of "emotional stimulation" (jingshen shang zhi ciji). "These regulations are very good," Lin remarked with acerbic wit. "Because they are offered material encouragement and stimulation, the workers do not feel as though they've completely sold out their bodily labor to work for the baotou. We suspect that other tea districts do not have such a perfect system."[52] Work songs recorded by Lin, however, indicated that workers were not so easily intimidated by these tactics:

> Without many leaves plucked, sit on the ground,
> who dares grab the flag and ring the bell,
> I don't care about the top wages,
> what can you baotou do with me?

Other songs displayed the workers' sense of humor about the wage system:

> Plucking leaves, my friends have no worries,
> with curled backs and bent waists, no sex either,
> both good and bad, pluck some baskets,
> with the top wages will also bring a girl.[53]

In the Wuyi Mountains, the cliff factories took care of many tasks that would elsewhere be undertaken in the market town factories, such as re-roasting, sifting, and sorting leaves. As a result, many of the pluckers transitioned into a second job by evening. During the busiest weeks, these men found their waking and sleeping hours dictated entirely by the continuous refinement process:

> Every day, the pluckers work on the mountains from 5 a.m. to 6 p.m. at night, twelve hours of nonstop climbing cliffs and crossing ridges and valleys, such arduous work. Even if the workers can get some rest, they must also spend half the night roasting and rolling leaves. Therefore, every night after eating supper, the workers sleep until the leaves are finished fermenting. The early ones get to sleep from around eight or nine until midnight, when they are awoken from their dreams by the sound of bamboo sticks being struck. All the factory workers are mobilized to roast and process the leaves plucked that day. Furthermore, the plucking laborers must also do the labor-selling activity of tea rolling. After the leaves are roasted, if they finish early, the workers can catch some more sleep. If the sun has already begun to rise, then the workers will not sleep. They eat breakfast and once again bring their baskets up the mountains to recommence their twelve hours of backbreaking labor. These pluckers sleep, at most, three to four hours each night. On days when the mountains are filled with mature leaves, the workers will go several nights without sleep. The bitterness of their lives can be called extreme.[54]

Inside the factory, the sorters were rewarded and punished based upon speed: "In terms of work efficiency, the fast workers can pick through seven baskets, and the least skilled workers can pick through four per day." Whereas the factory system rewarded faster than average workers by letting them sleep until the morning, the "slow ones work from dawn to dusk and have to use a oil lamp." The following song reflected the cycle of unending, sleepless work that fueled the expansion of the Chinese tea trade in the nineteenth century:

After Qingming ends the grain rains begin,
and my thoughts turn to Chongan, how pitiable,
day after day spent besides the bushes,
three nights pass without two nights of sleep.[55]

CONCLUSION

Within the study of Chinese history, scholars have long pursued the indigenous foundations for, and obstacles against, the spontaneous development of industrial capitalism. They have done so by tracking the emergence of capitalism's technical components, features of "proto-industrialization," including widespread markets, specialization, and free wage labor. Curiously, although these features have been unearthed as far back as the economic revolutions of the Tang and Song, industrial capitalism, they concluded, did not follow. For generations, the most popular explanations were to frame Qing China as a society stuck in a "high-level equilibrium trap" or patterns of "involution." Of course, several historians have since challenged these classic theses, and a brief survey of recent scholarship may help clarify the arguments of the current chapter.[56]

In his major work, R. Bin Wong (1997) reframed the late imperial period as running parallel to the proto-industrial patterns of early modern Europe, wherein greater market-oriented production led to successful population growth, albeit without mechanization. Wong had usefully resituated China within dynamic terms, but general criticisms of the proto-industry concept still applied. Perlin, for instance, argued that the "proto-industrialization" literature divorced households and villages from the broader historical context of long-distance trade, colonialism, and distinct patterns of capital, thereby producing flattened ideal-types and "neo-evolutionist" schema. Indeed, much of the revisionist scholarship has intentionally focused on Chinese history prior to the nineteenth century, in order to avoid, perhaps, the complications of the treaty-port era. By contrast, Peng Nansheng's recent descriptions of "semi-industrialization" (*ban gongyehua*) in China approached the long nineteenth century head-on. From the 1870s onward, he argued, Chinese rural handicrafts in certain eastern and central regions experienced forms of economic development in terms of tools and specialized techniques that were driven by long-distance markets and shaped by the backdrop of industrialization (defined as labor-saving machinery) elsewhere around the world. Peng's theory pointed to the emergence of particular economic patterns within pockets of Chinese society un-equivocally linked to the global context; he was interested in elucidat-ing "processes" rather than hunting for "results." The strongest exam-ples of semi-industrialization were cotton and silk—his primary case studies—alongside paper, oil, flour, and, indeed, the export tea trade.[57]

The current chapter builds on the insights from these newer ap-proaches. In particular, although I discovered Peng Nansheng's work very late in the process of my own conceptualization, I was pleasantly surprised to discover that we had separately arrived at similar conclu-sions. Whereas his research offered a broad analysis of regional pro-duction across treaty-port-era China, this chapter has foregrounded the specific experience of tea by highlighting similar phenomena in fur-ther depth. However, I also wish to emphasize that the point of depar-ture for my own analysis is that the most recent centuries of Chinese, indeed world, history have been distinguished not by the presence of any particular *technical* feature but rather the unprecedented degree to which the *social* compulsion to grow and produce for the world market has come to dominate everyday life. I have offered a discrete picture of the qualitative changes experienced by tea producers immediately fol-lowing a historic spike in demand from overseas, when merchants and overseers began to exert an exceptional degree of managerial discipline over workers. While the earliest tea merchants were merely itinerant guests indifferent to manufacture, by the turn of the twentieth cen-tury they had developed a standardized system for timed labor that demanded speed and coordination. Ultimately, it was these same social dynamics of competition-inspired intensification that would draw Chi-nese tea producers toward capital-intensive, mechanical methods in the twentieth century.

The techniques highlighted here were developed during the late 1800s, around the same time that tea plantations in India first emerged on the global market. For years, Chinese producers staved off their ri-vals to the west by economizing on human labor costs. Only by the last decade of the century were they unable to compete with the structural advantages afforded the colonial industry, which itself developed in re-sponse to the strengths of the China trade. It was in order to challenge Chinese tea's grip on the Euro-American markets that British planters sought recourse in exceptional government legislation to control labor costs, laws that proved decisive in the colonization of Assam, as the next two chapters demonstrate. In seeking to explain the eventual commercial success of the Indian industry, therefore, we must not only point toward the much maligned limitations of the Chinese tea trade but also its economic dynamism—the relentless competitive pressures exerted by the resourceful guest merchants and industrious seasonal workforces of Huizhou and the Wuyi Mountains, the two remote frontiers where the export tea trade of China had first begun.

3 A Crisis of Classical Political Economy in Assam

From Economic Liberalism to a Theory of Colonization, 1834–1862

TEA EXPORTS THRIVED in the decades following the Opium War, but although British consumers were happy to indulge their addiction to the Chinese beverage, members of Parliament and the East India Company worried about an indefinite dependence upon the Chinese market. Just as British free traders justified military adventures in China on the grounds of a "safe and unrestricted liberty of trade," Company officials used the same language to support experimentation with tea cultivation in India.[1] The governor-general of India, William Bentinck, first proposed experiments in an 1834 Minute by submitting a letter from a certain "John Walker," who wrote that Indian tea would "contribute to the consumption of British manufactures, and increase the prosperity of our empire in the East, and also annihilate the Chinese monopoly."[2] The supply of tea had become a matter of "considerable national importance," "intermingled with our habits and customs," and provided the government four million pounds in revenue per year. The Qing government's "jealous policy" of limited trade placed cumbersome limits on commerce. It was marked by "ignorance," "pride," "prejudice" and "corruption," but "it will be easy for us to destroy" through competition. The same bellicose rhetoric that "liberalized" the Chinese markets also laid the foundations for the Indian tea industry.

But Assam was not China. In Canton, British merchants relied upon an extensive network of inland commerce and specialized production that had developed over centuries. By contrast, the EIC found in the Brahmaputra Valley a land "covered with a jungle of gigantic reeds, traversed only by the wild elephant or the buffalo, where human footstep is unknown and the atmosphere even to the native[s] themselves is pregnant with febrile miasma and death." At first it turned to the Chinese teamaker to come to Assam and "instruct the natives," promoting "peaceful habits of industry among them." Bentinck, accepting that Indian tea must rely on "Chinese agency," authorized funds for travel throughout Southeast Asia to obtain "the genuine plant" and "actual cultivators." Over the next decade, a Tea Committee composed of English and Bengali capitalists employed a staff of 135 men, including 39 Chinese workers and 76 "native" apprentices, costing the government nearly 43,000 rupees per year. But if the Opium War had been supported by the principle of free trade, and the dominant ideology of rule within the empire was one of economic liberalism, then officials naturally expressed ambivalence about government involvement in commerce. In 1840, the new governor-general, George Eden, sought to hand over the tracts to "private enterprize," for the tea experiments had "reached a scale" that exceeded the limits of "a full, fair and efficient experiment." Henry T. Prinsep, member of the government council, expressed his reservations over migrant contract labor from China and eastern India. "The Government," he wrote, "should be careful of establishing a precedent for the transfer of laborers for a consideration which eventually may assume a shape not easily distinguishable from the transaction so much cried out against in Mauritius and in the Slave Colonies."[3]

There is a deep irony reading Eden's and Prinsep's words from the standpoint of the turn of the twentieth century. By then, the Indian tea industry had achieved spectacular economic success, "annihilating" its Chinese competition, but only after the colonial government had subsidized the planters with free land, revenue concessions, and a labor indenture system that directly contradicted Prinsep's warnings: "the same organized system of recruitment that was pursued by the planters of Mauritius."[4] Starting in the 1860s, officials legalized penal labor contracts that prevented migrant Indian workers from leaving employers under threat of prosecution. During the last decades of the century, the system shepherded nearly half a million migrant workers into Assam, a boon of cheap and immobilized labor critical to the industry's success. Assam tea thrived, in other words, based upon an economic strategy that stood opposed to the principles of liberalism espoused at its outset.

Extant historiography has largely depicted the Indian tea industry as a smooth and natural outgrowth of the collaboration between British planters and the colonial state.[5] Although critical of the human costs of "economic success," these scholars have unintentionally reinforced the impression given by champions of the industry itself, who attributed their accomplishments to an ideologically coherent, distinctively "British" approach to capitalist industry. A focused examination of political-economic thought and practice, however, shows that the origins of the tea industry were fraught with contradiction and controversy. British officials originally envisioned their industry as derivative of the Chinese free tenantry, whom they praised for their "commercial disposition." The ultimate turn to penal contract labor, by contrast, was justified as an *exception* to the norms of liberal political economy, a somber admission of the limitations of free and private enterprise. Over the next two chapters I will analyze this reversal of policy as a history of political-economic thought and a social history of global capital and local labor.

In the current chapter, I illustrate how Assam labor indenture emerged out of a crisis of political-economic principles in colonial India. During the initial 1830s experiments, the colonial government held fast to the doctrines of classical political economy, embodied in the twin ideals of free markets and free labor. Officials displayed an admiration for Chinese society as a collection of medium-sized commercial farmers who did not rely upon government intervention, and they hoped to re-create this model among the local Assam population. But planters complained from the beginning that the government did not provide support commensurate with the significance of tea. Only after a mid-century crisis of liberalism did officials openly criticize laissez-faire doctrine, embracing government intervention into the recruitment of waged workers. Thus, capitalist production in Assam was not created out of British liberal principles but rather out of the crisis of them.[6]

In the first section I describe the initial political-economic philosophy of colonial rule in Assam. Throughout the first half of the century, economic thinkers within the British Empire promoted "private enterprize" rather than government intervention. Champions of liberal and utilitarian reform in India—prominent among them Bentinck—held that human nature was universal and Indian society could be shaped in the image of England. In the words of a Calcutta businessman, "We may be assured that in buying and selling human nature is the same in Cawnpore [Kanpur] as in Cheapside."[7] Liberal reformers were above all optimistic. In the realm of economics, they argued that commercial value stemmed not from the land but from the addition of labor, as optimized by market mechanisms. They valued a strong rule of law and clear property rights. In Assam, Governors Bentinck and Eden both envisioned tea cultivation naturally taking hold among the local peasantry, as they believed it had in China, rather than through the monopoly of European corporations. These beliefs came out clearly in two topics of official correspondence, one revolving around the promotion of "free migration" from China into Assam and the other regarding the transition from government-sponsored experiments to privately owned plantations.

Labor indenture policies arose as a break from the established political-economic principles of Company rule. The second section explains how this rupture emerged out of multiple crises of colonial governance. A series of political rebellions, starting with the 1857 "Sepoy Mutiny," forced British officials to question the optimistic universalism of classical political economy. Instead, they saw Indian society as historically backward and culturally particular, a view captured in the work of Henry Maine. This pessimistic outlook was also adopted by proponents of indenture, who blamed the failure of labor markets on the "backward" habits of the Assamese. In particular, the bureaucrat W. N. Lees, influenced by the theorist of colonization Edward G. Wakefield, offered the most complete and self-consciously *illiberal* justification for intervention and indenture. He followed the same template laid out by other critics of liberalism: that culturalism and historicism should displace universalism, practical experience should displace abstract principles, and colonization should displace the free market.[8]

Bureaucrats in Assam turned to penal labor contracts in order to resolve an ongoing *economic* crisis of labor, and in so doing they contributed to a general *political* crisis of liberalism reverberating throughout the British Empire. In this chapter I expand on past studies on late imperial crisis, which have emphasized the codification of racial, religious, and gender differences, by demonstrating how the same crisis shaped *labor* policies as well. In turn, I also situate a rich social history of Assam within the history of economic thought, demonstrating how indenture was conceived not as a model for imperial policy but as an exceptional approach for an exceptional region, one that defied the "ordinary" dynamics of commercial society observed in Bengal, England, or China.

The exceptional status of Assam is analyzed more closely in the concluding section, which seeks to crystallize the main findings of this history of economic thought. In trying to theorize the special circumstances of colonies like Assam, the Americas, and Oceania, writers such as Lees and Wakefield repudiated an earlier faith in the market, but they nevertheless reinforced a central tenet of political economy: that the basis of modern capitalist production was wage labor itself. Whereas in Britain, Adam Smith's discovery of a "theory of value" reflected the ongoing development of an emergent capitalist society, in Assam and other colonies the same theory functioned as a lever for policy change. Because officials could not find a market for cheap labor in the colonial frontier, they created one themselves, thereby attempting to *make* Assam conform to the same laws of development as in the metropole.

THE TEA EXPERIMENTS

Assam and Political Economy on the Eve of the Tea Experiments

Once the British had annexed Assam with the Treaty of Yandabo (1826), David Scott (1786–1831), a Scottish official stationed in the northeast since the early 1810s, was appointed political agent to the governor-general in the Northeast Frontier of Bengal. For nearly a half century, the Brahmaputra Valley had been devastated by civil wars, and some estimates suggested that 80 percent of the productive valley had been abandoned. Analyzing Scott's initial attempts to manage this region can help us begin to grasp the prevailing principles of governance in India in this early period, as well as their limitations. Scott first sought to reform the system of revenue collection and to establish clear property rights in the region, but he also held fast to the principle of minimal intervention and expanding commercial activity among locals. Rather than unseat the Ahom monarchy, he sought to reform the system of administration while reinstalling the prince Purandar Singh into power. In upper Assam, he retained the *khel* system, which organized the peasantry by taxing their forced labor during one-third of the year. In lower Assam, his team instituted systems of collection similar to those in Bengal. Despite Scott's initial optimism, however, the Ahom administration was beset by corruption and embezzlement, and revenue could not cover state expenditures. Attempts to phase out corvée in favor of cash payments slowed down economic activity, as the peasantry began to rely on outside moneylenders and fall into debt. In Assam, market activity had not facilitated social improvement but only worsened conditions. Before his sudden death in 1831, Scott offered the first of several plans for a more interventionist approach. He proposed that the Company reinvest revenue into the region by establishing "sericulture demonstration farms" and purchasing opium and silk from local peasants. Scott justified this departure by arguing that classical political economy was valid only "in the ordinary state of political societies." Assam was an exception, and the government could not wait for improvements "by chance" and should actively nurture them "with certainty and at once."[9]

When Scott spoke of the "ordinary state of political societies," he was referring to the basic tenets of British rule in India. In 1765, when the East India Company acquired the grant of *diwani* of Bengal, its prevailing political strategy could be summarized, in the words of Eric Stokes, as one of "expediency." The Company was a commercial monopoly in origin, and administrators viewed their primary activity as revenue collection, which enabled the Company to purchase silk, indigo, sugar, and cotton piece goods from Bengal. Revenue collection as a support for trade became the Company's "absolute priority," but administrators did not envision a total revolution of Bengal society. Edmund Burke reinforced political caution during the trial of Warren Hastings (1788–1795), the first governor of Bengal, affirming the Whig belief that "arbitrary power" in government should be kept in check. This conservative approach coincided with the widespread dissemination and acceptance of political-economic thought in Britain and British India. Adam Smith's wildly popular *The Wealth of Nations* (1776) compelled subsequent generations of English readers to study and debate the merits of the new science known as "Political Economy." By the nineteenth century, Smith's views on individual liberty had become a "cardinal article of middle class faith," just as the English middle class formed the workforce of the Company. Further, the Company court of directors installed a course on the laws of society and economics into their syllabus for civil servants at the East India College at Haileybury.

Many officials would later recount studying economics on their own, and the names of the great economists of the day peppered the correspondence of high officials. Political economy "was part of the *psyche* of those who were ruling India from England."[10]

Smith had offered an optimistic vision of how individuals, freed from the yoke of custom and coercion, would naturally bring about a society-wide process of "improvement," what we today might call "economic growth." Two of the most significant tenets of his vision were his emphasis upon productive labor and the free market.

Smith argued that the most "civilized and thriving" societies were characterized by an "improvement in the productive powers of labour," namely the division of labor. He championed the possibilities of industry and manufacture by self-consciously dissenting from two earlier philosophies, that of the "mercantile system" and that of the French Physiocrats. The former held that value was contained in metals themselves, and its proponents focused on tariffs and trade surpluses. Instead, Smith emphasized the role of production, enabled by free trade. The eighteenth-century school of Physiocracy, by contrast, had already recognized the importance of labor but only that associated with the land. Only agriculture, they reasoned, created the physical utility ("value in use") of grains and raw materials. Smith had expanded their category of value to *all labor* that was embodied in a commodity, thereby yielding commercial profit ("value in exchange"). He thus abstracted value from a physical to a social characteristic. In his emphasis upon commodity-producing labor, Smith laid the foundation for classical political economy's theory of value: that productive labor was both the source and measure of value in society. How could these productive powers be unleashed? Smith's answer was the expansion of free markets. Through exchange, individual actors would marry the three factors of production—land, labor, and "stock," or, capital—producing a specialization of discrete skills, the accumulation of capital, and commodity production through the division of labor. The motor behind this "automatic mechanism" was human nature itself. For Smith, there existed "a certain propensity in human nature . . . to truck, barter, and exchange one thing for another."[11]

Notably, Smith was also fiercely opposed to aspects of the EIC. When he wrote *The Wealth of Nations*, the Company was mainly a trading company whose profits stemmed from a monopoly he criticized fiercely.

Smith's work helped mobilize opposition to the Company monopoly, phased out in the charters of 1813 and 1833. Company officials side-stepped criticism by claiming that, as a company-state, they ensured the widening of the marketplace in Indian society, free from the oppression of native landlords and despots. The Company's political-economic approach may not have adhered faithfully to the entirety of Smith's vision, but officials did selectively deploy Smithian arguments, namely, his abstract vision of development based upon trade and consequent improvement.[12]

During this early period, Company officials shared the belief that "government interference would retard the full development of human beings," and they argued that the role of the state was "minimal but not nonexistent," consisting in providing the "correct institutional structure": free trade, infrastructure, and, especially, the rule of law in protecting private property. By the turn of the nineteenth century, the latter two were firmly etched into the foundation of British rule. The two most famous models of revenue collection, the Permanent Settlement of Bengal (1793) and the *ryotwari* system of western India, were tied to different schools of philosophy—Physiocracy and romanticism, respectively—but they shared the view that private property was the bedrock of Indian "improvement." Back in Assam, David Scott's attempt to retain and improve the *khel* system had followed a similar pattern of codifying native structures into a transparent system of private property and revenue collection. Otherwise, wrote historian S. Ambirajan, "the idea of [economic] non-intervention was entertained and adhered to."[13]

The dilemmas Scott faced in Assam also revealed the dangers of minimal intervention in a region chronically short of capital. The Company's long-standing policy had been to bar British merchants from settling in India, citing the danger of unchecked European oppression. But by the first decades of the nineteenth century officials and economists began to argue in favor of expanding state reach and European investment. After all, if Smith had placed so much importance on widening market activity, then restrictions on the overseas movement of capital were an affront to free trade. Utilitarians such as Jeremy Bentham and James Mill argued that "colonization" in the form of direct British investment and management would benefit both sides. They attributed stagnation in Britain to a surplus of capital and competition, and they saw India as an outlet for hoards of wealth. English colonization would introduce important "knowledge, morals, capital, skill, and personnel" into, as Bentinck put it, India's "torpid population." Among the most ardent champions were the Bengali reformers Rammohan Roy and Dwarkanath Tagore, who, based upon experiences with indigo cultivation, believed capitalist industry would enrich the average Indian cultivator.[14] European investment was codified with the Company's Charter Act of 1833—the same legislation that liberalized the China trade—and proposals for British-led experiments with tea soon followed.

The push for colonization also reflected a tempered embrace of interventionist reform by officials. Insofar as India was burdened by custom and tradition, liberal and utilitarian reformers in Europe reaffirmed that the government's duty was to free people from the fetters of religion and feudalism, enabling them to participate in the world of exchange, rationality, and individual autonomy. Precisely because Company rule was less hampered by the various constituencies of England, its administrators treated India as "a laboratory for the creation of the liberal administrative state." Bentinck was himself an admirer of utilitarian reform. In 1827, on the eve of his departure, he had reportedly told Mill, "I am going to British India, but I shall not be Governor-General. It is you that will be Governor-General."[15] Under Bentinck's direction, the Company outlawed the practice of *sati*, or widow sacrifice (1829–1830), and Thomas Macaulay delivered his infamous "Minute on Education" (1835). Seen alongside these attempts at social reform, Bentinck's proposal to cultivate tea becomes legible as part of an attempt to liberate Indian society and nurture its improvement through law and free trade.

The tea experiments in Assam thus stood at the intersection of two historical patterns. First, across India, administrators turned to European investment both as a solution for the glut of British capital and as a tool for developing the Indian economy. In his original memorandum, Walker had written that Indian tea would address the imbalance from British textile industrialization: "The exportation of Manchester and Glasgow cottons and muslins to India has so deluged the Indian markets, that many thousands of the native weavers are ruined, and in the greatest distress," he wrote, and "the East India Company are much at a loss to provide some reasonable occupation for the natives, to promote peaceful habits of industry among them." Tea was an ideal

commodity, for the "inhabitants of India" had "little or no occupation excepting that of agriculture," and therefore "the cultivation and
preparation of tea would admirably accord with their sedentary and
tranquil habits." Second, in Assam, administrators faced an especially
poor and underpopulated region on the margins of Bengal. Scott's successor, Francis Jenkins, spoke forcefully about the need for a European
presence. Dispatched years earlier to survey the northeast, Jenkins had
written that "the settlement of Englishmen of capital on the wastes on
these frontiers seems to me to offer a better prospect for the speedy realization of improvements than any measures that could be adopted in
the present ignorant and demoralized state of the native inhabitants."
Before he had even learned about the wild tea plants of upper Assam,
Jenkins had contrived other strategies for cash crop promotion, advo-
cating for higher tax rates that would force the peasantry to convert
the "wastes and haunts of wild beasts into fruitful fields of sugarcane,
mustard, mulberry, lac, tobacco and vegetables."[16]

Bentinck delivered his memorial on tea in January 1834. At first,
he speculated about Nepal and the Himalayas as sites for experimentation, unaware of ongoing attempts in Assam, dating back to 1819,
to investigate whether indigenous tea plants could be identified. In
February, Bentinck appointed his Tea Committee in Calcutta, and by
May 1834, Jenkins wrote from Assam that "in the Singpho district of
Beesa," officials had learned of "a coarse variety of the tea plant" that
was "undoubtedly indigenous." He recommended appointing "some
well-qualified person" to come to the northeast "for the examination
of the soil in which it grows, as reported, and an inspection of the tract
of mountains between Cachar and Assam." By Christmas Eve the committee had confirmed, after years of speculation, that "the tea shrub is
beyond all doubt indigenous in Upper Assam," adding that "this discovery" was "by far the most important and valuable that has ever
been made on matters connected with the agricultural or commercial
resources of this empire."[17] In less than one year, Bentinck's tea experiments had settled upon Assam as their designated site.

Experiments with Laissez-Faire Development

Earlier generations of historians were surely correct to pronounce
that "British private enterprise in Assam was not the outcome of a

laissez faire policy."[18] Between 1834 and 1839, the Tea Committee founded an experimental tea garden in Sadiya; imported thousands of plants from China; and recruited a workforce from the local population as well as hundreds of teamakers from China and Southeast Asia. The experiments culminated in the production of tea that could be sold back in England, and afterwards members of the Tea Committee inherited the experimental tracts, converting their holdings into a limited liability company that for decades enjoyed, more or less, a monopolistic hold on the industry. Nevertheless, throughout the 1830s officials consistently expressed their adherence to the minimalist tenets of political economy. That officials had to repeatedly contradict such principles was a source of tension between them and the private planters. This latent conflict would eventually boil to the surface over the problem of finding supplies of wage labor. The historical problem addressed in this section, then, is not *whether or not* economic policy in Assam was actually laissez-faire, which it clearly never was; the more relevant question is *how did* the tension between laissez-faire theory and interventionist practice produce a new political-economic worldview that brokered labor indenture policies that were once unthinkable?

To better understand this ideological break, I examine two series of correspondence which revolved around policy proposals that ultimately failed but which also revealed the precarious nature of the Company's philosophy. First, Governor-General Eden hatched a plan to promote the "free migration" of Chinese tea farmers into upper Assam, with the expectation that the migrants would encourage locals to take up tea cultivation themselves and that Assam would "naturally" develop along the path of other Asian commercial societies, such as Bengal or China. Such policies would be considered laughable by the turn of the century, when Chinese tea was mocked for its primitive and unhygienic methods. Second, at the close of the experiments, the governor-general and other officials opposed the policy of handing over government tracts to the Assam Company on the grounds that it would encourage monopoly.

The Tea Committee's experiments were led by Superintendent of Tea Culture Charles Bruce, who established a nursery for imported Chinese plants in Sadiya, later relocated to Dibrugarh, both along the upper reaches of Assam. He also scoured the surrounding areas for wild tea plants, discovering tracts under control of the the "Muttucks" (Matak) and Singpho territories (figure 9). By 1839, he reported to Calcutta that he had documented some 120 total tea tracts across upper Assam. Throughout these experiments, colonial officials attempted to foster a spirit of enterprise among the various local groups. In May 1836, Jenkins wrote that Raja Purandar Singh, who years earlier had brought wild tealeaves to the Company's attention, "is anxious to retain one-half of the hill, that he may carry on the cultivation of the tea plants, ... and overseers of the Government should instruct his people in the management of the plant and manufacture of tea." In October, Bruce recommended "giving up the Suddeeah tea plants, and distributing them among the native chiefs and others that may wish to take them." Jenkins also added that, at this early date, "I do not contemplate the Government wish to do more themselves than to show the feasibility of producing a marketable tea within our own provinces, and thence I should judge that the sooner they can abandon the proposed tea plantation to private enterprise the better." Nathan Brown, a missionary who had followed Jenkins around the tea tracts, added that the "tea trade will produce a great change in the country—will fill it with a dense population, and convert these almost impenetrable jungles into the happy abodes of industry." It did not take long for these buoyant predictions to crash upon the shores of colonial realities. One year later, in 1837, Jenkins relayed that Bruce "complains of the apathy of the Singphoos," but he also added that serious discussions for internal labor migration were premature "in the present state." Bruce reiterated that he hoped the Singpho people could become industrious workers, writing in 1839, "If the cultivation of Tea were encouraged, and the Poppy put a stop to in Assam, the Assamese would make a splendid set of Tea manufacturers and Tea cultivators."[19]

In the meantime, the Tea Committee's main priority was to soundly learn the art of cultivation. They made plans to contract Chinese teamakers from Canton, schemes that yielded their own share of difficulties. In 1836, the government made an uneasy pact with four teamakers who hailed from Jiangxi, near the Wuyi Mountains of Fujian, and from them Bruce had first learned the basic steps in making black tea (figure 10). Over the next several years, "batches" of 50, 64, and 247 Chinese workers arrived in Calcutta from various parts of Malaysia. The entire experiment was later recalled in mocking terms. "Every man with a tail [the signature queue hairstyle required of Qing imperial subjects] was supposed to be qualified to cultivate, manipulate and prepare tea,"

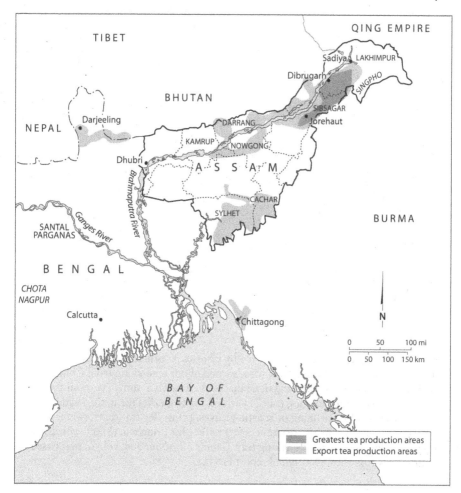

Figure 9. Export tea production regions in India at the turn of the twentieth century. The Tea Committee's 1830s experiments took place in the upper reaches of the Assam Valley, which grew into the colonial industry's area of greatest concentration. Cartography by Bill Nelson, based on *The Atlas of the World Commerce Maps, Text and Diagrams* by J. G. Bartholomew (London: George Newnes Limited, 1907), 82–83.

a local paper reported. Another observer recalled that the committee, "acting presumably on the belief that every Chinaman must be an expert in tea cultivation and manufacture . . . transplanted all the Chinese shoemakers and carpenters that they could induce to go from Cositollah and other bazaars in Calcutta to Assam; these men were nearly all from

Figure 10. Sketches on how to make tea by Charles A. Bruce, superintendent of gardens for the Tea Committee, who learned about teamaking from Chinese workers brought over from Jiangxi, China, to Assam. They show (1) stand for sun-drying, (2) rod for moving trays, (3) stand for withering tea in the shade, (4) cast-iron pan for steaming or roasting leaves, (5) trolley transport, (6) manual rolling as taught by Chinese teamakers, (7) basket for firing tea, (8) tray for dried or fired leaves, and (9) hand-picking tray. Ukers, *All About Tea*, vol. 1, 464, based on drawings from Bruce's original report (1838).

the sea-port towns of the Celestial Empire, and many had never seen a tea plant in their lifetime." Officials nevertheless evinced optimism that the free and entrepreneurial Chinese farmer ideal could be found. In 1839, Eden announced, "If any of the Chinese are inclined to settle as tea cultivators on their own account, they should meet with all possible encouragement. Nothing would be so beneficial to the Province as the introduction of a *skillful and laborious* Chinese tenantry." In his complaints about Chinese men brought in on contracts, Jenkins had cited the cost and unruliness of the hired men. By contrast, Eden spoke of cultivators who would "settle" on "their own account." Tenant farmer migrants would cost the government nothing, and those men would have every incentive to improve tea agriculture. These ideal teamakers would represent the sort of parsimonious class of merchants that political economy saw as the foundation for social "improvement."[20]

In reply to Eden's 1839 resolution, the Tea Committee forwarded a letter concerning a man from Fujian, China, known as Ting Kwoe, who wished to grow tea in Assam. The author of the letter was the Prussian missionary and Orientalist Karl Gützlaff, who had served as an interpreter for the British government during the Opium War. The intermediary between Gützlaff and the Indian government was Jardine Matheson & Co., which had already contracted thirteen workers from Fujian to be sent to Assam.[21] Gützlaff introduced his man to the government as "a very nice Fokeen man" who had "extensively been engaged in the Cultivation and manufacture of tea, and therefore wishes to proceed with a quantity of seeds entirely on his own account to Bengal to plant them himself and the only advance he stipulated is two hundred dollars." Ting offered to bring his brothers and son "to establish a free tea colony," and Gützlaff added that "as this is *the first instance of free emigration to the Tea hills,* Mr. Matheson thought it prudent to encourage this man that others may follow his example." Eden expressed "much satisfaction [over] the likelihood of a case occurring of free emigration from China to the Province of Assam of a Chinese family for the purpose of settling and Cultivating Tea on their own account." He was "prepared to afford every ligitimate [*sic*] encouragement to such letters."[22]

Unfortunately, Ting Kwoe's gesture turned out to be a swindle. He accepted the advances from Gützlaff but failed to show up on the arranged day to sail to Calcutta. "It appears that some fraud has been practiced on the Revd W. Gutzlaff with regard to the case of free emigration of a Chinese family," the government soberly noted. Further, the seeds that "Teng Kwoe the pretended emigrant" had sold to the Company for two hundred dollars, turned out to be "entirely useless and unfit for being sown."[23]

Undeterred, the government continued to pursue the elusive "free emigration" from China through other avenues. For years, officials speculated about employing Gützlaff to wear "a Chinese dress" and "penetrat[e] from Canton through Yunnan to Assam," "exploring the interior of China, and ascertaining the facilities which exist for such communication between it and Calcutta." Moreover, when Tea

Committee officials persuaded the Indian government to hire a Chinese translator, they advertised that he was "capable, better perhaps than any one else, to cause that speedy introduction into Assam of a skillful and laborious Chinese tenantry, than which nothing would be more beneficial to the province."[24]

The language of these proposals expressed an underlying political ideology that prized a natural, free market for labor that was innately "skillful and laborious." For many, the introduction of European management and capital was but a temporary means to an end, an interregnum before Chinese or Assamese peasants could run the industry themselves. Whereas historians have noted that the British colonial "liberal set out, on the basis of . . . [a] shared humanity, to turn the Indian into an Englishman," in this particular instance, Eden and his peers sought to turn the Indian into something akin to a "skillful and laborious Chinese tenantry." Officials were laudatory toward Chinese migrants based less on some racial logic than a perception of their practical habits, which were steeped in commerce. In his 1834 Minute, Bentinck wrote that he had traveled eastward and observed the "character of the Chinese adventurers there," concluding that "their superior energy, their industry, their spirit of speculation and calculation of profit," were "quite equal to that of any European nation." Bentinck and Eden were echoing an idea long established among early modern European thinkers, such as Leibniz, Voltaire, and Quesnay (see chapter 5), who expressed deep admiration for China. For his part, Smith had written that China, as well as Bengal, was "the exemplar" of "the natural progress of opulence," seamlessly combining its dedication to agriculture, manufacture, and commerce. These descriptions were of course merely speculative, and opinion would shift abruptly by the end of the century. But Bentinck's and Eden's comments nevertheless disclosed an optimism shared among officials that non-Europeans, whether in Assam or China, had the same underlying capacity to achieve economic development as their counterparts in the mother country. At this early phase of Indian tea, British officials targeted Chinese teamakers not simply because they were experts on production but also because of a social vision that de-emphasized the role of government and championed the equal capacities of all groups—whether English, Chinese, or Assamese—to improve.[25]

The same year as the Ting Kwoe incident, 1839, the identical rhetoric of free markets emerged in a controversy over what to do with government tracts after the conclusion of Bruce's experiments. Tea Committee members wrote to Calcutta suggesting that they inherit the land from the Company and operate it as a "private enterprize." Although the government had planned to parcel out the lands to private interests, the committee surprised Eden by entreating him to grant them the *entirety* of the upper Assam tracts as well as an act of incorporation to expand their initial capital of five thousand pounds. Eden initially rebuffed their proposal, arguing that it clashed with the principles of expanding rather than restricting market activity. He "laid stress on the necessity of guarding especially against the introduction of anything like a monopoly of tenure & cultivation, and on the absolute expediency of ensuring competition." Further, he did not want to allow a mere "three or four great associations" to "parcel out the whole Province amongst themselves." Six months later Eden reiterated that the government's position had always been that "the cultivation and manufacture of tea" would "more directly take the sounder and the safer course of the ordinary pursuits of commerce and of industry, in conferring benefits upon the community." This meant that "special care" needed to "be taken so as to exclude any hazard of our granting a monopoly to the first extensive speculation." Eden's ambivalence underscored the government's resistance toward permanent intervention in the early development of the industry. In the words of Prinsep, this whole dispute could be boiled down to the core question of political economy, which was to locate "the point where the Government experiment should terminate & that of the private speculator commence." Eden believed that the government needed to hand over tea manufacture to an open field of private merchants, a theory that would be tested over the next few decades when the "labor question" became the most pressing problem facing the nascent Assam Company.[26]

The First Decade of the Assam Company

By 1840, the Tea Committee had come to a compromise with the colonial government. The latter agreed to hand over some two-thirds of the tracts, including 160,000 plants capable of producing four thousand pounds of tea, while continuing its own experiments and encouraging the entry of other companies. The Tea Committee renamed itself the Assam Company, becoming in January 1840 one of the earliest joint-stock companies under British law, with nearly 80 percent of its shares in London. Its creation marked a departure from the model of medium-sized family farms in China that Eden had hoped to replicate. Over the next decade, any further physical reminders of Chinese teamaking gradually faded from Assam. The Assam Company remained the lone tea grower in India until the late 1850s, when it stopped importing workers from China, and the remaining men died or were repatriated. Superintendents experimented with their own, self-consciously "scientific" methods of tea cultivation, abandoning Chinese methods of sowing plants in clusters and instead placing them in rows. Most improbably, the company abandoned imported Chinese plants and instead emphasized indigenous Assamese varieties.[27]

As the company grew more confident in its techniques, it recognized that its most glaring problem was finding adequate numbers of workers. As early as the forties, the superintendent of the gardens wrote a letter that "attribute[d] the failures" of the gardens to "Small plants" and "Want of labourers." What were the most pressing problems with recruitment? First, attempts to indiscriminately recruit Chinese labor had ended disastrously. Second, as the company turned to local "Hill Coolies," these workers habitually absconded back to their nearby homes. Without stronger contracts, recruitment entailed paying an advance without the ability to enforce specific performance. Competition from other employers constituted a third problem. As the Government of India hired local workers to build infrastructure in Assam, the Assam Company could not match its wages. Other would-be workers busied themselves growing different crops that shared seasons with tea. In September 1847, an indigo planter wrote, "labourers and their families" from "the districts of Beerbhoom and Burdwan [in Bengal] . . . can be obtained in any number after the middle of November," after indigo season ended. Tea season, however, spanned spring and summertime.

These individual problems boiled down to the same matter: workers were faced with other, more enticing options. When the Assam Company's London board of directors suggested that "the Bengalee Coolies" had absconded due to excessive work, the superintendent replied "that such is not the case, those of the Kacharies have left on account of the reduction in their rate of pay." What about paying them more? The superintendent feared this would encourage "further demands" and declared he "preferred fighting the battle out." How much were planters willing to pay? In a tense exchange among board members, a London shareholder declared "in the strongest manner that it was idle to say that labour could not be readily obtained,—that he had lived for 15 years in India, & would pledge his word that sufficient labour could be obtained." He "warned the Shareholders that unless more vigilance was used," then "the Company's plantations would soon become a mass of jungle." In reply, the leaders of the Assam branch remarked sarcastically that the man should have "been good enough to point out the 'right means' which should be adopted to secure us a sufficient supply of labour *of the kind that we require, & at a cost that the Company can afford.*" The board added, "We can procure any number of unsuitable people *if* expense is no object."[28]

Such comments suggest that the "labor question" did not revolve around *absolute* but *relative* shortages of labor. This observation carries several analytical consequences. First, it sheds light on the British planters' strategy for expanding production by driving down labor costs—or, "fighting the battle out"—a constant feature of the Assam plantation system analyzed in chapter 4. Many historians have expressed skepticism over just how sharp the labor shortage really was, suggesting instead that the planters were simply being cheap. Second, as scholars of the global history of plantations have pointed out, "the concept 'labour shortage' possesses a specific politico-ideological meaning." It justified coercive and unfree work conditions by making the free mobility of workers seem aberrant and lacking ("short") while making the employment of wage labor appear normative and natural. The Assam Company's problem was not the physical absence of labor but rather the *absence of social conditions* that would compel locals to sign up for low-paying jobs. This latter question—namely, the historically specific conditions of a developed market for free labor presupposed in theories of political economy—would continue to rear its head in Assam throughout the rest of the century.[29]

By May 1850, as managers had begun to figure out the mechanics of cultivation and processing, Assam Company officials declared that the lack of affordable labor was the sole barrier to expansion. "The confidence of the proprietors in those who have the management of the Company," the minutes recorded, "is for the first time established." This confidence magnified the dispiriting prospects for mobilizing a proper labor force: "The Company has perhaps never been in a more unfavorable position regarding labor than at this moment." In 1853, the ongoing problems with labor were brought into stark clarity in a retirement letter from the outgoing director H. Burkinyoung. Offering philosophical rumination on the direction of the company, he wrote that the past decade had provided a new lesson in political economy: "In all cases Capital, which has been considered a primary, has proved to be only a secondary object, and that the primary want in all enterprize is the practical ability by which the application of capital is to be effected." "Application," he clarified, meant "the supply of labour." For Burkinyoung, labor was the "primary" concern that superseded capital itself in tea economics. He concluded that "no more striking illustration of the fact exists than in the Assam Company itself, when with twenty lacs of capital it failed to accomplish any significant practical results."[30]

The Assam Company continually discovered that the "labor question" circumvented its ability to generate value out of the plants and land. Burkingyoung's lesson would be echoed countless more times by other officers. The company superintendent, for instance, wrote, "I am convinced that a steady influx of labour from Bengal can alone enable the Company to advantageously extend its operations." In affirmation, the London board commented that the "great impediment" facing the Company was "present inadequate supply of labour." Later in the decade, when more firms had joined the tea business, the board wrote to the Government of Bengal that "the first and most important factor which militated against the more rapid expansion of tea planting was the acute shortage of labour in the province." If Smith had posited that the division of labor, and hence "improvement" of society, had been limited by the extent of the market, then the experience of the Assam Company pointed to the inverse formulation: that the refusal of local Assamese peoples to hire themselves out as labor acted as a limitation upon market activity. After several bad harvests in the forties, "the Company tottered on the brink of utter ruin." Even after it had begun to recover and pay dividends, production remained small, employing manual techniques not dissimilar from those of the independent peasantry. Thus, "until the 'sixties the tea industry was hardly a carrier of the fruits of the industrial revolution."[31]

THE HISTORICIST CRITICISM OF CLASSICAL POLITICAL ECONOMY

The Crisis of Liberalism

In May of 1857, soldiers in the Bengal army known as "sepoys" massacred English residents in the northern Indian town of Meerut and then marched to Delhi in the hopes of overthrowing British rule. The infamous "Sepoy Mutiny" stemmed from multiple grievances, from high taxation to the degradation of regional Indian elites, and it inspired further revolts throughout northern and central India before its suppression in 1859. Mughal rule was finally ended, as the emperor Bahadur Shah was exiled to Burma, and the British Parliament transferred the authority of the Government of India from the East India Company to the British Crown. Assam society was drawn into the revolt as well. In the fall of 1857, Assamese and Bengali intellectuals conspired to overthrow English rule in eastern India, and they counted among their supporters Assam Company workers, who, according to a report, believed "that the Europeans 'were to be cut up.'" But these plans never got off the ground, as British forces responded by arresting and prosecuting the conspirators by the next year.[32]

Far more consequential for the Brahmaputra Valley was the profound shift of political thought throughout the British Empire inaugurated by the revolts. British officials abandoned their earlier optimism of liberal reform and adopted a far stricter and more patronizing political approach. The revolts in India, paired with near-concurrent uprisings in Ireland, Jamaica, and New Zealand, forced officials to question their assumptions about the feasibility of social improvement, the reception of liberal reform in India, and the shared humanity between British and Indian people. The year 1857, Karuna Mantena has argued, "would come to mark a definitive turning point in the transformation of British imperial ideology . . . from a *universalist* to a *culturalist* stance." Inspired by the works of Henry Maine, officials began to emphasize the intractability of cultural differences, grounded in religion and social custom and organized through the logic of historical evolution. Instead of liberating Indian society, they now governed cynically in belief that India remained locked in native tradition.[33]

Historians of late-century India have focused on the culturalist agenda of post-1857 India by highlighting policies that codified notions of race, caste, tribe, religion, and gender. Officials also used the idea of cultural difference as a justification and "alibi" for greater imperial control. Andrew Sartori has demonstrated that custom and culture were also, for many colonial officials, categories of rational political-economic calculation. Similarly, I suggest that post-mutiny historicist thought was also mobilized to justify new policies of economic intervention, specifically, the authorization of penal contract labor in Assam. At the same time that ideas about cultural particularity and historical backwardness garnered credibility within the bureaucracy, officials in the northeast articulated formally identical arguments to justify the paternalistic and illiberal policy of labor indenture. The dislocation of imperial ideology in the sixties provided an opening to question the optimistic assumptions of political economy and its emphasis upon individual freedoms and market exchange. The marriage of culturalist political theory and paternalistic political economy was best embodied in the work of William Nassau Lees, a bureaucrat in Calcutta who laid out the case for government authorization and regulation of penal-contract-based migration to Assam.[34]

"Slavery of the very mildest form": William Nassau Lees's Theory of Colonization

William N. Lees was employed as an Orientalist at Fort William College in Calcutta, with dozens of translated Arabic and Persian texts to his name. He was also an amateur student of political economy. During the "cotton famine" caused by the United States Civil War (1861–1865), Lees began to investigate prospects for growing American strains of cotton in India when he stumbled upon information regarding the struggling Assam tea industry. Intrigued, he invested his savings into several small tea plots, and therefore, in his own words, wrote "both from the settler's . . . stand-point, and from a higher point of view." In 1863, Lees published a loosely organized, often rambling, political tract on the Indian tea experiments and was surprised to find it was widely read and positively reviewed, with a new edition reprinted soon after. In 1864, the new governor-general of India, Sir John Lawrence, invited him for breakfast to seek his advice, noting that he trusted Lees's opinion as a man who "shar[ed] the confidence of both tea planters and Government." The publication of Lees's tract also coincided with an ongoing speculative bubble and rush for tea lands in Assam. Starting in 1854, the government had liberalized terms for purchasing land, and by the end of the decade, fifty-one private gardens had appeared in the area. In 1861, new laws proclaimed that land in Assam should be sold under fee-simple terms, a change that created rampant speculation by replacing fixed rates with an auction system. The subsequent "tea mania" would cost investors millions of pounds and force the government to confront the region's "labor problem," as detailed in chapter 4. But even during the bubble's height, Lees foresaw that without addressing the flaws of a noninterventionist approach, the development of Assam was doomed.[35]

Lees's contribution to the history of tea was to articulate the ongoing labor problems through the theoretical language of political economy. His arguments in defense of government "colonization" anticipated pro-indenture arguments that became widely accepted over the sixties and seventies. As with Bentinck decades earlier, Lees suggested that greater British investment would provide an outlet for English capital while developing Indian manufacture. The current moment gave special urgency to such measures. The tea question mirrored the ongoing quest to find new global sources of raw cotton, which, one observer wrote to *The Englishman* in 1861, "appears to me to be the leading topic of the day." The supplies of both raw cotton and tea were threatened by the coincidence of civil wars erupting on opposite ends of the earth. Regarding cotton, Lees wrote, "The manufacturing interests of the Mother Country, consequent on the lamentable circumstances of the dis-United States of America, are in the throes of a crisis that threatens their annihilation." Raw cotton from the American South could be replaced by "India alone." At the same time, developing the Indian tea industry had become a national emergency, for the Taiping Kingdom in China "has shrunk up thousands of acres of fine tea crops" and so "what has occurred with cotton, *may* occur with tea."[36]

Lees argued that ventures to cultivate cotton and tea in India were possible "*By Government Intervention Alone.*" The true target of his political tract was the "*laisser-faire*" school of economic thought that viewed "the interference of Government a mischief, and the greatest hinderance to a nation's progress." In the face of the cotton and tea crises, this attitude was "tantamount to telling a ship-wrecked man that he must not catch hold of his neighbor." "It seems almost ludicrous to be talking 'first principles,' at this hour of the day," he railed, "but if people *will* preach, and act, as if they supposed the pharmacopeia of Economic Science, contained remedies for all the ills that trade is heir to, and pertinaciously ignore the fact, that the markets of the commercial world are subject to perturbations altogether outside and beyond the control of its laws, there is no help for it." Lees's text was no mere anti-intellectual screed, however. In his discussion of the tea question, he offered a complex and abstract analysis of classical economics and its presuppositions about human nature.[37]

Lees drew upon the ideas of Henry Maine, who was as influential as any figure "in shaping the practical work of nineteenth-century British empire." An English legal scholar who rose to prominence with theories expounded in his book *Ancient Law* (1861), Maine served as a member of the council of the governor-general of India, and he gave voice to the "crisis of liberalism" faced by the British Empire in the second half of the century. For Maine, the failure to foresee the revolts in India, Jamaica, and Ireland was ultimately an "epistemic" one. British policymakers, in their universalist view of human nature, had failed to ask questions about the true order of native culture and society, which in India were governed by religion and "caste sentiment." Within Maine's logic, India remained stuck in an earlier time, and administrators were wrong to apply English principles to governance in Asia. He stated that the history of law could be envisioned as a movement "from Status to Contract," and running parallel was the movement from communal to individual property. In modern society, property formerly held by families and households would eventually be divided into individual holdings. Because Indian society had remained communal, the colonial government's attempt to institute individual property rights had been a mistake. Lees, citing Maine, seized upon the same categories in his description of life in India. He wrote: "Even in Calcutta, the metropolis of British India, where Newton and Bacon, Shakespeare and Milton, have been familiar as 'household words,' for upwards of a quarter of a century, . . . native gentlemen, brought up in English schools and colleges, are unable to shake themselves free of this community of interests and property inherited with their birthright,—*because it is the custom of their country.*"[38]

Lees and Maine shared several key conclusions about colonial policy. First, both challenged the assumption that human nature was universally malleable. Departing from liberal optimism, they emphasized that even after a century of British rule, India remained stuck at a lower "stage of civilization," a result of climate and geological differences. "In India," Lees wrote, some regions were occupied by "wild beasts," others by "demi-savage races" and "semi-barbarous tribes." In the aggregate, India "may be said to be in the Agricultural stage of civilization." The lag behind Europe was even more pronounced in Assam, where the people were not even "like Hindustánis, nor yet like their neighbours, the Bengális." Second, they agreed that past attempts to impose policies borne from the experience of Britain were a mismatch with the social fabric of India. For Lees, "when we take into consideration, the area, the population, the number and diversity of races and languages, the divisions of caste, the different stages of education and civilization of its various provinces and districts, and countless other circumstances in which India is antipodal to England," then "if the same laws which regulate the system there . . . be applied here, they will be met by disturbing influences quite sufficient to upset the most accurate and nicely balanced calculations." For both, the revolts of 1857 demonstrated that efforts to transform Indian society had failed, and they saw the sepoys as ungrateful for the gifts of English education and law. "Had the people of India not been ignorant and superstitious," Lees wrote, "the rebellion of 1857 would have been an impossibility." Third, finally, the fundamental error with liberal reform was methodological. Maine criticized political economy for relying upon abstract deduction, beginning with general principles about human nature rather than paying greater attention to the "friction" of differences. Similarly, Lees wrote that political economy should not be "a standard of *infallable principles* [sic], to which all cases, occurring in nations in all stages of civilization, may be referred, as to an undeviating *Law!*" Both instead emphasized a "scientific" worldview that relied upon the ideas of historical evolution, comparison across human "stages," and the role of "culture," which acted as a brake upon political economy.[39]

Lees mobilized these culturalist and historicist theories in support of labor recruitment policies for Assam tea. He first asked how economic prosperity could be created and why government policies had failed to achieve it. He criticized the earlier emphasis on fixing land revenue collection (ca. 1790–1810), embodied in the cornerstone policies of the Permanent Settlement in Bengal and the *ryotwari* system in western India. The Permanent Settlement had not enriched the entire country but only the narrow class of zamindars, or native landlords, who failed to reinvest their wealth into the soil. It had misapplied the English model to a Bengal society where natives lacked education, escaped taxation, and acted out of narrow interest. Lees then dismissed the utilitarian push for increasing European investment (ca. 1820s–1840s), labeling such measures a mere "means to an end," again pointing to the conundrum of racial difference: "as long as the existence of the one race is exotic," he wrote, "the interests of both must in no small degree be antagonistic." Having eliminated policies centered on land and capital, respectively, Lees turned toward that last factor of production in classical economics: "That which first merits attention, and is of far more pressing importance than the title of property in the soil," he wrote, "is *Labour*." In doing so, Lees's argument mirrored Smith's own refutation of Physiocratic and mercantilist theories in his explication of value as a product of human activity.[40]

Lees believed colonial officials had ignored the government's duty to regulate labor. He echoed pronouncements by Burkinyoung and Assam Company officials who claimed that before European capital could transform the fertile soil of Assam, labor recruitment came first. The reason "population is the *most* valuable" was that "without labor, in this matter, Capital is as it were, locked up and useless." The Assam Company's "capital had literally been poured out upon the earth, and there allowed to rot." Lees further agreed that the Government of Bengal needed to recognize the proper order, or "relation of these elements." Instead of treating the question of Assam as "one of *labor* and *capital*," officials should treat it as "one of *Colonization*." Because labor was so foundational for economic development, government "interference" was necessary. The "secret of colonization" was that the divine law "Be fruitful and multiply" should be turned upside down: that "unless shoots from the parent stock *take root* and flourish in the new soil, . . . the object of the Divine law is not fulfilled—the wealth of the world is not proportionately increased."[41]

The nineteenth-century theory of colonization rested on a criticism of market dynamics to resolve labor shortages. On this point, Lees looked to another prominent theorist of the day, Edward Wakefield, a British politician who took a leading role in policies for settling Australia and New Zealand. As with Maine, Wakefield argued that political economy required more than deductive reasoning; it should take into account specific, regional differences, namely, the ratio of land to labor in different territories. Laissez-faire economics relied upon unfounded assertions that market mechanisms would operate on labor as they did for capital and commodities. But unlike money and goods, humans did not necessarily find their way to regions with high demand. Wakefield wrote that the works of Bentham, Mill, and David Ricardo shared a *"non sequitur"* in their line of reasoning. They had begun from the premise that capital was the foundation of wealth creation, and hence, productive activity was limited by the amount of capital available for investment. However, they mistakenly concluded *because* only capital could employ labor, then therefore capital *would necessarily* find labor to be employed. In 1830s Assam, Francis Jenkins had expressed the same belief when he wrote that there was "no great reason for holding out any inducements to [the] immigration [of foreign labourers] on the part of Government. The profits to be expected from immediate progress in the Culture of the plant will be a sufficient motive to speculators to bring laborers to Assam." This, Wakefield claimed, was a logical fallacy: "It is not true that all capital employs labour. To say so, is to say that which a thousand facts prove to be untrue. Capital frequently increases without providing any more employment for labour." This *"non sequitur* of political economy" was the fatal oversight that short-circuited liberal economic thought, a discovery that suggested that non-market solutions were needed where labor markets failed.[42]

The same argument became Lees's justification for indenture in Assam. He elaborated upon his position with two policy recommendations. First, the tea industry should require binding contracts because potential Indian migrants were not free, rational subjects who sought out employment opportunities on their own. Whereas much of India had a "teeming population," other regions remained "extremely underpopulated." Assam was a particularly tragic example, for the Assam soil "will literally produce *any* crop in luxuriant abundance," but the "indolent and lazy" local population allowed the "productive powers of the soil" to "lie almost wholly dormant." Lees echoed earlier frustrations with the Assamese locals. Potential migrant workers, however, were "the *poor*" of society, who did not have the resources to travel on their own. They required advances from garden managers, who in turn, required security that workers would stay: "Hence the necessity for a Contract law." Second, such contracts would require government regulation because experience demonstrated that migrants were being deceived under the current system. Lees chastised the former lieutenant-governor of Bengal, who stated in 1860 that the management of "importation of labor" was "*not for Government but for those immediately interested in the Tea plantations of Assam.*" This line was mere "abstract principle" that had a "practical" cost in "money and bloodshed," the "evil effects of which meet the traveller at every turn in Assam." In recent years, tea planters had employed labor contractors at the cheapest rates. The contractor "as rule" was "unscrupulous," for "as long as he puts money in his purse, whether it be human beings or the beasts of the field he has to deal with, the amount of dishonesty or cruelty he perpetrates, will not sit heavy on his conscience." Contractors preyed upon the "old and decrepit, the young and tender, the halt, the maimed, and the blind," and "even the infected, the diseased, and the dying, were pressed into the service of these most degraded of crimps." Without a government overseer protector or medical examiner the recruits were placed in unsanitary depots, "cess-pools" where they "contracted the germs of distemper and disease." The responsibility for these practices, comparable with the "horrors of the slave trade," lay on the shoulders of government officials and their "barren discussion of 'sound principles.'"[43]

Lees's paternalism marked a substantive departure from the universalistic optimism of liberal reform. "The natives of India are in a state of infancy," Lees wrote, and could be "enticed from their homes under delusions." They were "consequently in need of protection . . . in the sense in which the Law applies it to persons under age." As far as the question of individual liberty, Lees admitted that under the penal contract system, "the *free* laborer is reduced to a state of *bondage*." His justification was that principles required compromise and that, given the state of Indian society, a small sacrifice of freedom was worth the material benefits. He pointed out that penal contracts already existed anyway, luring away Indian coolies to destinations such as Mauritius and Reunion. Whereas Prinsep in 1840 had urged the Assam industry *not to* follow the example of the overseas sugar colonies, Lees asserted that domestic indenture at least had the benefit of keeping workers underneath the purview of the Government of India. "Living under the protection of English laws," he wrote, "their slavery will be of the very mildest form."[44]

Lees provided the most detailed defense of labor indenture in Assam, but he was not the only one. As new legislation passed in the 1860s, many other officials echoed his ideas in their correspondence and in the bills themselves. Similar arguments could also be found in other discussions of Indian policy. For instance, regarding the cotton trade, a writer for *The Economist* justified state-led efforts to promote cotton by positing that in India, the "primary presuppositions of political economy are not to be found." Indian suppliers were "fickle and shortsighted," "unaccountably apathetic" villagers in a "strange state of society" where "universal propositions" are not respected. The piece concluded, "There is no greater anomaly in recommending an unusual policy for a State destitute of the ordinary economical capacities, than in recommending an unusual method of education for a child both blind and deaf."[45] Lees's tract was historically noteworthy, then, not because of his singular genius but because of the eventual hegemony— the common-sense status—his ideas achieved within the colonial administration. If the turn to penal contracts in Assam was a particular solution to a regional problem, then it also became plausible as part of a broader, empire-wide crisis of liberalism, in which officials began to view Indian society in culturalist and paternalist terms, using political-economic arguments to justify intervention. The practical consequence was the beginnings of a state-sponsored labor indenture system for Assam tea almost simultaneous with Lees's articulation.

CONCLUSION: THE HISTORICAL SPECIFICITY OF THE THEORY OF VALUE

Before proceeding to analyze the practical operation of the penal contract system, this final section pauses briefly to further explore the theory of colonization, its implications for the body of classical political economy, and how to think about the recurrent idea of a "theory of value" as an object of historical analysis. Both Lees and Wakefield introduced their proposals for colonization by criticizing the canonical works of their predecessors. In his most irreverent line of argument, Lees challenged the status of Smith's writings as the "gospel" of the science, instead situating them at the head of a lineage of thinkers who had since superseded him. Lees meant "no disparagement," for to deify Smith would be even more insulting, as it would suggest that "civilized Europe" had "stood still" since the eighteenth century.[46] Nevertheless, both Lees and Wakefield remained committed to the broader project of political economy as the science of prosperity. Although the theory of colonization challenged certain classical assumptions, it also added to them historical and geographical depth, a reflection of the fact that these men were less concerned with explaining growth in eighteenth-century Europe, as most economic writers had been, than with the future capitalist development of societies formerly outside the global market, territories such as New Zealand, Australia, and Assam.

The theory of colonization championed by Wakefield pointed to a historical conundrum at the heart of classical political economy. Although Smith and his followers provided a cogent analysis of how markets worked under ideal conditions, they paid less attention to their historical conditions of possibility. In *The Wealth of Nations*, Smith had written about the question of a "previous" accumulation that generated the first hoard of wealth to be used as capital, but he shed little light on what those earlier processes actually looked like. Within the logic of accumulation, circulation presupposed production, which presupposed capital, which presupposed circulation and production. "The whole movement," Karl Marx would later comment, "seems to turn around in a never-ending circle."[47] Marx referenced the problems in Smith's previous accumulation in his own theories on the "secret of *primitive* accumulation," which he drafted around the same time as Lees's pamphlet. As with his contemporary Lees, Marx found in Wakefield an illuminating exploration of the role of labor in economic theory.

"It is the great merit of E. G. Wakefield to have discovered," as Marx concluded the first volume of *Capital*, "not something new *about* the colonies, but, *in* the colonies, the truth about capitalist relations in the mother country." Wakefield had observed "that, in the colonies, property in money, means of subsistence, machines and other means of production does not as yet stamp a man as a capitalist if the essential complement to these things is missing: the wage-labourer." He thus discovered that "capital is not a thing," such as specie or land, as previous economic schools had believed. Rather, capital was "a social relation between persons which is mediated through things." By social relation, Marx meant that the expansion of capital depended upon the availability and employment of wage labor. Although Wakefield challenged the naturalness of market exchange, he had otherwise reaffirmed Smith's basic claim that the value embodied in commodities was derived neither from market demand nor the earth but only from putting productive wage labor to work. In a "wasteland" without a lively free labor market, for instance, Assam, capitalist production was impossible.[48]

If Wakefield had argued that the classical theory of value operated only under contingent social conditions, then what was the historical context that enabled Smith himself to initially grasp it as a natural and universal law? Smith spent his adulthood in the commercial centers of Scotland—Glasgow and Edinburgh—with additional time in Oxford and Paris. During this period, Glasgow merchants, owing to their position in the Atlantic tobacco trade, had branched into various industrial sectors, including coal and lead mining, paper, glass, iron, linen, and cotton. In his 1763 lectures, Smith also referred to the "work houses" and "manufacturers" of "new works at Sheffiel(d), Manchester, or Birmingham, or even some towns in Scotland." His milieu entailed a type of early capitalist growth animated by extensive networks of merchant capital combined with labor-intensive manufacture—not unlike the world of Chinese tea production described in the previous chapter. As historians have speculated, eighteenth-century Scotland's combination of seemingly primitive highlands with the "more advanced Lowlands [where] social relations based on the market and free labor existed alongside the remnants of older forms of social organization" compelled Smith's generation of writers to muse about the various "stages" of development. Given this context of mixed labor forms, the initial pages of *The Wealth of Nations* appear disjunctive, insofar as Smith presented his theories as timeless and natural, with individuals offering their labor voluntarily, without duress or coercion. However, by the eighth chapter on wages, Smith admitted that independent producers were no longer "very frequent," and "in every part of Europe, twenty workmen serve under a master for one that is independent." Smith's depiction of commercial society could thus be grounded in the context of a Europe where wage labor was fast becoming the general norm. Notably, this was *not* a world of capital-intensive technological innovation; nevertheless, it could be described as a world of social and economic revolution.[49]

More conceptually, Smith's timeless depiction of "productive labor" as the source and measure of value contained several presuppositions about economic life historically specific to the modern wage. Smith's repudiation of the mercantilists and Physiocrats—reproduced in Lees's criticism of colonial policy—is significant here. Whereas those earlier schools envisioned value in the physical form of metals or corn, Smith saw value as something more intangible and social, as something rooted in the "quantity" of human labor embodied in commodities. He described labor in an abstract manner, as a substance "interchangeable" from activity to activity. Some have argued that this attitude of indifference revealed Smith's personal condescension toward real-life manual laborers.[50] At the level of concepts, though, the abstractness and non-specificity of his language also corresponded to the very character of waged work itself. The more human labor became a commodity sold on the market—as opposed to labor secured through clans, caste, or personal service—the more people found themselves available for hire in any number of trades, not just in agriculture but also mining, textile, or glass manufacture. As the social form of wage labor became *generalized*, the content of *labor itself* became abstract and uprooted from specific activities. It was this social phenomenon that was illuminated in British political economy's theory of value. In Marx's historical notes, he wrote admiringly that Smith's theory got at the heart of capitalist society:

> Indifference towards specific labours [labour in general] corresponds to a form of society in which individuals can with ease transfer from one labour to another. . . . Not only the category, labour, but labour in reality has here become the means of creating wealth in general.[51]

Marx was not suggesting, as in some crude "base and superstructure" model, that ideas were the epiphenomenal byproduct of external reality.[52] Rather, consciousness was itself as *real* as social practice; the two were inextricably connected. Smith's *subjective* articulation of the theory of value was as historically notable as—and historically corresponded with—the *objective* social form he was describing. It indexed, within the history of economic thought, the emergence of concepts adequate to the expansion of industrial capitalism.

Of course, to pin down the exact contours of this "correspondence" between wage labor in practice and the classical theory of value in consciousness remains an elusive problem for historians. My reconstruction of the social conditions behind economic thought is not meant to suggest that *just anyone* living in a capitalist society will inevitably reach the same conclusions as an Adam Smith. Rather, it is to suggest that the processes of capitalist accumulation have historically constituted the conditions of possibility for such ideas: that the classical theory of value would only make sense to someone living in a capitalist society. Observers situated in industrial centers such as London and Glasgow could find the theory intelligible and plausible insofar as it resonated with their own social context, where the economic power of manufacturing was expanding quickly and innovations in efficiency were the most exciting topics of the day. And, as we shall see in subsequent chapters, observers in commercial China and Bengal became attracted to the theory as well, for they recognized the same widespread phenomenon of market-dependent workers fueling commercial manufacture.

However, the theory shared a much less organic connection to mid-nineteenth-century Assam. There, the role of labor became a central political question due not to the prevalence of waged work but precisely its absence. Faced with unforeseen difficulties establishing a capitalist industry in the borderlands of Asia, men such as Burkinyoung and Lees modified the received tenets of classical political economy. They broke down its components until they could distill it to its most crucial ingredient. Government administrators then set about forging a reasonable facsimile in the form of a temporarily unfree penal contract system. Rather than a crystallization of already existing social relations, then, the classical theory of value acted in Assam as a lever for change. This scenario was not unique. It mirrored problems faced by planters in the post-emancipation societies of the Caribbean, the United States South, and European settler colonies, as will be discussed in chapter 6. From a comparative perspective, the Assam tea planters were not so different from their direct competitors in China, either. Just as planters in Assam needed to secure migrant contract labor, likewise, the Cohong merchants of Canton and the guest merchants of Huizhou and the Wuyi Mountains advanced loans to the peasantry and employed seasonal migrant workers through personal networks. As the next chapter demonstrates, there were many other parallels shared between the respective regimes of labor-intensive tea production in China and Assam. What ultimately set apart the Indian industry commercially, however, was a plantation system premised on the theory of state-backed colonization, one that directly contradicted the vision of economic liberalism championed in the beginning.

4 After the Great Smash

Tea Mania, Overseas Capital, and Labor Intensification in Assam

IN 1895, THE Indian Tea Association (ITA) sent advertisement copy to American magazines with the caption: "Ceylon and Indian tea is prepared entirely by machinery, which eliminates all chance of contamination from nude, perspiring, yellow men, and preserves its natural aroma, flavour and purity." The centerpiece depicted "the interior of a Chinese tea factory, with the process of hand-rolling in full operation," with Chinese workers "stripped to the waists" ("but there is nothing in the least bit offensive about it," added the representative).[1] Although this particular ad was rejected as being too "indecent" in imagery and language, it captured in the most vulgar terms the essence of the ITA's campaign at the turn of the century, as seen in countless other advertisements (figure 11). In line with new discourses on Chinese backwardness at the time, the ITA established the conceit that the astonishing rise of Indian tea and the attendant collapse of Chinese tea could be explained by the simple difference between labor- and capital-intensive production, between human and machine. From hygiene to flavor to strength, representatives of the Indian industry sang the praises of machine-made teas.

The ITA, a combination of British- and Indian-based agency houses with roots in the late 1870s, was tasked with promoting tea sales abroad while managing questions of labor and production in Assam. It quickly propagated triumphalist explanations wherein the technical question

A Second Story about Tea
From the Tropical Paradise of Tea Growing

DAY'S WORK DONE AND CHECKED

CEYLON was famous for its spices long before Tea became its staple product.

INDIA is the native country of the tea plant, as it is found growing wild there.

Virgin soil, and a sub-tropical climate, with careful culture, favor rapid growth of leaf, thus enabling the trees to yield frequent "flushes" of fresh, juicy and succulent leaves. Two tender leaves and bud are all that's used; these contain the concentrated essence and vigor of the whole plant, for Ceylon and India tea.

The growth and manufacture of this tea is conducted under skilled management, directing native labor, and it is prepared for the market entirely by machinery in the most careful and cleanly manner. It is this scientific manufacture or preparation which gives the teas of these two countries their uncontested superiority over those made by the hand labor of Mongolians in China and Japan.

On account of this exceedingly careful attention it costs a little more than cheap, ordinary teas, *but* as it is double strength it is the cheapest in the end.

Imported into North America
1894 5,379,542 Lbs.   1895 9,283,144 Lbs.

Figure 11. An ITA advertisement that appeared in *Ladies' Home Journal*, November 1896, which contrasts manually produced East Asian tea with the supposedly superior machine-produced South Asian teas.

of human- and machine-based production became intertwined with cultural oppositions between Eastern and Western civilization. Recall planter David Crole's statement that successful Indian tea sales represented the "triumph of the West over the Flowery Land," resulting from the "intelligence, science, and research" of "Occidentals." Ironically, many of these assumptions about the relationship between culture and capitalism were shared by subsequent generations of economic historians. Those scholars disagreed that the Assam plantations were capitalist, but they *did agree* that capitalism has been characterized by its civilized conduct. They fixated on the employment of labor indenture in Assam, arguing that colonial-era Asian plantations were precapitalist because, unlike factories in the metropole, they were limited by the "contradictions" of "unfreedom." A plantation that employed unfree workers, then, would be unable to respond to market fluctuations, and "low wages consequent on unfreedom" would result in "little incentive to adopt labour-displacing technology"—hence there would be "no increase in the level of the productive forces."[2] These historians shared with the ITA the mental association between capitalism and freedom: first, that capitalist development originated with European, specifically English, civilization, whose liberal political ideals stood opposed to the barbarism and unfreedom of Asia; and second, that what set capitalist development apart was the advent of technological innovations that liberated workers from labor-intensive methods.

In this chapter I challenge the assumptions underlying both accounts. In the late nineteenth century Indian tea initially thrived not because of its adherence to the ideals of civilization and freedom but precisely due to its reliance on an exceptional system of labor indenture. Behind the curtain of marketing campaigns focused on flavor and hygiene, British planters themselves attributed the rise of Indian tea to lower production costs from indenture. "This has been brought about," Crole acknowledged, "by India and Ceylon underselling the Chinese, and has only been accomplished by an enormous reduction in the price of tea."[3]

Starting in 1865, officials in India devised a system of regulated labor recruitment and penal contract employment for the Assam tea industry. It featured the restriction of worker movement, constant surveillance, and wages fixed by law rather than by the market. Penal contract laws provided planters both a subordinated migrant workforce and the legal impunity to intensify the production process. Politically, indenture was controversial due to its resemblance to African chattel slavery. It was unquestionably "unfree" by modern standards. Commercially, however, it was a dazzling success. During the last three decades of the century, as hundreds of thousands of workers were brought into the eastern Indian plantations, British planters opened up 170,000 more acres of land, and tea production skyrocketed to sixty million more pounds per year. By the turn of the century, Indian tea exports had surpassed those of their Chinese rivals, and the industry had become the leader in world production.

The spectacular economic results of this unfree labor system present several challenges to extant scholarship. Recent research has contested the presumed link between "free labor" and the origins of capitalist production. As with the ideal of merchant capital discussed in chapter 2, the ideal of free labor originated in the canonical theories of political economy and should be treated as an abstract simplifying assumption rather than a concrete empirical fact. Indeed, new work has shown that in both the "most advanced liberal market society of the nineteenth century," namely, western Europe and the northern United States, "wage labor, was, by modern standards, unfree labor." Nevertheless, employers in factories and on colonial slave-driven plantations extracted massive productivity gains through labor discipline. If the origins of industrial production were inseparable from the deployment of extra-economic coercion, legal scholar Robert Steinfeld argues, then "the traditional account of the rise of free labor is backwards."[4]

The story of Assam tea also forces us to rethink our categories for understanding capital itself. Assam labor indenture emerged from the ashes of an 1860s speculative bubble known as "tea mania." In the wake of its collapse, novel business entities known as "managing agencies" took over the industry, consolidating Calcutta and London capital and sinking it into infrastructural improvements, from land and buildings to, ultimately, an indentured labor force they treated as illiquid, fixed stock.[5] Several consequences emerge from this analysis. First, the paradoxical persistence of unfree labor into the late nineteenth century makes sense only by examining the simultaneous transformations of business forms, namely, the transition from independent gardens to managing agencies. Second, it becomes less tenable to claim that Chinese and Indian tea production represented two sides of a binary opposition between tradition and modernity, or barbarism and civilization. Instead, the two industries should be viewed as discrete points on a spectrum of distinct yet overlapping labor practices united by the overarching goal of accumulation for mobile and transnational capital. The Assam industry was first reorganized by trade-oriented managing agency houses that gradually dominated tea, a typical transformation from a merchant concern into an industrial one. As indenture laws brought more workers into Assam, the tea industry, during the initial burst of production, relied primarily on labor- rather than on capital-intensive methods to surge ahead. As in China, planters and managers in India regulated unfree employees through physical coercion, time-discipline, and a gendered and ethnic division of labor.

From a technical standpoint, the difference between manual and machine labor was of course massive. The point is not to efface this gap but rather to suggest that capital-intensive and labor-intensive industrialization were historically interdependent. British planters reaped the benefits of advances in mechanization only after decades of labor-intensive growth in the late century. Mechanization cannot stand in for the history of capitalism as a whole but rather is best resituated within the broader social compulsion toward rising productivity. It was not the cause but the result of social transformation.

In the first section below I detail the establishment of indentured labor over the course of the 1860s and seventies, showing how the *theoretical* problems articulated by W. N. Lees played out in *practical* terms during an 1860s speculative land rush known as "tea mania." Although the mania has been documented by several studies, they have overlooked its implications for a new post-mania political economy. Company records and case studies illustrate how the tea industry reorganized itself into large, corporate-backed entities known as managing agencies, which then pressed for more favorable recruitment laws. In the second section I analyze the tea labor regime by providing an alternative timeline of the standard technology-centered account of Indian success. Drawing on data collected by historian Rana Behal as well as concepts from the history of technology, I argue that although planters could boost productivity by employing machinery, such devices did not displace the labor force, which continued to grow into the new century. In the final section I discuss how the intensification of labor can actually help explain the rise and emergence of labor-saving machinery. The division of labor had already begun to treat human workers as a type of nonhuman machine, which in turn enabled labor substitution: a practical interchangeability that was reflected in the way planters spoke of machines as workers and workers as machines.

THE CREATION OF THE INDENTURE SYSTEM, 1861–1882

Tea Mania

At the start of the 1860s, W. N. Lees had articulated in theoretical terms the long-standing tensions between the abundance of cheap land and capital versus a paucity of wage labor in Assam. Only after the rush for tea lands during the rest of the decade were these problems laid bare for all to see. The mania had its origins with new regulations set forth by Governor-General Charles Canning in October 1861. On the logic that European ownership would accelerate the process of "improvement," Canning declared that all land in Assam should be sold at a low, fixed rate between two and five rupees per acre.

Critics blasted the new laws as too liberal and inviting dishonest speculation. Inside the auction house, lands for tea gained a reputation as a "money-spinner." Soon, a "madness comparable in intensity with that of the South Sea Bubble seized men's minds." Exacerbating this madness was a lack of solid information about the lands up for sale. The wasteland laws stipulated that before properly bidding, agents needed to first survey each territory. However, officials discovered "there is scarcely anywhere in the world more difficult ground to demarcate and survey than the forest jungles of Assam and Cachar." Applicants were allowed to bid based upon a "rough pen-and-ink sketch" of "an almost imaginary tract of land." Agents would advertise land five times its actual size, the planter Edward Money recounted. Other times, the successful bidders discovered that their garden simply did not exist. Other tracts would be "lumped together" with "three or four inferior jungly tracts" and sold far above "true value." Sometimes, the land was already occupied by local Assamese groups, in which case the government sided with the new European owners and kicked the locals off the land.[6]

The mania also discouraged actual cultivation. In "those fever days," planters paid "the most absurd prices" for "wild jungle lands," and many decided that rather than bringing lands to maturity, they would cash out when prices hit their peak. When J. W. Edgar, junior secretary to the commissioner of Assam, visited in 1863, he observed, "There used to be a saying in the mouths of planters that it was very doubtful whether it would ever pay to make tea, but that there was no doubt that it paid to make gardens." Planters would clear their land, plant a first inedible crop, and flip it for an advance seven or eight times the original price. New gardens sprung up so rapidly they became known as "mushroom companies." By one count, the total number had jumped from a handful to ninety-two by 1865. The pool of experienced garden managers was similarly depleted. Money wrote that "new gardens were commenced on impossible sites and by men as managers who . . . did not know a Tea plant from a cabbage." Many were described as "young men fresh from England," unprepared for life in Assam. Others were "a strange medley of retired or cashiered army and navy officers, medical men, engineers, veterinary surgeons, steamer captains, chemists, shop-keepers of all kinds, stable-keepers, used-up policemen, clerks, and goodness knows what besides!" In short, "people who had failed in everything else were thought quite competent to make plantations."[7]

Contributing to this mania was a new set of limited liability laws in colonial India. Newspapers reported that in this "dangerous epidemic," men who had found it "difficult to make a fortune out of their shops began to launch them on the share market" as limited liability companies. Looking back, registrars and judges characterized such ventures as a "house of cards" and "huge superstructures of fraud." Henry Hopkinson, commissioner of Assam, lamented that in Assam, the "tea remains" but the companies and their men "pass away, change with every season." Although most gardens still had not produced marketable tea, companies behaved "on the analogy of an unfinished railway line" and paid out dividends to shareholders, ranging from 5 to 15 percent. Confined to rumor and hearsay in Calcutta, owners, investors, and banks alike were swept up by the idea that every garden was "a veritable El Dorado."[8]

Prices for shares peaked near the end of 1863. Historian Shyam Rungta dated the collapse of the industry to May 1866, noting that two months later, fifty-eight of seventy-five tea companies were selling their shares at a discount. By the end of that year, ten more companies would fold, and thirty-three more within three years. In total, 57 percent of companies that were registered during tea mania were finished by the end of the decade. Almost one-half of total capital investments had been lost. Money described this decline as "the great smash." Investors soon overreacted in the opposite direction. "Gardens that had cost lakhs [hundreds of thousands] were sold for as many hundreds," Money recalled, "and the very word 'Tea' stank in the nostrils of the commercial public."[9]

Two major consequences from the fallout of tea mania are worth noting. First, it exacerbated the long-standing shortage of adequate wage labor in the minds of colonial bureaucrats, ultimately convincing them that legislation to facilitate migration into Assam was needed. A government inquiry noted that the "cry from Assam, both from speculators and *bona fide* tea cultivators, during the continuance of the tea mania, was 'Labour, more labour.'" Echoing Lees, the government concluded that workers were being recruited under terrifying conditions, to the detriment of both the migrants and their employers: "The halt, the blind, the insane, the hopelessly diseased—in fact the refuse of the bazaars, were all alike drafted to Assam. . . . In one extreme case the mortality in the garden was so excessive that the manager deserted it, leaving the dead unburied and the dying without help."[10] The remedy was a government-regulated system of migration.

Second, tea mania also cleared the path for the eventual colonization of Assam by a concentration of highly capitalized, British-backed entities known as managing agency houses. The managing agencies expanded far more aggressively than the first generation of companies had, clearing land, building infrastructure, importing "batches" of new workers, and establishing operating standards for large-scale cultivation and manufacture—measures that would set the stage for the sudden surge of tea production in the following decades.

The Expansion and Concentration of Managing Agency Capital

The Government of India responded to planter demands for a secure workforce by passing a series of labor indenture laws, first in 1863, followed by revisions in 1865, 1870, 1873, and 1882. Under these laws, a breach of contract by a tea plantation employee would be treated and punished as a criminal act, liable to imprisonment or enforced specific performance. These laws belonged to a body of legislation across the British Empire known as "master and servant" laws, which criminalized uncooperative workers through forced labor, prison, or worse. What set apart the Indian legislation were its provisions for recruitment from the rural areas of Bengal and central and southern India. Officials cited the remoteness of Assam and the lack of "communication" as justification for legislation "other than the ordinary law of master and servant."[11]

From the beginning, officials recognized that each new law was "a piece of class legislation." The master and servant laws, sociologist Marc Steinberg has argued, embodied the "materiality of the law": that legal and political institutions did not stand apart from economic processes but were deeply interwoven within them. During the eighteenth- and nineteenth-century birth of North Atlantic industrial society, lawmakers provided employers legal tools to shape a suitable workforce. In England as in the American South, these laws were "carefully designed to create labor markets that were less costly, more highly disciplined, less 'free'" than other markets, a "way of keeping people in their place."[12] This logic animated the Assam regime as well, though planters first needed to bargain with the colonial state.

Initially, the laws were highly regulated. Planters were required to hire government-licensed recruiters, known colloquially as "arkatis" (*ārkātī*, a derivative of "recruiter"), which increased costs and placed planters at the mercy of impersonal go-betweens. By the end of the seventies, the planters successfully lobbied to liberalize the laws in favor of "free migration," in which they could hire nonprofessional recruiters known as "sardars" (*sardār*). Act I of 1882 deregulated the recruitment system and also extended contracts from three to five years. A "watershed" law, it reinvigorated an industry that faced falling prices and declining recruitment. The passage of Act I reflected the increased size and influence of the planter class, which had consolidated power over the first decades following tea mania.

Recovery from the great smash began in 1867. By 1869, according to reports, "nearly all old gardens . . . were still not only in existence, but were, by careful management, yielding a profit to their owners." In 1873, the commissioner of Assam reported that tea was "no longer speculation, but an honest industry." Meanwhile Edgar in 1874 observed the presence of "very large concerns managed through paid agents." Those "paid agents" came to dominate the Indian industry during the last third of the century. Before tea mania, gardens in Assam had been managed by individuals, with the exception of the incorporated Assam and Jorehaut tea companies. After the bubble collapsed, agency houses gradually overtook management and sometimes ownership. No agencies had held a stake in tea before 1860, but by 1875, fifty-six of sixty-six tea companies were managed or owned by an agency.[13]

The managing agency house traced its origins to the first private European "agency" or "commission houses" that accompanied the East India Company into Calcutta during the eighteenth century. These firms provided services such as banking, shipping, and insurance, but their primary focus was to simply buy and sell goods on contract. In the 1830s, they began to oversee production, sinking money into fixed assets. Most predated the mid-century tea boom, managing a diverse portfolio of indigo, shellac, jute, cotton, and silk. In terms of form, the managing agency houses were not unique to the British. Sanjay Subrahmanyam and Chris Bayly have argued that they were "in a sense lineal descendants of the Asian portfolio capitalist," that is, of the state-backed merchant houses of the pre-colonial Indian Ocean world. Most infamously, they also served as the "country traders" who, in the decades before the Opium War, transported Indian opium to China in exchange for tea. That many of the large tea agencies first got their start as intermediary agents of commerce strengthens Banaji's and Perlin's claims that during the early phases of industrial capitalism merchants were a force for the integration of manufacture and trade. To the extent that British agencies *did* eventually intervene into production, they did so only after decades of opposition to fixed investments, a pattern not dissimilar to that of the guest merchants of China. Such philosophic ambivalence comes out clearly in specific case studies.[14]

Managing agencies consolidated gardens in Assam through several routes. In one pattern, older companies that had survived tea mania hired agency houses to manage their plantations on behalf of the shareholders, as exemplified by the oldest tea firm, the Assam Company. After experienced planters left in the late 1850s to form a rival concern, the London board relied upon a motley crew of inexperienced bureaucrats. Formerly the only game in town, the company floundered throughout the sixties, "living on its own fat." The Calcutta board recommended they hire a locally based managing agency to take over in Assam, and in 1867 they chose Schoene Kilburn & Co.[15] The rival Jorehaut Company had already hired its own agents, Begg, Dunlop & Co., in 1862. In both cases, financial affairs remained the responsibility of the metropole, and the managing agencies were tasked with overseeing the middle space between London and Assam.

A second route entailed managing agencies moving laterally into tea and then proceeding to buy property and manage it themselves. Observers in the mid-seventies described gardens that had been bought "for a mere song during the panic" and subsequently produced "enormous profits." This path was typified by Jardine Skinner & Co., whose founder, David, was the nephew of William Jardine of Jardine Matheson & Co. based in China. The Calcutta office of Jardine Skinner had attempted to acquire gardens during the height of tea mania, having purchased seeds in 1862 and bidding to run the Assam Company.[16] That same year, the Calcutta office expressed interest in new tea lands, to which the London office expressed opposition:

I trust you have not gone into this hastily,—& without satisfying your-self *thoroughly* as to the *adaptability* of the soil, climate &c. for the culture of tea. . . .

I remember the Coffee planting mania in Ceylon,—when parties went into it, & laid out vast sums in planting & preparing ground which turned out eventually utterly useless! . . .

Now there is a considerable analogy between the Coffee planting rage of those days, & what is now taking place with regard to tea in India—& men seem to be engaging in this latter culture evidently in profound ignorance of the subject.

When the tea mania would taper out, they warned, "the time will come, & that ere long, when a reaction will ensue, when it will be the 'devil take the hindmost,' & every one will be striving who shall get out first!" Once prices collapsed, the London office agreed to hold on to their lands, and they eventually produced marketable tea by the end of the decade.[17] Only after vigorous internal disagreement did these agen-cies begin to undertake responsibility over production itself.

The influx of managing agency houses into tea was in part powered by a new outflow of overseas investment from Britain into India. Forty years ago, Amalendu Guha's pioneering study of Assam claimed that "only a small part of the total investments in tea appears to have origi-nated from Britain's home savings." However, Guha's judgment was based on the records of the Assam and Jorehaut tea companies, which were exceptions to the rule. By contrast, the new generation of manag-ing agency houses drew upon a historic outflow of capital from British markets. From 1865 until 1914, the nominal capital of overseas invest-ment from Britain totaled over £4 billion or 60 percent of all money raised, a high point in the history of the empire. About £317 million, or 8 percent, found its way to India. Finance concentrated in the City of London had overtaken the traditional concerns of land and manu-facture as the most dynamic sectors of the economy. British bankers found "adequate compensation" in the empire's "invisible exports" of shipping, insurance, and capital. This ascendant financial class, houses such as Barings and the Rothschilds, constituted Britain's "gentlemanly capitalist class." In India, the largest private beneficiary of gentlemanly financial capitalism was tea. By the early 1900s, tea had been firmly established as a large, if not the largest, private sector of India. In 1911, there were more tea companies registered (927) than those of cotton (681 presses and 168 mills), coal (331), or jute (109 presses and 50 mills). In 1914, tea companies fetched £22.6 million of investment from British and Indian stock exchanges, numbers that swamped those of competing industries. Indian tea had matured into one of the most formidable and powerful sectors of the colonial economy.[18]

This particular pattern, in which an agency backed by British capital consolidated smaller gardens, was embodied by a third house, Finlay Muir & Co. The Glasgow firm had roots in cotton textile manufacture, with partners participating in the early century campaign to liberalize the Canton trade. After further involvement in silk, insurance, and jute, it moved laterally into tea. During tea mania, the company brokered loans for several companies but did not intervene into management. "At the beginning," the company historian recalled, "the firm were merchants purely and simply." As with Jardine Skinner & Co., its metropolitan partners were "chary of plunging too deeply into this attractive but risky speculation." By 1870, however, they had opened their first Calcutta office, and by 1875 they had added two tea gardens to their portfolio, transforming "from being merely agents to being principals."[19]

Finlay Muir & Co. made up for lost time by aggressively establishing new plantations while absorbing existing private gardens. This strategy is illustrated by the case of Patrick Buchanan. He had arrived in India in 1863 at the age of seventeen, one of those "boys fresh from school" during the rush for tea land. By nineteen, he was promoted to manager, and by twenty-five, he owned gardens in Sylhet, hiring Finlay Muir & Co. to manage them. Known for his "personal driving force," Buchanan expressed "a constant anxiety" over having "sufficiency of working capital." By the 1890s, he asked Finlay Muir & Co. to join him as partner in his company, and his gardens became a subsidiary of what was already known as the "Finlay Group" of gardens. By then, Finlay Muir & Co. was the managing agency with the most acreage under cultivation, and, according to the industry historian, it was well known that the company's ambitions were to create a tea "Empire" in India. By the 1920s, Finlay Muir & Co. was far and away the most productive managing agency, nearly tripling the next largest interest, and profitable enough to claim status as the fourth largest business group in all India.[20]

Several analytical consequences flow from this analysis of the origins of tea capital. First, it reinforces the argument by Steinfeld that freer markets in the nineteenth century paradoxically relied upon, and actively produced, regimes of unfree labor. The story of Assam tea makes clear that *metropolitan* capital actively funded the rise of *colonial* labor indenture, much in the same way that recent literature has demonstrated how London and northern American banks funded southern United States slavery.[21] Secondly, this inflow of investment strengthened the power of planters in India to push for friendlier labor laws. In 1878, the agencies formed the Indian Tea Districts Association (ITDA)—a forerunner to the ITA—and authored a joint memorandum to the Government of India requesting revisions to labor legislation:

> Tea culture alone, apart from other products, is capable of almost indefinite expansion. Land and capital can be found in abundance, and the sole impediment to its continuous development is the difficulty of obtaining an adequate supply of labour on terms admitting of its profitable employment. This hindrance to progress [arises] . . . from the excessive cost of recruitment and transport, largely due, in the opinion of all tea growers, to the stringency of the labour laws.[22]

The language and logic of this memorandum echoed sentiments from Lees's political tract twenty years earlier, and it inaugurated an internal government debate over indenture reform that resulted in Act I of 1882, rejuvenating labor recruitment and enabling the industry to continue expanding into the next century.

LABOR-INTENSIVE CAPITAL ACCUMULATION IN THE ASSAM TEA GARDEN

From Technology- to Social-Centered Historical Explanations

The suggestion to use machinery for tea production dates back to the first experiments in the 1830s, and machines for rolling and sifting teas first emerged in the 1870s. Standard accounts of the rise of Indian tea have often pointed to such innovation as the key factor that set apart the Assam industry. Historian Robert Gardella wrote, "From 1860 to 1900, an industrial revolution overtook the tea-garden factories [in India], as steam-powered capital equipment for withering, rolling, firing, and sorting black tea steadily replaced workers skilled in these tasks."

By contrast, the suffering Chinese tea trade was "sans industrial revolution." Talk of an industrial revolution for Indian tea dated back to turn-of-the-century campaigns by planters to promote their product. In 1910, the president of the ITA stated that in India "the hand is entirely dispensed with." Meantime in China, the "old process of hand rolling still exists . . . and when the arms are tired, the Chinese have recourse to their feet." Claims about hygiene were tied to those about productivity. Because Indian tea was produced more efficiently, planters argued, Chinese managers were forced to abandon their standards of quality. Crole wrote that "cheaper production" in Assam meant that "the Chinese cannot possibly put tea of the same class or quality on the market at anything approaching the same price."[23]

Such explanations have fixated on the technical capacities of machinery in isolation, at the expense of a broader analysis of the social and economic context in which they were introduced. They embodied what David Edgerton has called the "innovation-centric conflation of innovation and use" in histories of science and technology. Conventional histories, he wrote, have emphasized exciting and novel "innovation," thereby overshadowing the actual, practical history of "use." If we disaggregate innovation from use, then the story of an industrial revolution in Assam becomes less tenable. First, the nature of tea production meant it could never come close to full automation. The ITDA's 1878 memorandum admitted that the "peculiarities of the culture . . . are such that hand labour must always be largely employed, and rank as the governing factor in the cost of production." In 1883, the planter George Barker wrote that machinery for deforestation, hoeing, pruning, weeding, and plucking was "impossible to construct" without damaging the plants. A decade later, Crole wrote that in outdoor work "as yet little or nothing is performed by machinery."[24]

Second, to the extent that labor-saving machinery was ultimately effective, it was introduced too late, and its practical problems resolved too slowly, to explain the dominance of Indian tea before the turn of the century. The most impactful inventions aided in the three actions of rolling, drying, and sifting tea, but their most effective versions were introduced only in the late eighties, and they were not well integrated for decades. According to Barker, "there are so many experimental machines, full of faults, sent into the country, most of which have to be re-modelled before they will work." And Crole noted that bottlenecks arose, for "in most factories, we find there is only sufficient machinery to deal with a little more than the average amount of leaf, so that when a 'rush' of leaf comes, the whole resources of the tea-house are tried to their utmost and even overtaxed."[25]

Finally, such anecdotes dovetail with statistics, collected by Rana Behal, outlining tea industry productivity over the last two centuries. Although planters in the 1870s boasted that gardens could easily yield seven hundred pounds per acre, government data suggests that this productivity spike was long delayed, as the industry averaged only three to four hundred pounds through the end of the century—numbers roughly matching those of the Wuyi Mountains in China. Only after the first decade of the 1900s did per acre yields jump into the five to seven hundred range, a leap of such magnitude that it likely reflected, as a lagging indicator, the widespread integration of those technologies. The data also reflects that productivity per worker stayed relatively stagnant from the 1880s into the 1910s. Nevertheless, even if we concede that the general adoption of capital-intensive machinery *did eventually* result in productivity spikes after 1910, Indian tea had already left behind Chinese competition decades earlier (figure 12).[26]

So then how exactly did the Indian tea industry overtake its rivals during the intervening decades? As a starting point, we should note that the Assam plantations had already achieved an impressive feat by expanding production nearly sevenfold over three decades while maintaining steady rates of productivity. Because new gardens did not produce an average yield until after four or five years, planters must have offset the underperforming young bushes with higher yields from existing ones. Even without a surge in efficiency, constant expansion at steady rates resulted in the flooding of British and global markets with new teas, which forced down prices and pressured Chinese and Indian producers alike to cut costs. Prices for Indian tea, for instance, fell by over half their original rates. Under these conditions, whichever regional industry could best shed costs at the margins while sacrificing minimal quality would emerge victorious in the tea war between China and India. "Competition nowadays is so severe, and the profits, in the majority of cases, are cut so fine in consequence," Crole wrote, "that a manager who wishes to earn and enjoy success must see to it that advantages be taken of every detail whereby labour and time can be saved." Barker added, "Economy, even in the smallest details of

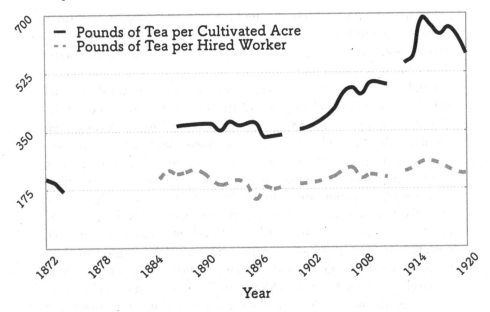

Figure 12. Average tea productivity by land and labor in the Brahmaputra Valley of Assam, 1872–1920. The data encompassed Darrang, Kamrup, Lakhimpur, Nowgong, and Sibsagar. Figures from Behal, *One Hundred Years*, 353–59.

working, must be rigidly practised in order to make a garden pay sufficiently well."[27]

The planters' pursuit of cheaper production entailed a combination of two distinct strategies. First, they increased the productivity of labor through better "management": both the clever work of more efficient arrangements—proposals such as using better seeds and manure, planting tea bushes closer together, pruning branches, and selling old and unproductive lands to focus on the highest yielding soils—and the physical terror of coercion and discipline.[28]

Second, tea planters, backed by penal contract legislation, cut costs by simply paying employees less. Economists have often argued that technological innovation arose as a response to the high cost of wages, and this dynamic, conversely, explained why labor that is relatively cheap discourages innovation. Historically, however, there was no forced choice between raising productivity and "sweating" labor. Assam planters used both as viable strategies for cutting costs. Many planters deducted from wages illegally by subtracting advances, punishing workers for lower output, ignoring statutes for wage increases, or selling rice to workers at higher rates. Henry Cotton, the chief commissioner of Assam, found "no room for doubt that employers have been endeavouring to effect economy in working at the expense of the labour force." Aside from this illegal activity, the state regime itself artificially suppressed stipulated wages, freezing them at five rupees per month for men and four for women. Nominal wages remained flat well into the twentieth century while real wages declined until 1926. As basis for evaluation, we can look at the wages of free agricultural workers elsewhere in Assam. In 1894, the critic Reverend Charles Dowding claimed that the planters paid less than half the market rate for workers, a figure confirmed by official reports early in the next century. As a result, Dowding wrote, the tea industry enjoyed a "fictitious value" due to "that most vicious of all forms of protection, namely, exceptional legislation, enabling it to obtain labour at less than its value in the open market." The implications of these figures are far reaching. With tea prices declining steadily and with labor costs representing, by far, the bulk of a plantation's expenses, this 50 percent discount on labor could easily account for the difference between profit and loss, enabling a much more aggressive policy of expansion than otherwise possible with a free labor system. During these formative decades, the sweating of wages was as crucial as technological innovation for the purportedly civilized success story of Assam tea.[29]

Despite the modest gains of new seeds and mechanization, then, planter spokesmen were too hasty in boasting that machinery had "entirely dispensed with" manual labor. The labor force grew virtually every year from the late 1870s into the early twentieth century. Indeed, one of the surest indications of the industry's unsustainable labor intensity, Behal has shown, was a death rate that always exceeded the birth rate, a phenomenon officials attributed to onerous work pressures.[30] Without recourse to a true industrial revolution, planters relied upon extreme practices that shared features with the type of labor-intensive accumulation observed in the China trade. In the remainder of this chapter I explore these connections through an investigation into the most pivotal strategies for labor intensification, including: physical coercion, time-discipline and piece wages, and a racialized and gendered division of labor. Finally, I show that these practices of labor-intensive accumulation can also help account for the eventual dominance of labor-saving mechanization in the new century.

Physical Coercion

Coercion was not unique to the Assam tea industry, as the indenture laws were modeled on those of overseas British colonies that had imported Indian migrant labor after the abolition of African slavery. Before the twentieth century, more broadly, almost all forms of labor relied upon coercion to varying degrees. Workers in Euro-America rarely fit the normative descriptions of labor offered by neoclassical and orthodox Marxian economics, in which individual agents, separated from family, property, or master, freely seek out employment in the marketplace. Instead, most were organized through systems of what sociologist Michael Burawoy described as "patriarchy" and "paternalism": employees were fully dependent on a specific subcontractor or employer, often from the same family or community, and often older and male. This profile fit the labor systems of the Wuyi Mountains described in chapter 2. The baotou was in charge of leading migrant workers from Jiangxi into Fujian, negotiating on the workers' behalf, and overseeing the daily work schedule. To keep them on task, the baotou relied upon superstition, custom, and outright bullying. The term "baotou" ("head" of contract labor) also suggested paternalism in the sense of the worker's "close surveillance by" and "dependence on a specific employer."[31]

In Assam, many of the same duties were undertaken by individuals known as sardars. The Persian term "sardar" mirrored the Chinese "baotou" insofar as it originally meant "leader," such as a village elder, but during colonial times it took on the duties of labor management and recruitment (in the twentieth century, when Chinese reformers described the Indian labor system, they used the same terms *bao* and *tou—chengbaozhe zhi kuli tou*, or "head of contracted coolies"—to describe the sardar). What set the Assam industry apart from Qing China, where state intervention into the economy was relatively minimal, was its reliance upon legal and juridical force. Penal contract laws provided planters both the formal code and implicit authorization to physically prevent workers from striking, rioting, or abandoning employers. Planters described these activities through euphemisms, for example, "governing coolies," "coolie management," and "coolie-driving." As with Lees, the planter Barker employed historicist and culturalist claims to justify indenture. There was "no similarity on any one point in the two modes of looking after European and Eastern labour," he wrote, "nor will any amount of theorizing be able to break through the intensely practical manner in which natives have had to be dealt with for the last one hundred and fifty years." Crole compared the management of Assam tea labor with the manner in which "planters of the Southern States used to consider the slave-labour of their cotton and tobacco plantations."[32]

Magistrates most commonly punished workers with a sentence of "rigorous imprisonment." A report in 1883 noted that "adult tea coolies" were imprisoned at a rate three times greater than the general population. In the minds of workers, imprisonment, or *phatak*, evolved into a metaphor for the plantation system as a whole. Even without bringing a case to the local magistrate, planters immobilized their workforce by surrounding them with sardars and officers known as "chowkidars" (*chōkidār*). In 1873, the Assam official Edgar recorded that "Chowkeydars were posted at every possible outlet from the cooly lines, which in some instances were enclosed by high palisades outside which the coolies were not allowed at night."[33]

Actual documentation of these disputes was far outnumbered by unreported cases in which employers bypassed procedure and punished workers directly. Planters would announce a reward of five rupees to anyone who caught and returned a "runaway cooly," employing "savage hillm[e]n" as bounty hunters and even sending out dogs. Initially, the employment of bounty hunters, known as "black-birders" and "coolie-catchers," was illegal. However, the 1865 law authorized the power of private arrest on the grounds that the political and legal infrastructure of Assam was inadequate. Barker wrote that on the gardens, the "sahib [European] acts as judge and jury." Several magistrates noted in their reports that a manager had taken "the law into his own hands" in order to whip or cane his workers.[34]

When Edgar first visited the tea districts in 1863, he noted that "the practice of tying up and flogging coolies" when they failed to meet "the amount of daily task" assigned them was "almost universal." The Act of 1865 had instituted regular inspections, but similar incidents continued to surface, which suggests that physical punishment was now simply concealed from oversight. But not all planters saw the necessity for circumspection. Representatives from the Allyne Garden and Dilkhosh Tea Estate had written directly to the deputy commissioner of Cachar requesting to formally legalize "severe flogging" for disciplinary purposes! Their request was never met, but neither did the government disincentivize the practice effectively.[35]

In 1900, Cotton, the chief commissioner of Assam, broke from precedent and forcefully criticized the penal contracts, calling for a system of free labor. As reward for his honesty, Cotton was terminated from the government, but his landmark report remains a crucial record of the extreme horrors of the plantation. For instance, a Mr. Cattell was "charged with wrongful confinement of the wife and the daughter of a chaukidar coolie, and with severely assaulting him." He was fined 150 rupees. On a plantation known as the Phulbari Garden, a "coolie woman" who had absconded "was recaptured" and "flogged in the most barbarous manner at the order of Mr. T. J. Walker, the manager, by three of the garden employés in presence of all the labourers on the estate." The fine was five hundred rupees. In the upper Assam district of Sibsagar, a Mr. Greig responded to reports that his "coolies had been stealing firewood" and proceeded to strike a worker "some blows on the head with a stick. The coolie fell down and died on the spot." Greig was acquitted by a jury trial. Within this system, Elizabeth Kolsky has argued, planters were given "protection *from* law rather than protection *under* law."[36]

These examples suggest that physical punishment was hardly rational from an economic perspective, weakening the very workforce planters depended upon. Nevertheless, planters defended it as a necessary tool for maintaining economy on the tea garden. Barker described the use of force as a response to workers who "shirked" duties through "dextrous manipulation." He recommended "various forms of punishment—from a good thrashing to making him do two to three times the amount over again." Crole estimated that tea planters had been able to extract greater efficiency from their employees through better management. "In Upper Assam," he wrote, "coolies accomplish much more work now than they did twenty or thirty years ago. The daily task ('nirrik') for such work as hoeing, for instance, has increased from 25 to 30 per cent more than what used to be demanded of the coolies."

As in the Chinese tea districts, British planters, under the pressures of competition, organized tea production around abstract notions of time and productivity.[37]

Wages and Time-Discipline

By the 1880s, planters had instituted a regular schedule of labor management that entailed daily tasks. The unit was the *nirikh* (lit. "rate" or "price") that Crole spoke of. By completing a nirikh, workers would be paid the statutory wage known as "hazri" or "hazira" (*hājri, hājirā*). These abstract units were the building blocks of a regime of time-discipline. Garden managers organized tasks and wages around the periodic striking of gongs, enforced by the chowkidar and sardar. As Barker outlined:

> During the rains, the gong is beaten at five o'clock every morning, and again at six, thus allowing an hour for those who wish to have something to eat before commencing the labours of the day. . . . Few of the coolies take anything to eat until eleven o'clock, when they are rung in. The leaf plucked by the women is collected and weighed, and most of the men have finished their allotted day's work by this time, so they retire to their huts to eat the morning meal and to pass the remainder of the day in a luxury of idleness, . . . except for the unfortunate coolies engaged in the tea-house. . . . At two o'clock the women are turned out again to pluck. . . . About six o'clock the gong sounds again, the leaf is brought in, weighed, and spread, and outdoor work is over for the day.[38]

As in China, managers in India ensured workers were continuously on task, but the Assam system also featured regional idiosyncrasies. The Bengali social novel *Sketches of Coolie Life* (1888), to be discussed in chapter 6, confirmed Barker's description of the gong system but with a twist:

> The gong in the middle of the garden rang out "ding! dong!" and announced it was six o'clock. In almost every garden, six o'clock p.m. is the time for rest. However, when the gong strikes six o'clock, it is not quite six o'clock. In this country, it is often the case that six o'clock is set to whenever the sun sets. In this manner, when it strikes six [actually 5 p.m. elsewhere], the coolies bring their baskets of leaves on their head and come in from the gardens, lining up in rows to enter the tea-house.[39]

The novel's author, Ramkumar Vidyaratna, was one of the few writers during his day to spend extensive time living among the gardens of upper Assam. When Vidyaratna wrote that six o'clock was "not quite" (*thik nā*) six o'clock, he was referring to the practice of setting clocks on the gardens differently from those elsewhere across India. This practice was known as "garden time," and the principle was similar to the concept of daylight savings: in order to maximize time spent working while the sun was up, companies adjusted clocks backward by one hour so that the workers could complete tasks earlier. The government did not establish a uniform Indian Standard Time until 1906; before then, clocks in India were set by railroad stations, telegraph bureaus, and government offices. That tea gardens sidestepped these institutions and established their own garden time reflects how they regarded themselves as exceptional spaces with their own set of laws and even time zones. The significance of these moves was not lost on working populations. Around the same period, measures in Bombay to extend the working day were met by protests and strikes by cotton factory workers. In the more repressive environment of the Assam plantations, such protests were unthinkable.[40]

Planters paired the dense work schedule with a system of wages aimed at maximizing efficiency similar to the piece wages of Chinese tea. The industry's official historian wrote that the hazira was paid to a worker for completing a set of tasks that "might be expected to take the field worker, according to his or her diligence, about four to five hours to perform." In fact, the hazira system resulted from a willful misinterpretation of policies intended to *protect* tea laborers. The 1865 law stipulated that workers were guaranteed a fixed salary based on a nine-hour workday. The planters reinterpreted this law and converted the figures into a system in which wages were wholly contingent upon the completion of individual tasks. The term "hazira" literally means attendance, and in the context of the law, hazira probably designated a system of wages guaranteed to workers who were "in attendance," regardless of productivity. Over time, planters began to use hazira to denote individual and specific tasks, remuneration for which would not be delivered until the task was done. The original meaning of hazira was thus inverted along the same lines as the relationship between concrete and abstract time outlined in chapter 2: whereas originally workers were paid for time regardless of output, they were now paid for their output regardless of time spent.[41]

The aim was to push workers to finish tasks faster than average, which, once generalized, then allowed planters to raise the average daily quota, resetting the cycle. Postone described this as the "treadmill effect" of industrial remuneration. Crole had openly stated that planters had raised the burden of nirikh by 25 to 30 percent since early days, and J. Berry White, a medical officer in Assam, estimated in 1887 that "tasks for hoeing and plucking have in 10 years increased by one-fifth." Another observer suggested that planters, "endeavouring by every possible means to reduce expenditure" by "taxing to the utmost the working power of the coolies," had in some cases doubled work quotas. Workers were paid less than the stipulated minimum wage, a fact that planters did not deny and in fact praised as a spur to greater diligence (figure 13).[42]

Figure 13. Assam tea plantation workers clearing land for large-scale cultivation. *Assam Tea: A Pictorial Record* by Balmer Lawrie & Co., Ltd., ca. 1950s. Berkshire Record Office, U.K.

Vidyaratana's novel revealed how the hazira system also served to immobilize workers by preventing them from finishing their contracts. In one scene, a tea worker has been captured trying to flee, and he explains that his employers manipulated hazira rates to keep him indebted to the gardens:

> [The sardar] showed me a piece of land and said, "look, today you will be hoeing this chunk of earth. If you are able to finish this, then that will count as one day's worth of work. If you can finish within two *prahar* [six hours], then you will receive one payment of hazira, that is, one full day's worth of work. If you can do more, then you will get 'double hazira.'"
>
> ... Even before I was done, my body was exhausted, and I could not work hard anymore, my entire body fell sick. What could I do? ... I finished one-quarter hazira by the time the lunch gong rang at 11 o'clock. In the afternoon, I finished another quarter hazira. One full day's work left me pouring sweat from head to foot, just to finish one half hazira. In other words, based on how much I could work in one day, I was due a monthly wage of five rupees, or five paisa per day. But in Assam, one cannot pay for goods with anything less than ten paisa. Therefore on the first day I already accrued a debt of five paisa for food and lodging. Day by day, my debt increased, and when my agreement expired, the sahebs calculated that I was thirty to forty rupees in debt. In theory, when a coolie finishes their contract, they can return to their country, but this was impossible.[43]

The piece-rate system represented another form of physical confinement, providing legal pretext to bind workers to the gardens. Different aspects of the labor discipline regime thus overlapped and were mutually reinforcing. These first two dimensions of labor intensification blended together with a third: the planters' strategy of organizing the workforce through the social categories of race and gender.

The Racialized and Gendered Division of Labor

By the 1880s, Barker wrote that the only local Assamese people employed by planters were the Kacharis, originally from the southeast region of the Brahmaputra Valley. He praised them as "powerful men and willing workers, and, more extraordinary still, fond of filthy lucre." As with the "ol' Jiangxi folk" in the Wuyi Mountains, different groups on the Assam tea plantations developed reputations for the specific work they appeared naturally suited to perform. For the task of drying tea, the Kacharis were seen as intrinsically more capable than their Bengali peers: "Even at their best Bengalis cannot compare as tea-makers with Assamese, all of whom seem to be born adept at the industry."[44]

The most prominent objects of this ethnic typologization were recruits from central India designated by colonial officials as the "Dhangar." Starting in the 1860s, after planters had resigned themselves to the intractability of local labor, they began to aggressively recruit from the regions of Chota Nagpur and the Santhal Parganas, on the western side of the Bengal Presidency, today the states of Jharkhand and Chattisgarh. From 1885 to 1905, 690,076 migrant workers were brought to Assam, of which 43 percent were from the two central regions, with a peak of around 60 percent in the late eighties. By some estimates, 20 percent of the Ranchi district in Chota Nagpur had found its way to Assam. "The great hunting-ground for recruiters is Chota Nagpur," Crole wrote. Thus, the "coolie worker" was "just as much an alien in the land" as the British planters.[45]

The history of the Dhangar in Assam constituted, for anthropologist Kaushik Ghosh, but one component of a more complex story in which colonial officers sought to codify categories of caste and civilization in the pursuit of waged labor. Colonial officials first recorded the Dhangars' existence as a sort of prehistoric aboriginal during the first quarter of the nineteenth century, targeting them for ex-slave sugar plantations in the Americas and the Indian Ocean. In 1837, Jenkins had suggested recruiting the "more industrious races from Chota Nagpore" for Assam tea. In the minds of British officers, Dhangar signified the *lack* of caste, which meant they did not face the same dietary or labor restrictions shared by other peasants in India. Officials speculated that Dhangars were accustomed to a state of physical deprivation and less likely to express dissatisfaction with plantation discipline. The Dhangars were thus idealized as the perfect worker. In turn, their eventual preponderance among the Assam labor force reinforced their reputation as the group most naturally suited to such work. "The demand for cheap labour and the discourse on race and primitivism quickly fetishized the Dhangar into the solution to the labour crisis of the plantations," Ghosh wrote. "The more the Dhangars were fetishized, the greater the demand for them. And as the demand grew into 'a mania' the fetishism fastened itself deeper in the colonial consciousness."[46]

This feedback loop resulted in the literal valorization of primitivism as a commodity (figures 14 and 15). Migrants were judged for their

Figures 14–15. Workers on the estates of the Jokai (Assam) Tea Company. The captions emphasized the "racial types" of the "aboriginal tribes" and "primitive people" recruited from central India, and photographers portrayed them as ethnological objects on display. *Assam Tea: A Pictorial Record* by Balmer Lawrie & Co., Ltd. ca. 1950s. Berkshire Record Office, U.K.

"extremely dark" skin and their "woolly hair." Planters would make offhand comments describing them as "black." The recruits were reputed to be "simple-minded" but with bodies that were "strong and hardy." The more a worker conformed to these stereotypes, the more planters were willing to pay. "Planters, in a rough and ready way, judge of the worth of a coolie by the darkness of the skin," Crole wrote. Though the category "Dhangar" disappeared by the end of the century, it was later transmuted into the modern terms "aboriginal" and "tribal." As in other parts of the world, such ethnic and racial categories had been historically shaped by the social division of labor among different regions and groups.[47]

Similar patterns emerged with the recruitment of women to Assam. The tea plantations developed a gendered division of labor in which, outdoors, women plucked leaves while men hoed and, indoors, women sorted leaves while men fired and packed them. The workforce was nearly 50 percent women in the nineteenth century, a higher ratio than in the Chinese trade, the overseas colonies, or other industrial sectors in India. At the outset of the 1830s experiments officials assumed that migrant workers would be exclusively single men, but planters soon realized they needed to re-create the conditions of village family life in order to secure a self-reproducing population. They preferred a system of recruitment that brought "family batches, with a high proportion of women and children" because they were more likely to settle down in Assam. The planters could not follow the model of the Calcutta jute mills, for instance, in which men from rural districts traveled to the city and women remained home to earn income through sideline activities. In the specialized tea districts of Assam, tea *was* the entire economy, and whole families were attached to its production.[48]

This pro-natal policy meant offering maternity benefits and special bonuses for bearing children. Recruited workers would often be forced into impromptu "depot marriages," in which agents simply paired off workers regardless of caste or preference. In their defense, planters portrayed marriages as free and voluntary. Crole wrote that "coolie women were emancipated" by marriage "as in all other parts of the world."[49]

In another parallel with the Chinese tea districts, we encounter the notion that wage labor liberated women from the burden of family responsibilities; and once again this claim requires closer examination of the specific conditions of work. In Assam, officials found, labor commodification delivered neither gender equality nor liberation from the norms of womanly duty. For instance, a 1906 inquiry expressed alarm at the low birth rate of women in the gardens. They discovered that women were seeking abortions because they wanted to avoid the double burden of garden work and child rearing, from which men were free. The report recommended extending maternal benefits, as well as a policy of "weekly parading of pregnant women," with prosecution for those who had abortions. This double burden, Samita Sen has shown, was no different from the general condition of women workers across eastern India, where upper-caste values emphasized female domesticity, both exacerbating the burdens for women workers and depressing the value of their labor as inappropriate for civil society. Women workers were thus paid less, treated as disposable, and considered less skilled.[50]

The gendered hierarchy of skill emerged clearly in planters' descriptions of the garden schedule. Women were paid 20 percent less than men on the justification that their work was lighter and easier and also, conversely, that women were a natural fit for feminine tasks. Barker described the women pluckers as "the nimble-fingered ones." Crole described plucking as "easy work" that "does not require any physical strength." By the twentieth century, this association between women and tea production became central to modern advertising campaigns for Indian tea, which pushed images of "dark-skinned, subaltern women," with heads covered, "nimble" fingers, and "wrists braceleted," naturally suited to serve European consumers. Of course, plenty of counterevidence suggested there was no natural link between gender and the distribution of tasks. In Assam, planters would deal with a "rush" of leaves by having the men "taken off the other work altogether for as many days as may be found necessary, in order to pluck the whole day."[51]

Women's work was nevertheless fetishized, not dissimilar to the fetishization of the Dhangar. Women were originally assigned to do womanly tasks, and as a result, those tasks were performed almost exclusively by women, reinforcing the mental connection between the two. A feedback loop created the appearance that plucking tea was a natural and innate talent found within women themselves. A woman's predisposition for labor was similarly commodified, as she gained social value from performing her tasks efficiently. Crole noted that "many good workers earn double pay during the height of the season, and such are eagerly sought after as wives by the coolie men." Women were crucial to the Assam industry's profitability during its meteoric rise, as they represented one-half of the workforce—the industry's largest expense—but were the significantly cheaper option. By the turn of the century, at the same moment Assam became the world leader in tea, women outnumbered men in the Brahmaputra Valley tea plantations for the first time.[52]

Labor Intensification and Mechanization

Until now, I have suggested that Indian tea propelled itself past its Chinese rivals owing not to its technological innovations but to its exceptional regime of labor intensification. In this final section I bring together these two historical processes, as the story of labor-intensive gains—and, more broadly, a framework that begins from an analysis of labor—can also help account for the eventual rise of capital-intensive innovations in the twentieth century. Labor intensification not only antedated automated production temporally but also laid the *social* basis for the invention and integration of those machines. Understanding this relationship first requires looking beyond the technical dimensions of the history of mechanization.

In analyzing the history of commercial technology, social theorist Harry Braverman argued, one could distinguish between an "engineering" versus a "social" approach to machinery. The former highlighted how different technologies in an isolated, decontexualized comparison have been exponentially more efficient than manual production. For instance, in the last few decades of the nineteenth century, planters boasted that new models for tea refinement had raised productivity over manual labor by four times (1870s), ten times (1880s), and upwards of thirty times (1890s). However, this type of technical analysis was incomplete, for writers who divorced inventions from their social context were "reifying" the history of human innovation while overestimating the agency of machinery. In addition to an "engineering approach," Braverman championed the "social approach" of viewing machinery "in relation to human labor," conceptualizing the two as continuous and overlapping. He had in mind the social organization of the workshop and the phenomenon of the division of labor, which historically predated and gave rise to industrial production. The earliest champions of political economy, for instance, had equated "industry" not with labor-saving devices but with the rational organization of specialized tasks in a collaborative setting. Those writers did not view the advent of new machinery as a new historical stage or mode of production but as a "companion" to specialization.[53]

This vision resonated with how Assam planters themselves understood the evolution of tea production. The first Indian gardens inherited the methods of Chinese tea production and thus relied upon a division of labor from the outset. Assam planters attested to the benefits of higher productivity and skills resulting from specialization. "After a season or two's experience," Crole wrote, "one knows intuitively whether the leaf is liable to 'heat' at all, either from acquaintance with the effect of the weather, or from the feel of the leaf on the chungs. This knowledge can only be attained by practice." The contribution of British planters was to further break down the production process. Planter manuals detailed countless attempts to streamline production by cutting out superfluous steps or exploiting unused space and energy. In the minds of planters, the progression from streamlining manual techniques toward labor-substituting machinery was evolutionary in character, "simply the natural development" from primitive to modern techniques.[54]

The subdivision of tasks further enabled planters to replace simple human motions with the most advanced machinery of the age. As both economic theorists and Assam planter manuals acknowledged, this individual process was only possible because managers and overseers had already diminished the worker into something less than fully human. In Assam, planters described (1) machines as workers and (2) workers as machines. Both analogies disclosed something fundamental about the continuity between humans and technology in the industrial labor process.

First, at the individual level, the subdivision of complex tasks into simpler ones helped engineers imagine ways to complete the same simple motions with automated devices, what economists have described as "roundabout methods of production." Because the tea refinement process was too complex to be substituted by a single device, planters subdivided its components into individual movements that were partly replaceable. Workers were only asked to perform simple manual operations applicable across different processes, such as rubbing, rolling, cranking, shaking, and pressing. As managers divided labor into

"motions which extend across the boundaries of trades and occupations," they treated labor itself as an "interchangeable part," and more
easily substituted by tools. For instance, the machines used for drying
and sifting tea were also employed in the processing of coffee, minerals, and agricultural and chemical products; only rolling machines were
specially invented for tea. As labor became an abstract unit for measuring value, the content of work itself also grew increasingly abstract,
removed from the particular qualities of the tealeaf. Thus, the first
rolling machines in the 1860s only prepared leaves for a final rolling
and still relied upon human energy. Only with the 1887 Jackson Rapid
Roller did planters eliminate hand-rolling altogether. Once planters
had reduced workers into a collection of simple and discrete motions,
the benefits of replacing them with an automated device were clear,
especially given planters' complaints about laziness, insubordination,
and shirking. No wonder that Barker described the tea-rolling machine
as a "willing labourer that does the work as efficiently and ten times
more quickly."[55]

Second, at the collective level of cooperation and coordination, the
practical interchangeability between human and machine enabled
planters to envision a scaled-up apparatus in which individual devices
could be combined as interlocking parts, displacing workers as the
centerpiece of the production process (figure 16). Having subdivided
production into simple tasks, planters recombined them into a chain of
subsidiary motions while retaining control over the larger process. The
division of labor intensified the demand for productivity, for now each
individual depended upon one another to meet the expected speed of
production. "No change can be made in the tea-house work," Barker
wrote, "which goes on steadily."[56]

This darker aspect of the division of labor was openly acknowledged
during the earliest decades of industrialization. In the 1820s, Euro-
American political economy's depiction of the division of labor began
to turn away from an optimistic image of spontaneous and rational
free agents working in concert, as in The Wealth of Nations, toward a
picture of grim discipline. Victorian writers, such as Charles Dickens
and Elizabeth Gaskell, criticized industrialization for reducing workers
to mere "hands." Influenced by developments in thermodynamics and
natural selection, natural philosophers described nightmare scenar-
ios wherein machines overtake human workers. Metaphors between

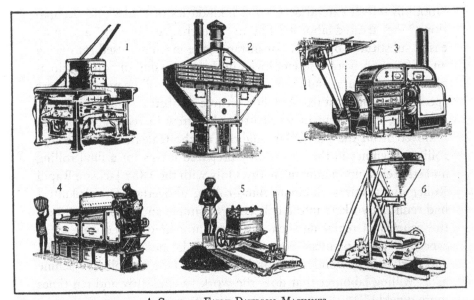

A GROUP OF EARLY DAVIDSON MACHINES

1. "Sirocco" tea roller.   2. Up-draft "Sirocco" drier.   3. Down-draft "Sirocco" drier.   4. Large tea
sorter.   5. Tea packing machine.   6. Packing machine with hopper.

Figure 16. Early tea-processing machines designed by Samuel Davidson in the late nineteenth century, including (1) a tea roller, (2–3) driers, (4) a sorter, and (5–6) packers. The placement of the workers as accessory parts to the central machinery reflects how inventors imagined they could displace human labor from the heart of the production process. Ukers, *All About Tea*, vol. 1, 481.

humans and machine parts peppered the analysis of Charles Babbage, Andrew Ferguson, and Andrew Ure, whose unironic description of the factory as a "vast automaton, composed of numerous *mechanical and intellectual organs* operating in concert and without interruption" caught Marx's attention as the perfect description of the essential logic of the capitalist division of labor.[57]

Managers in Assam, likewise, strove to shape their plantations into one of these "productive mechanism[s] whose organs are human beings."[58] Samuel Baildon, an Assam planter, wrote:

Labour is the great machinery by which tea-land is made valuable; and it is costly machinery, too, especially for Assam tea-planters. Now, no man would be fool enough to buy a machine, and then wilfully damage it; and precisely the same thing may be said of tea-planters in regard to their labour.

Baildon expanded this point, stating, "The great machinery upon which all industries are dependent, is labour." In an echo of Lees, he proclaimed that providing planters land without labor was "equivalent to asking men to make bricks without straw." From another perspective, the industry critic Dowding wrote that the tea gardens featured a "machine-like organization" that concealed its dependence on enervating work processes. "When we hear of the machinery of a tea-house actually running day and night without stopping, for several months," he wrote, "we may admire the organization; but we feel perfectly certain that to supply leaf to that machinery the whole garden must be worked at high pressure," which "no doubt has a direct influence on the death-rate."[59]

Even champions of the division of labor admitted that it had corrosive effects on its participants. Adam Smith wrote that specialization rendered workers "as stupid and ignorant as it is possible for a human creature to become." In Assam, Barker described hand-rolling without machinery as "interminable, never-ending drudgery." Thus, whereas commentators have for two centuries attributed the impersonal experience of the industrial labor process to the gradual development of technology, observations from the earliest days of industrialization suggest that the phenomenon predated, and even set the social foundations for, the introduction of automation.[60]

Perhaps the most persuasive proof was the fact that these dehumanizing aspects could also be observed in the tea factories of China, where the labor process was far less mechanized and automated. In his 1930s survey of the Wuyi Mountains, researcher Lin Fuquan described the rolling and roasting of tea as a spectacle of cooperative labor. "Although the schedule is packed," Lin wrote, "the division of labor and cooperation is very orderly, not sloppy at all." Each basket of tealeaves needed to be roasted and rolled two times each and in alternating order: roasted, rolled, roasted, and rolled. Managers divided workers into units of two roasters with one pan each, with alternates standing by to substitute on a rotating basis. Each roaster was assigned two teams of two rollers, who took turns rolling leaves and sending them back to the roaster. Here is the process the tea master oversaw:

Group A receives the first batch of roasted leaves and rolls them for the first time. After those leaves have been roasted a second time, Group B will roll them a second time, just as another batch of leaves is roasted a first time and then delivered to Group A to be rolled a first time. By the time Group B finishes rolling the first batch and sends the leaves off to another room to be baked [the next step in the process], Group A will have just finished rolling the second batch, and those leaves will be roasted again and delivered to group B. They are synchronized *like a machine* [*ru jixie*].

Lin followed in a long tradition of economic thinkers who saw the division of labor and mechanization as continuous in their shared social dynamics. Synchronization entailed a sense of timing and rhythm that united the individual parts into a collective whole: "the sounds 'lift from the pan!' [*qiguo!*] (what the roasters yell toward the rollers when they are done roasting) and 'pick up!' [*jiebei!*] (what the rollers yell toward the window of the roasters when they are done rolling) echo all night long." Inside the factories, "time was organized by the rhythms of tea rolling." To pass the night and also stay on schedule, "the workers all sing songs together."[61]

It may be objected that, from within an "engineering approach" to economic history, there was still a great disparity between the technical capabilities of the Chinese and Indian industries, as the latter eventually dominated the former in terms of sheer productive force. However, from the "social approach" perspective, both workforces were subjected to the same objectifying dynamics of division, specialization, and reintegration. The differences between the two were quantitative ones, therefore, rather than the qualitative opposition between tradition and industry that has commonly appeared in historiography. Though labor-saving machinery would ultimately give Indian tea an unmistakable technological edge that Chinese reformers came to admire, the devices were not the source but the result of the *social technology* of labor rationalization shared in common across the tea belt of Asia.

CONCLUSION

By the early twentieth century, the British industry's position atop global tea sales appeared permanent, and its dominance invited simple and reductive explanations for the divergent fortunes of the Indian and

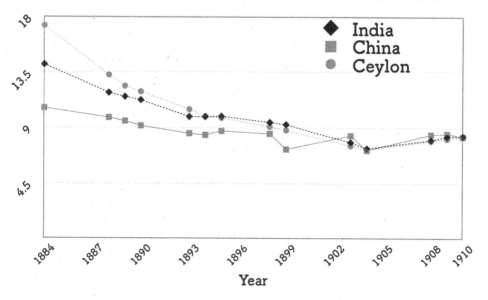

Figure 17. The price of tea imported into the United Kingdom from Asia, in pounds sterling, 1884–1910. Figures from British House of Commons, various "Tea and Coffee" Reports, 1900, 1903, 1908, and 1910.

Chinese trades. In 1914, an article in *The Times* praised the "scientific culture" of the Indian plantations, with the result that "the world has a larger and much cheaper supply of teas than if it had to rely upon China teas alone." It concluded, "The great hold that India has on the world's tea market is given it by the cheapness of its products."[62] This explanation was correct insofar as the rise of Indian tea was driven by efforts to cut production costs. However, the process of competition was more complex than simply offering the same product at a lower price (figure 17).

Industry insiders acknowledged early on that patriotic propaganda would have limited appeal to consumers without better techniques. Yet the fall in prices alone could not explain the timing of Indian tea's ascent, for its products actually remained on average more expensive than their Chinese competition until the new century. A crucial factor in favor of Indian tea was the subjective perception of each regional industry as they settled into distinct market niches. In the 1880s, the expanded production of Indian and Ceylon tea sent prices tumbling by one-half. "Competition in trade," wrote Baildon, "has become so keen—suicidal almost." In response, Chinese growers, already operating at maximum efficiency, sacrificed quality. Both British and Qing observers documented the abundance of Chinese "cheat" and "lie tea," which included mixtures of branches, dust, and non-tea plants, topped with a coating of blue and green dye to fool consumers. Of course, Erika Rappaport has pointed out, nonhygienic work conditions were shared by producers in South Asia as well. Meantime, British planters responded by pushing their workers to higher levels of efficiency. By the turn of the century, those spectacular mechanical innovations in drying, rolling, and firing tea—as well as advances in manuring and soil treatment—had been successfully incorporated, yielding massive leaps in productivity. As a result, Indian tea settled into the status of a high-quality luxury good, whereas Chinese tea increasingly became seen as a cheap filler. This stratification worked to the British planter's advantage.[63]

Starting in the 1880s, British marketers encouraged consumers to blend teas from India and China together in order to offset the high prices of the former. "Grocers have told me that they would be virtually closing their doors for the sale of tea if they were only to offer high-priced Indian produce," Baildon noted. Indian teas were initially a luxury item, but following the path of coffee, sugar, and Chinese teas, they were now being gradually democratized from the aristocracy to the middle and working classes, a transition facilitated by the cheaper leaves from China. The grocer's solution was to put in "as much strong Indian tea as can be afforded, with a balance of weak leafy China tea."[64]

Blending aimed to moderate not only Indian tea's high prices but also its dense flavors, which were considered too strong if brewed alone. ITA ads announced that Indian and Ceylon tea required "only about half of what is used in the case of China and Japan teas." "But for so mixing them," Baildon wrote, "there would be no market for them." If true, such economy could explain how South Asian teas could undercut competition that was cheaper by the pound. Notably, however, the British colonial planters themselves despised blending, for they feared English consumers would never fully appreciate the distinct flavors of South Asian varieties. But for now they had no choice. The irony, then, was that Chinese tea producers *enabled* the rise of their Indian competitors. "Instead of despising China tea because it is weak, and thin, and impure," Baildon wrote, "they ought to be thankful that it is so bad, because therein exists the safety of their present unassailable position."[65]

By the turn of the new century, such animosity extended to the consuming public at large. Euro-American consumers had come to look down upon Chinese, as well as Japanese, teas, and they also took aim at the entire apparatus of cultivation and manufacture behind the product. This attitude signaled a sharp departure from the original beliefs guiding the creation of the Indian tea industry, which was founded on a reverence for authentic Chinese methods. In the 1880s and nineties, the rise of Indian tea had sent Chinese tea sales into a tailspin, and metropolitan capital that was formerly invested in the Chinese market now migrated elsewhere, including Assam. As one industry thrived, the other collapsed. It was a process embodying geographer Neil Smith's apt metaphor of the "seesaw movement of capital": the uneven process by which the development of one region simultaneously brought about the underdevelopment of another.[66] This was an abstract movement, however, one that mystified Chinese merchants, whose only recourse was to continually try whatever means possible to cut costs in the face of tumbling prices. Burdened with their own crisis of profitability, Qing officials in the 1890s, in a parallel with colonial officers in India decades earlier, were now forced to reevaluate their own prevailing principles for understanding the laws of motion governing economic life.

5 No Sympathy for the Merchant?

The Crisis of Chinese Tea and Classical Political Economy in Late Qing China

IN HINDSIGHT, FOREIGN officers in the Imperial Maritime Customs (IMC) could see that troubling signs in the Chinese tea trade had surfaced decades before the real crash. "The deterioration of Chinese tea was first noticed about the year 1870," the commissioner of Customs reflected in 1891. Black teas fetched their highest prices during the sixties, a brief apex quickly followed by a steady decline. Overall volume of sales would climb well through the 1880s, and only after the 1888 season did many realize the gravity of the situation (figure 18). One Qing official recalled, "In 1887, Chinese tea occupied five-sevenths of the market. In 1889, Indian tea suddenly surpassed Chinese tea on the British market. This was unthinkable [*chuangjian*]!"[1] Once sales began to dwindle, they fell fast and hard.

The 1880s and 1890s were a time of crisis for Chinese tea. Bewildered provincial governors and foreign customs officials described declining sales as a "disaster" that risked the trade's "prompt obliteration." A tone of alarm filled correspondence between foreign officers, who delivered a report on the trade to the Guangxu Emperor (1871–1908) in 1888. This "falling off in the quantity of tea exported from Foochow," Edmund Faragó, the IMC commissioner, reported, "constitutes the most important change that has occurred in the province during the last 10 years." Many farmers had abandoned tea cultivation, a "painful sight," wherein "sweet potatoes or some other common

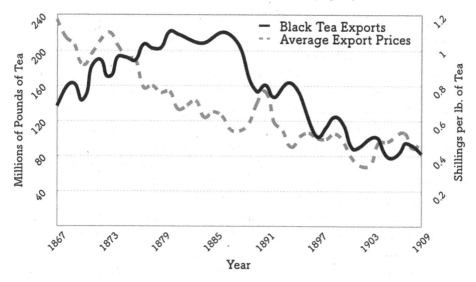

Figure 18. China black tea export quantities compared to export prices, 1867–1909. Figures from Lyons, *Maritime Customs*.

vegetables" grew next to abandoned "tea shrubs." Similar scenes were documented across other important routes connecting the central tea districts to Shanghai via the inland entrepôt Hankou. One Qing official wrote, "Last year was the worst season in Hankou so far. All of the four big merchant groups counted losses, almost three million *liang*. This is unprecedented. Onlookers are certainly dumbstruck, but those in the middle are even more baffled!" Another observed, "Those in the thick of the trade appear lost, as if they are in cloud and fog" (*yunwu zhong*). In Fuzhou, "the big, rich merchants have posted losses. They're afraid of what could happen next." The same sense of anxiety and confusion haunted the Qing state, for it understood that its fiscal destiny was inseparable from the export trade. The tea trade had provided a valuable source of revenue throughout the last century, when the empire had battled foreign wars, internal rebellions, and a jarring outflow of silver.[2]

The current chapter contends that paying greater attention to this sense of disorientation during the 1890s tea crisis yields key insights for understanding the transformation of political-economic thought in modern China. If chapter 2 illustrated changes in the practices of tea production in rural China, then this chapter turns its attention to parallel changes in consciousness. The stimulus of competition from South Asian tea, crystallized in the crisis, pushed Qing thinkers to abandon dominant mercantilist notions of wealth as something acquired through overseas trade and instead visualize it as something produced by labor. But they did not simply return to earlier imperial discourses that valorized agrarian production for domestic consumption. Those older views saw wealth as something physical, rooted in the earth, and hence finite. Instead, global competition compelled a minority of Qing officials to see wealth as something socially determined, originating from the skill and productivity of human activity, hence capable of infinite expansion through innovation.

The economic thinker Chen Chi (1855–1900), a member of the Ministry of Revenue, was exemplary of this transformation. In the nineties, at the same moment he attempted to explain dwindling tea sales, he grappled with ideas found in the earliest Chinese translations of classical political economy from western Europe. Notably, Chen's attempt to reconcile European classical economics with Chinese thought was far from the mainstream of the late Qing. His analysis was more experimental than systematic, but it was historically noteworthy precisely because Chen, amidst the chaos of the 1890s, landed upon creative applications of political economy that would endure in Chinese history. Chen discovered in Smithian thought abstract "natural" and "heavenly" laws that resonated with his concrete, personal experiences presiding over a commercial Chinese society in crisis. He described his own approach as the *dao* ("way"), or the "principle for producing wealth" (*shengcai zhi dao*), a set of ideas that corresponded to the theory of value posited by Adam Smith and embraced by Lees in India. The same theory that was so central to the creation of Assam's indentured labor force therefore provided a foundation for efforts to overhaul Chinese tea production. In both cases, it emerged most clearly amidst efforts to understand and overcome economic crises. However, as the story of Assam tea has illustrated, the discourse of classical political economy became most intelligible and plausible under historically specific social conditions. In India, colonial officials had rejected the application of Smithian liberal economics in a "wild" frontier such as Assam, insofar as political economy's universal assumptions were circumscribed by the persistence of native custom. They found they had to make Assam society conform to economic laws premised on wage labor. By contrast,

Chen discovered in the classical theory a powerful tool for grasping his immediate social context. In turn, this *subjective* transformation of economic consciousness suggests that late nineteenth-century China was far more enmeshed in the *objective* everyday social structures of global industrial capitalism than previously imagined by observers and historians alike.

The historiography of late Qing economic thought has largely centered on the fatalistic question of whether or not the imperial bureaucracy was too traditional to rescue itself. From the time of the Tongzhi Restoration (1860) until its ultimate demise in 1911, the imperial court teamed up with prominent local gentry to initiate a succession of military, commercial, and political reforms. Those experiments, known today as the "Self-Strengthening" or "Foreign Affairs" movement, have largely been viewed in tragic terms. The first generation of historians posited an incompatible mismatch between the superficial application of modern "Western" ideas with an underlying Confucian system and a precapitalist peasant economy. However, recent studies have been more sympathetic, emphasizing the Qing reformers' sophisticated grasp of scientific knowledge, even as they lost key military battles. The story of Chen's response to the tea crisis suggests an even deeper degree of congruity between Chinese and global circuits of economic thought.[3]

Chen was able to ground his understanding of classical political economy within the shared social patterns of capitalist production and exchange that rendered such ideas plausible. For him, the dynamics of industrial capital did not merely represent something that China should aspire to in the future. Rather, Chinese society was *already* subjected to the same pressures of competition faced elsewhere in the world; it *already* depended on the same employment of market-dependent workers for accumulation; and it was a society in which the value of commodities was *already* determined by the skill and productivity of human labor that went into them, regulated by the same global division of labor shared by counterparts in Indian tea, French silk, and British textiles. In his mind, China was *already* an active participant in the world of modern capital accumulation. These social dynamics, in fact, had already been intuitively grasped for decades by peasants, workers, managers, and merchants on the front lines of the export tea trade. But only in the midst of crisis were they articulated in such clear and theoretical terms by Qing writers.

In the first section below, I analyze the initial set of official responses to the fall in sales of export tea, from around the 1880s to early 1890s, and I situate them within a longer tradition of Qing statecraft. At first, officials sought to stimulate tea sales by lowering transport taxes and costs, a reflection of a merchant-focused economic worldview. This initial approach had evolved out of the imperial bureaucracy's growing appreciation of economic circulation. Economic thinkers of the high Qing (1661–1796) had developed a grasp of markets that rivaled their European counterparts in sophistication. In its best years, the Qing was, in Peter Perdue's terms, a "developmental agrarian state" founded on the twin pillars of "agricultural production" and "commercial exchange." The goal was not the accumulation of profit for its own sake but rather the augmentation of state resources and the improvement of people's "livelihood." The theoretical assumptions underlying such policies mirrored those of early modern English mercantilism and French Physiocracy, among others, as these regions were united by similar patterns of commercialization and agrarian development.

By the close of the nineteenth century, however, these stock principles had come under challenge by foreign military aggression, the loss of fiscal autonomy, and recurring civil wars. Within the imperial bureaucracy, the ideals of livelihood and fiscal health were now joined by the goal of competitive accumulation. In the second section I briefly outline how global competition forced Qing officials to consider methods for revolutionizing the production of export goods such as tea and silk. In basic terms, the Qing state shifted its focus from livelihood to accumulation, a "fundamental break" in Kenneth Pomeranz's words.[4] This also entailed a shift of emphasis from commercial circulation to the productivity of human labor. As they examined their overseas rivals and their practices of vertical integration and mechanized production, observers began to view China's own methods as anachronistic.

Chen Chi, one of the sharpest voices who articulated this new view, is the focus of the third section. Over the course of the years 1895–96, Chen worked frantically, completing an influential imperial memorial on tea that codified the bureaucracy's focus on reorganizing production; finishing a treatise on political economic principles as they applied to China; and in the reformer paper *Chinese Progress*, publishing summarial translations of a textbook written by Cambridge economist Henry Fawcett, a disciple of John Stuart Mill.[5] The common thread was Chen's attraction to the classical theory of value: the notion that wealth was not an innate quality of physical goods in circulation but rather embodied by human labor, determined by the relative productivity of real-life workforces. Chen's "principle for producing wealth" built upon but also departed from the economic orthodoxy of Qing China. He was attracted to it insofar as it enabled him to make sense of fundamental questions dogging Chinese society: why Chinese exports had been leapfrogged by overseas competition, why policies of greater merchant freedom failed to revive trade, and how the rationalization of human labor could yield limitless riches, not only for China but for humanity as a whole.

THE INITIAL RESPONSE

Sympathy for the Merchant

Our knowledge of how the Qing state dealt with the late nineteenth-century tea crisis depends largely on twentieth-century compilations of exemplary "statecraft" (*jingshi*) memorials. Many of these writings are unattributed and lack precise dates, but what materials have survived tell a story of how the conventions of Qing economic thought were reconfigured through efforts to grasp recurring commercial hardships. A good overview of the Qing state's first response to the tea crisis can be observed from a pair of memorials by Liu Kunyi (1830–1902), governor-general for the crucial tea markets along the upper Yangzi River. Liu recounted that during the 1860s, when tea sales were brisk and profitable, the Qing state had begun to levy the transport tax, or *lijin*, on the domestic movement of tea. The *lijin* was initially created to fund Qing efforts versus the Taiping Kingdom, but in subsequent decades it remained a crucial source of revenue for an indebted Qing state. The *lijin* subsumed the earlier Ming and Qing practice of taxing tea through the sale of merchant permits. Further, because export taxes were now regulated in conjunction with foreign powers, the only taxes that the Qing could unilaterally reduce were those for domestic transport. As tea prices fell in the seventies and eighties, the merchants lobbied for lower tax rates, and in the nineties, Liu recommended further cuts: "According to reports, the tea merchants face a tough and painful situation. They are losing on investments, and they request further tax reductions." Liu reasoned these cuts could solve the merchants' ills, because "the key is to solicit more business and to make the tea trade appear less daunting to merchants." He explained that many merchants were hemorrhaging losses, a threat to the health of the empire. "Recently the rise of foreign tea has begun to cut into our profits. The prices in Shanghai are now manipulated [cao] by foreigners. Once sales stop, losses will spread, and our silver notes will become worthless pieces of paper. This is a very real possibility."[6]

Liu Kunyi, one of the most prominent Qing officials of his day, argued that the tea crisis resulted from heavy burdens on the circulation of goods. He was not alone, as similar theories were proposed from the 1880s until the empire's demise. Many suggested that the long-term benefits of lowering taxation would result in greater overall amounts collected, but the Qing state, desperate and fearful of losing revenue, did not budge. Nevertheless, the solution was so popular among reformers that the foreign IMC characterized general opinion this way:

> The gentry and merchants argue that high-class China Teas have a rich flavour and strong aroma, and that it is upon their good qualities that the European Tea dealers depend in mixing them with Indian and other Teas (to give tone to the mixture); that the injury suffered by the China Tea trade is entirely due to the excessive pressure of taxation, and that the fact that, in spite of this heavy taxation, the trade has not been of late years entirely usurped by their rivals, is due to the superior quality (of Chinese teas).[7]

In their focus on taxation, officials and merchants were at first indifferent toward questions of production. This position originated from the perspective of the coastal "warehouse merchants" stationed in Fuzhou, Shanghai, and Hankou, men who specialized in the purchase, transport, and distribution of tea without being directly involved in production and consumption. Initial solutions for the tea crisis were centered on the merchants—as opposed to the peasants or inland factories—largely because the tea business was *itself* centered on, and controlled by, these men. Tellingly, Liu Kunyi concluded his memorial by stressing that the emperor sought to demonstrate "humaneness" (ren) and "sympathy with the suffering of the merchants" (su shangkun). For over one century of Qing political writing, the stock phrase "sympathy for merchants" (xushang) as well as its double-negative imperative "not to fatigue the merchants" (leishang), William Rowe has argued, served as two of the "pervasive idioms in official rhetoric, powerful discursive weapons used to validate a wide range of procommercial policies," down to the late nineteenth century.[8] The initial response to the tea crisis emerged out of this "sympathy for the merchant," which entailed two levels of logical reasoning: first, the officials had a political interest in supporting the merchants' profits, and, second, Qing political economic theory held fast to the belief that the chief activity responsible for the creation of wealth was the increased freedom of merchants to circulate goods and money.

First, in terms of short-term political solutions, late nineteenth-century statesmen linked their own fate with that of the merchants, not out of an inherent stake in private wealth but because a healthy tea trade boosted the state's own economic interest. The empire had lost nearly 400 million dollars of silver during the first half of the century, and it had suffered mightily from inflation, incurring "vagrancy, corruption, poverty, and riots." It had also increased its expenditure on military measures, relying less upon the land tax and increasingly more on transport duties. Further, Qing officials could scarcely imagine solutions other than empowering the coastal tea merchants, for these men controlled the capital of the trade, and they were by far its biggest and most visible beneficiaries. By one estimate, the thousands of export merchants known as "compradors" earned over 530 million silver taels in the half century after the first Opium War, outpacing the per capita accumulation of the Qing gentry by perhaps a thousandfold. Further, a cursory look at the organization of tea demonstrated that the enterprise was organized and operated by the coastal merchants. In a memorial written by the Hankou tea merchant guild, for instance, the authors suggested that, of everyone involved in the trade, they themselves were the most crucial element. "The farmer and his family," they wrote, lacked capital. From "the beginning of the year to the end, [the farms] have to devote all their energy and care to the setting out and cultivation of the plants, and yet they cannot secure their daily bread." The merchant's capital, by contrast, was indispensable: "When Tea merchants have lost their original capital there will be many difficulties in carrying on the trade." They focused their complaints upon the various costs that made them less competitive with "the Indian producers": "a grower's tax," "Likin [lijin] charges," and "the money paid for carriers, freight, boat hire, coolies, purchasing chests and their lining, and providing food for labourers."[9] If the Qing state desired more revenue, then its first priority should be to protect the merchant's return on capital.

Second, underlying this union of interests, the Qing bureaucracy had gradually devised a peculiar set of economic principles over the previous two centuries, and the late Qing "sympathy for merchants" reflected one of two main positions finely balanced within the economic orthodoxy. While writers in China had for millennia venerated the role of agriculture as the physical foundation of people's livelihood, Qing thinkers had supplemented this with praise for commerce and circulation as activities central to wealth creation. This broader context is worth further exploring here in order to better understand the field of political possibilities in the nineteenth century, including both the traditionalist opponents of the export tea trade and also a third response focused on improved methods of production, which I spotlight in the second half of this chapter.

Roots and Branches: The Political-Economic Theories of Qing China

Among historians, the most common comparison for Qing political economy has been the eighteenth-century school of thinkers known as the Physiocrats. In Europe, the French school reached its peak of popularity in the 1760s, exerting a significant influence on Smith, who alternately admired and criticized their agro-centric worldview. The Physiocrats, in turn, cited imperial China as inspiration. François Quesnay (1694–1774)—called the "Confucius of Europe" by students—wrote that Bourbon France ought to take a cue from Qing China, where "agriculture has always been held in veneration, and those who profess it have always merited the special attention of the emperors." The Physiocrats were the first in Europe to envision an aggregate, bounded entity known as the economy, sketched out as a "circular flow." The "key variable" that enabled expansion was "the capacity of agriculture to yield a 'net product.'" Writing from within an agrarian society characterized by small farms, Quesnay promoted improvement by entrepreneurial farmers, and he championed trade free from monopolies and taxation. For Rowe, the Physiocrats and Qing orthodoxy shared the "distinctive coupling of a belief in the primacy of agricultural production with a desire to stimulate maximum commercial exchange." Similarly, Perdue argued that the Qing Empire paired "high yields of agriculture" and "low levels of taxation." Just as the Physiocrats sought to promote improvement in France, the Qing was a developmental agrarian state that "encourage[d] the fullest possible exploitation of landed resources, including foodstuffs and minerals."[10]

The high Qing worldview rested upon the twin pillars of agriculture and commerce. In order to grasp the origins of this balancing act, one must start with the long-standing veneration for the earth. Writers since ancient China had praised the role of agriculture, most often through the idiomatic pair *ben* and *mo*. The terms literally mean "roots" (*ben*) and "branches" (*mo*), but in Confucian thought, they also connote the opposition of the "fundamental" and the "peripheral." In most contexts, *ben* referred to agriculture, the foundation of a Confucian polity, and *mo* referred to commerce and crafts, peripheral and secondary pursuits. Praise for agriculture, according to Hu Jichuang, had not necessarily been accompanied by condescension toward other fields until the rise of the Legalist tradition and the publication of the *Han Feizi* (written by Han Fei, 280–233 BCE). Soon, it became orthodox to simultaneously denigrate commerce and industry as "peripheral" and praise the "fundamentals" of agriculture. For instance, during the Tang, the concept of the "four classes"—scholar (*shi*), farmer (*nong*), artisan (*gong*), and merchant (*shang*)—was codified into law. Officially, the merchant was "conceived of as a disturbing factor, and as a potential danger to the established order."[11]

By the seventeenth-century Ming-Qing transition, however, official discourses on the merchant had grown far more charitable. Increased commercialization since the Song had elevated the social status of shopkeepers and artisans, a phenomenon reflected in the emergence of ethical "merchant manuals" that attracted urban audiences in market towns. This trend had parallels in other commercialized regions around the world. In seventeenth-century England, pamphlets celebrated merchants as "the most honourable profession," presenting them as the "heart and soul" of a new, "truly self-conscious commercial society." In Tokugawa Japan, Ishida Baigan (1684–1744) justified the profit-making activities of trade by using a logic of "enlightened self-interest" not dissimilar to well-known examples in western Europe. Such similarities appear uncanny, insofar as they emerged without direct intellectual correspondence. What united these authors was their shared experience of commercialization, which, in the minds of observers, linked the expansion of trade with the accumulation of wealth throughout society.[12]

By the eighteenth century, official Qing discourses recognized the significant role played by merchants, and "the social and economic values of commerce achieved a broad consensual authority they had never before enjoyed." Attempts to stock the granary system were a clear example of the state's appreciation for the laws of supply and demand. The granaries provided affordable food for the entire population year-round: officials purchased grains during harvest time, when prices were low, and sold them back to the public during the dire winter months. Imperial debates featured an intense discussion over the market as a mechanism for redistributing goods. Helen Dunstan has argued that these officials demonstrated a mature "market consciousness." Officials then pivoted from describing the positive effects of grain markets in particular to argue that circulation in general had beneficial properties. Thus, according to Rowe, "circulation" would become "an unambiguously positive keyword in [the emperor's] administrative correspondence, used to validate a wide range of policies." Circulation was said to improve livelihoods, create jobs, and promote the accumulation of wealth. Although Qing officials continued to ritualistically invoke moralist rhetoric, wrote Dunstan, their "core arguments about market function and how state involvement could affect it were technical and economic, not Confucian." Further, although officials praised the roots of agriculture, they now rarely trivialized commerce. That phrase was often replaced by the ubiquitous "sympathy for merchants."[13]

Sympathy, however, had its limitations. Quesnay had similarly praised circulation for "stimulat[ing] agriculture," but he maintained that trade itself was "unproductive" and "sterile." He offered qualified support for commercial circulation only insofar as it aided in agricultural production, and Qing officials displayed a similar ambivalence. The Qing did not advocate for a fully unregulated market, for the objective remained less of "letting the market accomplish its task than of making it do so." And it did not embrace the endless pursuit of wealth as an end in itself but instead constantly returned to promoting the production and distribution of material natural resources. Officials visualized wealth as something that could be physically lifted from the ground, especially in the phrases "exhausting the profits of the earth" (*jin dili*) and "extracting profits from its source" (*jun liyuan*). More fundamental was the term *minsheng*, often translated as "livelihood," which became the "most basic and pervasive term" in Qing political discourse. For Rowe, *minsheng* clearly referred to "the material conditions of life" and "standards of living." Livelihood was originally limited to grain to feed the people, but it also extended into other sectors, such as cotton and sugar, which stimulated overall production. Nevertheless, whenever trade came into conflict with grain production, the latter won out over the former. During food shortages, the empire ordered farmers to convert cash crop fields back into sites of grain production, and they prohibited grain exports in order to protect domestic supplies. The notion of wealth as physical, natural, and, hence, "finite," Rowe wrote, remained central to "imperial orthodoxy" during this period.[14]

Again, this tendency in Qing thought was not unique, as Physiocrat-*like* ideas were widespread across the early modern world. In Tokugawa Japan, Kumazawa Banzan (1619–1691) and Ogyū Sorai (1666–1728) promoted a return to the land, with rice instead of gold as the national currency. The Ottoman writer Mustafa Naima (1655–1716) composed a theory of society that viewed the peasantry as the only productive class, providing food to the rest of the social body. In India, the Mughal Empire crafted a revenue system aimed at occupying wastelands and steadily improving agricultural productivity. Indeed, when East India Company officials sought to reinvigorate agriculture in Bengal, they viewed the pre-colonial zamindar landholder as the Mughal equivalent of the entrepreneurial *fermier* theorized by the Physiocrats. Across multiple contexts in the global history of economic thought, then, the tenet that agriculture is the primary source of economic value found a receptive audience wherever commercial agriculture served as the foundation for social welfare. Physiocratic thought had intuitive appeal in agrarian societies, Ronald Meek has suggested, for "no one could deny that agriculture was historically prior to industry and commerce" and "the production of a surplus in agriculture could easily enough be visualized in physical terms." It is worth stressing again that these parallels emerged despite the fact that these writers across Asia could not have read the works of the French school.[15]

The Disorientation of the Nineteenth Century

If eighteenth-century Qing political economy practiced a balancing act between commerce and agriculture, then the nineteenth-century shock of wars and foreign treaties tipped the balance in favor of unqualified support for overseas trade. As British and other foreign merchants flooded the Chinese market with opium and textiles, Qing officials had to confront the deleterious impacts of a negative balance of trade. The first prominent Qing thinker to express this idea was Wei Yuan (1794–1856), who argued that the illicit opium trade had caused great damage to the Chinese economy, causing inflation and stymieing the flow of money and goods.[16] His analysis borrowed from English-language mercantilist ideas, specifically, that the accumulation of specie signified national strength. As such, officials repurposed older concepts of "circulation" and "merchant sympathy," aimed at the optimal distribution of goods, to now champion commercial strength in the global arena. The balance of trade became the dominant framework for political-economic discussions throughout the rest of the century, and overseas exports such as tea, formerly subordinated to domestic livelihood, became more important than ever.

Within the debate over the tea crisis, the balancing act between commerce and agriculture was now abandoned, as writers often picked one side versus the other. On the side of commerce, we can locate the initial set of solutions to the tea crisis, represented by Liu Kunyi's memorial, expressing sympathy to merchants and promoting circulation through lower taxes. Around this time, the reformer Wang Tao (1828–1897) most clearly articulated a rejection of the Confucian ben-mo hierarchy. He wrote that "circulation" was "what is fundamental. Everything else is peripheral." He elaborated, "Ever since ancient times, China has emphasized agriculture and looked lightly upon commerce, valuing grains and denigrating money." However, the West had succeeded precisely by taking the opposite approach of the Confucians: "In the West the roots are abandoned, and the branches are prioritized. How can it be that in trying to provide for our own people with our own produce, we still rely on trade with foreign countries?"[17]

On the side of agriculture, many traditionalist voices advocated rescuing the roots from the branches. Within the tea crisis, the most prominent voice was Bian Baodi (1824–1893). Bian had been on the front lines of two major export markets, serving in Hankou during the 1880s before assuming the governorship of Fujian and Zhejiang in 1888.[18] "Recently," Bian wrote, "tea merchants have found sales stagnant. Each year is worse than the last." This was accompanied by social unrest: "Each time after the tea market closes, all sorts of people will scatter along the roads to the mountains, where they will hide and then kidnap unsuspecting pedestrians." Bian believed it was "best to let bygones be bygones and instead focus on the future." He drew up orders to ban tea cultivation in areas that could be used for growing grains, limiting tea to "those areas which already have tea." He used the same Legalist language of roots and branches to remind the court of its fundamental mission:

There is no better source for nourishing our people than clothing and food. Speaking honestly, our fundamental task [*ben*] is to ensure the most important activities, that is, agriculture and sericulture. . . . We all know that in times of a famine, tea cannot be eaten, and in times of cold, tea cannot be worn. It is an unimportant, peripheral crop [*mo*], and it is detrimental to our fundamental task of agriculture.[19]

Bian Baodi's ideas shared the worldview of eighteenth-century economic thought, but by the time of the 1890s tea crisis, his were the exception, now anachronistic. Nevertheless, viewing the pro-circulation and pro-agriculture responses together is instructive, for they demonstrate both the flexibility and limitations of high Qing political-economic discourse. For all their disagreements over policy, the mercantilists and the traditionalists shared in common certain Physiocratic assumptions about wealth rooted in the physical and material qualities of goods. This assumption would soon be challenged by global competition and its emphasis upon productivity as the new basis of wealth and power.

THE SECOND RESPONSE: FROM CRISES OF CIRCULATION TO CRISES OF COMPETITION

By the end of the century, Qing officials no longer believed tax cuts alone addressed the fundamental problems facing tea. As the crisis worsened, officials delved further into its underlying causes. From an initial focus upon high prices, they examined production costs and eventually the process of tea production itself. In this section I address this transition by briefly examining the historical relationship between capitalist competition and modern economic thought. For Qing officials and Chinese merchants, the rise of Indian tea was a jarring external stimulus that forced them to pay closer attention to their rivals to the west. Competition also forced Qing observers to deepen their analysis from mercantilist concerns over taxes and transport costs into the opaque realm of production. Competition naturalized the patterns of capital accumulation and mechanization, giving them the appearance of natural and lawlike movements that could be codified into philosophical and metaphysical principles of economic behavior.

It may be useful to first clarify the dynamic of competition in historical terms. In much of neoclassical economic scholarship today, competition between firms is described as a state of "equilibrium" devoid of antagonism and historical change. However, a long tradition of economic thinkers from Smith to Joseph Schumpeter to Friedrich Hayek recognized in competition the opposite tendency. Schumpeter wrote, "In capitalist reality as distinguished from its textbook picture, it is not [price competition] which counts but the competition from the new commodity, the new technology, the new source of supply, the new type of organization." For these thinkers, competition was not a state but a process, not an equilibrium but an antagonistic rivalry. Schumpeter called it "creative destruction," and Marx, "a fight among enemy brothers." As economist Anwar Shaikh recently put it: "Firms within an industry fight to attract customers. Price is their weapon, advertising their propaganda, the local Chamber of Commerce their house of worship, and profit their supreme deity." Such antagonism was also recognized by observers on all sides of the rivalry between Chinese and Indian tea producers. In British India, Governor-General Bentinck's original 1834 Minute on tea aspired to "annihilate" and "destroy" the Chinese monopoly, and the planter David Crole had of course pronounced British efforts as waging a "tea war."[20]

Within the Qing context, the most notable voice was Zheng Guanying (1842–1922), an ex-comprador turned imperial bureaucrat. In his influential treatise *Words of Warning to a Prosperous Age* (*Shengshi Weiyan,* 1894), he popularized the phrase "commercial warfare" (*shangzhan*). In earlier decades, "commercial warfare" referred to policies of taxing commerce as a means to fund military measures. Zheng redefined it as an embrace of economic competition *as an end in itself,* a weapon for matching and overpowering China's rivals. He argued that decades of self-strengthening, in which Qing officials focused their energies on building regional arsenals in Fuzhou, Shanghai, and Tianjin, had proved fruitless. The "other races" (*bizu*) continued to laugh at China. It was clear that "to study military warfare cannot compare with studying commercial warfare." Such an attitude marked a sharp departure from high Qing economic thought, which, Rowe wrote, may have recognized the "natural principles" of supply and demand but also emphasized "the Confucian ideal of social harmony" over "unfettered struggle in the marketplace."[21]

Zheng Guanying's discussion of "commercial warfare" exemplified how modern economic competition forced participants to look beyond circulation and examine questions of production and technique. Extending the logic of military battle, he cited a dictum from *The Art of War* by Sun Tzu (Sun Zi, 544–496 BCE): "If you know your enemies, and if you know yourself, then in one hundred battles, you will have one hundred victories" (*zhibi zhiji baizhan baisheng*).[22] In commercial terms, Chinese merchants and producers could wage war only by studying and emulating their rivals, particularly for the most profitable Chinese exports, silk and tea. Outlining the logic of commercial warfare, Zheng wrote:

> The idea of "commerce" [*shang*] means exchange. If we send out profits but do not bring enough back in, then the others will have commercial gains and we will suffer commercial losses. . . . However, the successes and failures of commerce do not depend solely upon the scarcity of goods. One must also look at the level of skill in industrial arts [*gongyi zhi qiaozhuo*]. If one can use manufacture to buttress commerce, then the clumsy can be converted into skilled, the coarse can become refined. . . . But if we focus only on commerce without manufacture, then even though our land is fertile with many treasures, even if the natural products of our provinces grow more plentiful every day, we would still be throwing away our own profit for others to grow richer. If we wish to make an effective plan, then we must not overlook the combination of commerce and manufacture.[23]

Zheng was not alone in turning from trade to production techniques. In the last half of the 1890s, commentaries on the tea crisis grew fixated on the methods used by the Indian plantations. This information first entered state consciousness with the IMC's 1888 report on tea, which included passages from Robert Fortune and the planter texts from George Barker and Edward Money analyzed in chapter 4. Qing reformers grew self-conscious about the relative lack of mechanization in their own tea districts. Famed reformer Zhang Zhidong (1837–1909), who once wrote that Chinese tea "remained superior" due to the quality of the soil, now claimed that "because our human-labor-based methods [*rengong*] for firing and processing tea are imperfect, they fall short of the quality of machine-made tea." Another official commented, "Chinese people do not have manufactured goods that attract the attention of foreign merchants," and instead "it was only tea, this natural form of profit in China [*ziran zhi li*], that foreigners considered indispensable."[24] Qing officials had internalized the British colonial planters' propaganda and its rhetoric pitting East versus West as the evolutionary opposition between manual versus machine, traditional versus modern methods.

Qing writers also began to think differently about the nature of wealth itself. Earlier, they expressed confidence that the "rich flavour and strong aroma" of Chinese tea, namely, its physical utility, placed it beyond reproach. Now, many believed that this attitude had bred laziness and negligence. One official complained, "frequently, we just look at whether or not the weather is good in order to measure how much tea can be grown. We look for how much it will rain and then resign ourselves to our fate." Instead of physical utility, the real source of economic strength lay in diligence and skill:

> Westerners work harder, they conduct research, and they use human ability to conquer nature. Chinese people, however, are greedy for the fruits of nature [*tian zhi gong*], but they are content with being lazy. In terms of what human labor can accomplish, heaven sets no limitations. The only concern is whether humans themselves work hard enough.[25]

Others were more optimistic, maintaining the customary notion of wealth as physical utility but also combining it with new knowledge about superior techniques in India and Japan. Chinese tea production was defective for now but capable of improvement:

> The myriad of things [*wanwu*] each have their own appropriate nature. Chinese tea results from processing a natural source of profit. Foreigners, however, use human powers to plunder from the work of nature. . . . Their soil is not suitable for tea, so they struggle against nature, and ultimately their flavor is worse. The problem is that Chinese processing is not yet refined, and others look down on it. If we commit ourselves to reform, justice will prevail and we will fetch high prices and be competitive.[26]

Another memorial suggested that the merchants' confusion resulted from their inability to understand simple supply and demand. The merchants "wasted their time cursing the Westerners for squeezing prices, or they wasted their time bemoaning how much better things were in the past." As another memorial put it, "Foreign merchants have never once cheated Chinese merchants. . . . Rather, it was the Chinese merchants, in fact, who cheated themselves first! Who knows how much their miscalculations have cost them?"[27]

As the crisis deepened, tea merchants did not so much "exhaust the earth" as they exhausted the sympathy of Qing officials. Earlier, officials had looked for ways to explain the seemingly random and chaotic movement of prices, settling on a theory based on the arbitrary behavior of foreign bullies. Now, officials suggested that the core determinants of price were the impersonal, objective laws of labor and capital inputs. Juxtaposed against the rationality of such laws, Chinese merchants appeared petty and rash. If officials began to scapegoat native merchants instead of foreign traders, their attitudes were premised less upon the *subjective* whims of individuals and more upon the *objectivity* of natural economic laws.

This lawlike quality of modern economic life constitutes a second historically significant dimension to capitalist competition. Out of the tea crisis, Qing thinkers began to articulate a more general notion of wealth akin to the classical theory of value, attributing it not to physical utility but to the social determinations of relative labor productivity. Although this famous theory has attracted heated debate among economists, much less has been said about what, historically, allowed this theory to gain traction in everyday economic life—why it appeared plausible to anonymous merchants and planters in places outside cutting-edge industrial centers like England. Market competition can help to answer this question. By participating in competition, tea producers in China unconsciously internalized many of the assumptions behind political economy's theory of value.

Throughout this book, I have suggested that the history of capitalism is best conceptualized not as a particular set of technologies or class relations but instead as a general social dynamic shared across commodity producers, a dynamic that has also, in modern times, come to appear natural and lawlike. For Marx, it was only with "free competition" that the "inner laws of capital—which appear merely as tendencies in the preliminary historic stages of its development—are for the first time posited as laws." Unlike in other economic systems, in which prices or labor allocation may be determined by some authority, such as an official, landlord, or village custom, market competition is far more confusing precisely because it is regulated by nobody in theory and hence everybody in practice. Prices are determined by a potentially infinite multiplicity of firms, and the field of competition appears as a state of anarchy that nevertheless obeys certain inescapable principles. As Marx put it, the "inner law" regulating the determination of value by labor appeared as a "blind natural force . . . asserted in the midst of accidental fluctuations." In mundane economic life, real actors such as Chinese tea merchants or British tea planters encounter specific pressures to adopt a new competitor's techniques of production, "posited as external necessity." These concrete, individual pressures ultimately add up to abstract and general concepts, patterns, or laws governing accumulation. Observers do not arrive at them "as a result of a rational social convention," Diane Elson has explained, "but from an unplanned historical process" of "iterative" competition. For instance, the British planter Baildon had written that due to competition, "the cost of production must come down. . . . This cannot be considered a pessimist view, but a hard fact." In China, the IMC's report to the Guangxu Emperor had included a passage from a British lecture stating that the "command of the Tea supply . . . *will finally rest with whatever country can produce it at least cost,* a law that applies to all commodities."[28]

In China, one of the most distinctive thinkers to give voice to these natural economic laws was the Qing official Chen Chi. His suggestions for industrializing tea were grounded in his own understanding of the abstract, cosmological principles of trade and production. A close study of Chen's thought illustrates how these external patterns of competition corresponded to transformations of consciousness.

SOME THINGS COME FROM NOTHING: THE POLITICAL ECONOMY OF CHEN CHI

In his official capacity, Chen Chi enjoyed a relatively unexceptional career as a mid-level bureaucrat within the Qing government. He attained provincial graduate status (*juren*) in 1882 and thereafter occupied various posts in the Ministry of Finance for less than two decades until his death. His biggest claim to fame has been his close friendship with Zheng Guanying and his collaboration with famed reformers Kang Youwei and Liang Qichao, as he participated in the two men's ill-fated Hundred Days of Reform (1898). What has been overlooked is Chen's role as one of the earliest thinkers in China to engage with the tradition of political economy. Many scholars have highlighted Yan Fu's translation of Smith's *Wealth of Nations* (1900) as a milestone in the introduction of European economic thought into China. However, the earliest widely read work was in fact an 1880 translation of Henry Fawcett's *Manual of Political Economy* (1874 edition), undertaken by the state-funded School of Combined Learning (*Tongwen Guan*). Chen Chi incorporated ideas from this early draft into his own set of writings, published during the years 1895–1896.[29]

Why was Chen so drawn to Fawcett's text? Chinese intellectual life was radicalized by the Qing military's humiliating defeat in the first Sino-Japanese War (1894–1895), spurring greater openness by the Qing court to outside ideas. Over the next year, Chen, who normally would not have had a direct line to the emperor, submitted three imperial memorials outlining measures the Qing bureaucracy would need to take in order to modernize the Chinese economy. Among them was his memorial on the tea trade. Whereas many other reformers agreed that the Qing state needed to adopt "Western methods," such as democratic political institutions, Chen and a handful of others turned their attention to the school of political economy. He interpreted the rise of Japan as simply the most extreme example of the superiority of Western methods, and he argued it was incumbent upon the Qing court to investigate new techniques overseas and study translated works at home.[30]

If eighteenth-century Qing economic thought held on to notions of wealth as physical, natural, and finite, then Chen Chi broke from tradition by experimentally incorporating political economy's view of wealth as intangible, socially determined by the productivity of labor, and hence capable of infinite expansion. He exhorted tea merchants to integrate commerce with production (branches with roots), rationalizing labor and investing capital into labor-saving machinery. Past generations of scholars have lumped Chen Chi with other late Qing thinkers known as "Westernizers," and they explained his enthusiasm for classical economics through his devotion to "Western learning."[31]

Despite his enthusiasm, they have stressed, the marriage between British classical economics with Chinese realities was incompatible. However, we should bear in mind that there were many examples of thinkers outside of Europe at this time who read political economy but did not embrace it. For example, Lees and Wakefield argued that much of Smithian thought *did not* apply to the undeveloped territories of the Americas, Australia, and India (see chapter 3). That Chen was able to locate in China a corresponding social referent to the abstract textual principles he found in economic translations, therefore, is noteworthy. Political economy's theory of value resonated with Chen not due to some fetish for foreign ideas, I suggest, but because he recognized in China the everyday social structures that it sought to explain.

The Memorial on Tea

In January 1896, Chen Chi submitted a memorial to the imperial court on "matters relating to tea." Many of the individual recommendations echoed ideas found earlier in the report from the IMC and in the work of other Chinese thinkers. As a whole, however, Chen's memorial represented a pivot from the conventional focus on lowering taxes toward novel state-centered attempts to vertically integrate tea production with commerce. The memorial circulated widely, traveling to the Guangxu Emperor's Grand Council, which commented that Chen's work provided "penetrating analysis written with clarity." The court ordered the memorial be distributed to all the provincial governments of the central and southeast districts, including Anhui and Fujian. "In general, tea is one of the big sources of profit for China," the emperor concluded. "In the southeast, the livelihood of merchants depends upon it. Provincial governors and local officers can not overlook tea."[32]

The memorial featured two halves. First, Chen Chi described the three major problems hurting the trade: the rise of South Asian tea, the scattered character of undercapitalized Chinese merchants, and the tug-of-war between tea peasants and inland factories. He criticized the tea-growing peasantry for hoarding tea and raising prices when dealing with the inland factories. Their selfish behavior hurt the profits of the trade, for "the merchants found themselves caught between, on the one hand, mountain peasants raising their sale price and, on the other, foreign traders in Shanghai who were lowering their buying price. The peasants would occasionally earn a profit, but the tea merchants always lost money." As for the merchants, he wrote that they were too "scattered" to withstand the "foreign merchants' oppression":

> With only a few thousand *jin* of money, these small merchants lacked capital, and so they sought to sell their goods quickly, and they resorted to producing fake tea. When prices fell, they rushed to sell. Foreign merchants started to bully the ignorant and weak. They started to push down prices, be selective, and manipulate numbers. Pretty soon, they wrested away control over the trade. The fresh leaves of this year must be sold before next year. If overseas merchants do not buy then the Chinese merchants have no profits; and the Chinese merchants borrowed half their capital, which they must return—all these factors mean that Chinese merchants rush to cut prices to keep the business of foreigners, and so they slash prices to an extreme![33]

Chen outlined four solutions: tea-rolling machinery, motorized boats for transport, a guild warehouse, and a reduction on transport taxes. He sought to connect the various components of the tea trade in order to lower prices without sacrificing quality. Chen was also among the first to recommend that the emperor send Chinese researchers to colonial India to study tea production, a venture undertaken later in 1905 and again in 1934 (see chapter 7): "It would be best to allocate funds and to select two tea masters, one Chinese and one foreign, to secretly go to India, to test out and study their methods for tea production, buy machines and then set them up in the mountains of China." Once the experiments bore results, the government should provide financial support to encourage using machines. At the end of his memorial, Chen summarized his approach as the "simultaneous promotion of the branches and roots" (*benmo bingju*):

> Regrettably, in China, bureaucrats and merchants have traditionally remained separate. "Worship the roots and suppress the branches," as the saying goes. Bureaucrats have been indifferent to the successes and failures of merchants, feeling neither happiness nor sadness in their hearts. But if we adopt this attitude and try to compete with the Western powers, then that would be like trying to catch a thoroughbred by riding a mule. It would wipe out all wealthy merchants from China, and we would cede all commercial power to the other races. We would be in dire straits, living off others' crumbs, just like those colonized countries Burma, Thailand, and Vietnam.

As with the mercantilists of the nineteenth century, Chen defended the merchants against traditional pro-agrarian prejudices. But continuities in merchant sympathy were also paired with novel suggestions to reform the tea merchants' own behavior by widening their scope of activity to include production as well. In one of the memorial's crucial lines, Chen wrote, "The tea merchants and mountain peasants will be entirely united and coordinated." This phrase, *yiqi hecheng*, which literally meant "continuous as one puff of breath," was his early attempt at describing what we today might call vertical integration. Chen Chi held a vision of Chinese merchants behaving like the industrial tea capitalists of British India, overseeing every aspect of cultivation, manufacture, processing, packaging, and transport. When he wrote that the tea merchants were too cheap and short-sighted, he was pushing them to invest their capital into fixed infrastructural improvements. When he remonstrated the peasantry for their recalcitrance, he was summoning them to subordinate themselves to the merchants as an efficient labor force. He was articulating a social dynamic that had already begun to quietly emerge in the commercial districts—in which tea production was being transformed by guest merchants along the principles of industrial time-discipline—but to a stronger degree.

The Supplement to the Wealth of Nations

Chen Chi's memorial on tea emerged out of his larger analysis of the problems facing Chinese society, which he had addressed in a rough draft on political economy written earlier that year. *The Supplement to the Wealth of Nations* (*Xu Fuguoce*; *The Supplement* for short) included sixteen chapters dedicated to agricultural reforms and the cultivation of specific crops, including tea, which the Qing Empire should promote. *The Supplement* was Chen Chi's true contribution to the history of economic ideas in modern China; its chapters were welcomed by reformer study groups and collected in influential Qing anthologies on practical matters of statecraft.[34]

The Supplement opened with a justification for the study of English economic thought, especially Smith, on the grounds that China and "the West" shared a common human fate, with trade as the crucial bridge. Chen echoed popular themes on the importance of trade, but he also introduced what he called a "principle for producing wealth," which attributed to labor a special role in creating wealth. It was an idea inspired by political economy's theory of value, the consequences for which he fleshed out in his specific analysis of how tea, silk, and sugar could become more competitive with their industrial rivals across the ocean. These sections demonstrated the intuitive appeal of political economy's theory of value, insofar as it corresponded with Chen's own observation that Chinese society was increasingly mediated by the exchange of labor embodied in cash crops produced for the world market. Finally, returning to the big picture, Chen concluded that if the "principle for producing wealth" were true, then Chinese officials should dispense with old shibboleths of imperial economic thought, such as the finitude of physical and material wealth.

The Universality of Political Economy

In the opening pages of *The Supplement*, Chen speculated about the differences between China and the West, landing on the notion of a shared synthesis of economic principles. Chinese poverty and weakness, he wrote, stemmed from the past sixty years since the first Opium War, during which the fundamental differences between China and the West had become manifest: "Whereas China seeks principle [*li*], the West seeks quantity [*shu*]. . . . Whereas China understands substance [*ti*], the West understands function [*yong*]. Whereas China is refined [*jing*], the West is crude [*cu*]." Until now, these philosophies "mutually repelled" one another, and it appeared the two "would never merge and unify and thereby change." Nevertheless, he claimed, both regions were now united through trade, and they even had a shared history. Years ago, China featured great texts, but they had been destroyed when the Qin (221–206 BCE) burned their books and buried their scholars. These ideas had traveled westward, and during the Ming (1368–1644), several "remarkable people" emerged in Europe. They

> used old methods to build new tools and learn new principles, establish new methods, and write new books. They were able to harness fire and water as energy and thereby create steamships, trains, firearms, telegraphs, and various machines. They applied these to agriculture, mining, manufacture, and commerce, enhancing the people's convenience, and greatly enriching the nation. They took these new machines and methods into China, and China was unable to resist.

Because "all under heaven is on the same track," and "all books are being read together," then logically "all activities are now interlinked." This was "the beauty of the Will of Heaven." Chen quoted from the *Book of Changes*: "exhaustion yields change, change yields development, development yields longevity" (*qiong ze bian, bian ze tong, tong ze jiu*). He concluded that "there is no distinction between the ancient and new, inside and outside, Chinese and foreigner, thing and self, there have only been people." As a result, "there are no boundaries, only oneness."[35] For Chen, the universal optimism of political economy, championed by East India Company officials in the early nineteenth century, resembled the boundlessness of Daoist philosophy.

Chen had seized upon a narrative device popular among writers of the late Qing: that the European Renaissance and the English Industrial Revolution originated from the lost wisdom of ancient China, which was now being reintroduced into China through global trade. In his study of late Qing thought, Paul Cohen characterized this argument by Chen and others as an "ingenious . . . exercise in intellectual gymnastics."[36] For Cohen, such "gymnastics" were unnatural, concealing a fundamental incommensurability between Western and Eastern—modern and traditional—values. Certainly, the claim that modern industry in England originated from pre-Qin China was dubious. But to fixate on the literal meaning of Chen's story would be to overlook the validity of his underlying proposition: that in the current moment, economic laws were neither uniquely Western nor Eastern, for global trade and investment had united a multiplicity of world societies underneath the same competitive pressures. It was this competition that initially compelled Qing writers to study the works of British classical political economy, and it was those works, in turn, that enriched their observations about the economic realities of China.

Elaborating on these laws, Chen Chi mixed quotations from Daoist and Confucian classics with his description of Smith's *Wealth of Nations*. Smith was "a virtuous man" whose book "exhaustively described the principles of commerce." Equipped with these ideas, "English commerce became so powerful that it is now strongest in the whole world." That Britain, those "three islands of only thirty-five million people," could become so rich could "be entirely attributed to this one book *The Wealth of Nations*." Thus, whereas past historiography has interpreted late Qing thinkers through a "culturalist" framework, emphasizing incompatibility between China and the West, Chen had stressed the opposite theme: that China was unified with the world through shared economic practices. Cultural difference did not determine political possibilities; rather, it was global interactions, and trade in particular, that shaped the limits of belief, custom, and knowledge.[37]

The Principle for Producing Wealth and Its Plausibility

In the second half of the preface to *The Supplement,* Chen Chi situated the key theoretical insight he drew from Smith within the context of Chinese history:

Back in the day, a friend once told me: "ever since the days of the Three Kingdoms, there have been users of wealth [*caiyongzhe*], movers [*yi*] and looters [*duo*] of wealth, but there has not yet been any producers of wealth." Who are the movers? those who simply take without producing. Who are the looters? those who tax. However, no one has yet figured out a way to move and loot wealth from overseas and return it to China. If one were to conceive of the principle for producing wealth [*shengcai zhi dao*], then it must be this: where the ground originally had nothing, where among humans originally there was nothing, suddenly there are things. Agriculture, mining, manufacture, commerce: these are how the Chinese people can expand their livelihood, like pouring a vast ocean to fill up a leaking goblet [a reference to the balance of trade]. These are how they can open up a source of profit for the common people, to increase taxes for the nation. These are how China can enhance its industry, to stem the power of foreign nations.[38]

Historians of Chinese economic thought have recognized Chen's "way" or "principle for producing wealth" as his version of political economy's theory of value. Just as Smith had introduced his own ideas by rebuking those of the mercantilists and Physiocrats before him—and just as Lees and Wakefield, in chapter 3, had asserted the primacy of labor by dispelling theories centered on land and money alone—Chen criticized the pro-merchant and agriculture-centric tendencies of Qing governance popular in previous generations. In terms of the former, he decried merchants and tax-collecting officials as "movers" and "looters" who did not produce anything. And in terms of the latter, he widened the limits of what counted as productive labor from agriculture to include mining, manufacture, and commerce. Notably, Chen included "commerce" as a form of productive labor, a departure from the Smithian view, perhaps reflecting Chen's attempt to reconcile these categories with Chinese thought.[39] But in subsequent chapters, he clarified that commerce ultimately was separate from, and rested upon, the activities of production:

> The basis of commerce is agriculture. When agriculture thrives, then hundreds of things grow, and flows of profit can be extracted. The source of commerce is mining. When mining is opened, then the five metals will be abundant, and wealth will thrive. The content and form [tiyong] of commerce is manufacture. When the arts of manufacture flourish, then ten thousand goods will proliferate and accumulate, and through transport and circulation they will fill the four seas.[40]

But even as historians of Chinese thought have praised Chen for his ability to grasp the basics of classical economics, they wrote that his understanding was limited and "feudal," for Chen continued to view wealth as something physical and material. Possible evidence for this interpretation was the fact that the phrase "production of wealth" (shengcai) was already widely used in imperial China, most notably by Song-era thinker Wang Anshi (1021–1086), who meant it as material agricultural production.[41] However, an examination of Chen's other writings suggests that when he used the term shengcai he was not invoking Wang Anshi but instead the classical economists and their imagination of "wealth" as the result of human labor, hence intangible and socially determined.

Chen Chi's engagement with economist Henry Fawcett is instructive. In 1896, in the same year he wrote his memorial on tea and was composing The Supplement, Chen also finished a series of short retranslations and summaries of political economy in the reformer newspaper Chinese Progress (Shiwu Bao), founded by Liang Qichao. Chen believed he was summarizing Smith's magnum opus, but in fact it was Fawcett's Manual of Political Economy, translated into Chinese in 1880. For the purpose of my claims, this confusion of author identity is inconsequential, for Fawcett's work had been chosen precisely because it summarized the main tenets of the classical tradition in didactic terms. In order to grasp what Chen meant by "the production of wealth" in his own treatise, we should look to how and where Chen used the term to translate Fawcett's categories.

First, Chen translated a short summary on the nature of wealth in the following way:

What people eat and use, having a lot and having nothing, moving quickly and moving slowly, having enough and not having enough, trading with each other and getting something in return—these are all part of what can be called "wealth" [*cai*]. . . . [But] if it cannot be traded, then it is not wealth. Water is matter, but there is no place without it, and no people who do not use it, so water is not wealth. However, in a large town, where land is sparse and people crowded, rainfall does not supply enough water, and they must rely upon human power [*renli*] to transport it. In that case, water is wealth.[42]

This section used the classic water-diamond paradox to demonstrate that wealth was not only the utility innate to physical goods (Smith's "value in use") but also something socially determined by labor and exchange ("value in exchange"). His articulation combined the duality of production and exchange—similar to roots and branches in imperial Chinese economic thought—into a single, contradictory category specific to the social patterns of modern capital, insofar as it was predicated on the effectiveness of "human power." In turn, Chen employed this same dual notion of wealth in his own concrete explanation of the principle for producing wealth. In his *Supplement*, he described how introducing machinery would both enhance the "convenience," or use-value, of people's lives *and* "greatly enrich" (*dafu*) the nation. In the prefatory passage on the "production of wealth," he used a similar parallel structure to stress that *shengcai* benefited the material "livelihood" of the people *as well as* "opened a source of profit."[43]

Second, Chen used the phrase *shengcai* to translate the classical distinction between productive and unproductive labor. As examples of productive labor, Chen listed human activities that produced commodities, such as growing wheat, forging cooking tools, and sewing clothes. By contrast, unproductive labor consisted of people who did not produce anything with commercial value. Smith had given the example of servants and churchmen. Chen changed this example to "Buddhist and Daoist temples," which "produce not one thing, contributing little to this world." He concluded, "According to the 'principle for producing wealth,' there are those who harm without profit, who use things up without achieving anything. They truly are a parasite [*du*] upon the people and the nation." The "wealth of the nation" he wrote, turned on the productivity of those whose labor was "profitable" (*youyi*).[44]

To be clear, then, what I am suggesting is that Chen Chi, although living in a radically different time and place, sought to follow the path of Smith and political economy before him by critically engaging previous intellectual traditions centered on the twin pillars of agriculture and trade—embodied in the bifurcated responses to the nineteenth-century tea crisis—in order to advance a vision of human-labor-powered industry as the future basis of wealth.

But if Chen Chi's notion of wealth was aligned with the classical economists, then it is worth asking why he found this ostensibly foreign and abstract set of ideas plausible. As suggested in chapter 3, political economy's theory of value emerged out of, and best corresponded to, the historically specific conditions of a British setting where wage labor had increasingly become a social norm. A theory that attributed value to *labor in general* corresponded to societies organized around labor that had been *generalized*, that is, wage labor. However, economic historians such as Philip Huang have argued that imperial China was prevented from becoming capitalist precisely due to the absence of this wage labor population. As proof, he cited the first full surveys conducted in the early twentieth century, which placed the number of full-time wage workers at 10 to 20 percent of the population. But as Kathy Le Mons Walker has argued, "estimates of the rural labor force based only on calculations of wage workers at once obscure the significance of" other forms of labor that contributed to the accumulation of capital.[45] The generic sociological category of wage labor used in the surveys, in other words, had been misleading. Productive labor within the logic of capital was simply any human activity that produced a commodity in exchange for payment. This definition could include all sorts of workers who were productive but would not be counted as "free" and "independent" in survey data: women's and children's household labor, debt-bondage, tenant farmers, sharecroppers, and casual and seasonal gang labor. *These* groups in China may not have fit the classic definition of an urban proletarian, but they certainly contributed to Chen Chi's intuition that wealth in Chinese society was the collective product of a general workforce, one scattered across various makeshift factories, peasant households, and tenant farms.

In the commercial regions of China, a collection of domestic, sideline, and casual workers who contributed to the accumulation of merchant capital had become increasingly visible since the seventeenth century, as illustrated by the snapshots of the tea, silk, and cotton trades seen in chapter 2. Although most remained tied to the land, many households were integrated through the production and exchange of goods via regional markets. "The entire production process" of the household, Walker wrote, "came to be mediated by commodity exchange." As early as the seventeenth century, Pan Ming-te has argued, households survived by borrowing high-interest loans from creditors, relying upon household female labor to produce silk and cotton, and, consequently, making the most cost-effective calculations about labor inputs and expenditures. Peasants produced for the market to survive, and "sidelines and handicrafts were the backbone" of this economy.[46] Even though official discourses continued to venerate the production of grain, the everyday reality for the peasantry was the compulsion to produce whatever commodities would pay the best. As they relied more on advances and loans from moneylenders, they grew less independent, increasingly embedded within social relations that, to varying degrees, resembled that of employers and employees.

Chen Chi understood the degree to which the Chinese peasant now depended on cash crops for survival. In addition to tea, cotton, and silk, Chen recommended introducing wine, coffee, and rubber into the countryside. When describing coffee and tobacco, he noted both were labor-intensive crops, and although they offered little use-value for direct consumption, they yielded value through trade. A field of three to five *mu* (between 0.5 to 0.8 acres) would earn "fat profits, with enough left over to feed a family of eight, who would be well-fed and clothed, without any worry of starvation or cold." Chen also took for granted the availability of disposable labor. In his description of the silk industry, Chen recommended building the same silk-reeling machines used in France, adding that with "one request, crowds of female workers would quickly gather." In his description of growing camphor trees, he described that a large number of itinerant salt refinery workers had recently lost their jobs, and they could be tasked with planting and caring for trees throughout the empire, while also instructing the locals on how to harvest them. Throughout his work, then, Chen presupposed the wide availability of families with nothing to offer but their time and labor.[47]

Within the context of Chinese tea, we have already seen that manufactories for refining *maocha* reached up to hundreds, perhaps over one thousand workers during the peak seasons. As for the peasant cultivators, piecemeal evidence from the nineteenth century suggested that for much of the boom years, households that grew tea had become dependent upon credit markets. An 1839 report noted that peasant households employed a mixture of family and hired work for plucking leaves and that they relied upon advances from coastal merchants. In the 1870s, the English photographer John Thomson noted from his travels that tea farms in Fujian were "small, seldom exceeding a few acres in size, and are rented by the poor from the landowners of the district. . . . The men who grow that tea which is a source of so much wealth to China very rarely possess any capital at all themselves." And even households that controlled their own labor were subjected to the same competitive demands to calculate the value of their family members' schedules in terms of cost and output, despite the absence of formal wages.[48] Such examples give substance to the hypothesis of generalized social forms outlined in this book's introduction: that although not everyone in China was a waged worker, everyday life for pockets of Chinese society increasingly assumed the social patterns of laboring for survival. These dynamics would persist into the twentieth century, when surveyors documented them systematically for the first time (see chapter 7).

When Chen looked at these regional commercial networks, he could visualize what Smith and Fawcett had described: that the basis of profits did not come from the earth but from the various forms of employed labor that went into it. Further, another tenet of modern capital—the necessity for an efficient and disciplined workforce—recurred throughout his analysis. In his memorial on tea, Chen remonstrated the tea peasants for being stubborn and recalcitrant instead of an obedient workforce. In his *Supplement,* he described a world of potential workers who required acculturation to the temporal rhythms of industrial production. The coastal areas featured "thousands upon thousands of people without work" and lacking official instruction. The economic benefits of crops like coffee and tobacco were clear, but he worried that these "wandering people" (*xianmin*) were "the type of people who, in planting and cultivating trees, will do the job crudely and irresponsibly. They will pay lip service, but in the end the lazy peasants of all under heaven [China] will not produce any results." His solution was greater vigilance and involvement from officials and experts. After a few years of supervised work, these projects of import substitution would yield results that would "nourish the people," "expand livelihoods," and also overturn the national imbalance of trade.[49]

The Infinite Improvements of Labor

A final corollary to Chen Chi's "principle for producing wealth" was that if economic value was the social product of human labor, then what made one form of labor more profitable than another was its combination of quality and quantity. In *The Supplement*, he described the "production of wealth" as "where among humans originally there was nothing, suddenly there are things." In his retranslation of Fawcett, he wrote that wealth came from activities that "depend upon human power." Such observations seem to contradict portions of his memorial on tea, where he criticized the inland factories' employment of human labor as inferior to the machinery used in India. But of course, such machinery did not actually replace human labor; rather, it enhanced the latter's overall effectiveness. In the memorial on tea, he continued, "only by using machines to roast leaves will the fire be even and proper and all products will be perfected. . . . One person could do the work of ten, and we could produce ever greater amounts." Chen's theoretical equation between economic wealth and human labor pointed to labor-saving machinery, which in turn required capital investment.[50]

Chen noted, however, that many Qing officials feared that mechanization would be detrimental to economic activity:

> Writers today often say . . . if China also uses machines, then how much more market space can there be? If goods are cheap and prices low, then ultimately there will be no profit. Those people with this type of "frog in a well" [*jingwa xiachong*] mentality, this self-destructive [*yuanyu congque*] attitude—they are the ones truly guilty of keeping China poor and weak.

As a counterexample, Chen cited the western European experience, where new machines and factories had led to higher profits and wages. In China, too, mechanization would not exhaust existing wealth but create new sources: "If in China we opened factories in every province, then tens of millions of poor people will suddenly have plenty to eat and be warmly clothed, they will be able to provide for their wives and children. Those people who in the past relied upon manual labor to feed themselves will also be able to avoid hardships. Those who worried about freezing or starving will enjoy these great riches." The capacity of human labor was itself a source of endless wealth. "The great achievements and virtues of the heavens truly are unimaginable and without limit!"[51]

Chen applied this theory to different cash crops. Aside from tea and tea-rolling machines, he wrote that if the silk trade employed motorized filatures, then Chinese companies could sell their goods for twice the price. He made similar pronouncements about paper, sugar, and cotton. More generally, he praised the English pursuit of "agricultural science," which entailed new methods of cultivation and "new machines" that turned "barren into fertile soil, desolate into productive land. One person was now enough to meet fifty people's labor, and one *mu* of land could match fifty *mu*" (about eight acres).[52] As with British observers of the tea war and his friend Zheng Guanying's articulation of commercial warfare, Chen identified the efficiency of production as the key to competitive success.

Such solutions were presented as objective, universal laws. Pressures to mechanize were a "command" (*ming*) from the "will of heaven" (*tian zhi xin*) that applied equally to China as to the rest of the world. Chen spoke of the benefits of raised productivity for human progress as a whole. "If you are still wearing grass and eating trees," he wrote, "if you don't even wear fur or cook with fire, and someday you want to wear fancy official robes, live in mansions, and become civilized—then in that case, how can you provide for people's basic livelihood unless you figure out how to make one person do ten or hundreds of people's work?"[53] Although Chen's objective was to craft a program for reviving a Chinese society in crisis, his analysis and solutions emerged from the conviction that China should be understood as a constitutive member of the capitalist world, insofar as it obeyed the same economic laws, and was tethered to the same fate, as those of their overseas rivals.

CONCLUSION

It is a well-known criticism that most histories of economic thought share a presentist approach, gravitating toward past writers whose ideas most closely match today's orthodoxy. It therefore bears acknowledging that although Chen Chi's engagement with political economy was prescient in many ways, his was still the minority view in his time, and its widespread acceptance was far from predetermined. Among officials writing about tea, Bian Baodi interpreted the fall in sales as a cautionary sign to return to the Confucian ideals of noncommercial agriculture. Other traditionalist economic thinkers during this time, such as Liu Xihong and Zeng Lian, warned against adopting Western methods of building railroads and factories, instead championing the ways of the "ancient sages and kings," wherein societies remain materially wealthy because men farm outdoors while women weave indoors.[54]

But the clearest sign that Chen's reformist views remained far from universally accepted was the fate of the 1898 Hundred Days of Reform. Chen's 1896 memorial on tea affairs had been made possible by the political opportunities opened up by the Qing defeat in the Sino-Japanese War, after which reformers had continuously pressured the court to overhaul its political system. In 1898, the Guangxu Emperor finally agreed to put some of their proposals into action. From June to September, he empowered a coterie of leading thinkers to replace the imperial education system with a more practical curriculum grounded in Western ideas and to establish new bureaus overseeing economic reforms. Chen Chi participated on the margins, regularly exchanging letters with leaders Kang Youwei, Liang Qichao, and Tan Sitong throughout the process. But the new policies alarmed court officials, who responded by imploring the emperor's aunt, the Dowager Cixi, to return from retirement and pronounce herself regent of the empire, sidelining the emperor and executing many of the reformers. Though living in Beijing, Chen was able to avoid the Qing court's crackdown without physical harm—but he did not escape unscathed. His brief biography noted soberly that he spent the remaining two years of his life "with a bottle at his side, beneath a lamp, crying loudly as if singing a song, in a daze."[55]

History would be more kind to Chen's actual political economy, and his tea memorial would enjoy a wider audience in following years. It became a touchstone in discussions over reviving the tea trade, praised by the imperial court, distributed to local provincial and county officials, and later canonized within compendia on Qing statecraft. That these local bureaucrats welcomed Chen's memorial is testament to how much his analysis resonated with the tea districts and their constitutive social structure. One recipient was He Runsheng, local magistrate of Shexian in southern Anhui, the hometown of the Jiang family of Fangkeng Village. He Runsheng commented that "the opinions on the problems and solutions to tea . . . outlined are entirely correct."[56] Another official in the tea districts wrote:

> Last year I happened to read the memorial on tea by Mr. Chen distributed by the Grand Council. In order to recover the financial strength that has been lost, he recommended getting rid of old Chinese customs and adopting new methods from overseas. . . . If we are able to get those involved in the tea business to implement these policies, then how could the tea business not be revived?[57]

Other positive responses came from the governors of Anhui and Jiangxi, located in the heart of the export tea districts.[58] For instance, De Shou, Jiangxi provincial governor, applied Chen's analysis to central China. After outlining Chen's solutions with approval, he provided his own examples from experience. He agreed that the human-labor-based methods in the region were inferior:

> Methods for making tea in China rely upon human power and a combination of weather and timing. There are women who pack, roll, and fire tea. There are tea masters who inspect and manage the firing of tea as well as the crude labor beneath them. Currently, most of these people are without jobs.

De Shou also exhorted the merchants to purchase machinery to compete with their rivals. "It is necessary to give orders to everyone who has capital, everyone who stands to profit," he wrote. "In order to improve the future of Chinese tea, they must introduce machinery into the hills in order to make brick tea."[59]

Chen's memorial also featured an internal tension that foreshadowed future directions in the economic thought of China. Chen's solutions were still ostensibly merchant centered, and his memorial invoked the phrase "sympathy for the merchants."[60] Chen supported the merchants because, within a historical moment dominated by mercantilist concerns over the balance of trade, the state prized revenue from taxing trade, and economic life in China was organized through merchant groups rather than powerful factories. The actual content of Chen's program, though, was subtly critical. Mercantilist thought, he argued, remained at the superficial level of fetching better prices in circulation rather than improving efficiency in production. Although pledging sympathy for China's fraternity of tea merchants, Chen also attempted to transform them into modern industrialists.

Local officials approved of Chen's veiled criticisms, for they themselves had grown fed up with the self-interested teamen. He Runsheng lamented that if merchants were left to their own devices they would never come up with the same solutions. "If we first consult with merchants before implementing these policy proposals," he wrote, "then they definitely will never see the light of day. Out of every ten merchants, not even one will clearly see the big picture. . . . Merchants are not committed every year. If it's profitable, they'll join in. If it's not, then they'll leave." The magistrate concluded, "The merchants only do what is convenient for themselves."[61]

As the tea crisis dragged into the twentieth century, Chen's distinctive thread of economic thought gained wider acceptance. If he had grasped the technical dimension of modern capital, as a pattern of continual reinvestment into improving production, then only in the twentieth century did reformers bring out its full social implications, which took the form of a campaign to eliminate the old merchant classes. As perhaps the most acute indication of a sea change in economic thought, reformers, economists, and social scientists collectively denounced the comprador treaty-port merchants as a parasite on the Chinese peasant economy and nation as a whole, turning the high Qing "sympathy for the merchants" upside down into an outright antipathy.

II COOLIES AND COMPRADORS
Tea and Political Economy at the Turn of the Century

IT WOULD BE useful at this point to briefly take stock of the interwoven story of competition laid out thus far. In the previous chapters I have presented a reinterpretation of the global tea trade while also demarcating the place of Chinese and Indian tea within the broader history of modern capitalism. Combined, they challenge an Anglocentric yet canonical historical interpretation that has long persisted within Asian and, indeed, global historiography. In that technicist view, capitalism was equated with a high level of technological sophistication and a specific set of class relations founded upon free labor and first located within England. By contrast, the stories here have demonstrated how both purportedly independent peasant households in China and unfree indentured workers in India, regardless of levels of mechanization, produced economic value as part of a circuit of capital accumulation spanning the globe. Mediation by competition, in turn, created impersonal pressures to raise the productivity of human labor, a dynamic that inspired new, increasingly abstract and cosmological theories of value premised upon labor itself, resonant with the ideas of classical political economy.

These findings should dispel any easy formulas about the incompatibility of capitalism with itinerant merchant capital or immobile unfree labor. Both were crucial to patterns of intensive capital accumulation in the Chinese and Indian tea districts. If the preceding chapters have challenged these commonplace historiographical conceits, then the two that follow explore how these categories emerged in the intellectual history of modern Asia in the first place, tied to the structural transformations of social and economic life in eastern India and coastal China. These final chapters will be more essayistic in nature, for, as the global market grew more crowded, the histories of Chinese and Indian tea became less interwoven. British planters in Assam joined forces with their rivals in Ceylon by the 1890s. Their main concern was no longer toppling China in particular but rather expanding into new consumer markets in Europe, the United States, even domestically in India. The Chinese industry, meantime, simply looked to pick itself up from a position of despair in the face of multiple new competitors from across Asia.

Among the new tea producers, the Dutch East Indies industry featured the longest history, as the colonial government had experimented with cultivation as early as the 1820s. Officials focused upon Chinese varieties and traveled to China to bring back seeds, tools, and, in a parallel with the Assam experiments, human teamakers. Tea became incorporated into the "Cultivation System," or, colonial policies requiring cash crop cultivation in order to accumulate revenue for the metropole. The industry's turning point did not come until the last third of the century, when the colonial state abandoned its experiments and liberalized land laws for private entrepreneurs. Dutch planters, in consultation with London brokers, switched from Chinese to Assamese varieties, and they traveled to colonial India and Ceylon to study their methods. Officials also promoted tea cultivation by smallholder farmers, who came to supply millions of pounds of raw leaves for the plantation factories. By the new century, these measures resulted in substantial growth for the nascent industries of Batavia, Java, and Sumatra.[1]

Meanwhile, the Japanese and Taiwan industries were jumpstarted by British and American trading houses—including Jardine Matheson & Co.—which expanded out from the China trade in search of more supply sources. They arrived in Nagasaki and Yokohama in the 1860s, bringing with them Chinese assistants ("tea boy[s] from Shanghai") to assist in the refinement process. The new Meiji state (1868–1912) prioritized tea as a national industry, finding its greatest gains in the area of Makinohara in Shizuoka prefecture. In a remarkable story, the regional industry was developed by former samurai retainers of the last shogun, Tokugawa Yoshinobu, and by local farmers and transportation workers displaced by the political transition. Shizuoka has remained the top tea-producing region in Japan ever since, and it was also where Chinese reformer Wu Juenong studied new production techniques from 1918 to 1921. Japanese green tea made inroads into the American market by the late century, but soon the industry's emulation of Chinese methods became a liability. On the advice of European, American, and Chinese experts, Japanese producers liberally applied Prussian blue dye, but they were later targeted by the Indian and Ceylon industries' campaign against "Far East" teas as adulterated and unsafe, as seen in chapter 4. While Japanese green tea had inflicted damage upon Chinese producers, it, too, now became a casualty of British colonial black tea producers.[2]

In Taiwan, tealeaves had long been harvested as a wild plant by aboriginals and then, after large-scale migration from Fujian in the 1700s, cultivated as a side industry, plucked and sold raw to China at low prices. The new Anglo-American firms established the first refineries in 1864, and the Taiwan export industry took off by the seventies, unseating Fuzhou as the top producer of oolongs for the U.S. market. By the 1880s, the Euro-American and Taiwanese merchants had been displaced by Chinese capital from Hong Kong, Shantou in Guangdong Province, and Xiamen in Fujian. The latter in particular, known as *mazhen* houses (based on the English "merchant"), coordinated the re-export of Taiwan teas and controlled the trade in a fashion similar to the tea warehouses in Shanghai. But they too were expelled when the Japanese Empire gained control in 1895, turning the northern port of Danshui into a hub for direct export to the rest of the world. The colonial government also established research stations to develop fully oxidized black teas (*hongcha*), and in the 1920s, the Mitsui *zaibatsu*, or, "financial clique," invested heavily in Taiwan tea. Sales suffered due to competition from India, Java, and Ceylon teas as well as boycotts across China and Southeast Asia against Japanese imperial goods.[3]

Finally, in the British colony of Ceylon, planters had built estates for coffee around the same time as the 1830s tea experiments in Assam. In 1869, they discovered a leaf fungus known as *Hemileia vastatrix*, or, the coffee leaf disease, which ruined the industry with alarming speed. Planters scrambled for substitute crops, cycling through cinchona and cocoa before landing on tea. The leftover infrastructure from coffee—including the labor force—along with the island's compatible natural conditions enabled tea to succeed almost instantly. As with Assam tea, "King Coffee" and Ceylon tea thrived by employing a migrant labor force, namely, the Tamils of south India. Just as colonial officials in eastern India promoted recruitment by sardars, seen as insider village authorities, the planters in Ceylon promoted kanganis as figures of customary prestige but who came to serve straightforward commercial functions as recruiters, creditors, and plantation overseers. Without the penal contract laws of Assam, Tamil coolies were bound to plantations through informal mechanisms of immobilization, especially debt bondage. This system enabled Ceylon tea production to jump three-hundred-fold to nearly forty-six million pounds over its first full decade of operation, the 1880s. At the same time, rising exports by all the world's major tea-producing regions and colonies were matched by falling prices, squeezing profitability, and placing a premium upon new methods, new technologies, and new commercial and political strategies to fight for any edge in the new century (figure 19).[4]

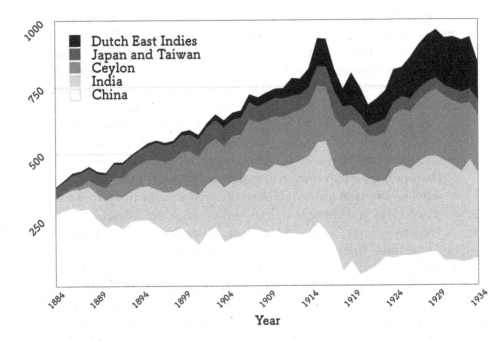

Figure 19. Exports from all major tea-producing regions, in millions of pounds, 1884–1934. Figures from Lyons, *Maritime Customs*; Hsiao, *Foreign Trade Statistics*, 117–21; ITA Report (1920), 403; (1931), 375; (1940), 201; Wu and Fan, *Chaye Wenti*, 169–71; Teramoto, *Nihon Chagyōshi*, 16–17; Chen Ciyu, *Taibei Chaye*, 243–46.

Thus, the nineteenth-century direct rivalry between Chinese and Indian tea had grown into a multisided, global affair by the final decade. Each new regional Asian industry featured strikingly similar stories of immediate success by emulating Indian or Chinese methods later met by falling sales due to cutthroat competition. Nevertheless, the two original export tea-producing regions of coastal China and eastern India remained connected by the types of social changes and political questions nationalist thinkers wrestled with at the turn of the new century, problems concerning how the changing fortunes of empire would affect their tea industries and, conversely, the role of tea within larger projects of political economy, national development, and resistance to foreign capital. The object of these last two chapters is to provide a glimpse into how Indian and Chinese observers around the turn of the century made sense of the jarring upheavals of the previous decades of intensified global integration.

6   Coolie Nationalism

The Category "Freedom" and Indian Nationalist Campaigns against Labor Indenture

IN LATE JUNE 1878, a forty-two-year-old Hindu pundit named Ramkumar Vidyaratna (1836–1901)—or sometimes simply "Swami Ramananda"—boarded a steamer stationed in the lower Assam town of Dhubri and bound north by way of the Brahmaputra River. He was traveling on behalf of the liberal Sadharan Brahmo Samaj, based in Calcutta, delivering sermons on religious reform across the Himalayas and the northeast. Of all his destinations, Assam was his favorite. Although most Bengalis were "struck with fear" at the mention of the region, Vidyaratna wrote, he found it "as captivating as a painting. . . . It would be no exaggeration to call it a treasury of nature [*prakritir dhanāgār*]."[1] On that particular ride, however, Vidyaratna's ethereal thoughts were punctured by the jarring presence of the foreign-dominated tea industry. In addition to private passengers, Vidyaratna noticed on board over fifty coolie workers contracted for employment on the tea gardens. He struck up a conversation with a man from Orissa and asked how he had wound up on the ship. The passenger replied:

> There was a man on the road near a large market. He told me he could find me work in the house of a saheb [European]. . . . I'm Orissan, I don't know Bengali, and I don't understand Hindustani. So I went with this man to the saheb's house. Whatever the saheb asked, I would reply with "yes, yes." And I signed my name on a piece of paper. I thought, I'm

going to get some good work [kārja]! But babu, right now I'm in this terrible state. . . . For wages [arthopārjaner janya], I abandoned my family and friends and came to Calcutta. . . . I had no clue that I would wind up in such a terrible state. God! I will never see my family again![2]

Ten years later, Vidyaratna would re-create this eye-opening experience in his social novel *Sketches of Coolie Life* (*Kuli Kāhinī*, lit. "The Story of the Coolie," 1888), a work celebrated by Indian nationalists as their own *Uncle Tom's Cabin*. In Vidyaratna's fictionalized version, an indentured coolie who had come to Calcutta looking for a "job" (*chākri*) to feed his family is discovered chained up in the lower hull of a steamship. Another character in the novel—a surrogate for both Vidyaratna and the reader—responds to the man's story by proclaiming: "Oh my! Who says that the Christian government has abolished slavery? This is a system of slavery! I have been blind for so long, but now it is clear before our eyes. The British government is civil and moral in word, but not in practice."[3] Vidyaratna had drawn a clear lesson from his encounter years earlier: Indians today were freely traveling to Calcutta to seek out waged work (*kārja, arthopārjan, chākri*), but instead of encountering a civil (*sabhya*) and moral (*dhārmik*) system, they were being tricked into slavery (*dāsatya*).

Vidyaratana's political awakening in the 1870s and eighties coincided with a sustained, decades-long campaign by Indian nationalists to expose employment on the Assam tea gardens as an anachronistic system of unfree labor. In the last decades of the century, Vidyaratna and members of the Samaj wrote expository journal articles in both Bengali and English that unmasked the deception, physical abuse, and sexual violence that characterized the plantation. They condemned it as slavelike and immoral, a symbol of European imperialism's political, cultural, and economic domination of native coolies. Recruitment of indentured workers had been liberalized by Act I of 1882, but after decades of political pressure, the provincial and imperial governments gradually rolled it back through a series of reforms in 1889, 1893, 1896, and 1901. By the new century, officials themselves began to publicly advocate for total repeal. In a climate of rising nationalist sentiment and a depressed global market for tea, the penal contract system was dismantled for good in 1926.

Curiously, although indenture was crucial for Indian tea's economic success, its demise has received sparse attention in previous studies.

Rana Behal and Prabhu Mohapatra argued that indenture was repealed due to its "inherent [economic] contradictions": overproduction combined with falling prices had threatened profitability, and competition for new workers led recruiters to charge higher fees, producing the paradoxical condition of a "high cost for cheap labour." However, their explanation rested upon the assumption that planter-capitalists were rational and clear minded about their self-interest. As Behal himself later demonstrated, the industry was still highly profitable when indenture was repealed. Most planters resisted abolition kicking and screaming. In the 1920s, on the eve of abolition, legislators could only extract, at best, a "grumbling assent . . . from capitalism."[4] It would be difficult to imagine the planters had reached a consensus on the system's objective untenability.

Instead, as I demonstrate in this chapter, the ultimate push to end indenture revolved as much around liberal political-economic ideology as it did around pure accounting. Indian nationalists, living in an increasingly commercial and industrialized society, pushed for abolition on the reasoning that a free labor system was more economically rational than indenture. Most prominent were the Sadharan Brahmo Samaj and the Indian Association, two groups foundational to the long history of Indian nationalism. Famously, historians within the Subaltern Studies school have criticized earlier studies for glorifying these thinkers in an elitist and hagiographic manner. My approach in this chapter, however, is to ground their ideas about indenture within the dense structural changes in the social and economic life of eastern India at the turn of the century. Central to the campaign against the penal labor contract was the same opposition between slavery and civil society—or, free versus unfree labor, monopoly versus free markets—found in Vidyaratna's work, as well as in countless plays, articles, essays, and speeches from the same period.

Although scholars of colonial Asia have argued that both foreign officials and nationalists alike viewed the category "coolie" in paternalistic terms, in this chapter I suggest an alternative interpretation. For liberal nationalist critics of tea indenture, the tea coolie was a ready participant in the capitalist world of exchange, thwarted only by the illiberal and coercive regime of colonial indenture. They challenged the unfreedom of indenture on the grounds that "free labor" was a modern and natural way of organizing society, insofar as workers in India were increasingly becoming a commodity for exchange. In articulating their views, nationalists constantly made comparisons between Indian tea coolies and the enslaved Africans working on British- and American-run plantations, drawing on the abolitionist movement's emphasis on free mobility. They also adopted the same historicist logic of arrested development originally advanced by colonial officials—that the Indian peasant had *not yet* evolved into a modern subject of exchange—to argue instead that coolies *had already*, in fact, matured into capitalist subjects who were ready to sell their bodily labor as their only capital. By the mid-twentieth century, this political-economic claim continued to evolve, from championing the mobility of Indian tea labor to that of Indian tea capital. With the abolition of indenture, Indian economic nationalism turned its focus to tea plantation ownership.

This story addresses historiographical and historical questions that have persisted throughout the current study. Historiographically, the increased commercialization of Indian society made the ideal of "free labor" appear natural and universal. It is this naturalization in the twentieth century that explains why so many historians have argued anachronistically that nineteenth-century indenture was anti-modern or precapitalist. I suggest, however, that the embrace of free labor ideology among nationalists in Bengal indexed their own immersion within the social patterns of modern accumulation. As with Chen Chi, Indian nationalists borrowed from political economy in order to achieve their own political ends. What these distinct intellectual trajectories in China and Bengal illustrate is not that Asian economic thought was merely derivative of Europe; rather, political economy, originally seen as a foreign body of thought, gradually attained widespread plausibility as a set of universal and natural principles corresponding to the ongoing expansion of capitalist production and waged employment into new territories worldwide.

In the first section below, I revisit the original justifications for Act I of 1882 by situating government discussions during the preceding decades within the broader contradictions of "coolie" discourses in colonial India. Act I was a compromise between two official images of the "coolie." On the one hand, workers were owners of commodities and capital—their labor—and hence deserved economic freedom. On the other, Indian migrants were seen as "demi-civilized" and unaccustomed to market exchange. The colonial state offered indenture as an exceptional, "transitional" legislation that would facilitate exchange while enforcing it through criminal prosecution. In the second section I show how Indian nationalists protested this legislation while retaining the same assumptions about the naturalness of the labor market. In particular, Vidyaratna's *Sketches* inherited the opposition of slavery and freedom from trans-Atlantic abolitionist debates earlier in the century. Here I also challenge the historiographical claim that Indian nationalist writers, in their opposition to the tea plantation, were romanticizing traditional village life and gender roles. Instead, nationalists accepted the premise that village life was no longer tenable in rural India, and to emancipate the peasantry, they turned to the "ordinary laws" of labor supply and demand. In the third section I demonstrate that the evolution from archaic indenture to modern freedom served as the dominant framework for the twentieth-century abolition of indenture. The conclusion places this campaign within the broader context of anticolonial nationalism and its turn toward the "indigenization" of the colonial capitalist economy.

THE COMMODITY FICTIONS OF COLONIAL INDENTURE LAWS

The category "coolie," Jan Breman and Valentine Daniel have demonstrated, has been ideologically contested throughout history. It originated in precolonial South Asia but assumed new meanings during colonial rule. Initially a Tamil term for payment (*kūli*) and the name of a Gujarati tribe (*Kuli*), "coolie" became a generic nineteenth-century term that described menial Asian labor in highly paternalistic terms. Within colonial discourses, it embodied the contradictory qualities of immobility, hence requiring active recruitment beyond market incentives, and instability, hence requiring extra disciplinary measures to regulate behavior. These contradictions meant, especially in Assam, that the "task was to mobilise an essentially immobile work force only to re-immobilise it by tying it to the enclaves of capitalist production."[5] Within the archives of Assam tea, this paternalistic view proliferated in the 1860s, at the same time W. N. Lees articulated his justifications for self-consciously illiberal policies of colonization. For the classical theorists, Lees had written, labor would naturally find its way to the underpopulated regions of Assam, for workers acted out of self-interest, unfettered by bonds of custom or guild. But such a workforce had yet to materialize in Assam, as the locals turned out to be "demi-civilized," "semi-barbarous," and stuck in the "agricultural stage of civilization." Indenture was necessary because, just as legislation could protect workers from deception by recruiters, so too did employers require protection from absconding coolies.

Such paternalism also subsequently animated the correspondence between government officials, clashing with their stated goal of fostering a free labor force. In 1873, the lieutenant-governor of Bengal, Sir George Campbell, discovered that gardens in Sylhet on the eastern border of Bengal and Assam had been successfully recruiting workers without penal contracts. He asked the Bengal Council to encourage planters to employ workers in the same manner, a "system of free emigration" that would exist "side by side" with the penal contract system. He wrote, "if he goes without any binding contract, when he reaches the labor district he ceases to be an emigrant—becomes an ordinary laborer, and may then enter into any contract he chooses, like any other local laborer under the ordinary law of contract." Under these circumstances, "these people, who are now in a state of quasi-bondage . . . will become free men and free women."[6]

But almost no planters took up Campbell's suggestion, refusing to hire without the security of a penal contract. In the following years, officials searched for explanations as to why Indian peasants were so unwilling to travel. One wrote that within Assam, "inhabitants of the hills have a great objection to leaving their own country even for short periods . . . the disinclination evinced by the masses to leave their native country is owing to their demi-civilized condition." Henry Hopkinson, commissioner of Assam, wrote that the average Indian or Assamese farmer was simply different from their counterparts around the world. Unlike an American who "*lives by exchange*," Assamese farmers earned and spent only a fraction of the money an American did. With this phrase, Hopkinson was referencing an idea central to Adam Smith's work, that in a "commercial society," individuals rarely produced for their own consumption and instead "exchang[ed] . . . the produce of his own labour" for that of others. "Every man thus *lives by exchanging*, or becomes, in some measure, a merchant," Smith had written.[7]

The most telling comments emerged from a correspondence in 1880 that presaged the passage of Act I of 1882. Throughout this debate, incited by the Indian Tea District Association's 1878 memorandum, interlocutors expressed contradictory ideas about the political-economic status of migrant labor. On the one hand, Steuart Bayley, the new chief commissioner of Assam, believed that "immigration must be spontaneous, not organised by Government." On the other, special legislation was justifiable because the "circumstances of tea-gardens are still so far exceptional," he wrote, "as to require exceptional treatment and exceptional legislation." He described Indian migrants as childlike and unable to understand their material self-interest:

> We know, moreover, what are the habits, feelings, and prejudices of the population whose emigration we most desire to assist, and we know by the experience of colonial recruiters, tea recruiters, and Government recruiters that, speaking generally, it is impossible to persuade these particular classes to emigrate. . . . The agricultural classes, and more especially their wives and families [are] unwilling to cut themselves adrift from the system of village life which appears to them as necessary to their existence as the air they breathe, and without which they deem in their helplessness that life would not be worth having.[8]

Other commenters were skeptical that the Indian people could ever find it in their nature to perform free and spontaneous migration:

> It is not exactly known how new Provinces are first peopled in India, but (in the case of the Central Provinces) there is reason to believe that Hindu settlers were first drawn down by invitation and aid from the local princes. . . . There was no such thing as spontaneous settlement, as understood in European colonies, by means of independent adventure.[9]

Here, it is necessary to complicate Breman's and Daniel's claim that officials viewed coolies in strictly paternalistic terms. Officials also framed the penal contract *as if* migrants were fully liable merchants who *could* live "by exchange." Bayley emphasized that under any reform, a worker "*should be free to take his labour wherever he pleased.*" Elsewhere, he warned against any "special system of labour, where the labourer is not free *to take his labour where he likes.*" The notion that migrants were "carrying" their labor as an external asset or commodity was a common refrain within British imperial debates. In 1838, a Calcutta recruiting firm justified overseas indenture by arguing, "It is a question involving the rights of British subjects . . . to *carry their manual labor* to the most productive market." Decades later, a member of the Legislative Council of India quipped in an offhand manner: "It appears to me that the only justification for these labourers being under a penal contract at all is that it is to their interest that they should *be brought up* to the labour-district, that they cannot *bring themselves up* there as they have not the means."[10]

This ideological construction of the worker as a merchant who carries and sells its alienated labor as a commodity has attracted the attention of many scholars. For instance, Karl Polanyi famously described it as a harmful "commodity fiction."[11] How this fiction was created is a question that will be addressed below. For now, it is important to stress that colonial officials both envisioned Indian migrants as the owners of their labor, in the form of a commodity, but also circumscribed their freedom by deploying paternalist logic. Ultimately, this mixture of universalism and paternalism provided the theoretical justification for labor indenture. It was a solution halfway between free and forced labor. Act I of 1882 proclaimed:

> The classes which furnish the emigrants in both cases are extremely ignorant, and the interference of Government is required to secure that they are not imposed upon; . . .
> On the other hand some regulation of the contract between the labourer and his employer, and some more effectual means of enforcing it than a civil action, is demanded by justice. . . . The employer is compelled by law to guarantee to the coolie a minimum wage; and it is only equitable that the law should provide him with the means of obtaining the due fulfilment of the contract by the coolie, *whose only capital is his labour,* and who ought not be allowed capriciously to withdraw himself from the service of the employer who has paid for his introduction.[12]

These tensions between commercial exchange and paternalism, Samita Sen has argued, produced the most infamous and harmful innovation of the law: the deregulation of labor recruitment in order to encourage "sardari" recruiting. Until then, most labor was secured through professional recruiters, both European and Indian, known as "arkatis." A labor inquiry reported that the arkati "has been described by different witnesses as the scum of the earth, a heartless scoundrel who would boast that he could by ill-treatment make any one 'willing' in a few minutes to emigrate to Assam and who was feared as much as a man-eating tiger." In the 1870s, officials learned about an alternate option, employing garden "sardars" to recruit through personal networks. As detailed in chapter 4, the Persian term "sardar" was an umbrella term for village figurehead, and in the context of tea, it came to mean a labor contractor or jobber. This vision of sardari recruiting, Sen wrote, reproduced the same contradiction of paternalism and market universalism. On the one hand, the sardar's function dovetailed with paternalist assumptions about the Indian's aversion to migration. "Sent down from the garden to his 'own village' to recruit among his kinfolk, caste-fellows and village neighbours," the sardar was "valued as an 'insider.'" On the other hand, if the sardar had earned the consent of fellow villagers, then sardari recruitment brought the entire system closer to the political-economic ideal of free, spontaneous, and self-interested migration. It was the perfect vehicle for the government's envisioned "transition" to free labor.[13]

But it turned out a disastrous compromise. In order to promote this new system, Act I ended formal regulations on registration and transport in the recruitment districts of Bengal. Deregulation resulted in a free-for-all in which all distinctions between professional arkatis and informal sardars disappeared into a "nexus" of predatory recruitment.[14] Arkatis began to employ sardars as subcontractors, recruitment networks expanded into new regions, and prices for coolies skyrocketed. Act I resulted in a staggering number of new migrants but also a spike in mortality rates for workers and prices charged by recruiters. It was this spectacle that caught the eye of Indian nationalists in Calcutta, who fixed their attention on the tea industry as a symbol of racial domination endemic to colonial rule.

SLAVERY AND FREE LABOR IN THE
ASSAM TEA GARDENS

Although it was Assam's distinct topography and climate that British planters found uniquely suitable for cultivating tea, the industry remained alien and exotic to local society for much of its early history. The main actors had come from outside the region, traveling from as far away as Glasgow or Jiangxi, and the campaign to end labor indenture was no exception, pulling in the political interests of the rest of eastern India. The imperial headquarters were of course in Calcutta, and the bustling city served as a hub where capital, management, expertise, and labor were collected from the surrounding region and shipped up the Brahmaputra River. Fittingly, the most vocal critics of indenture were Calcutta's nationalist intelligentsia, who voiced their opinions through the English- and Bengali-language nationalist press. Notable critics included the social-reform-oriented Sadharan Brahmo Samaj and its sibling political organization the Indian Association. It was these Calcutta organizations, along with a host of other regional groups of urban intelligentsia located in Pune, Madras, and Bombay, who eventually formed the Indian National Congress (INC) by the end of the 1880s.[15]

As historian Bipan Chandra stressed, the movement against tea indenture was far from a proletarian struggle against capital, a proposition made obvious once we examine the social composition of the activists. Both the Samaj and the Association consisted of upper-caste elites, earning their income from land, law, or government. Ananda Mohan Bose, founder of the Association, even "amassed a modest fortune" from his investments in Assam tea. The original Brahmo Samaj, founded by Rammohan Roy in 1828, was the most famous and successful organization in the early years of Calcutta political life. It was composed of high-caste and wealthy urban elites, and although they expressed their devotion to the tenets of social reform, their practical unwillingness to depart from traditional marriage practices produced a series of splits in 1866 and 1878. The result was the creation of a younger, more reform-minded Sadharan Brahmo Samaj (*sādhāran*, lit. "universal" or "general"). Two years earlier, the new Samaj's founders had also established a political association as a vehicle for reform. The Indian Association was an outgrowth of politicized, middle-class, and English-educated graduates who had studied overseas or at elite Indian institutions. Both the Samaj and the Association self-consciously departed from an older politics, embodied in the British Indian Association, which was narrowly representative of only the most conservative elements of Indian society, such as rentier landlords, merchants, and professional pleaders. By contrast, the newer Indian Association held the conviction that since the "illiterate masses could not speak for themselves and the aristocracy spoke only for themselves," then "only the middle class, strategically placed, could speak for all."[16]

Members of both the Samaj and the Association paired a liberal critique of entrenched power and rentier landlordism with an economic outlook that embraced the universality of such liberal concepts as equality, freedom, and property. In their criticism of colonial rule, they did not challenge British political economy as such but took aim at its hypocritical "perversion" by racism. Nationalist economist R. C. Dutt wrote, "Economic laws are the same in Asia as in Europe. If India is poor to-day, it is through the operation of economic causes. If India were prosperous under these circumstances, it would be an economic miracle. Science knows no miracles. Economic laws are constant and unvarying in their operation." Dwarkanath Ganguli, who served as assistant secretary in both the Samaj and the Association and who became one of the most prominent critics of tea labor indenture, opened his investigative articles with an almost apologetic paean to the trade: "Tea-cultivation in Assam is a grand industry and it has largely contributed to the material prosperity of the province. . . . If in securing all these advantages the emigrant labourers were subjected to such hardships as were not beyond human endurance, we would not probably have raised our voice." Although the nationalists were critical of British policy, many agreed with the tenets of economic liberalism.[17]

The actual history of nationalist criticism of tea began in 1874, when the Calcutta writer Dakshinacharan Chattopadhyay published his play *The Mirror of the Tea Planter* (*Chākar Darpan*). Although some accounts suggest the script was never staged, its cutting depiction of planter cruelty attracted attention in both Bengali- and English-language papers, and the government banned future "seditious" dramatic performances. Later criticism was led by the Samaj and the Association, and the most well-read and historically influential work during this period was by Samaj member Ramkumar Vidyaratna. He had lived for years among migrant workers on the Assam tea plantations and, upon returning to Calcutta, published a series of articles in the Bengali paper *Sanjivani*, combining his stories into the novel *Sketches of Coolie Life*. Excerpts from Vidyaratna's work were sent to the governor-general of India, Lord Ripon, and circulated among the planters themselves, one of whom, according to legend, stood up at a meeting of the ITA and proclaimed, "The contributor to the *Sanjibani* will be the first victim to the planters' gun." Vidyaratna received threats from "not only the white planters" but also from Indian clerks, lawyers, and agents employed by the tea companies.[18] Decades later, the prominent nationalist Bipin Chandra Pal (1858–1932) recalled the novel's wide-ranging impact:

Uncle Tom's Cabin was a favourite book in those days with the educated intelligentsia of Bengal. . . . We readily compared the condition
of tea garden labourers in Assam to that of Negro labour in America
before the Emancipation. . . . In my boyhood and early youth I had come
across starving and sick coolies from the tea gardens. All these early
experiences came up to my mind when Pandit Ramkumar Vidyaratna
published his *Cooly-Kahini*.[19]

Sketches of Coolie Life follows Adarmani, a woman from a Bengal village, and her daughter Kritartha as they are recruited to work
on a tea plantation in the fictional Assam town Sonitpur. At the outset, Adarmani's family is burdened with debt and rent demands. Her
opium-addicted husband Nidhiram gives away her jewelry and then
loans out their two sons to a neighboring village for farm work in
order to secure fast cash. Dejected, Adarmani is swayed to travel to
the tea gardens when two female recruiters regale her with wondrous
stories about the riches and comforts of life on an Assam tea garden.
The novel follows the mother's and daughter's harrowing journey from
Dhubri to Assam, the torturous conditions on the garden itself, their efforts to escape, and ultimately their release from the plantation with the
mercy of the kind-hearted English junior planter. The final scene features Adarmani's opportunity to tell her own "story"—or, *kāhinī*—to
a courtroom, where her tales of woe bring the jury and judge to tears.
In the following sections, as I delve further into the story's details and
ideological structures, it will become clear that the story's underlying
theme, running parallel to abolitionist literature, was its characters'
pursuit of "freedom" (*swādhīnatā, mukti*).

"Freedom" in *Sketches of Coolie Life*

From its first glimpse of the tea gardens, *Sketches of Coolie Life* depicts Assam as a space of confinement and unfreedom:

On all four sides, Sonitpur is surrounded by mountain peaks that are so
tall they seem to be looking in on the misery of the coolies, as their tears
of sorrow and sadness ooze down to wet the soil. These tears from the
tea gardens of Sonitpur flow all the way into the Brahmaputra River.
Beneath the mountains is a country of forests, and in these forests there
lurk tigers, rhinoceroses, bears, and other animals.[20]

The coolies are not only hemmed in by the dangerous world of the jungle, but their fate on the garden is worse than that of natural prey: "When a herd of cattle see a tiger, they will be afraid and stupefied, but they will flee. When tea garden coolies see a saheb, they are not allowed to flee. That is the only difference between lowly versus 'free' animals [i.e., humans]." Soon, the story quickly establishes the comparison between tea coolies and the historical institution of slavery:

> With the sunrise, a terror appears in the hearts of the coolies who live in the tea gardens. Their faces are stained with the shadow of melancholy. They fall into despair and live in fear of being hit and struck. In sum, the life of a coolie—past, present, and future—is one of being plunged into the dark depths of slavery [dāsatya].[21]

The term dāsatya has much older roots as a term to denote submission and servitude, but it also became the standard Bengali translation to describe African chattel slavery in the nineteenth century. The characters in Sketches of Coolie Life constantly associate penal contract labor with African slavery in the British colonies and the United States. Other critics of indenture did so as well, with the common phrase "slave-law" emerging frequently. Ganguli had titled his series of articles on Assam "Slavery in British Dominion," proclaiming: "It is pure necessity that has obliged us to make use of this very expressive name, for none other would adequately convey to the minds of our readers any idea of those horrible sufferings to which the emigrants in the tea-plantations of Assam are subjected."[22]

Though the terms "freedom" and "slavery" were consistently used to mark opposites and extremes in nineteenth-century political discourse, the actual content and meaning behind the words were liable to shift. What exactly distinguished freedom from slavery? For many, indentured tea labor resembled slavery because the deceptive tactics denied workers willful consent. Another argument was that the work conditions were subhuman, as stories of coolies who were physically beaten and forced to live in squalid conditions trickled out. In Vidyaratna's novel, the head planter tells a doctor that he does not allow his coolies any medical leave: "What, do you think of the coolies as humans (mānush)? Don't you know that once upon a time in America, civilized English would treat slaves, that is, coolies like hunting dogs? We do the same here."[23]

Other critics emphasized that the category of "slavery" extended beyond the problems of consent and mistreatment. The Reverend Charles Dowding, a friend of the nationalists, wrote: "When we say that a state of semi-slavery exists, it is no answer to declare that coolies are well fed, housed, and clothed, even if it were universally true; or that they are given the best of medical attendance when ill . . . for all this could be said quite as correctly of slaves in America."[24] More fundamental than the ills of deception and abuse was the penal contract itself and, as Breman and Daniel put it, its attendant "re-immobilization" of workers. In theory, a "free" worker could also be subjected to mistreatment, but what distinguished the tea "coolie" was the legal right of planters to enforce contracts through imprisonment, physical beatings, and sending out bounty hunters to chase them if they escaped. In *Sketches*, this element of immobility forms the basis of the slavery/freedom distinction. In one scene, Vidyaratna described a scene of chained coolies crowding into a steamer bound to Assam from Calcutta as "the life of slaves" (*dās jīban*). In another dialogue between evil British planters, he compared the penal contract with slavery on the grounds that both enabled planters to arrest runaways with impunity, with the tea planters in envy of the slave owners' power:

> In the days of the cotton trade in America, how did the businessmen treat the Negroes? In Bengal, that other land, what did our indigo-planter brothers used to do, indeed, what do they still do? There, it was the dark races [*krishnabarn*], and here, too, it is the dark races—that is, whether in America, whether in Bengal, or whether in this country [Assam], in all lands, it is the dark races who do this work. . . . In America, they had laws for runaways, and we have runaway laws, too. But the distance between the two is like heaven and earth. According to our laws, we can only imprison coolies for six months. In America, a runaway slave could be punished for life.[25]

One of the clearest demonstrations that "slavery" and "freedom" were categories of mobility, rather than treatment, came from a scene featuring the doctor of the tea plantation, Narendranath Ghosh. His English employer orders the guards to prevent him from leaving, as he has already threatened to publicly expose the horrors of the plantation. After being caught and sent back to his room, Narendranath walks to the dispensary and fetches a bottle of medicine he intends to swallow whole. He exclaims in a monologue:

Let's see how much you are able to confine me. My movements [*ātghāt*] have been obstructed, my free being [*swādhīn jīb*] has been turned into an unfree beast [*adhīn pashur mata*]. . . . Today, I tried to run away, but you forbade me, all parts of me are now completely subordinated to you. I have sold my freedom, and I can't take any more, so enough!

After finishing the medicine, Narendranath "becomes free," breaking out from the "birdcage of his soul" (*prānpākhi piñjar*). "He was free," Vidyaratna wrote, "in this heavenly world, he had bought his great freedom." When the police arrive the next day, they find his suicide note, which reads: "I have arrived at the final limit of freedom. . . . My wish is that this morning I can see the sunlight of freedom."[26]

Here it is notable that Vidyaratna and other nationalists framed the idea of freedom through the timeless, almost religious language of "souls" and morality. Indeed, for much of the nineteenth century, the political idea of "freedom" was popularly seen as a humanitarian cause, a "transcendent moral crusade" that overrode immediate and short-term pecuniary interests. Historian Thomas Holt, however, has suggested a more critical account of the politics of free labor, interrogating it as "a product of the social relations of its time." Yes, the concept of freedom could be traced back to earlier figures, for example, Thomas Hobbes and John Locke, but it achieved hallowed status as a foundational political principle only with the rise of trans-Atlantic abolitionist movements, which provide a useful reference point for understanding developments in Assam at the end of the century.[27]

The British abolition of slavery in 1834 marked a turning point in the political trajectory of the category "freedom." The ideological appeal of abolitionism was inseparable from its proponents' personal attempts to grapple with the "ongoing capitalist revolution" in western Europe and the United States. This revolution entailed the expansion of production, calls for free trade and the end of monopolies, and the "freeing" of labor from households and artisan guilds into urban workshops. Abolitionists, in working out how individuals should relate to one another if not through custom, family, and tradition, latched onto the category of "slavery" in order to "locate the outer boundaries of freedom." Over time, elites crafted a set of arguments asserting that free labor systems were comparatively better *in economic terms*.[28]

Trans-Atlantic abolitionists, Holt wrote, were committed to the political-economic ideal that self-interested behavior should be unhampered by such "artificial and arbitrary constraints" as unjust taxation or limitations on mobility. Slavery's greatest sin was the way it retarded the worker's rational pursuit of profit. Following "their mentor Adam Smith," they believed "there was no question that free laborers, having the greater incentive for efficient and productive work, were more profitable to employ than slaves." The contrast between slavery and free labor generated at least two practical conclusions about the character of the latter. First, "if slavery meant involuntary labor for the master's benefit, freedom meant voluntary contracts determined by mutual consent, which theoretically should guarantee the enjoyment of the fruits of one's labor." Second, if "slavery meant subordination to the physical coercion and personal dominion of an arbitrary master, then freedom meant submission only to the impersonal forces of the marketplace." Free labor thus emerged out of newly prevalent ideas about the naturalness of free exchange. Political economy's "notion of Exchange" in the eighteenth century, legal scholar Patrick Atiyah has noted, brokered a marriage between the concepts of "freedom of trade" and "freedom of contract." Restrictions on either "simply protected (or exploited) some groups at the expense of others." In order for Smith to equate free trade with free labor, he treated labor itself as a commodity that obeyed the laws of supply and demand. Thus, the immobilization of labor was not only "contrary to natural liberty and justice" (a quote from Smith) but also condemned "on grounds of economic efficiency."[29]

"By the mid-nineteenth century," Adam McKeown wrote, "the stark dichotomy of free and enslaved that had emerged from the African slave trade dominated most conceptions of migration." But though abolition sanctified the principle of freedom, politicians and commentators had difficulty transplanting the mandate of antislavery into other contexts. What, precisely, labor would look like in a world without slavery was up for debate. "Freedom" was "an abstract concept, difficult to define in substance" and "liable to misuse." Abolitionists and subsequent policymakers adopted the strategy of defining free labor as the opposite of slavery, Madhavi Kale noted, but the actual meaning assigned to them remained fluid and "plastic."[30]

For instance, in the former slave-owning plantation colonies of the West Indies and Mauritius, sugar planters experimented with hiring workers from overseas, including workers from China and India. The system of indentured labor in Assam developed almost two decades after that of the sugar colonies, but officials in India seemed to move in step with broader, empire-wide shifts of opinion. Initially, indentured labor was seen as too close to slavery, and by 1839, antislavery organizations in Britain had successfully lobbied to end the indentured migration of Indian workers overseas. It was around this time in Assam when H. T. Prinsep, first seen in chapter 3, warned that the Indian tea industry should not employ workers under labor contracts "not easily distinguishable from the transactions so much cried out against in Mauritius and in the Slave Colonies." Prinsep was not opposed to migration in general, for elsewhere he had complimented overseas labor migration as a "powerful agent of civilization." However, public consensus forced him to weigh whether or not contracts were coercive and slavelike.[31]

By the middle of the century, however, British officials had come to justify penal contracts as an acceptable form of free labor. The British government reauthorized indentured Indian migration to Mauritius in 1842 and to the West Indies in 1845. Officials and planters appropriated the concept of freedom to their own side by arguing that outlawing overseas indenture would deny the "workers' right to sell their labor at the most favorable terms available." Many of these same arguments were deployed by colonial officials in India to justify indentured migration to Assam from the 1860s to 1880s. Lees, for instance, argued that the abolition of indenture would mean the "Indian laborer [was] being prohibited by law from *the freedom* of carrying his labor where he pleases." This usage of the idea "freedom" to justify penal labor contracts may appear bizarre from a contemporary perspective, but that only serves as testament to how the boundaries of freedom have long been unstable and historically contingent.[32]

Late nineteenth-century Indian nationalist critics such as Vidyaratna represented a distinct next phase in this back-and-forth debate over the meaning of freedom. The Indian nationalists' intervention was to clarify that freedom was not determined by questions of abuse or consent. Rather, it turned upon whether or not workers could leave their employer without the degrading threat of criminal prosecution. Criminalization had been justified on the grounds that Indians were demi-civilized, and the nationalists wished to close that civilizational gap. In doing so, they affirmed the normative idea of labor as a commodity for exchange. As with the abolitionists, they presupposed that markets for free wage labor were becoming the norm of economic relations in their immediate context—this time, in the surrounding stretches of colonial Bengal. This point is best illustrated by engaging recent historiographical interpretations of the gender politics of Vidyaratna and of the nationalist movement against indenture.

Wage Labor in the Anti-Indenture Movement

Previous studies on nationalist writing have argued that its authors viewed tea coolie workers in the same condescending, paternalistic terms as did colonial officials. For instance, in their seminal studies on Assam tea's indenture system, Samita Sen and Prathama Banerjee criticized Vidyaratna's *Sketches of Coolie Life* on the grounds that it implicitly upheld traditional gender relations that confined women to the household. According to Sen, the tale of Adarmani and Kritartha turns on the opposition "between family/marriage" versus "wage work." The novel's subtext is to chastise the two female protagonists for abandoning their traditional role in the village and home and thereby to punish them for choosing "plantation employment" along with the "sexual violence [of] European plantation bosses." Thus, Vidyaratna presented "the world of capitalist wage labour" as "a cauldron of vice, crime and disease while by contrast the rural world of family-based peasant production gained idyllic characteristics in increasingly nostalgic retelling." In her interpretation, Sen placed Vidyaratna's work within the schema of late nineteenth-century anticolonial nationalism presented by political theorist Partha Chatterjee, who argued that the nationalists divided thorny social questions into two domains. The "outside," "material" domain was dominated by men, and it concerned Western notions of politics and economics; by contrast, the "inner," "spiritual" domain was a bastion of native autonomy, where tradition and female domesticity could be preserved. Sen's interpretation certainly resonated with much of the anti-indenture literature and its traditionalist view of women. However, a closer analysis of the liberal political-economic logic underlying *Sketches* suggests other political directions that contravene this reading.[33]

Broadly speaking, Sen was correct that scenes portraying women as passive victims were ubiquitous across anti-indenture literature. The most popular scenario depicted sexual attacks on female workers by their English employers. An 1888 article in the nationalist paper *Hindu Ranjiká* noted that "the tea-gardens are, in fact, worse than hell. Beautiful women are first ravished by the manager, then by the clerk of the garden, then by the doctor, and last of all by the sirdar." These stories were framed in moralistic terms, suggesting that the women should feel ashamed for losing their caste and chastity. In the play *The Mirror of the Tea Planter*, the female worker Sarama is forced to visit the European planter's bungalow. When she returns to the stage, her clothes are tattered, and she appears to have been beaten. She exclaims, "The saheb has touched this Bengali's body with his hands, do I still have caste [*jāti*]?" She ends her monologue by announcing to her sister-in-law, "Sister, if you ever see my mother and father, then tell them their beloved Sarama has been expelled from her caste [*jātibhrasta*] and has given up on life." In *Sketches*, similarly, Vidyaratna described the female protagonists through the prism of chastity and corruption. After the daughter Kritartha is beaten and raped by a British planter, she wakes up to pangs of guilt, for she is no longer an "ideal chaste woman" (*ādarsa satī*). As for Adarmani, she flees the garden and testifies in a courtroom that she wants nothing to do with the planter, "that non-Hindu" (*yaban*). She declares, "Chastity, I will not lose chastity [*satītya*]! Let my life be destroyed, let my children die by my side, let me look at my dead children's faces, but I will not lose my chastity!" These scenes attest to Tanika Sarkar's observation that in nineteenth-century anticolonial literature, women's chastity stood in for the purity of the nationalist project itself. "The politics of women's monogamy," Sarkar wrote, was "the condition of the possible Hindu nation." Sarkar's insight shed greater light on the opposition between freedom and subjection (*adhīnatā*) so central to Vidyaratna's *Sketches*. "*Adhinata* became a peculiarly loaded word," she wrote, "fraught with a double guilt: the sin of submitting to foreign domination, which necessarily conjured up the associated guilt of submitting the woman to a state of subjection."[34]

Within *Sketches*, the passage that conveyed this theme most clearly was the scene in which Kritartha is approached by the planter in his bungalow. She announces to him:

Saheb! I would choose death over you. Rather than remain your slave in this bungalow here, it'd be better to die! Shame! Shame! Foreigner! Foreigner! Sinner! [*go-khādak*, lit. "beef eater"] Am I in a sinner's home?

Whatever he touches must be washed with water from the Ganges! Whatever room he enters must be atoned for! Am I going to become a foreigner? Absolutely not! Do not try to tempt me. Greed for money, for clothes, for jewelry, these things have destroyed us, they have ruined our family. Is this the reward for money, jewelry, and good clothing? If I had known earlier that the price of money was slavery, that the value of jewelry was the sale of honor [*satītya bikray*], that the value of good clothing was the destruction of one's caste, then I would never have agreed to this terrible work![35]

Kritartha's speech unites many of the central oppositions that run throughout the novel: slavery versus freedom, foreigner versus Indian (Hindu), and money versus honor and chastity. In this way, it undoubtedly affirms Sen's interpretation that *Sketches* relied upon a division between the "outer," "material" world of wage labor versus the "inner," "spiritual" world of sexual purity.

But as Sen also acknowledged, *Sketches* was riven with a tension between this moral condemnation of the plantation versus the economic necessity to seek waged work outside the village. In the same speech, Kritartha concludes: "Shame! Shame! I am a coolie, I am your servant, you are the boss, am I supposed to do this work? Let me go, I will spend my life doing coolie work [*kulir kāj*], but I will not do any of these terrible things, I will not sink into hell." It is not waged work itself that degrades Kritartha but the specifically unchaste conditions of the Sonitpur tea garden. Nationalist literature at the time abounded with similar distinctions between the immorality of indentured labor versus the general legitimacy of wage labor. An 1888 editorial in the paper *Sanjivani* cautioned that despite demands for reform, "Nobody wants Government to put a stop to the voluntary emigration of coolies to Assam." Another writer stated: "While making efforts to put an end to [oppression] ... everyone should see that kindness for the coolie is not carried so far as to bring about a stoppage of coolie emigration."[36]

What was the role of waged work within the nationalist vision? When Kritartha tells the planter that she is a coolie and is willing to spend her life "doing coolie work," the reader is asked to recall the social circumstances under which she and her mother were originally convinced to come to Assam. Vidyaratna's descriptions of village life suggested that migrants traveled to Assam precisely because of the pernicious effects of rural poverty upon women. By the time of Vidyaratna's novel, Sarkar argued, Bengali novels had long featured "the well-worn theme of the drain of wealth . . . recreated within indigenous society: there is a drain within a drain, so to speak, with the wealth, talent and leadership siphoned off from the village—the real India of authentic peasant and familial virtues."[37] These novels bemoaned how women, imagined as a repository of traditional values, were encroached upon by the cash nexus of landlords, usurers, urban babus, and, in this case, tea plantation recruiters. In the early chapters of *Sketches of Coolie Life*, Vidyaratna did not describe the Bengali village in romantic or nostalgic terms but as a site of misery and precariousness. At a lake nearby Adarmani's and Kritartha's village, the local women wash rice for dinner while trading tales of hardship:

> One woman spoke up, "in the heat of this hellish world [*porā sansār*], I have been worked to death." On the other side, a woman said, "there's already so much work in this world, but taking care of the children makes me even more anxious. If I didn't believe in God then I wouldn't find any comfort." From the other side of the lake, another spoke up, "in this hellish world, so much work has piled up that all day long I toil at the cost of my own life [*prānpane*], but I also cannot not work so much!" "Oh sister, there's no time for such talk. Evening is coming, and my man and my kids are about to come back from the fields. Let me go home and cook, or else what are they going to eat?"[38]

Arduous labor for women is contrasted with the male figureheads who do not work, who spend their days smoking opium, and who, in the case of Adarmani's husband Nidhiram, are naively hoodwinked by petty thieves. It is no wonder Adarmani cannot resist the female recruiters' stories of luxury in the Assam gardens: "As if possessed by an evil spirit [*bhūtgrasta*], Adarmani's existence had been corrupted. Her heart had been dried up, but her eyes still had tears and her face was dirty. Now this great temptation pulled on her mind, and she could not stay grounded in common sense." Even if Vidyaratna's novel suggested that Bengali peasants had enjoyed a better life in the village, it also bemoaned the unsustainability of that existence.[39]

The same trope of village poverty pushing migrants to Assam reappeared throughout most anti-indenture literature. In the play *The Mirror of the Tea Planter*, one bad rice harvest dooms the protagonists into succumbing to the local rent collector's scheme of luring peasants to sign penal contracts. In the short story *An Autobiography of*

a Tea Coolie (Chā-Kulīr Ātmakāhinī, 1901), the narrator opens with
a description of the systemic problems facing the Bengal countryside:
"In the past, this village was among the most prosperous in the district,
but now, because of malaria, the village has been completely stripped
of its beauty. Those educated and capable of earning a living have left
for Calcutta and other places. Now, of those still in the village, almost
everyone lives by agriculture and have nowhere else to go. Other villages in Bengal are in the same lamentable situation."[40]

Such descriptions have a historical basis in the economic stratification
that afflicted colonial Bengal. After the Permanent Settlement of 1793,
which distributed rent-collection rights to various zamindars across
the Presidency, the Bengal peasantry was hit by a "rent offensive" of
higher rates through the first half of the next century. The overall burden of these increases had stabilized by the end of the century, Sugata
Bose has shown, but it remained especially high in western and central
Bengal, which featured a higher level of inequality between zamindars
and rich peasants versus smallholder tenants. Those areas, bordering
on the Chota Nagpur Plateau, were also where much of the Assam tea
labor force was being drawn from, where the authors of anti-planter
criticism set their plays and stories: Bankura, Hooghly, Nadia, and the
24 Parganas. There, the combination of "high rents, uncertain harvests
and a demographic arrest (owing to malaria epidemics from the mid-
nineteenth century until about 1920)" drove peasant households into
poverty. It thereby created an agrarian workforce of aboriginals and
lower-caste groups who "supplied much of the labour on the agricultural lands, invisible to settlement statistics" as sharecroppers, day laborers, and farm servants—such as Adarmani's sons. This "invisible"
workforce paralleled that of Qing China described in chapter 5, providing the backdrop to a more dramatic nationwide growth in employment in the major urban sectors of cotton, jute, and coal—the latter of
which grew sevenfold over the last two decades of the century alone.
Thus, the "vision of self-cultivation by peasant smallholders" could not
be sustained, for indebtedness to zamindars and moneylenders, as well
as the attendant transformation of family into wage labor, was already
common.[41]

In the stories and plays about indentured tea coolies, the uncontrol-
lable and seemingly alien pressures of high rent and dwindling income
were personified in the figure of the rent collector, depicted in the most

contemptuous manner. In both *Sketches* and *The Mirror of the Tea Planter,* the protagonists are driven into indenture after being harassed for rent and tax payments by the zamindar's employees, the gomastha (*gomastā*) and naib (*nāyeb*), respectively. Historically, Bose wrote, these figures formed the "seigneurial sergeant class" of middlemen and village leaders, who "colluded with the zamindars to fleece the peasantry and were allowed to hold land at favourable rates." In *Sketches*, it is in order to pay the land tax to the gomastha that Adarmani's husband loans his sons to the neighboring village. Vidyaratna described the collector as "the messenger of death [*Yamadūta*]. He had no mercy [*dayā*], no compassion [*māyā*], no politeness, and no hint of civility." When the family explains they have recently lost everything, he threatens to seize their property by force if they do not pay their rent, including a 20 percent "tip" (*pārbanī*), by the end of the day.[42] In *The Mirror,* the protagonists open the play with the following exchange:

SARADA: Brother, the rice paddy didn't grow, what will the women eat?

BARADA: That is one thing to worry about. On top of that, if we again fail to pay rent to the zamindar, then our calves will be sold.

SARADA: Our zamindar is not a terrible person. But, you see, the naib, that fellow, he is a total bastard.

BARADA: It is because of those naibs that the tenants [*prajāder*] are so miserable. If they just tried to make the zamindars understand our situation a little, then would the zamindar try to tax the tenants to death?

SARADA: Brother, you don't understand. If they do not collect rent [*khājnā*], then how could the collectors earn any profit [*lābh*]?[43]

Even if Indian nationalist writers denounced the tea plantations as slavelike bastions of sexual immorality, their criticism was counterbalanced by an acknowledgment of the structural patterns in the countryside—the impersonal pursuit of "profit"—that were normalizing outside hired work as a general survival strategy. In *The Mirror,* the wives of the farmers encourage their husbands to supplement their income from cultivation with an outside job (*chākri*). In *An Autobiography,* the protagonist chastises himself for immoral behavior—liquor, opium, and women chasing—that resulted from being too lazy to find honest work (*kājkarma*).[44]

Nationalist writers, therefore, were not championing the preservation of traditional family life in the village. Rather, they accepted the naturalness of waged work, and they promoted free wage labor as a normal and modern way of organizing social relations. They agreed with colonial officials that Indian villagers had no choice but to think of themselves as self-interested subjects of exchange, as individuals who should improve their lot by selling their own labor for the products of others. Ganguli had praised the tea plantations for enriching Assam and "giving employment to nearly 3 lacs of emigrants including their children." Similarly, the economist Dutt wrote, "Many wild wastes in hills and valleys have been thus converted into gardens, and hundreds of thousands of poor people have found employment in these gardens."[45] It is not hard to see the similarities between the Indian nationalists and the political-economic vision articulated by Chen Chi in China. Both discourses saw wage labor as a natural organizing principle for economic life, corresponding to the widespread, albeit informal and unaccounted, commodification of work in the putatively traditional villages of eastern India and coastal China.

But as I have suggested above, Vidyaratna did not limit his discussion of freedom to a principle of capitalist rationality; he also treated it as a metaphysical principle. For instance, he used the term "freedom" to depict how the tea coolies relish their weekly opportunity to buy household items at the bazaar, describing the pleasure of exchange as something as natural as fish in water. At the market, the coolies express pure joy (*ānanda*) and delight (*ullāsh*) "not for salt, oil, betel nut, or tobacco . . . but only for freedom—for that thing that was lost, making them beggars." Market exchange, beyond its *objective* rationality as a determinant of price, then, also resonated with the *subjective* feelings and desires of tea garden workers. Contra Chatterjee's interpretation, then, the nationalists' political-economic claims about free labor were not limited to the "outer domain" of the material world but also the "inner domain" of spirituality. "In practice," B. C. Pal wrote, labor indenture meant planters could act as the "absolute masters of the body and soul of their labourers."[46]

In a scene late in *Sketches*, a virtuous English planter vocally supports abolishing indenture laws, defending the workers' virtue against charges of absconding:

But why do the coolies flee? If the coolies received good treatment on the gardens, if they had enough to eat, then they would never flee. Like

I was saying before, if we treat the coolies well, then the gardens will run smoothly. And I still insist that in order to make the gardens operate well, then the contract labor laws aren't even necessary.[47]

In pursuing this line of argument, Vidyaratna was once again following the lead of abolitionists decades earlier, who claimed that economic incentives were more efficient than extra-economic coercion, for workers share with merchants the inner propensity to pursue self-interest through exchange.

Translated into policy terms, the demand by nationalist literature was to treat employees "freely" as a commodity to be sold and purchased. In 1888, the Indian Association sent a memorial to the Government of Bengal urging members to "allow the emigration of coolies into Assam to be regulated by the law of supply and demand without the aid of legislation." Years later, Dutt noted the swelling momentum among the Calcutta intelligentsia against penal contract legislation, writing, "Responsible and high administrators have desired a repeal of the penal laws, and have recommended that the tea-gardens should obtain workers from the teeming labour markets of India under the ordinary laws of demand and supply." He added, along similar lines, "much oppression and many acts of cruelty are reported from time to time; but the Government of India does not care to brave the wrath of capitalists by withdrawing these penal clauses, and leaving the labour market free as in other industries."[48]

Indian nationalists, therefore, subscribed to the same "commodity fiction" as colonial officials. They also agreed with the logic of the abolitionists that freedom meant submission to market forces. Whereas scholars such as Polanyi have emphasized the baleful implications of this commodity fiction, in this chapter I have suggested the possibility of analyzing and accounting for its historical emergence. What made the appearance of labor as a commodity increasingly plausible for observers in Bengal, as elsewhere across the British Empire? Was it the increased visibility of wage labor beyond a certain threshold? The statistical preponderance of wage labor in a market society? For Marx, the answer was located in a dynamic process, a temporal trajectory in which workers increasingly were treated, and saw themselves, as commodities. The crucial mechanism was the ever-widening spiral of accumulation that reproduced asymmetrical economic relationships between capital and labor. In the labor market ("the sphere of circulation"), Marx wrote, labor employment appeared as an act of exchange between equals who own commodities for sale: wages exchanged for labor. The flipside of this formal equality, however, was practical inequality in the "abode of production": the unequal distribution of economic surplus into the capitalist's profit and the worker's wages. Under these conditions favorable to capital, employers could continually use their profits to hire more workers. Employees, meantime, would "freely" return to seek more work, because they had received only subsistence remuneration. This *practical inequality* all but guaranteed the continued and expanded reproduction of the capital-labor relationship, along with its outward *formal equality*: "The constant renewal of the relationship of *sale and purchase* merely ensures the perpetuation of the specific relationship of dependency, endowing it with the deceptive *illusion* of a transaction, of a contract between equally free and equally matched *commodity owners*."[49]

In the context of Assam tea, it was no secret that the basis for any free labor system would be the continued poverty of the peasantry. One nationalist paper noted, "If the Coolie Acts in force are repealed, there will be no reason to fear that coolies will not be found to work in Assam, for livelihood in the North-Western Provinces has become so dear and difficult that many poor people will, of their own accord, come to the tea gardens." Decades later, during the final legislative debates over repealing indenture, a Bombay attorney assured skeptics that "it should be enough to point out for the safety of those who want to guard capitalism that capitalism is already guarded much more by the poverty of the people than by industrialism." Although the purportedly free wage workers were not being physically coerced into the jute factories and collieries of Bengal (though often they were), they were still under economic duress during times of both employment and unemployment, a theme highlighted in nationalist short stories and novels. They were not actually free *not to work*. As a symptom of the historical instability of the category "freedom," then, the line between free and unfree labor proved historically less tidy than imagined by its champions. The difference could be reframed as one of being bound either by the physical "chains" of the contract or by the "invisible threads" of the labor market.[50]

But although the line between the two has been blurry, one could also discern long-term patterns at play. Initially, capitalist production and exchange were compatible with many varieties of "inherited" work patterns, from independent peasant to sharecropper to slave, but as regular exchange has continued, it has naturalized the free purchase and sale of labor, producing an apparent evolution from archaic unfree toward modern free labor. In the late nineteenth century, these ideas grew increasingly natural in the minds of Indian nationalists. As with trans-Atlantic abolitionism decades earlier, the nationalists' denunciation of backwards and inhumane practices reflected how they were grappling with the transformation of economic and social relationships in their immediate surroundings. The more villagers fell into conditions of economic dependence, the more they sought employment in an apparently spontaneous manner, and the more market-based labor relations appeared natural and legitimate. Whereas colonial officials earlier argued for the necessity of exceptional legislation, nationalists championed ordinary economic laws. Whereas officials had described Indian migrants as childlike and demi-civilized, nationalists stressed that, as subjects of exchange, they had fully matured. And whereas Act I of 1882 was envisioned as a transition to fully free labor, the nationalists sought to complete the transition by repealing all penal contract legislation. For all their immediate disagreements with the colonial government, the nationalists also accepted and appropriated its historicist logic. This theme of free labor's modernity would thereby go on to play a central role in the twentieth-century abolition of indenture.

THE TWENTIETH-CENTURY DEMISE OF INDENTURE

The colonial Indian government gradually dismantled the regime of tea labor indenture over the first decades of the twentieth century. In 1901, the government attempted to restore regulated recruitment, but it discovered that even earlier policies were simply unworkable by then. In 1903, a series of tea plantation riots spurred yet another investigation into the relations between planters and workers. In 1906, the Assam Labour Enquiry Committee produced the most comprehensive report on tea labor in nearly four decades, and its authors confronted the prospect that the very institution of the penal contract was beyond reform.

The 1906 report drew heavily on the same normative claims about the naturalness of free labor regulated by the ordinary laws of market dynamics championed by the Bengal nationalists. A member of the Viceroy's Council provided an account of the recruiter system that could easily double as a plot summary of Vidyaratna's earlier novel:

> a horde of unlicensed and uncontrolled labour purveyors and recruiters sprang into existence who, under the guise of assisting "free emigration," made large illicit gains by inducing, under false pretences, ignorant men and women, chiefly from the most backward districts of Bengal and the Central Provinces, to allow themselves to be conveyed to Assam, and by practically selling these people to the planters for the purpose of being placed under labour contracts in that Province.[51]

Such hyperbolic rhetoric surrounding the "shadowy figure" of the arkati, McKeown has argued, was part of a broader rhetorical turn at the turn of the century targeting the deceptive Asian broker. The trope was symptomatic of an emergent twentieth-century "construction of the free, self-motivated individual as the proper subject of immigration law and theory." Of course, McKeown pointed out, these descriptions rarely assigned blame to European actors, instead finding the Asian broker a convenient object of moral castigation. Brokers "were increasingly depicted as artifacts of non-Western and premodern cultures opposed to the rationality and transparency of modern markets." The point here is not to deny that the arkatis did, as a matter of fact, engage in unscrupulous and exploitative practices. Rather, it is to question how the limits of permissible behavior were being drawn. For many politicians, the real crime committed by the arkatis was the threat they posed to the political-economic ideal of "free markets, free choice, and free mobility."[52]

Free labor also posed a challenge to the indenture regime in practical terms. According to the 1906 report, potential laborers who would otherwise come to Assam were instead being directed toward other "industrial activity" in the "docks and jute mills of Calcutta." Over the previous decade, coal output had nearly tripled, and jute and shipping had each doubled. A "marked decrease in population, the opening of new railways and the starting of new industries," the authors reported, have "told strongly against recruitment." Further, the worsening reputation of Assam was deterring workers from traveling. "There are stories of witchcraft, of leeches and continual rain," they acknowledged, "which obtain ready credence amongst classes already biassed against Assam by the bad name which has been given to it." If the penal contract laws of the previous century were justified as temporary stopgap measures, then the 1906 Report suggested that the time had come to retire them. "Conditions are changing," the authors wrote, "the coolie is becoming more independent, and he is not ready to submit to the restraint which such a contract involves." The report's authors echoed the sentiments of the nationalists, writing, "The freedom of the labourer is the most certain means of drawing people to Assam and keeping the labour force contented on the gardens." The government's affirmation of the principle of free labor was not so much a repudiation of the rationale behind earlier penal contract laws—as the defensive planters perceived them to be—but rather a realization of their goals.[53]

As a result of the report, special legislation for the recruitment of Assam tea labor was abolished in 1915. But indenture was not completely erased from the legal code. Several years before the first special law for Assam in 1863, the government had passed the Workman's Breach of Contract Act, or Act XIII (1859), which enabled urban employers to enforce contracts through prosecution, and it had been used intermittently in Assam. The authors of the 1906 report decided not to challenge this law, for it could serve as a "stepping stone towards free labour." By 1917, however, Madan Mohan Malaviya, a high-ranking veteran of the INC, raised the idea of repealing Act XIII.[54]

In 1919, the International Labour Organization held its first conference in Washington, D.C., with the stated aim of raising the conditions of labor around the world. It provided an opportunity for Indian nationalists to pressure the government to catch up with changing global standards of what counted as modern. At government hearings that year, Malaviya reminded officials that "we are now in the 20th century," that indenture was "mediaeval in outlook," and that "modern conditions require its total repeal." The Chamber of Commerce for the United Provinces of Agra and Oudh concurred that Act XIII was "strangely in discord with the spirit of the times and quite out-of-date in the present days of free and emancipated labor." For Malaviya, the central development that distinguished the current moment was the universality and normalcy of free waged labor in Indian industries:

> I have seen that the Jute mills round Calcutta, and the Buckingham Mills in Madras and the Nagpur Mills have made most excellent provision for the accommodation of their labour. At Jamshedpur too, at the Tata Iron Works, they have made very satisfactory provision for such accommodation and it is going to be improved still further. Labourers willingly go to these places. There are thousands upon thousands of persons

willingly working at Calcutta, Madras, Bombay, Jamshedpur and Nagpur. . . . Now I am certain that if the state of things which exist to-day
existed in 1859, nobody would have thought of enacting Act XIII of
1859. Therefore taking the reverse of it, now that such a state of things
does exist, the Government ought to repeal that Act.[55]

Nationalist thinkers provided the line of argumentation, but the actual ultimate push to abolish indenture came from the workers themselves. The tea industry had profited handsomely during the First World
War, as the British government purchased large "blocks" of tea to guarantee a domestic supply. But in the war's aftermath, the global market
experienced a glut of production; the ITA reported 1920 as the "most
trying" year it had ever experienced. Its problems were exacerbated by
the fact that indentured workers were seen as a fixed investment and
firing them would "represent a partial loss on capital." The planters'
strategy was to limit production and cut wages, their largest expense,
but their squeeze efforts also inspired protest and strikes. The activities
in Assam intersected with a nationwide ferment of political activism inspired by new Congress leader Mohandas Gandhi's call for nonviolent
noncooperation as well as the pan-Muslim Khilafat movement. By this
time, nationalist politics had long veered away from its 1890s roots
as an organization of bureaucratic and reformist professionals. Disil-
lusioned by the failure of orderly, constitutional measures, Gandhi and
other leaders promoted *hartals*, or popular demonstrations, to protest
British policies. Assam tea workers, who had met with noncooperation and Khilafat activists in the street markets near the gardens, chose
to strike and abandon their employers en masse. During the largest
exodus in the Chargola Valley of lower Assam, nearly nine thousand
workers left their employers, demanding the planters pay their return
to their villages. Throughout the exodus, they chanted, "*Gandhi Maha-
raj ki jai!*" ("Victory to the revered Gandhi!").[56]

The strikes and riots inspired yet another colonial inquiry into the
conditions of tea labor. Writers of the 1922 report suppressed the clear
political ramifications of the protest, arguing that the strikes were
purely "economic" in nature. Nevertheless, they conceded that there
was no longer any justification for labor indenture, which they acknowledged as "unsuited in many respects to modern conditions" and
"modern feelings." The penal contract was an "anachronism" that had
been "responsible for the frequent occurrence of these regrettable incidents on Assam tea-gardens."[57]

The final repeal of Act XIII (1859) in 1926 brings the story of the Assam indenture system full circle, raising the similar themes of liberal political economy as those animating the original justifications for the system. If late nineteenth-century colonial rule had been grounded in the historicist charge of backwardness, then the response from nationalists was the equally historicist claim that India, once undeveloped, had now evolved into a modern society governable by market exchange. In a long expository appeal to abolish indenture, a nationalist writer named M. Krishna wrote, "It is my earnest hope that everyone who has the welfare of India at his heart will take up the matter at once and procure for the labourers the least of their rights, viz. the right to sell their labour without compulsion, the right to know, and the right to try to improve their lot."[58]

Even as officials accepted the end of indenture as a fait accompli, many voiced their displeasure with a policy that was based on abstract theory. In 1926, with labor indenture in its twilight, one member of the Council of India subtly mocked anti-indenture sentiments as "all arguments of principle and theory of an irreproachable character." Another stated they were "unobjectionable from a theoretical point of view" but ignored "the practical advantages of the system." Another speaker, an Indian industrialist, followed a speech from the union leader N. M. Joshi by arguing sharply, "It might have been very different if Mr. Joshi . . . actually studied the problem on the spot, and had gone into the practical difficulties of those who have to organise labour and handle labour. . . . He has visualised from his office room only one set of circumstances, only one set of labourers, in Assam or any other part of India and generalised from this."[59] Although they clashed on the desirability of indenture, both sides agreed that its abolition had been justified less upon its empirical unfeasibility—after all, its near-five-decade track record spoke for itself—than upon the ideologies and principles of free labor, ideas perfectly consonant with a strand of liberal political economy that had now become common sense for nationalist economic thinkers.

CONCLUSION: COOLIE NATIONALISM AND NATIONAL CAPITAL

The Bengali nationalists at the turn of the century had presented their campaign in moral and humanitarian terms, appealing to their readers' anger and disgust over violence witnessed on the tea gardens. But the campaign also sought to push a specific vision of Indian society. It involved a better life for the tea workers, but it was also concerned with the organization of capital. First, many of the arguments in defense of free labor pointed to its economic rationality: free and happy workers would not agitate for higher wages and the tea gardens would run smoothly. In government reports, planters agreed with officials that unfree labor had inflated the price of coolies and that broker fees were wasteful. According to the nationalists, business based on free labor was simply more profitable.

Second, in addition to the operation of capital, the nationalists were primarily concerned with capital's *ownership*. Limitations upon Indian economic activity were unfounded because Indians had evolved into subjects of exchange. For the nationalists, the tea industry's profits were the fruit of the labor of Indian coolies, and the scandal of indenture was that it enabled British planters to unjustly extract surplus value from them. In 1919, the nationalist Malaviya wrote that the tea worker "has suffered a great deal in the past owing to the operation of this Act . . . out of which the capitalists have made much at his expense." Krishna stated that the problem with indenture was less its inhumanity than its economic exploitation: "The point is not that employers should pay workmen enough to keep them in comfort, but that the workmen should get the legitimate price of their labour power. Let the toilers live in comfort or discomfort, only let them be paid the fruit of their toil." On this point, the criticisms of indenture overlapped with the general, more well-known discourse on the "colonial drain of wealth" from Britain to India, as the plight of Indian tea labor would gradually give way to a politics of Indian tea capital.[60]

The drain thesis contended that British officials and companies had systematically shut out Indian entrepreneurship over the nineteenth century. During its early decades, colonial rule in Bengal had witnessed the coequal participation of British and local aristocratic businessmen. The most prominent entrepreneur of the era, Dwarkanath Tagore, envisioned an "all-encompassing interracial partnership of Britishers and Indians." For instance: both Tagore and Rammohan Roy had echoed Bentinck's promotion of "colonization"; the original 1830s Tea Committee included two Bengali capitalists, Radhakant Deb and Ramkamal Sen; and Tagore himself made an early bid in the 1830s to take over the government tea tracts and run the first private Indian tea company. However, the region underwent an economic crisis from the 1830s onward, culminating in 1848 with the collapse of the Union Bank, a joint venture between European and Indian shareholders for funding indigo. By the twentieth century, Indian capital had largely been excluded from the largest manufacturing concerns, a pattern especially acute with tea: in 1895, 171 of 182 tea companies were owned by non-Indians. Indian writers had begun crafting the drain theory by the 1870s. In his contribution, Dutt focused on trade policy, arguing that British officials lowered duties on imports of British manufactures and raised them for Indian exports, destroying Indian industry and converting India into a mere plantation for raw materials, paying special attention to Assam. "The indigo and tea exported were mainly grown and prepared by British capital and by Indian labour," he wrote. "The profits of the capital went to the shareholders in England; the wages of labour remained with the people of India."[61]

By the turn of the century, the drain thesis had become common sense, an "article of faith," in Ajit Dasgupta's words, among the Indian elite. In Bengal it became the theoretical basis for the 1905–1909 Swadeshi Movement against British rule (repeated later in the 1920s), which relied upon boycotting British goods and offering extra support for Indian, swadeshi ("own country"), industry. The Swadeshi Movements are useful as an anchoring point for grasping the broader framework of nationalist criticism that embraced the cause of the tea coolies. The goal of economic nationalism in this era, Manu Goswami has shown, "was a movement for the *nationalization* of capital, not its abolition."[62] Bengali nationalists assimilated the struggle for the emancipation of Indian labor into the broader struggle for the development of Indian capital.

This is best illustrated by revisiting the context of the 1920–1922 labor exoduses that took place under the banners of noncooperation and Khilafat. Many workers absconded from the plantations in the name of Gandhi, but as Shahid Amin has demonstrated, during this time there emerged a sizable gap between the leadership and Gandhi, on the one hand, and the mythological status he attained in the rumors circulating across India, on the other. Gandhi, in fact, had visited Assam in August 1921, at the height of the strikes, but he declined to meet with the protestors who invoked his name, visiting only with the British planters at a private club. There, he allegedly "disclaimed all connection [with the strikes] and stated he would give immediate instructions for its discontinuance." Indeed, during this period of nationwide peasant and labor agitation, the Congress leadership avoided class-specific grievances for fear of alienating capital; several Congress leaders in Assam, it turned out, were tea planters themselves.[63]

The nationalist leadership was concerned with the plight of the Indian tea coolies as a controversy over Indian versus British rule, but its sympathies stopped short of supporting newly emergent movements to help labor win economic concessions from capital. That fight would be taken up by plantation workers and union organizers on their own over the next two decades. As for the economic nationalists, they increasingly made clear that they believed the Indian tea coolie stood in for the larger predicament of economic immobility shared by *all Indians* under British rule. In a 1901 address to a general meeting of the Congress held in Calcutta, the writer B. C. Pal proclaimed of the ongoing controversy over tea labor indenture: "This question, Mr Chairman, is an old question—the world wide question of the conflict of Labour and Capital. . . . Prince or peasants, Mr Chairman, we all of us stand in the position of labourers in this country, and they stand, all stand in the position of capitalists." For Pal, the "coolie" was a symbol of the degradation faced by the general Indian population. But rather than depict the Indian people as a class to be emancipated *from capital*, many nationalists sought emancipation for India through the opportunity to freely sell and purchase labor and property *as capital*.[64]

By the 1920s, British planters were cognizant of greater nationalist sentiments across India, and they opened themselves up to the idea of Indian ownership in the tea industry. By the 1950s, the postcolonial Indian government could push for the transfer of ownership from British to Indian hands as part of proactive measures to territorialize the Indian economy and its profits. Strikingly, a half century after Pal's pronouncement of India as a nation of coolies, a prominent voice in the Indian planter community optimistically looked back on independence as the movement from Indian tea labor to Indian tea capital: "We were kept as hewers of wood and drawers of water; we were not allowed to develop our industries and we were exploited by our foreign masters for the benefit of their nationals. . . . Of the dark clouds of England's exploitation, the brightest silver lining has been the tea industry, which is India's fortunate legacy from foreign rule."[65]

Political economy had provided the language for a liberal criticism of monopoly and slavery as well as a vision of the tea industry as a vehicle for national emancipation. Although the Indian tea industry was initially characterized by the polarization of British capital and native labor, by the twentieth century, it increasingly featured the indigenization of tea capital, followed, eventually, by the indigenization of tea consumption.

7 From Cohong to Comprador

China's Tea Industry Revolution and the Critique of Unproductive Labor

ON MAY 12, 1905, an imperial expedition of nine men departed from Shanghai, bound for the tea-producing regions of Ceylon and India by way of Saigon and Singapore. They had been sent by the governor-general of the Liangjiang region, which encompassed Jiangxi, Jiangsu, and Anhui, to study overseas methods transposable to China's own tea districts. The project belonged to the Qing court's final efforts to forestall collapse in the aftermath of the aborted Hundred Days of Reform (1898) and the Boxer Uprising (1899–1901), the calamitous ending of which saddled the empire with insurmountable foreign indemnities and loss of control over its revenue system. The "new policies" (*xinzheng*) of the century's first decade aimed to reform the Qing's economic, military, and political institutions, on the belief that China needed to study foreign methods in order to stave off imperialism. During the same year as the tea expedition, the Qing court sent five ministers to study the constitutions of Japan, the United States, and Europe, and in that decade some ten thousand Chinese students enrolled abroad in Japan.[1] The historical irony was that the court itself was now spearheading the very same outside policies that it had rejected as heretical one decade earlier. To these examples, then, we can add Chen Chi's original 1896 memorial urging the tea industry to investigate new methods pioneered in colonial India, finally taken up nine years later, five years after Chen had already passed away.

The expedition's twenty-seven-year-old secretary, Lu Ying (1878–1969), documented the group's adventures: a British planter's majestic estate in Ceylon, an elephant ride through Darjeeling, and the crowded alleyways of Calcutta. While in the metropolis, Lu Ying was brought by an acquaintance from the Chinatown to meet with members of the Indian nationalist intelligentsia, the same men involved in championing *swadeshi* politics:

> I became familiar with how the Indian people have recently developed ideas about self-rule. In the midst of conversation, one said to me: "originally, we Asians were connected as one. Sadly, in recent centuries, the Western powers have invaded the East, and interaction with your esteemed nation has been cut off." What a surprise![2]

This comment hinted at a nascent Pan-Asian consciousness shaped in opposition to European rule; the same men told Lu Ying that they found inspiration from Meiji Japan's military victory over the Russian Empire the same year. His reaction of "surprise" suggests Lu Ying had not fully considered how Qing China and colonial India faced similar political situations, despite the obvious economic links that had brought him to Calcutta. He was perhaps overly confident about the Qing Empire's odds for survival; back in China, many of his peers had for years agonized over the prospect of being "carved up" (*guafen*) in the same manner as the colonized world.[3] Indeed, only two years after Lu Ying returned in 1909, the Qing Empire collapsed for good, and China was plunged into warlordism and chaos. A new generation of young thinkers in Republican China (1912–1949) found themselves forced to develop their own "ideas about self-rule."

As with *swadeshi* politics in India, Chinese nationalists saw indigenous economic development as fundamental for any challenge to foreign imperialism. Indeed, throughout much of the middle twentieth century, nationalists outside the North Atlantic world gravitated toward state-protected industrialization as their defense against an exploitative global market. Their inspiration, models, and material support were transnational in nature. Chinese nationalists seeking to revive the tea trade found their greatest source of inspiration from their competitors in colonial South Asia. While in Darjeeling, Lu Ying was deeply impressed by the tea plantation's technological and organizational innovations. "A factory that produces one-thousand pounds a day," he wrote, "only needs twelve or thirteen people. This is because the machines, compared with humans, save much labor." Planters benefited from "companies of massive wealth," "state support," and "trains and large ships." Hence, "production costs are low, and their prices fall lower and lower. They are quickly squeezing out Chinese tea." Once back home, Lu Ying set out to revive the Chinese tea trade along the lines of its Indian rivals, inaugurating a three-decade-long effort to bring about a national "tea industry revolution" (*chaye geming*)—a phrase that is perhaps more appropriately imagined as "an industrial revolution for tea."[4]

The context for such revolution was the radically altered economic landscape for tea. Chinese producers were now competing with not just India but also Ceylon, Japan, Taiwan, and the Dutch East Indies. In the 1860s, tea represented over 60 percent of the Qing Empire's earnings from overseas exports. By the 1930s, that number hovered around 5 percent. "The past sixty years of the Chinese export tea trade's history has been nothing less than the history of the Chinese tea trade's defeat," wrote the agricultural economist Wu Juenong, a central figure in this chapter's story. The black tea markets of the United Kingdom now belonged to South Asian producers, and the green tea markets of the Soviet Union and the United States had been "handed over on a platter" (*gongshou rangren*) to Japan and Taiwan.[5] For Chinese reformers, catching up would require absorbing the methods of their foreign competitors, much as British planters had imported Chinese tea production to Assam a century earlier.

Despite optimistic talk of revolution, though, the records of reform during Republican China's Nanjing Decade (1927–1937) are filled with frustrated voices bemoaning policy "failure," "corruption and decay," and a sense of being "cut short."[6] Wu Juenong compared his experiences to a play whose curtain had been lowered before reaching intermission. Instead of revolution, the dominant theme was withering criticism of middlemen agents known as "compradors" and, especially, the treaty-port merchants known as "tea warehouses" (*chazhan*). Well into the final decades of the Qing, export merchants had enjoyed a high social standing. But in the new century their reputation was turned upside down. They became scapegoats for economic underdevelopment, labeled "exploitative" (*boxue*), "monopolistic" (*longduan*), "unproductive" (*fei shengchan*), and "parasitic" (*jisheng*). Nationalist writers demonized them in sensational, moralistic language, calling them "devils" (*mogui*), "pests" (*mao*), and "bugs" (*chong*).

Many historical studies of Republican China have interpreted these reports as unmediated evidence of traditional China's involutionary merchant culture. In my view, such anti-comprador critique *itself* deserves to be analyzed as a historical object, for it indexed new social tensions between commerce and industry in China. My argument entails examining prewar Republican efforts to revive the Chinese tea trade while also providing a socially grounded history of the category "comprador" within the economic thinking of reformers.

Inspired by Lu Ying's early travels to South Asia, Wu Juenong and his team of agronomic surveyors conducted fieldwork surveys in the export tea districts during the 1930s, revealing how social relations there had become mediated by the accumulation of capital. They discovered bonds of commercial and financial dependence spanning the peasantry, inland factories, treaty-port merchants, and foreign firms. In chapters 2 and 5 I presented evidence suggesting the imprint of modern accumulation in the rural Chinese tea districts, but it was these twentieth-century surveys that substantiated it in detail for the first time. Contrary to many studies that have claimed the Chinese peasantry was precapitalist due to its reliance upon noncommodified family labor, these surveys suggested that the lending practices of rural China represented a disguised form of wage labor that shared much in common with the industrialized world.

This recognition was the point of departure for the reformers' broader criticism that the tea merchants' circulating capital was not doing enough to develop the productive capacities of the countryside—that the tea warehouses were simply extracting value from peasant labor in a parasitic manner. Although the opposition between peasants and merchants has long been featured in Chinese political thought, then, I suggest that anti-comprador criticism offered a historically novel articulation premised on a distinctive notion of what counts as productive labor, one that overlapped with classical political economy. The demand for faster, capital-intensive production appeared so natural to nationalist reformers that they quickly lost patience with merchants who failed to follow suit. The export tea merchants, lionized in the nineteenth century for their contributions to the Qing economy, became parasitic compradors in the twentieth century, a reversal that made sense only in a world of competitive accumulation.

In basic terms, the twentieth-century comprador and tea warehouse merchants were, in a vacuum, simply behaving as they had done since the eighteenth century. What had changed was not *their own* practices but the surrounding political climate. This was a transformation of ideology grounded in a transformation of economic organization extending beyond the boundaries of Chinese history. Notably, the "comprador" category has also found resonance in contexts outside of China, from Latin America to India, East Africa, Egypt, and Turkey. The twentieth-century demonization of the comprador was the Chinese-specific articulation of a problem global in scale and distinct to the modern world.[7]

In the sections that follow I begin by introducing the comprador both as a real, historical institution and as a theoretical category in modern Chinese history. Past historians have argued that the compradors' sudden collapse in reputation stemmed from cynical political partisanship and nationalism, but I suggest this decline was actually rooted in changes in global political economy. Next I explore institutional efforts to revive the tea trade, starting from Lu Ying's return to China and focusing on the 1930s surveys and experiments led by Wu Juenong. I analyze the political-economic assumptions behind their criticisms, showing how anti-comprador hostility was rooted in the categorial opposition between productive labor versus unproductive circulating capital. In the final section I highlight Wu Juenong's efforts to realize his vision of native industry by reorganizing village producers into agrarian cooperatives. In response, the tea merchants fought back through extreme tactics, giving these theoretical conflicts a real, living form and disclosing the historical stakes of the attempted tea industry revolution.

A HISTORY OF THE COMPRADOR: FROM THE CANTON SYSTEM TO THE SHANGHAI WAREHOUSES

In his brief history of the tea trade, Wu Juenong described the twentieth-century treaty-port merchants, known as tea warehouses, as the evolutionary successor to the Hong merchants and compradors of the Canton trade. During the height of that system, European compa-

nies dealt exclusively with the thirteen Hong merchants known collectively as the Cohong. Europeans adopted the Portuguese term "comprador" ("buyer") to refer to the Chinese employee hired to represent
their interests, known in Chinese as the *maiban*.[8] The Cohong disappeared after the first Opium War, but the comprador system continued to evolve in subsequent decades. As the new treaty ports of Hong
Kong, Xiamen, Fuzhou, Shanghai, and Hankou came to be dominated
by a handful of American and British firms, they relied upon Chinese
agents and middlemen to establish control over the inland circulation
of goods and money. These in-house compradors took over the role of
the eighteenth-century Hong merchants (figure 20). Compradors were
employed, for instance, as Jardine Matheson's army of "teamen," and
similar examples have been documented for the silk trade.

Throughout these changes, the Hong merchants and compradors
were viewed in positive terms, admired by both European partners and
the Qing bureaucracy. A British trader wrote, "The famous Co-Hong
of Canton . . . was an association of the highest commercial rank, and
possessed a monopoly of the foreign trade, granted by the Government because it was to be trusted." Domestically, eighteenth-century
Qing thinkers regarded the Canton trade as "manifestly a good thing,"
profiting both state and the people. During the nineteenth-century
Self-Strengthening Movement, the export merchants' reputation grew
stronger, as they financially supported state initiatives to modernize the
military and economy. Local officials proposed projects that were "designed to tap" the capital of the compradors, including the purchase of
large-scale ships and artillery and the creation of joint-stock companies
for shipping, mining, and textiles. These comprador-reformers were
seen as vanguard economic and political figures, embodied in the stock
imperial phrase "sympathy for the merchants."[9] Compradors were seen
as great patriots; their interaction with European companies was not
attacked as imperialist collaboration but rather what distinguished
them as visionaries and pioneers of Chinese capitalism.

As the new century neared, the practice of hiring in-house compradors had largely disappeared, as illustrated by the disappearance of
teamen from the upcountry trade of Fujian by the 1870s. With the export trades growing more complex, many ex-compradors established
their own independent firms in the treaty ports: the "silk warehouse"
(*sizhan*) in the case of the silk trade and the tea warehouse for tea, both

Figure 20. In-house comprador (*center*) employed by the Fuzhou-based English tea trader John C. Oswald, 1890. School of Oriental and African Studies Archives, University of London. John Charles Oswald Collection, MS 380876, by kind permission of SOAS Library.

of which played a major role in overseas commerce by the 1880s.[10] For instance, the Jiang family of Shexian, Anhui, regularly dealt with the Shanghai warehouse agent Tang Yaoqing. In Wu Juenong's mind, the tea warehouses had simply superseded the social function of the old comprador system. He called them "compradoresque [*maiban xing*] middlemen merchants," and he depicted the overall setup of the tea trade as a "trinity" (*san wei yiti*) of foreign firms, compradors, and tea warehouses. As support for his theory, we need only note that the most famous and celebrated compradors of the nineteenth century—Zheng Guanying, Tong King-sing (Tang Jingxing), and Xu Run—each started his own independent tea warehouse.[11]

In the early twentieth century, the compradors became a popular target of criticism. At the same time that the traditional in-house comprador receded from economic life, writers began to speak about the "comprador" in metaphorical terms, designating any Chinese employee of a foreign-owned firm, such as the comprador who worked for banking, insurance, and shipping companies. By one estimate, the numbers of compradors had climbed from 250 in 1854 to 700 in 1870 and up to 20,000 by the new century. It was during this time that the Republican government of Yuan Shikai collapsed into warlordism, ultimately requiring an alliance (1923–1927) between the nationalist Kuomintang (KMT) and Chinese Communist Party (CCP), known as the first united front, to reunify southern and eastern China. Despite political differences that would eventually erupt into civil war, the two parties shared many political convictions, not least of which was a distrust of China's compradors as harmful to national development. In his classic novel *Midnight* (1933), Mao Dun depicted the comprador Zhao Botao as the archnemesis to his protagonist, the national industrialist Wu Sunfu. The pulp short story "The Strange Comprador" ("Guai Maiban," 1924) portrayed these merchants as shape-shifting petty crooks. A young Mao Zedong placed the comprador class at the center of his analysis of imperialism (1926), and decades later, the ideology of Communist Party rule expanded the label "comprador" into a designation of ideology and culture, leveled at any accomplice to imperialism or enemy of the party.[12] Accusations of "comprador thought" (*maiban sixiang*), "comprador culture" (*maiban wenhua*), "comprador tendency" (*maiban qingxiang*), and "comprador economics" (*maiban jingjixue*) were leveled against the historical figure Li Hongzhang, reformers Hu Shih and Liang Shuming, and ousted party leaders Lin Biao and Deng Xiaoping, among others.[13] The film *The East Is Red* (1965), which crystallized the party's self-mythology of its rise from the ashes of old Chinese society, opened with a shot of Chinese porters lugging crates of silk under the yoke of imperialism, embodied by a European merchant and his comprador partner.

How can this dramatic inversion of reputation—from patriotic businessman to imperialist collaborator—be explained? Many historians have suggested it emerged from Communist Party orthodoxy and blind nationalism. Marie-Claire Bergère pointed out that the distinctions between "comprador" and "national capital" were incoherent. Empirically, "there were no Chinese businesses independent of the foreigners" during the Republican period, and hence, this "clear-cut opposition" was "completely artificial." The categories of "national" and "comprador capital" were therefore "no more than political labels" propagated by the Communist Party.[14]

Such explanations may be too hasty. Certainly, by the time of the Cold War, the comprador concept had taken on a life of its own, a catch-all marker of imperialist collaboration. However, the political fortunes of the comprador had already been decided earlier, in the 1920s and thirties. During those decades, a variety of authors, regardless of nationality or political party, came to agree that the comprador was an *economic* anachronism. It was a time of "political and intellectual flexibility" across KMT and CCP divisions, Margherita Zanasi has demonstrated, long before the calcification of orthodoxy in subsequent decades, and the category "comprador" "offered a common language" across parties. Rather than cynical ideology, the division between "national" capital and "comprador" capital, Zanasi suggested, turned upon ethnic identification (*minzu*). But while ethnicity and nationalism certainly explained much of their appeal, it is worth noting that anti-comprador sentiments were also held by overseas observers from Japan and the United States.[15] During this pivotal period, then, antagonism toward the comprador was shared across most political divisions, rooted in some form of social objectivity.

I suggest that, more than cynical label or ethnic distinction, anticomprador criticism signaled a deeper transformation in economic perception: how writers imagined the position of China in the world and what, accordingly, constituted the normative principles of economic life at the time. Anti-comprador critique stemmed less from changes in the behavior of the compradors *themselves* than from reformers' new expectations and idealizations of peasant labor, upon whom they now pinned their hopes. As peasant labor grew significant in the minds of reformers, the merchants' reputation suffered. Anti-comprador criticism was not only based on a *spatial* distinction between national and foreign powers but also turned on a *temporal distinction* between nineteenth-century commercial capital versus modern industrial capital. This change in perception becomes clearer as we examine the reforms surrounding the export tea trade, one of the quintessential fronts of anti-comprador criticism.

WU JUENONG POSES THE AGRARIAN QUESTION OF CHINA

Lu Ying's return to China in 1909 marked the onset of serious attempts to transform the production and circulation of Chinese tea. He set up a workshop in Hubei, followed by two more in Sichuan and Jiangxi, each of which taught new methods for cultivation and introduced machines from India. To fund his plans, Lu Ying relied upon his connections with his friend Zhang Jian, a famed cotton magnate who also served as the minister of agriculture and commerce. On Lu Ying's earlier visit to India, the mountainous tea districts of Darjeeling had reminded him of Qimen county (often spelled "Keemun" in English) in Anhui, near Shexian, Huizhou. The region originally produced the green teas common to Huizhou, but in the 1870s, its merchants started to market a full-bodied Qimen black variety (*Qihong*), which quickly caught the attention of domestic and foreign consumers. Lu determined "only Qimen black tea, with its unique and fragrant aroma, was worth focusing on. . . . As long as we hoped to revive the Chinese trade, we needed to start with Qimen black tea." Over the 1910s and twenties, Lu Ying initiated several experiments in Qimen, but amidst political uncertainty, his projects fell dormant. In the meantime, Lu Ying promoted overseas education for aspiring agricultural modernizers. "In the tea districts," he recalled, "there was no education about the science of tea. I called for more agrarian, industrial, and commercial education, the reform of old methods, and the scientific study of cultivation, processing, and marketing." He arranged for students to travel to Japan, where the Meiji and Taishō governments had commissioned resources for green tea production. The most notable beneficiary was Wu Juenong, a man who has since been hailed as the most important figure in twentieth-century efforts to revive the Chinese tea trade (figure 21).[16]

After Wu Juenong spent several years studying tea production in Shizuoka, Japan, he returned to China and conducted rural fieldwork surveys, spearheaded experiments with cooperative production in Qimen, and, after the Communist Revolution (1949), served as vice minister of agriculture and the director of China's first nationalized tea company. But the easiest way for us to understand who Wu Juenong was is to start with the origins of his peculiar pen name. Born Wu Rongtang, he grew up in a middle-class farmer family in Shangyu, Zhejiang Province. "In my hometown, there were many peasants in the mountains who grew tea," he recalled in his memoirs. "Because the peasants' lives were so difficult, and because they knew nothing about scientific cultivation, tea farming was backwards, small scale, and only a side occupation." By 1918, when he left for Shizuoka, he had begun writing under a new name, "Juenong," which translates as "awakening the peasant."

Figure 21. Wu Juenong in the 1930s. Courtesy of Wu Ning.

Regarding "peasant" (*nong*), he recalled late in life: "Why did I choose this name? My entire life, the issue that concerned me most was the living conditions of the peasantry and their ability to produce." As for "awakening" (*jue*), the best clue came from his groundbreaking essay "The Agrarian Question of China" (1922), in which he concluded: "In our nation, most peasants are in a slumber, a deep, deep slumber. There is no one to guide or lead them, so who will be able to wake them up? For now we say, there is no other way than for the awakened [*juewu*] young men and women to go 'back to the village.'" This was the task he had assigned himself with his new name.[17]

The metaphor of "awakening," John Fitzgerald has shown, was a central and "ubiquitous" concept during the tumultuous New Culture and May Fourth (ca. 1915–1937) eras of Chinese history. Throughout the 1910s and twenties, as China became enveloped in a civil war between warlords, a new generation of thinkers contemplated forms of reform and revolution that would both unify the country and bring it into the modern world. Wu Juenong was unmistakably a product of, and active participant in, these intellectual circles. He spent the 1920s in Shanghai, where he befriended vanguard thinkers Lu Xun, Mao Dun, and Chen Han-seng, while also publishing influential articles on feminism and agrarian movements around the world. His lead essay "The Agrarian Question," published in *Eastern Miscellany*, the most widely circulated journal in China, represented perhaps the first usage of the phrase in Chinese, and it was later distributed by a young Mao Zedong in his early work as a Communist activist.[18]

Wu Juenong's opportunity to "fulfill his lifelong dreams" of reorganizing the Chinese countryside would arrive only after the KMT's and CCP's first united front had taken back the Yangzi Delta region in 1927. However, in the early hours of April 12 in Shanghai, the underground Green Gang, under the direction of new KMT leader Chiang Kai-shek, initiated a reign of "white terror" against the CCP—a campaign Wu Juenong publicly denounced—driving its remaining members first to Jiangxi and then ultimately Yan'an, Shaanxi. There, over the next two decades, a young Mao Zedong would craft his own political-economic vision for China, one that paralleled the ideas of many left-wing members of the KMT, including Wu Juenong, which will be revisited below.[19] Meantime, in Nanjing, the Chiang-led KMT state enjoyed a decade-long respite from battle, during which it attempted to build a new culture, military, and economy for China. A powerful current within the Nanjing government was a group of economic reformers—most notably, Wang Jingwei, Chen Guangfu, and T. V. Soong—who focused on rural development as opposed to Chiang's urban-focused militarism.

In 1928, the American-educated Soong was appointed minister of finance, and in spring 1933, he created the National Economic Council (NEC) (*quanguo jingji weiyuanhui*). He traveled to the U.S. and negotiated for a loan of $50 million that would furnish the NEC with independent funding (later reduced to $17 million). Soong pushed for programs of "economic control" (*jingji tongzhi*): government intervention into, and regulation of, sectors vital to national wealth. The most famous NEC projects focused on cotton and silk production, but the same funds also supported Wu Juenong's experiments to reinvigorate the tea trade. In 1931, Qimen officials approached Wu about bringing Lu Ying's abandoned tea experiments back to life, and the next six years, until the outbreak of the second Sino-Japanese War, constituted what Wu Juenong called the most productive and "satisfying" years of agrarian reform in his life. During that time, the efforts of his teams exposed the potential for radical improvement to the existing economic system, laying the foundation for radical changes after the war.[20]

In Qimen, Wu Juenong's first measures entailed fieldwork surveys to understand the economic conditions of tea. His team of reformers fully mapped for the first time the dynamics of the tea trade as it extended from the coastal treaty ports down to the peasant household. What they discovered was the crucial problem of finance capital, as it was advanced from the warehouses to the peasantry.

"THE MAGIC OF ADVANCES": THE SOCIAL SURVEYS OF THE HUIZHOU TEA DISTRICTS

In their major policy statement published in 1935, Wu Juenong and his research partner Hu Haochuan explained the need for surveys by comparing their work with that of a doctor seeing a patient. A doctor does not simply hone in on a particular symptom but should begin with a comprehensive four-step procedure examining appearance, hearing, cognitive ability, and pulse. Although everyone "is conscious of the sickly tea industry of China," no one has yet performed the necessary procedure of examining the "ins and outs" and the "big and small" details of the industry. "In order to understand the various conditions that afflict the tea industry," they continued, "we must begin by relying upon fieldwork surveys" (shidi diaocha).[21]

Their goal was to understand why the Chinese trade was suffering, but simply addressing tea as a matter of trade was inadequate, they wrote, for the real problems were located in production. Asking how to boost Chinese tea sales also meant asking why the peasantry were so poor and why the tea factories were so incapable of improvement.

In their investigations, the surveyors discovered that the tea picking and refinement processes in the countryside bore striking resemblances wherever they went, whether in Anhui, Fujian, Hubei, Hunan, Jiangxi, or Zhejiang. They drew abstract charts to illustrate the movement of credit and tea through the trade routes:

Inland tea districts   Treaty ports

tea peasants → tea peddlers → tea factories → tea warehouses → foreign firms

1. The tea peasants. Also called "tea households" (*chahu*), "mountain households" (*shanhu*), and "garden households" (*yuanhu*), the families grew tea on their own farms and sold the semiprocessed leaves (*maocha*) to the factories.

2. The tea peddlers (*chake, chafan, chahang*), itinerant middlemen, traveled between village farms and market towns, delivering the raw leaves from the peasants to the tea factories.

3. The tea factories (*chahao, chazhuang, zhuanghao, chachang*) were established year to year in mid-level market towns. The factories purchased *maocha* from the surrounding hinterlands and employed seasonal workers to turn the leaves into a finished product.

4. The tea warehouses (*chazhan*) in Shanghai and other treaty ports inherited the functions of the old Cohong and comprador systems. Originally simply buyers and sellers, they eventually added the functions of finance, providing loans to the inland tea houses and keeping close ties with foreign traders and banks.

5. The foreign trading companies that purchased and marketed tea were American, British, French, Indian, and Soviet companies.

The approach adopted by Wu Juenong's team contrasted sharply with similar, more famous surveys conducted at the time by the Department of Agricultural Economics at Nanjing University. Those works adhered to the methodology pioneered by Cornell University agronomist John Lossing Buck, treating the household as an entrepreneurial enterprise rather than as a node within the circulation of capital.[22] By contrast, Wu's team argued that although peasant households and inland tea factories *appeared* as independent firms, they were *in fact* enmeshed in crippling relationships of financial dependence. Whereas Buck presumed that the peasant was a petty capitalist, Wu Juenong's team concluded that the peasant shared more in common with a waged worker. The latter's methodology made visible the various barriers to capital accumulation that were hidden within Buck's approach.

The Peasantry

Wu Juenong's team undertook the first attempt to comprehensively account for the scale and organization of the tea trade. Based on data from the 1915 census, they calculated that 1.5 million households were engaged in tea cultivation, totaling 9.1 million people. After adding women, children, and hired workers, they concluded—admittedly, polemically so—that some 17.9 million people in China, both employees and dependents, relied upon tea for survival, about 3.6 percent of a nation of 500 million. The Nanjing University team noted that most of the Qimen households they interviewed were full or part owners. Such distinctions were imprecise, however, and the surveyors warned against reading too much into them: "It is unavoidable that many people did not want to tell the truth, especially those families who had some savings. Further, of those families in debt, many were not perpetually stuck in debt but simply relied upon casual borrowing and lending."[23]

Tea-growing families needed to, first, cultivate and pick the leaves, then, second, put the leaves through an initial round of drying and wilting, converting the fresh leaves into semiprocessed *maocha*, before selling them. For peasants on the verge of debt, the lack of ready cash proved an obstacle to production, which required working capital for manure, equipment upkeep, and a hired workforce. The surveyors wrote: "the tea households which live on the mountains have very small and narrow rooms. They don't have any special facilities for processing tea, and they all just use their homes. They don't use any specialized tools or woks fixed in one place." The actual amounts of expenditures and revenue represented low stakes. "It is clear," wrote the surveyors, "the investments are small, and generally, in all the counties, the profits are thin." Families faced several natural risks, including poor weather conditions and insect blight. After one Zhejiang county was hit by pests one year, the "helpless tea households pooled together money to perform a Daoist ceremony, pleading with whatever god of insects to pardon them." The biggest threat to their livelihood, however, remained market prices. The surveyors initially assumed that the peasant household would first obtain working capital to cultivate the tea shrubs planted on their own land and then sell their product to the tea factories during the season. They discovered how most households were able to survive only by relying upon outside loans, sometimes borrowing three times in a year.[24]

As the leaves were plucked, the peasants converged on the Qimen marketplace to sell their *maocha* (figure 22). Surveyors complained that the peasants were too casual, transporting the leaves in cloth bags, bamboo baskets, sometimes even clay pots. As a result, the leaves were

Figure 22. Bales of plucked tealeaves at a local market. Tea Industry Photograph Collection, ca. 1885. Baker Library, Harvard Business School (olvwork710897).

harmed, either too dry or overly oxidized. Wu Juenong recalled: "'As the spring rains fall, the tea peasants suffer as if their hearts are sizzling in oil [*xin ru gunyou jian*].' When I was in the village, I would hum these words to myself daily, because every day I would see tea peasants on the road with their backs hunched over and carrying cloth sacks on their shoulders, knocking on the door of every tea factory." Sometimes, the peasants might walk several miles before finally selling off their harvest. At the start of the season, Qimen peasants enjoyed a competitive market, but as time passed, prices were prone to collapse, and merchants resorted to nasty bargaining tricks: "Most of the factories do not obey the rules laid out by the merchant guilds, so they slash prices and manipulate scales as they please. . . . It is enough to shock any observer." Faced with diminished demand, peasants had little lever-age. "Tea factories take advantage of the fact that the peasants cannot delay selling raw tea. If they hesitate just a little, then the leaves will spoil and become trash." Even if peasants successfully raised prices, the merchants could push them back down as a cartel.[25]

The Inland Factories

The factories that purchased the raw leaves were originally simply retail "shops" (*hao*). Over time, they took over responsibilities for re-fining leaves and became de facto specialized workshops, as typified by the Jiang family of Shexian. The factories needed facilities for only sev-eral months per year. Their normal operation expenses included "rent-ing buildings and tools, wages for workers, firewood, and payment for transportations and duties." Their profit margin also depended on how skillfully they could negotiate down the price of leaves from the peasants. In the central regions of Hubei and Hunan, the factories were larger, and the managers funded their operations from personal wealth or partnerships. But in Huizhou, the factories were small, and Wu Jue-nong's team observed that only two or three Qimen houses could sup-ply their own capital. The rest of the 180 factories relied upon loans from the Jiujiang and Shanghai treaty-port merchants. Those factories pooled together loans from the coastal cities with local partners; some-times even the peasants would contribute their raw leaves as capital, claiming dividends from the gross profits.[26]

The tea factories were highly ephemeral, set up at the outset of each season and dissolving at the end. Few laid permanent claim to buildings and tools, a practice that stood in stark contrast to the capital-intensive plantations of South Asia and Japan. As one manager explained: "Our financial situation is a lot like cooking rice. If you take one liter, then two people can get through one meal. But if three people are eating, then understandably you'll feel only half full." They roasted leaves in rented buildings, in their family ancestral hall, and even inside rooms in their house. The most colorful example came from the Tunxi green tea districts, where workshops were called "snail factories" (*luosi chahao*) due to their "temporary and unfixed nature, just like snails who roam far and wide." The same title applied to the peddlers who ran between the tea families and the houses, known as "snail guests."[27] Because the tea factories were dependent on outside capital, their nature was almost as transitory as that of itinerant peddlers, separated by a difference of degree rather than kind.

The Tea Warehouses

Finally, the surveyors discovered that the "compradoresque" tea warehouse merchants were the key to understanding the entire trade. The treaty-port warehouses held the inland factories in thrall to them, but for years the precise mechanics of this relationship escaped the grasp of both inside participants and outside observers. In 1931, a report filed by the Shanghai Commercial Savings Bank noted, "The tea warehouses . . . play the role of brokers yet earn such great profits. How they do so is guarded as a top secret [*huimo rushen*]. Outsiders find it difficult to discern the truth."[28] The breakthrough in analysis by Wu Juenong's team was to foreground the movement of credit. It was precisely the sense of confusion and abstraction in the marketplace, surveyors claimed, that enabled the treaty-port merchants to take advantage of their inland partners. If the political economy of tea could mystify most urban economists, then the circuit between countryside and treaty port must have appeared downright opaque to the average peasant, who occupied the unenviable position of speculating on international tea markets while living hundreds of miles away from Shanghai. Though they approached each season with a cautious attitude, the peasantry always wound up bearing the brunt of each fall in price.

As heir to the comprador system, the warehouses' initial role was to play broker between the inland factories and foreign firms (figures 23 and 24). In 1915 Shanghai, thirty-eight international firms participated in the trade, most from Britain, with others from Russia, Germany, France, Italy, and India. The warehouses became an "objective necessity" in an anarchic marketplace. Foreign firms placed their orders based upon early samples, with weeks passing between initial order and final delivery. To avoid cheating, firms relied upon Chinese guarantors. The warehouse merchants solidified their own reputation while policing membership into their guild. Initially, they simply served to purchase and sell finished products, but as greater demand spurred more production, inland factories looked to the warehouses for capital as well. As a result, the tea warehouse "gradually left its position as a pure broker

Figure 23. Gouache painting of a tea warehouse during the days of the Canton trade. Note the European merchants in the foreground. Copyright 2018 by The Kelton Foundation.

[*yahang*] and suddenly became a credit institution [*xinyong jiguan*]." Before plucking began in April, the warehouses sent agents into the countryside. They met with prospective peddlers and factory managers, drafting agreements based on personal trust, last year's performance, and the market forecast. Each warehouse was expected to lend out between one and four million *yuan*, but the warehouses themselves were not heavily capitalized, possessing between thirty to one hundred thousand *yuan* in cash. In preparation, they sought out loans from Shanghai banks or local native banks with an interest rate of about 10 percent, which they passed on at 15 percent.[29]

The crucial point was that because the warehouses were both brokers and financiers, they claimed at least three different sources of profit. First, in their role as lender, they charged a 15 percent rate of interest. Second, as transportation agents, they charged over a dozen small fees for handling tea, transport taxes, rental space in Shanghai,

Figure 24. A tea warehouse at the turn of the twentieth century. Tea Industry Photograph Collection, ca. 1885. Baker Library, Harvard Business School (olvwork710941).

and weighing expenses, all of which took off another 5 percent from gross profits. The third source derived from the complexity of the financial agreements between factories and warehouses, instruments in which the warehouses' two roles were blended together. The complexity escaped even some of the surveyors, who treated the warehouses as a typical middleman lender, uninvolved in the production of tea. For instance, Fu Hongzhen, a surveyor who had joined Wu Juenong in Qimen, described the risks faced by warehouses. "When sales are good and the houses do not lose money," he wrote, "then the warehouses can merely sit there and collect a monthly interest of fifteen percent." They thus had "special powers" (*tequan*) over the debtors. Nevertheless, Fu warned, the warehouses needed to be judicious in their loans, for "when the market fails, then the warehouses must also shut down with the factories. When the factories win, the warehouses win. When the factories lose, the warehouses suffer."[30]

What Fu Hongzhen had failed to consider was that the warehouses also acted as agents on behalf of the factories, and they enjoyed immediate access to the factory's only assets: the tea itself. Thus, the warehouses held all the cards—and they almost never lost. They monopolized market information, they owned the factories' debts, and they handled the factories' stock. "The function of the loan is not simply to claim interest," Wu Juenong noted. "It also allows them to control the distribution and sale of tealeaves, such that all of the factories' power to sell is monopolized by the warehouses." As the Shanghai bank survey put it, the warehouses were both a "brokerage institution" and an "institution for financial adjustment." Fan Hejun, another surveyor, clarified how the warehouses took advantage of their dual roles. Typically, the warehouses would first distribute advance loans to the factories, and after the first harvest, they would switch roles and act as agents selling leaves to foreign companies on behalf of the factories. But before distributing profits back to the factories, the warehouses would switch roles again, and as financiers they would deduct the principal and interest from the profits on sales. The first sale of the season would go toward paying off one-half of the advances, the second sale would pay off the rest, and only with the third sale would the factories receive any net revenue. In effect, this meant the tea warehouses enjoyed "first dibs" on the share owed to the factories. They were almost always protected from losses. "The nature of this type of loan," Fan concluded, "is no different from what the banking world calls a collateralized loan [diya fangkuan]." These "stable and dependable" loans were "not dangerous at all to the warehouses."[31]

A comparative perspective may be helpful here. American economist Gerald Jaynes coined the term "post-harvest payment scheme" to describe the economics of the postbellum (1862–1882) South. With the dearth of circulating credit after the Civil War, planters and freedmen workers negotiated a type of staggered payment scheme, similar to sharecropping, wherein planters would initially pay the workers only subsistence levels of wages, with the rest of their paycheck and any profits distributed only after the crop was transferred and sold. In a successful year, the workers would be fully compensated. Short of that, any gross revenue would first be claimed by the planters, which left the workers exposed to the risk of earning no further income. The planters effectively invested in capital inputs for cotton production but only paid for a portion of labor costs, just enough to keep the freedmen alive. Jaynes cut through the confusion of these arrangements and characterized the underlying relationship this way: "By far the most important and ironic aspect of post-harvest payments was the fact that they made the laborer a creditor of the planter!" A similar post-harvest payment scheme developed between the tea factories and warehouses of China. The factories, relying on the advances of the warehouses, would first ship tea to Shanghai to be sold. In exchange, the warehouses gave the factories promissory notes that could be redeemed at the end of the season. All profits were first appropriated by the warehouses. As with the freedmen in the American South, the inland factories were exposed to the risk of a bad season, in which case their promissory notes would lose value. The warehouses shared almost none of the risk, and the factories had no recourse. The actual effect was to enable the warehouses to borrow the factories' labor, embodied in tea, without the requirement to fully pay them back. Surveyors wrote that the warehouses "understood clearly but played dumb" about how they accumulated so much wealth by the end of each season. They used the "magic of advance loans" (xiandian shengchanjin de moli) to "fish" for profits.[32]

By the mid-thirties, the Great Depression took its toll on the export markets, and capital began to dry up. The inland factories and brokers began to extend the same relationships of credit and debt—the magic of advances—to the peasant households themselves. The peasants of Tunxi, for instance, had come to depend on tea in order to survive the winters, when they would run out of food. For these families, there was no option other than to borrow grain reserves from the peddlers, an arrangement known locally as "lending grain silver" (fang liangyin). This grain silver was to be returned with interest, and again the terms were confusing and harsh. First, monthly interest was 2 percent based upon the current market price for grains, unless prices had fallen, in which case the lender charged the original market price. Second, for every dan of grain borrowed (133 pounds), the family needed to pay half a yuan of silver. Third, the lenders had the right of first refusal to purchase the family's tea crops. Formally, the peasants were supposed to repay the grain silver loans through cash and not by direct barter. But the tea peasants had in effect granted the peddlers and factories a lien on their harvest, for they could not pay off the debts until after they sold their maocha, either to the tea factories or directly to the snail guests. On average, tea accounted for 60 percent of the families' incomes, a dependence that was reflected in the fact that most families did not repay their grain silver loans until June or July, well into the thick of tea season.[33]

In Tunxi, surveyors affiliated with the Nanjing school run by Buck stated that "the local tea land is almost entirely owned by the tea families, only very few pay rent." However, if the peasants had mortgaged out their tea to the lenders in advance, then their options were already constrained, and their status as independent farmers appeared less reality than fiction. They were not selling tea as an asset over which they had ownership; they were merely returning the initial advance along with the labor they added to it. As with the so-called free labor workforce of rural Bengal discussed in chapter 6, economic duress circumscribed any straightforward notions of freedom or independence for the Chinese tea peasantry. Though Nanjing University surveyors failed to note these relationships in the Qimen black tea districts as well, Wu Juenong did not:

> Everyone knows the saying "grains at the start of the year cannot reach year's end." It's especially true in Qimen. . . . The money they get from tea in the spring will already be eaten up by year's end. The only solution is to sell next year's *maocha* in advance.[34]

Jairus Banaji has shown how this type of advance system could be viewed as a disguised form of wage labor, and Kathy Le Mons Walker has illuminated similar dynamics in the Yangzi Delta. The advances reproduced the same relationship of dependence that characterized the formal waged economy: instead of a salary, the peasants received a partial loan; and instead of returning profit in the form of a commodity, the farmer would provide interest in the form of their crops. Whether agrarian interest or industrial profit, both represented net economic surplus. The complex loans were designed to protect the creditor at each stage. Wu Juenong wrote, "'The sheep's wool is skimmed off of the sheep's body': these huge losses from falling prices were always transferred onto the body of the direct producers."[35] Over the decades of fierce competition, global political chaos, and world depression, the tea warehouses faced the lightest risk. The thirties were a period of tumultuous world markets, and the decline of the tea peasantry occurred so predictably that it appeared almost preordained.

By moving backwards from the tea peasant to the factory and finally the warehouses, Wu Juenong's team came to understand that the story of the impoverished peasant and the undercapitalized factories—and therefore the underlying obstacles to reviving the tea trade—made sense only within the context of an abstract web of circulating advances. Wu Juenong and Hu Haochuan creatively summarized their diagnosis of Chinese tea by listing the three deadly "isms" that befell it. First, the warehouses practiced a "handcuff-tea-ism" (*bangcha zhuyi*). They used all sorts of tricks to control information, money, and tea, and they actively maintained the separation between inland producers and coastal buyers. Second, the factory managers found this level of "oppression" unbearable, but "they, too, enjoyed power over another relationship of debt, which allowed them some form of resistance." They could "turn around and pass it onto the tea-growing mountain households." The factories extracted extra revenue from the peasants through their own set of "tricks." The factories' attitude was: "Something has been stolen from home, so they go out and commit a robbery. . . . This 'compensation-ism' [*quchang zhuyi*] was, in substance, a 'steal-tea-ism.'" Finally, there were the peasant households. Because they had no others to exploit, their only recourse for "breaking even was to let go of responsibilities, to be careless in plucking and refining tea, to spend very little on their operations." The common saying among peasants was: "The big fish eats the small fish; the small fish eats shrimp; the shrimp has nothing to eat, so it must eat mud!" The surveyors felt sympathy for the producers, who were forced to embrace a "cheat-tea-ism" (*qiaocha zhuyi*). Here, Wu Juenong's team provided an in-depth explanation for Chinese tea's declining quality. They proclaimed a final diagnosis: "The sickness of the tea industry lies in these three habits: handcuffing, stealing, and cheating tea. Without a massive overhaul, this disease cannot be cured [*bukejiuyao*]!"[36]

MAKERS AND TAKERS: THE CRITIQUE OF THE TEA WAREHOUSES AND THE CATEGORIES OF POLITICAL ECONOMY

Although the 1930s surveys conducted by Wu Juenong and his team were grounded in empirical data and firsthand observation, their conclusions were not universally shared. During the same period, Buck's

Nanjing University team, using the methods of American agronomy, claimed to see only a collection of atomized "farm business operators" whose situation did not demand radical overhaul but only "rational and scientific social planning" at the edges. We can posit, then, that Wu Juenong's team framed its findings from within a particular set of values and economic principles. This was occasionally revealed in its descriptions of the merchants' profit as "not fair and just" and as a violation of "the ethics of commerce" (*shangye daode*), "uniform fairness" (*yiwei de chiping*), and "justice" (*gongdao*).[37] As with the Indian nationalists' rhetoric of "freedom," the Chinese reformers used the transhistorical language of morality, but really they were wrestling with social problems that were historically specific.

What can the language of anti-comprador criticism tell us about changes in twentieth-century China? To begin with, the tea reformers' particular criticisms of the tea warehouse merchant were a microcosm of a general condemnation of the comprador merchant across the national economy. Two themes in particular stood out. First, the surveyors characterized the tea warehouses' commercial and financial functions as "unproductive," meaning they did not add any value to the tea commodity. Wu Juenong and Hu Haochuan described them as merchants who "reap without working" (*bulao er huo*), and they referred to their financial practices as "unproductive loans." Similarly, Tsuchiya Keizō, a member of the Mitsui Bank's Shanghai branch, noted that Japanese companies in China had long ago abandoned the comprador system, because it was a "useless thing" (*muyō no mono*).[38]

Second, the tea researchers claimed that the warehouses actively harmed the industry's growth by draining away capital that could be invested into production. Worse than innocuous dependents, the warehouses were "parasitic merchants."[39] A local publication in the Tunxi districts pushed the host-parasite metaphor further, stating:

> Tea peasants and tea workers are the foundation of the tea industry. This foundation has long been eaten away by those [merchant] devils. . . . The ancients would say "things must first be rotten on the inside before the bugs appear" [*wu bi zifu er hou chongfu zhi*]. The new competition from foreign tea is certainly scary, but it cannot wipe away the inner strength of our Chinese tea. Exploitation by those devils, however, can certainly cause our entire tea industry to collapse.[40]

Labels of "parasitism," too, were echoed in general discourses. A study titled *China's Comprador System* (1927) published by the Commercial Press in Shanghai stated: "In polite terms, we can say that the compradors lack patriotic enthusiasm. In cruder terms, we can simply say they are a pest on the nation [*guojia zhi mao*]." The same study described the compradors as an outmoded institution that will either be "promptly eliminated by natural selection" (*ziran zhi taotai*), or, because it was a "superfluous organ" (*pianzhi*, lit. an extra thumb), be "chopped off" by the foreign merchants. It concluded by describing the merchants as an "appendage" (*fuyong zhi wu*) on the "skeleton" of China. The appendage metaphor was also used by Mao Zedong, who wrote that the landlord and comprador classes were "appendages" of the international bourgeoisie. The most vivid expression again came from the tea reformers, who described the warehouse merchants as "an ulcer that has developed into an extra appendage" (*ju cheng fugu*).[41]

If so many voices agreed that the tea warehouses, and the compradors more generally, were unproductive and parasitic, then their criticism logically turned on a specific definition of what counted as productive. In the western European tradition, it "was realized by the mid-eighteenth century," Helen Boss Heslop has argued, "that *any restrictive definition of the economy and the economic implies a boundary with a non-economic world*," and the converse was also true. This boundary could be drawn along many different criteria. In earlier periods, "productive" encompassed, for instance, any activity wherein one realizes their own potential; as foreign trade, which transfers overseas wealth into domestic society; or, under the prevailing notion of productive within various early modern economic schools, as labor that results in physical utility, envisioned in the crops that were converted into tax and rent. It is noteworthy, then, that the twentieth-century reformers adopted the modern definition associated with political economy and outlined by Chen Chi (see chapter 5): a productive worker created not only physical utility but also commercial profit, determined by productivity and embodied in commodities. Smith is often credited with establishing this definition, one that also relegated all nonproductive actors, from kings to servants to churches and temples, to the status of "Smithian parasites." In the context of the Chinese tea trade, a telling passage came from an article in a reformer paper that stated, "If we seek the actual roots and origins of [profits from tea exports], then clearly it is the tea peasants and laborers who are the true creators [*chuangzaozhe*]" of value.[42]

This definition of productive labor—as labor productive of profit in exchange—also implied a similar distinction between productive and unproductive capital: the only productive capital was that invested into commodity production, excluding capital in transport, distribution, and finance.[43] The compradors of China could be labeled "unproductive" and "parasitic" insofar as (1) they provided not labor but capital and (2) their capital was not invested directly into production but only used to extract profit from exchange and loans. Any value in the tea trade had actually been "created" exclusively by peasants and tea factories, later appropriated by the tea warehouses. If, for Wu Juenong's team, the key to understanding the immiseration in the tea districts was the opposition between peasant and comprador merchant, then underlying these concrete figures was the more abstract political-economic binary of productive labor and circulating capital.

From a comparative perspective, this rhetoric brings to mind other examples of anti-commercial and anti-financial discourses in modern world history. Modern anti-Semitism, Moishe Postone argued, relies upon an opposition of industrial capital, described as concrete and "'natural' artisanal labor," versus abstract and "'parasitic' finance capital." Another example came from the drain theory of India, described in chapter 6. Its proponents depicted British colonial rule as a "vampiric" force that had "drained, looted, and pillaged" wealth from Indian peasants and artisans to British corporations and banks. Dadabhai Naoroji wrote, "English capitalists do not merely lend, but with their capital they themselves invade the country. The produce of the capital is mostly eaten up by their countrymen."[44]

The idea that "labor in general" formed the substance of economic value, I have suggested, was a modern one. It corresponded to the historically specific conditions of generalized wage labor. Within Chinese history, the historical specificity of such discourses appears most acutely when juxtaposed against the treaty-port merchants' favorable reputation throughout the eighteenth and nineteenth centuries. This transformation of economic categories was tied to transformations of practice. In Marx's history of classical economic thought, he argued that earlier forms of circulating capital, including merchants, trading companies, and lenders, *had been* crucially important in previous eras of capital accumulation. Simply think of the English East India Company. Merchants extended networks of trade across vast bodies of water, opened up new frontiers and highlands, and expropriated land and labor by exposing them to the global marketplace. Most recently, Sven Beckert has described this era as the period of "war capitalism." However, the work of classical political economy signaled a new pattern of accumulation that was to become hegemonic, one premised upon hiring large workforces in a central factory system and continually upgrading the methods of production. Classical writers took these social patterns for granted, abstracted from their experiences in manufacturing centers such as Manchester and Glasgow. As the independence and dominance of "large-scale industry" marginalized the activities of merchants and traders *in practice*, the latter grew less relevant *in theory*. Tied to a definition of value animated by labor, Smith and Ricardo were "perplexed" and "embarrassed" by the possibility that commerce and finance could once independently create value. Merchants were "demoted" from their earlier significance and were now viewed as the mere "servant of industrial production." In Marx's words, the classical thinkers saw the world "from the standpoint of the capitalist mode of production and within its limits."[45] Similarly, Chinese writers criticized the comprador system because it fell outside the narrow equation of "value = labor," and this was as strong an indication as any that they had naturalized the same standpoint of the capitalist mode of production as that of the classical economists.

Marx's notes represented more schema than fact, a hypothesis that was later fleshed out by historians in their explorations of the early modern worlds of Islam and the Mediterranean. This story also dovetailed with the trajectory of the Chinese tea trade. During the eighteenth and nineteenth centuries, networks of merchants from the treaty port to the hinterlands promoted both the extensification of tea manufacture into new households as well as the intensification of labor. Merchants were the crucial agents who made the golden years of the tea trade possible. Similarly, the major account houses of the silk trade promoted extensive cultivation of cocoons in the countryside, supervised new types of woven fabrics by household women producers, and invested in modern machine filatures in Shanghai and Wuxi.[46] These and other export brokers *had* intervened into and "improved" export production during its expansive nineteenth-century phases. This was, not coincidentally, the period in which merchant activity was held in highest regard among Qing officials.

But if the political economists demoted merchant capital due to industrialization in western Europe, then how can we account for a parallel shift in Republican China, where large-scale industry remained negligible? The role of competition was crucial here, too. Chinese reformers constantly measured the Chinese tea trade against its overseas rivals, from Lu Ying's travels in the early 1900s to Wu Juenong's exploratory trip across East, Southeast, and South Asia in 1934.[47] Practices of labor-intensive manufacture in Huizhou and the Wuyi Mountains had been outpaced by new forms of capital-intensive production in Assam and Japan, and reformers came to grasp the connections between the immiserated Chinese tea districts on the one hand and the objective pressures of competition from overseas on the other. If the processes of capitalist production historically constituted the conditions of possibility for political economy's theory of value—if the theory only made sense to someone living in a society centered upon capitalist production—then Chinese nationalist reformers could grasp it because they saw themselves not merely as citizens of China but also embedded within patterns of industrialization on a global scale.

Within the history of Chinese tea, this reimagining of production along capital-intensive lines began with the late Qing tea crisis of the 1890s. After Lu Ying's travels to Ceylon and Darjeeling, reformers began to speak about tea through a new set of concepts that gave primacy to labor.[48] Lu Ying had divided industrial activity into the component categories of agriculture, manufacture, and commerce; or, within the context of tea, cultivation, refinement, and marketing. "From growing and refining to marketing tea," he wrote of the colonial plantations, "everything is directly handled by one company, and even the overseas distributors are shareholders. But if we look back at our own country, tea production is scattered like sand, . . . resulting in layers of exploitation, with no potential for unity and improvement."[49]

Decades later, Wu Juenong continued to use the same tripartite scheme. Of course, these terms were not new to Chinese political thought: they were the three non-gentry occupations within Confucianism. The novelty was the integration of all three, with manufacture at the center. Wu Juenong explained why this reorganization of economic life marked a break with the past. In the opening pages of his 1935 co-authored treatise, he drew a subtle distinction between two possible interpretations of the Chinese term *chaye*, which could be translated as an abbreviation of either "tea trade" or "tea industry":

> The noun *chaye* was not invented until tea attained such a lofty position within the export trade. In our national consciousness, *chaye* has always been seen as nothing more than a commercial undertaking. . . . [In fact,] *chaye* spans from cultivation to harvest, from manufacture to the final product, all the way to transport and marketing—really, it is an enterprise [*qiye*] that consists of all three branches of agriculture, manufacture, and commerce.[50]

Wu Juenong's distinction between commercial undertaking and enterprise corresponded to the binaristic opposition between merchant and industrial capital in political economy. The latter was so novel as a stand-alone concept that Wu borrowed the term "*qiye*," a loanword from Japan (*kigyō*), to do it justice.[51] The clearest expressions of what Wu Juenong meant by "enterprise" came in his descriptions of what it *did not* mean. He wrote that Chinese "producers still do not understand the principle of enterprise with regards to expenses, and they do not invest effectively." Because of the warehouses' "unfair and unjust" methods, "the tea producers simply cannot earn a profit and the meaning of enterprise [*qiye de yiyi*] has been lost."[52] He concluded by offering the following remarks on what truly capitalist production would look like:

> Why have the black tea–producing nations India, Ceylon, and Java been able to gain business so vigorously? Why have Japan and Taiwan, who produce green and oolong teas, been able to compete and expand their position? The reason is their wealthy resources and their effective methods. Within modern capitalist society, the saying goes that "if you have money you can make ghosts do your work" [*youqian neng shi gui tuimo*]. Only with wealth and resources can you have effective methods.[53]

Money to make ghosts do your work. This phrase dated back to the twelfth century, and Wu Juenong had repurposed it to describe the essence of modern enterprise: the accumulation of past profits and their reinvestment into the improvement of living human labor. More broadly, historians have observed that Wu's distinction between enterprise and commercial undertaking had already emerged in the late

Qing. In 1890s political circles, Wellington Chan noted, "a growing distinction was made between *shangye* as commercial enterprise and *shiye* as industrial enterprise . . . [which] reflected the growth of social distinctions between the two groups of merchants."[54]

The emergence of these categories in Chinese economic thought helps explain why reformers criticized the comprador merchants in moral and transhistorical terms. The production of commodities and the principles governing them began to appear as a timeless and natural part of human activity. This inversion of history can be seen as a form of reification intrinsic to the practices of capitalist production. In the actual history of the tea trade, it was the merchants—the foreign firms, tea warehouses, and inland guest merchants—who were originally responsible for the expansion of trade and production. However, this *history* ran counter to the *logic* of capitalist production. Within the latter, the process of wealth creation begins from the farmers, workshops, and other producers whose activities constitute the substance of value. Commodity production appears to have emerged prior to commerce: a timeless feature of human civilization that obeys "eternal natural laws independent of history."[55] The pressures of capitalist competition, with its unrelenting emphasis on production, naturalized this anachronistic view. That it would become the foundation for transhistorical and moral discourses on the treaty-port comprador suggests just how deeply the social logic of industrial production was already woven into the social fabric of early Republican China.

TEA COOPERATIVES AS LABOR-INTENSIVE INDUSTRIALIZATION

For both Chinese and Indian thinkers grappling with the problem of "imperialism" in the tea trade, national liberation did not entail rejecting modern industrial capital but rather an embrace of its beneficial practices. Whereas Indian nationalists spoke of emancipating the indentured tea coolie as a bridge to the indigenization of capital, Chinese reformers sought to eliminate the Chinese comprador in order to strengthen the peasantry and, by extension, national industries. The best path for "improving production and marketing" and hence "competing with the tea industries of the great powers," wrote Wu Juenong, was "none other than the promotion of cooperatives."[56]

Rural cooperatives were a widely popular idea throughout the Nanjing Decade. The earliest discussions began during the May Fourth era, and the cooperative was eventually popularized by the government in the 1930s. From 1923 to 1935, the total number exploded from nineteen to more than twenty-six thousand, attracting a wide variety of political actors and ideologies. For the Nationalist government and modern banks, they were a sound financial investment and a force for tempering social radicalism. For famed conservative Liang Shuming, they offered protection for the traditional Chinese village, and for educator James Yen, they were a vehicle of Christian social uplift.[57] The version promoted by Wu Juenong's team unfolded from its definition of industrial enterprise. Its members sought to transplant the principles of the Indian plantations into rural China, but unlike the British colony, they did not have access to robust financial markets. In lieu of liquid wealth, they looked to pool and share resources, a peculiar form of capitalist enterprise for a peasantry that lacked capital. It was a quixotic undertaking that would require a new social ethic to substitute for material resources. At the end of its first season, from 1933 to 1934, the Qimen cooperative reported:

> If we wish to fully break apart this web of exploitation, we must use the "all for one, one for all" [*renren wei wo, wo wei renren*] spirit of the cooperative methods, to exhort and lead the peasants to unite and struggle together. . . . Qimen peasants have always held onto the idea that they should first plan for themselves. They greatly lack cohesion [*jiehexing*] and the ability to unite [*tuanjieli*]. But what they truly lack, more than these, is capital.[58]

For the technical dimension, Wu stated, "The goal is for members to produce with their own property, to manufacture by themselves, to market goods by themselves." The cooperative, by eliminating middlemen merchants and pooling together village resources, would run more efficiently, making Chinese tea competitive globally. Wu Juenong believed that the question of quality was less important than the question of speed. The "quality" of the Chinese leaf remained better than the black teas of South Asia and the green teas of Japan, with the only difference the "large amounts of English and Dutch capital" and "capitalist methods" harnessed by those competitors. If producers in China could successfully incorporate capital improvements, then they too

could offer "excellent goods at low prices."[59] These were lofty technical goals, but at first the main focus remained social organization.

Lu Ying had established a "model tea garden" in Pingli Village of
Qimen in 1915, but it quickly fell into disrepair. Nearly two decades
later, Wu Juenong established the first tea producer cooperative, known
as the Anhui Province Tea Improvement Center, on the same site. The
first season produced only a small amount of tea—fifty-nine total
boxes—but organizers were satisfied. A report from the first year stated,
"The goal was to create a foundation to stimulate a mass movement
for cooperatives." The authors stated that at first the peasantry, though
sympathetic and curious, "hemmed and hawed" for several months
without joining the cooperative. The staff then decided to aggressively
recruit new members. Their new policy was: "To the outside world,
we would take on the name cooperative, but internally we would rely
upon the same people to run everything." The center's main function
was to operate a tea factory that processed *maocha* purchased from
nearby households. As they bought leaves, they simultaneously added
the seller's name to the list of members, giving them a share of profits
but without charging them fees. "This type of 'nonprofit cooperative
experiment' naturally was a very dangerous approach," the authors
acknowledged. Organizers lacked enough funds to pay the peasants for
raw leaves, so they volunteered to forgo their salaries for four months.
"Afterwards, however, in a year that would otherwise be considered
lean, we discovered that this method was surprisingly effective." Within
Qimen, "there arose an enthusiastic surge of response."[60]

Over the next few years, the cooperatives garnered support from
the government and modern banks, and organizers experimented with
substantively improving tea production itself. In July 1934, the NEC
and the Ministry of Industry renamed the cooperative the Qimen Tea
Improvement Center, with an executive board occupied by national bureaucrats. As Wu Juenong traveled overseas, his protégé Hu Haochuan
took over as director (figure 25).[61] The next year, Hu invited outside
technicians and engineers to improve tea production.

If the first season's goal was simply to prove the viability of the economic model without altering production itself, then in subsequent
years, Hu Haochuan and his team turned their attention to scientific
experiments. An engineer named Qian Liang recalled being hired to
work in Qimen in 1935. He and his colleagues set up a "chemical

Figure 25. Wu Juenong (*left*) and Hu Haochuan (*second from left*) at the Qimen Tea Improvement Center in the 1930s. Courtesy of Wu Ning.

experiment laboratory," where they conducted experiments to determine what made for the best quality tea. In one instance, an engineer tried to re-create the flavor of Japanese Gyokuro tea, which is fired at lower temperatures and for long periods. That day, the entire staff stood around the stove for more than ten hours watching the leaves together, excitedly "rubbing shoulder to shoulder until the experiment was complete." "That one tea season," Qian recalled, "was one of the most memorable in my life." Another engineer, Feng Shaoqiu, described how the cooperative began to employ foreign-made machines. In 1936, they purchased two small-scale machines from Taiwan, one which rolled leaves and one which dried them by ventilating heat. In 1937, they purchased several machines from the German Krupp corporation, including a large-scale rolling machine, a sifting machine, and a drying machine, all of which had been designed to be used in colonial India. Feng reported several bottlenecks resulting from relying on a hybrid of industrial machines and older manual methods but that such setbacks were part of the normal evolution of industrialization. The first year had resolved the "question of quality," and year two meant "taking measures to resolve the question of quantity." To address the lack of a wilting machine, they built their own makeshift version, putting aside a special room and piping in warm air from conventional heat sources. Machine-based tea production was able to "phase out the backwards methods of feet rolling and sun drying, improving quality and raising quantity."[62]

In the 1930s, Chinese tea sought to achieve the same industrial revolution that its counterparts in Assam had pursued forty years earlier. But as suggested in chapter 4, the history of technological innovation requires paying attention both to individual breakthroughs as well as their generalized adoption. On this latter question reformers felt the pressures of comprador capital. Feng concluded that although the cooperative had resolved the technical question of improvement, it could not escape the "rot of the social system" embodied in the tea warehouses. The cooperative members may have at first successfully avoided lenders by deferring salaries and rounding up alternate sources of support, but the problem of capital grew unavoidable in the following years, as the success of the cooperatives tempted government expansion.[63] After the NEC inserted itself in 1934, it aggressively established new cooperatives around the tea districts of Fujian, Hunan, Hubei, Zhejiang, and Jiangxi. Nearly forty new cooperatives were added in two years. As Wu Juenong wrote years later,

> Because we had not finished planning an organizational structure for marketing to Shanghai, the middlemen merchants were able to simply extend and intensify their usual skimming methods from the inland mer-

chants to us. . . . Most cooperatives lost money, and potential investor banks were scared off. Thus, the tea cooperative movement found itself stuck in an interrupted state.[64]

Wu feared that the peasantry, faced with these difficulties, would abandon the experiments. "Once the people in charge ran into a conflict between ideal and reality," he recalled, "they couldn't help but fall back onto old habits, focusing on small details at the expense of the big picture, in the end losing a great opportunity." However, he stressed that one could not say "the idea of the cooperative itself is a mistake" but only that the current surrounding context, the social and economic system of China, was unable to "fully absorb a new way of thinking."[65] These social tensions between the reformers' producer-focused cooperatives and the older, merchant-centered financial system were finally laid bare in the Shanghai tea merchant strike of 1936.

THE 1936 SHANGHAI TEA WAREHOUSE STRIKE

On April 23, 1936, the headline of the Shanghai-based *China Press* read: "Tea Hongs Strike in Protest Move." Unlike a typical worker strike, in which employees withhold their labor, this strike was organized by the fourteen most powerful tea warehouse firms in Shanghai, which withheld their capital. Unless the government rolled back its latest proposal, they would not honor the promissory notes that they had distributed to tea factories and peasants in Anhui and Jiangxi. At the start of the season, the warehouses had issued one-half of the value of their advance loans to the countryside, with the rest to be paid only after they received the tea. In the meantime, throughout the credit-starved rural economy, those first notes traveled as valuable currency, even greasing the wheels of the cotton trade. As noted by one local Chamber of Commerce, "The livelihood of several millions of tea growers, collectors, and merchants depends upon the unimpeded circulation of the loan drafts." The Shanghai merchants announced that in the city alone, over forty other businesses relied upon the warehouses for their operations, and the warehouses directly employed twelve hundred people from Anhui who worked as porters. On top of this, interviews with Anhui officials suggested some two hundred-plus factories, each with dozens of workers, were involved in the trade—to say nothing of the countless family farms that survived by cultivating and selling *maocha* to them. The urban merchant strike thus threatened to plunge the rural districts into "imminent financial chaos."[66]

The merchants were protesting the Nationalist government's recent plans to integrate the entire tea trade within a central agency, known as the Anhui-Jiangxi Committee for Marketing and Transport ("Committee"). The controversy even pulled in some of the most prominent officials in the Nanjing government, T. V. Soong, head of the NEC, and H. H. Kung, minister of finance.

Then, in early May, just ten days in, the strike ended. The government claimed that the original plan was a "misunderstanding," and they announced a "compromise" by allowing the tea warehouses to play their original role as broker and creditor. A major story that had dominated the headlines of China's premier commercial and financial center suddenly disappeared from view. So what was all the fuss about?

One month later, an anonymous writer published a commentary in the left-wing economic journal *Rural China* (*Zhongguo Nongcun*) arguing that the stakes of the tea warehouse strike could not be discerned from "simply looking at superficial accounts in the newspapers."[67] Instead, one "needed to look at concrete facts" and analyze the "essence" of the tea policies beneath the surface. This author praised the original policy as part of a broader program of "economic control" necessary to revive China's export trade. The government's plan was to offer the inland tea factories loans backed by modern banks at an interest rate of only 2 percent, rather than the warehouses' customary 15 percent. The warehouses would be forced to lower their own interest rates or risk going out of business. The goal was to transform the usurious warehouses, part of the "feudal social structure" of China, into a modern institution. According to the Committee, this would enable the factories and peasants to claim their "true profits" (*zhenzheng liyi*), accumulate savings, and "create a plan to revive the entire tea trade." As H. H. Kung told reporters, "We want to improve quality. On the international market, we don't want Chinese tea to lose out because of lower quality, so we propose this policy for Anhui and Jiangxi tea along the lines of economic control policies in silk."[68]

But the warehouse merchants complained to the press that the 2 percent loans would cause them to "bleed" money, and besides, the government plan violated the principles of free and legal commerce. Above all, they argued that different agencies had lied to them during the winter, when they denied any plans for economic control were in the works. The government had waited to surprise them long after the passage of the Qingming Festival in early April, when the merchants had already begun distributing advances to the countryside.[69] From the government's perspective, the timing was strategic, reducing the warehouses' bargaining power: the firms had no choice but to cooperate in order to recover their principal. However, what the government did not expect, according to this author, was the warehouses' willingness to engage in a suicidal "counter-offensive strategy" equal to "self-annihilation," namely, their emergency decision within a matter of days to cancel the value of all of their issued credit, bankrupting the entire tea trade if the government did not relent.

For this anonymous writer, this "pledge to fight to the death" demonstrated that the warehouses understood that their very survival was at stake. He explained that the 2 percent loans were out of the question for the warehouses, for they themselves borrowed at even higher rates from foreign firms and urban banks. Although the government's plan appeared conciliatory, really it was designed to eliminate the firms altogether. As a result "the tea warehouses would have 'warehouses' but no 'tea'! [*you 'zhan' er wu 'cha' le*]."

But beyond the numbers on a contract, beyond "the surface" of the government simply "giving the warehouses a tough time," was a more fundamental "battle taking place behind the curtain" between dueling economic philosophies. Whereas the warehouses were but a "remnant of feudalism," the proposed Committee represented an earnest effort to rationally integrate production, distribution, and finance, with the shared aim of improving the competitiveness of the tea trade and the livelihood of its workers. In wiping out the middlemen merchants, the original proposal carried an "anti-imperial, anti-feudal significance."

Unfortunately, there was a complication, a plot twist that transformed the strike from a heroic drama into a "tragicomedy where one is unsure whether to laugh or to cry." The government had expected to gradually phase out the warehouses, for it was itself too weak to replace them overnight, which explained why the tea firms were ultimately emboldened to strike. For its funding, the state relied upon the Shanghai banks and, by extension, the interests of modern finance capital. As a result, "after one strong attack, the government promptly backed off." The Nanjing government's compromise was to bring the warehouses into the new Committee, enabling the firms to act as the "compradors" and "runners" for the state agency and split the profits with the Shanghai banks, ultimately changing nothing.[70] Meantime, the tea peasantry had already sold many of their leaves for a pittance during the chaos of the strike, leaving them worse off than before. Consequently, the tea peasantry had begun to riot in the villages, and they were attacking and "smashing" tea factories in Qimen. Under policies of *economic control*, this author put it, "the poor tea peasantry has been *controlled* to death."

The pseudonymous author of this scathing commentary, it was revealed decades later, was none other than Wu Juenong himself. In the mid-thirties, after overseeing the Qimen tea cooperative and then traveling across Asia and Europe, Wu had returned to China and helped the NEC plan the "economic control" of tea, envisioned as an expansion of his cooperative experiments. His privileged access enabled him to talk in detail about the significance of different rates of interest, discovered during his own survey work, as well as the interagency tug of war between left-wing economists, conservative bureaucrats, and bank representatives. In his mind, the whole episode clarified a line of demarcation between different elements in the Chinese economy. The tea warehouses and Shanghai banks stood on one side as unproductive circulating and finance capital. If the merchants had developed a reputation as parasitic appendages, then the urban banks, similarly, were "building a path towards the villages, using low rates of interest to directly suck the blood of the peasantry." On the other side was the reformers' vision of developing the productive powers of labor through accumulation and investment, institutionalized in the Committee, and symbolized by the Chinese tea peasant. This vision remained unfinished. If the policies of economic control had begun as an "anti-feudal, anti-imperialist drama," then only halfway through the performance, he concluded, the "main protagonists—the tea peasants—had been yanked from the stage. The performance could not even reach intermission without being wrapped up unexpectedly."

What lessons could be drawn from the Shanghai tea warehouse strike? Within its immediate context, the strike fit neatly within a long list of examples demonstrating the baleful effect of KMT leadership upon rural initiatives. Kate Merkel-Hess has demonstrated how the independent rural reconstruction movement of the twenties was weakened by national leadership from 1932 onward. Throughout the 1930s, Chen Yixin has shown, the KMT-led cooperative movement was plagued by problems of coordination and co-optation by local elites. And Zanasi has examined similar problems with the NEC's attempt to organize cotton production in the Yangzi Delta. These stories exhibited common themes: local leadership undermined by top-down governance from Nanjing; rural goals subjugated to the interests of urban industry and finance; economic development sacrificed for Chiang Kai-shek's projects of militarism and anticommunism; and peasant agency circumscribed by the KMT's reliance upon landlords and gentry. The most famous cases concerned the Nationalist state's attempted reforms in rural Zhejiang, Jiangsu, and Jiangxi, and these dynamics applied equally well to Wu Juenong's proposed tea marketing committee for Anhui. Wu later blamed "covert rule by the KMT's reactionary faction."[71]

Seen together, these examples seem to support the well-worn conclusion that early twentieth-century China remained hampered by traditional, imperial-era social structures founded upon the arbitrary power of self-interested elites. Only with the Communist Revolution in China and land reform in Taiwan, then, was industrial development finally achieved. But the tea warehouse strike of Shanghai also presents new details that complicate this schema. First, the strike did not so much demonstrate the persistence of traditional, *precapitalist* social elements as instead the tensions between *different historical forms of capital accumulation*, from nineteenth-century merchants to twentieth-century banks to the future prospects of state industry. Second, understanding the relationship among these forms thus requires a wider view of history. As with unfree labor in colonial India, comprador capital in China was once widely accepted, if not embraced, in the late nineteenth century before steadily being condemned as anachronistic and incompatible with the modern world. This reversal said less about the inherent conservativism of the tea merchants, who had once played a vital, dynamic role in bringing China closer in line with the rest of the world, than about the rapidity and intensity with which the global economy around them was changing—more specifically, how young Chinese reformers were engaging with international developments and translating them back into their own contexts. This sea change of economic thinking signaled real historical changes in economic life, it must be stressed, not simply a dress rehearsal for the real thing decades down the road. New political-economic concepts corresponded to new, material tensions in Chinese society, made palpably clear in the tea warehouse strike of 1936. Those fourteen Shanghai firms demonstrated to observers that they were as powerful as the Chinese government itself, and they threatened to destroy millions of *yuan* and the livelihood of tens of thousands of workers and peasants in order to forestall further change. In India, the nationalists' embrace of political-economic thinking had resulted in the abolition of labor indenture, as part of a project of developing national capital. With the abolition of comprador capital, Chinese reformers were attempting to do the same, and they would continue to pursue these goals for many more years to come. Ultimately, it was the compradoresque Shanghai tea warehouses, with their pledge to fight to the death, that understood the weighty historical stakes of that project better than anyone else.

EPILOGUE

The dream of a tea industry revolution was unexpectedly given new life during the Second World War. Over the summer and fall of 1937, Japanese forces entered the Yangzi Delta, occupying Shanghai, and chasing the Nationalist government to Chongqing in western China. Fortunately for the inland tea districts, they remained untouched. Nationalist officials viewed the export tea trade as a crucial source of support for war. They coordinated sales to the Soviet Union for money or, sometimes, direct barter for weapons. Ironically, the tea trade during the war actually outperformed the previous decades. Precisely because the Shanghai tea warehouses were sidelined by battle, officials could fill the vacuum by redirecting transportation to Hong Kong, just downstream from the original Canton system. Reformers successfully implemented policies of economic control, integrating local peasant cooperatives with national agencies for distribution. Tea sales and prices jumped by over 30 percent, in some cases breaking new records. Though the trade was finally suspended in 1942 when Japanese forces shut down Hong Kong, the four-year experiment left Wu Juenong optimistic once again about the viability of progress. He spent the remainder of the war teaching new techniques in the tea districts, including two years in the Wuyi Mountains, and he organized university-level courses at Fudan University in occupied Shanghai, where he invited an older Lu Ying to return and lecture. "One day in the near future," Wu wrote, "the Japanese devils will definitely be chased out of China. Our tea peasants definitely need to maintain this vision, and we must encourage them to re-plant and nurture their tea plants in order to prepare for future development."[72]

During this time, Wu Juenong also fended off suspicion that he was secretly a member of the Communist Party. At this time he is said to have protected many party friends who wrote for the left-wing *Rural China* and who went on to help establish the People's Republic of China (PRC, est. 1949), including prominent names such as Qian Junrui, Sun Yefang, and Xue Muqiao. But Wu himself was never a party member; his connection with the Communists was instead one of shared economic ideals.[73]

After settling in Yan'an in 1935, Mao Zedong and the Communist Party had set out to build a small-scale socialist society that could serve as a new national model. Their theory was known as "New Democracy," first articulated in 1940 and reemphasized in 1949, after the outbreak of a civil war and with the Nationalists retreating to Taiwan. It entailed a two-stage vision of revolution. The first was a New Democratic revolution, named so because it followed the Euro-American path of bourgeois democracy but substituted the leadership of the monied classes with that of the people. The most crucial task was to fend off imperialism through economic development, indispensable for the transition to real socialism. Despite divergences in long-term goals, New Democracy's immediate tactics resembled the rural development programs shared by many left-wing KMT thinkers, including Wu Juenong.[74] Instead of complete dissolution of property, the party would first create a united front of workers, peasants, and the "national bourgeoisie" in order to liberate China from global imperialism. Mao wrote in 1949:

> The national bourgeoisie at the present stage is of great importance. Imperialism, a most ferocious enemy, is still standing alongside us. . . . China must utilize all the factors of urban and rural capitalism that are beneficial and not harmful to the national economy and the people's livelihood; and we must unite with the national bourgeoisie in common struggle. Our present policy is to regulate capitalism, not to destroy it.[75]

New Democracy shared with many KMT officials' theories the distinction between national versus imperialist, or comprador, capital. Both sides emphasized that a new China needed to promote the peasantry as national capital's social foundation, and both promoted socialized agriculture in the form of cooperatives. Such continuities, however precarious, help explain why Wu Juenong was brought on as the PRC's vice minister of agriculture in 1949. His specific task in Beijing was to run the new national China Tea Company, the government's first state-owned import-export company at the time and among the biggest today. China Tea coordinated marketing activities into one institution, finally eliminating the compradors and the tea warehouse system. Over the next few years, it integrated marketing with the cooperatives established in the 1930s, and it imported tea machinery from South Asia and Europe. In 1950, Wu Juenong addressed his employees and other comrades engaged in the project of reviving tea: "Today, we have already driven out the feudal forces, bureaucratic capitalism has been toppled, and imperialism no longer exists on our soil."[76] It was an exceedingly optimistic moment for Wu and fellow left-wing economic thinkers who had survived the war. It was also the endpoint of a much longer protracted struggle over the previous decades, during which time the real revolution was taking place in the realm of political-economic concepts and politics, if not yet in practice.

Conclusion

IN HIS SPARE time while a student in Japan (1918–1921), a young Wu Juenong often collected materials on the tea industries of China and the rest of Asia. He would later use this research to challenge propaganda from the British and Japanese industries claiming that Assam, not China, was the true birthplace of tea. At the same time, Wu developed a deep curiosity about the remote Brahmaputra Valley and the otherworldly tea plantations he had read about. In late 1934 he found an opportunity to visit Assam in person for the first time. Buoyed by the optimism of the Qimen tea cooperative's first season, Wu set out on behalf of the National Economic Council to study tea production in Japan, Taiwan, the Dutch East Indies, Ceylon, and India. In his diary and in published reports, Wu supplemented his personal impressions of Calcutta and Assam with a detailed history of Indian tea. He recounted how Robert Bruce had stumbled onto a wild plant in 1823, how Governor-General Bentinck had formed the Tea Committee in 1834, how British merchants had "completely copied our country's methods" from "our country's" tea workers, and, finally, how one of the "major events in the history of Indian tea," the "conflict and bloody tragedy" of the rapacious recruiter system, had transpired, becoming a political cause later taken up by the "revolution of Indian nationalism." While traveling, Wu Juenong studied the industry's English-language materials closely, mainly pamphlets from the ITA and memoirs by Robert

Fortune detailing his adventures through China in the 1840s. Decades later, Wu recalled to family members, "Fortune's travelogues were written very colorfully, and reading them not only helped me learn English and history; most importantly, they helped me understand China and Chinese tea through the eyes of a foreigner."[1]

A major object of this book has been to demonstrate how global competition brought together the Chinese and colonial Indian tea industries, forcing its Asian and European participants to study their immediate surroundings through the eyes of their rivals and the rest of the industrializing world. Aside from Wu Juenong, we have seen British colonial governors who perceived Assam using analogies with China and western Europe, as well as Indian nationalists who compared the tea coolies' fate with that of enslaved Africans in the Americas. Each recognized that understanding the events unfolding in their own locale was impossible without simultaneously situating themselves within the global circuit of tea and colonial commodities. Perhaps nothing captured this point better than the near-perfect symmetry of, first, colonial officers from India traveling to study Chinese methods and then, almost exactly one century later, Chinese reformers visiting the Indian tea districts to do the same.

What did these expansive connections add up to? The modern history of tea was not a story of global homogenization nor of the uniform dissemination of ideas from the West to the Rest. Instead, world competition gave rise to a set of shared, mutually constitutive pressures and uneven rates of profit and accumulation. It thereby produced regionally distinctive tensions exacerbated by the marketplace and manifested through idiosyncratic labor practices and ideological forms. After all, it was precisely the divergent fates of Chinese and Indian tea, and the attendant desire to catch up with one another, that motivated firms and officials to critically scrutinize their rivals' histories and behaviors. Given this analytical frame of global connections, I conclude here by synthesizing the various stories from the Chinese and Indian tea war into a handful of observations about history and historiography.

First, this book has given substance to a reconceptualization of capitalism's history more flexible and globally oriented than past approaches. The social changes associated with the Chinese and Indian tea trades did not match the classic image of industrial revolution arising spontaneously in a single country. They featured neither mechanized production nor free proletarian workforces, at least initially. Instead, Chinese and Indian tea relied upon local brokers known as arkatis, sardars, and baotou; draconian penal contracts in Assam and arcane technologies and rituals in China; and labor-intensive regimes that reinforced divisions along the lines of sex and ancestry. Such arrangements were makeshift, a combination of outside wealth and local customary practices that were "inherited," Marx put it, from earlier times. Rather than asking *whether or not* China had capitalism or Assam was capitalist—or whether or not one could discern the presence of particular technologies and class arrangements—this book has sought to understand *in what ways* these regions participated within, and were also being shaped by, transnational circuits of production and circulation, with their attendant social logic of intensive accumulation. This conceptualization more helpfully captures the unevenness of the last several centuries of economic history while also providing the shared basis for exploring connections and parallels across far-flung locales.

Second, this view from two marginal sites in rural Asia also illuminates new conclusions about the rise of the modern economy. In particular, there is evidence to support the hypothesis that putatively backwards and marginal social formations were at times more predisposed to industrial production than their metropolitan counterparts were. For instance, Mintz's study of sugar demonstrated that planter colonies in the Caribbean developed industrial production before continental Europe did. The sugar crop required the integration of cultivation and refinement, colonial regimes more brutally disciplined the workforce of indentured and enslaved people, and the structural separation of consumption from production encouraged large-scale specialization. Many of these traits were shared by the Assam tea gardens featured in this book. In China, similarly, the renowned social historian Fu Yiling argued decades ago that industrial commodity production first emerged in the remote mountainous frontiers rather than in the commercialized "riverine" cities. Those frontiers—a class that included Huizhou and the Wuyi Mountains—were often replete with poorer minority groups, such as the famed "shed people," who were dependent on specialized production for survival, were underwritten by outside merchants, and focused on extractive primary commodities such as tobacco, sugar, indigo, and tea. Together, these examples join a growing body of scholarship suggesting that traditional accounts of the modern world have gotten things "backwards," in Steinfeld's words. Practices and circumstances that were seen as anachronistic and traditional during the twentieth-century era of mass production may have in fact played a crucial role in the initial emergence of modern economic life.[2]

Third, beyond challenging the Orientalist categories of economic backwardness and tradition, this book has sought to account for their emergence through a critical history of political-economic thought. In China and colonial India, the crucial period spanned the turn of the twentieth century, when observers and participants in the tea trade began to speak about each region through the language of natural comparative advantages and timeless civilizational traits. These ideas were crystallized in the birthplace of tea controversy, when imperialist propagandists had rationalized the ascent of Indian tea by describing an innate, natural connection between the plant and Assam. In the fall of 1935, as Wu Juenong walked through the fields of an Assam tea garden, he offered what appeared to be a counterposed explanation. Indian tea, he wrote, had succeeded due not to its ancient roots but to the industry's novelty, manifest in its productive young plants; history, in fact, had worked to weigh down the Chinese trade, embodied in its decrepit tea bushes, which had been plucked for centuries, and in its exhausted farms, now stripped and barren. But, rather than resignation to fate, Wu proposed planting new trees in China and adopting new, scientific techniques. Doing so could alter "the destiny [*mingyun*] of our Chinese tea."[3] Tea, in other words, was not just a gift of nature but also the product of arduous human labor. Wu Juenong's was an explanation rooted in the tenets of political economy, of course, and it echoed observations about the value of human labor voiced earlier by other participants in the trade, from Assam Company planters in the 1850s to Qing reformers in the 1890s tea crisis.

However, political economy often produced its own naturalized economic theories as well, framed through conceptions of value. Chinese and Indian writers appropriated different aspects of political economy and expressed them through timeless and cosmological language. Ramkumar Vidyaratna decried penal contracts as immoral and slavelike, in violation of the "ordinary laws" of supply and demand and free labor. Chen Chi preached the *dao* of productive labor, which he pronounced the "will of heaven." Even Wu Juenong had been seduced into making statements that Chinese tea had remained traditional and unchanged for thousands of years. Seen in this light, the birthplace of tea theory, while certainly marketing propaganda, could also be viewed as an absurd, logically extreme version of political economy and its ahistorical naturalization of competition and uneven development. Such unevenness had been reified literally as a physical property of the Chinese soil and climate, if not its civilization and culture.

By contrast, this book has sought to account for such abstract economic thinking through a concrete history of economic life. I have argued that Chinese and Indian thinkers embraced the timeless ideals of political economy due, partly, to the latter's correspondence with dynamic social changes found within their immediate surroundings, especially the expansion of varieties of commodified work in rural China and Bengal. In these Asian hinterlands, new ideological forms and economic realities were unfolding together, intertwined and indissociable. The paradoxical conclusion to the tea war, then, was a modern history of backwardness: that so-called unproductive comprador capital and unfree penal labor contracts may have been indispensable to the early years of expansion for Chinese and Indian tea, respectively, but by the new century they were denounced as anachronistic and unfit for the modern industrial world. Seen through the categories of productive and free labor, aspects of Chinese and colonial Indian society have appeared parochial and unchanging to generations of observers and historians. Yet I have suggested that these appearances were the historical product of the ongoing social, economic, and intellectual revolutions of capitalism. Their plausibility discloses to us, therefore, that their authors were already immersed in capitalist social patterns spanning Asia that were global and dynamic in character.

Finally, this book can only speculatively gesture in the direction of another major question, namely, the historical relationship between transnational competition and national ideology, starkly apparent by the final two chapters of this story. How can we articulate the relationship between competition and nationalism? One hypothesis comes from sociologist Neil Davidson, who has argued that the former requires the latter in a functionalist sense, in order to justify itself "in terms of a higher aspiration than increased profit margins."[4] His hypothesis certainly resonates, for instance, with British attempts to push unpopular Indian teas in England by drawing upon patriotic sentiments. For Chinese and Indian nationalists, however, we find a history of reformers who developed an early sense of ethnic solidarity but first fumbled through different strategies—such as military modernization or religion—*before* landing on national capital as their response to foreign rule. There was thus no tidy sequential relationship between the economic goals of accumulation and the political sentiments of nationalism. Nevertheless, whatever the precise mechanics, the links between the two became impossible to ignore by the twentieth century. These nationalized forms of accumulation also provide us here a useful bridge to understand subsequent developments in the global tea trade in the second half of the last century. By then, the terrain of battle was no longer free trade liberalism nor empire but a postwar family of nations.

*

Entering the Second World War, the Indian industry had solidified its position as the world's largest tea producer and exporter. After the war, producers across Asia were forced to confront a new field of competitors, as export tea production was taken up in the Soviet Union, Latin America, and eastern Africa, especially Kenya. Tea, formerly an exotic Asian medicine for European luxury consumption, was now a mass commodity whose production and consumption spanned the world's continents.[5]

In India, the major transformation has been the indigenization of tea production and consumption. For some time, there had emerged a middle stratum of Bengali clerks, lawyers, and brokers within the industry who clamored for greater social mobility within its ranks. By the time of Indian independence, they framed the indigenization of tea capital in terms of national emancipation, and the new state promoted Indian ownership accordingly. In many ways, the Indian elite inherited the exclusionary tactics of the British colonial capitalists who preceded them. Different legislation restricted the mobility of foreign capital to move in and out of the new nation, requiring businesses to apply for licenses, provide minimum social benefits, and retain minimum levels of Indian ownership. As a result, from 1958 to 1977, the share of foreign-owned tea land fell from 46.5 to 32.5 percent, and foreign-owned production from 52.9 to 38.4 percent. The government also took aim at the managing agencies. It was unsurprising, one observer noted, that Indian tea witnessed a "pilgrimage to East Africa where costs were lower, yields higher and opportunities for profit inviting."[6]

From the 1950s into the sixties, the world tea supply nearly doubled, and the share of Indian tea fell from one-half to one-third of the global market. It was during this period when the habit of drinking tea picked up considerably among Indian consumers. In the colonial era, domestic marketing had been stymied by tea's strong association with imperialism. Indian consumption only took off in the 1970s with the development of cut-tear-curl, or, "CTC" tea, in which serrated steel rollers shred leaves into smaller particles, strengthening their flavor. The CTC machines represented a technical advance, Philip Lutgendorf has shown, as the resulting product "doubled the 'cuppage,'" from about three hundred to six hundred cups per kilogram of dry leaves. Cheaper and stronger CTC produced a vibrant "chai" drinking culture, and the share of domestic consumers for Indian tea climbed from 30 percent in 1947 and one-half in the 1970s to 70 percent by the end of the century.[7]

The postwar history of Chinese tea has been more erratic. In the 1950s, Wu Juenong remained at the forefront of tea reform efforts in the new state, but later that decade he became one of many officials sidelined for his "capitalist outlook" in anti-rightist purges. The last memory of his time in power was the Great Leap Forward (1958–1961), when he could only be a spectator as cadres and workers destroyed the tea fields of central China. As part of Mao Zedong's campaign of spontaneous collectivist activity, cadres invited "urban cobblers, barbers, public bath attendants, and fruit vendors all to scale the mountains and pluck tea."[8] Villagers even uprooted old tea bushes in order to fuel backyard furnaces used for smelting iron into steel. The ineffectual backyard furnaces, of course, have long been seen as a symbol of the economic missteps made during Mao's time in power, and it was only fitting that in their haste to build a new China, they sacrificed the most valuable commercial crop of the preceding era.

What happened next? According to the official narrative, Chinese tea did not recover until the 1980s period of market reform. However, in-depth economic research undertaken during the 1970s to 1990s suggests an alternative timeline: that the 1980s gains in tea were actually the fruits of successful policies in the 1960s and seventies, at the height of the Cultural Revolution (1966–1976). After the disastrous Great

Leap Forward, central authorities reasserted control over agriculture, and from 1965 to 1977 the area under tea tripled; in the most productive years, the gains in land equaled the entire tea area of Kenya or Sri Lanka *in total*. Central agencies supplied millions in loans, thousands of tons of chemical fertilizers, and thousands of tons of steel for constructing equipment. There is an irony here—potentially—that Wu Juenong's original suggestion to replant the tea fields with new bushes was accomplished against his will during the Great Leap Forward, yielding windfalls in the 1970s and eighties. These details dovetail with an emerging revisionist scholarship on the Cultural Revolution that suggests that during that period, "Red China" successfully implemented its own "green revolution." If true, the green revolution could also count among its gains the realization of the tea industry revolution theorized in the 1930s by Wu Juenong and his friends.[9]

Today, as with the turn-of-the-century tea war, the world's top two tea producers are China (1.9 million tons in 2014) and India (1.2 million). But much has changed in the interim period, and the two industries have experienced many historical reversals since the 1930s. The newest frontiers for consumption are no longer Euro-America but the middle classes of China, India, and other so-called developing markets, who can now afford costlier gourmet teas grown with ecologically sustainable conditions, fair labor and trade practices, and artisanal, manual refinement techniques. In a surprising reversal of its condescending attitude toward Chinese methods, the Indian industry has partly adopted Chinese-style segmented supply chain production, in which individual farms pluck their own leaves before selling them to independent "bought leaf factories." The main advantage, anthropologist Sarah Besky has argued, is the extreme flexibility in labor standards, offering a cheaper and lower-quality alternative in a cutthroat industry. In fact, a spokesman for the Indian industry recently expressed admiration for Chinese tea on many fronts: "The Chinese are far better than us in terms of agriculture practices, machinery, processing units and products," the Darjeeling estate owner remarked. "There are many lessons to learn for India from China while China has nothing as such to learn from us."[10]

Such historical ironies strengthen the claim of this book that the political-economic principles of high industry at the turn of the century may have presented themselves in natural, almost metaphysical language, but they have since been revealed as ideologies specific to a discrete, if massively important, historical era. For students of history, it makes little sense to interpret the long-term temporal and spatial scope of capitalism's history through the exclusive lens of the mid-twentieth century, anachronistically projecting its expectations onto distinct places and eras. Instead, we are better served with a more temporally and spatially flexible notion of modern accumulation. I am of course not arguing that the ideals of twentieth-century industry should be distrusted as mere fictions. Such ideologies were resonant and widespread for good reason, corresponding to tangible and palpable social pressures in their time. Understanding their historical formation helps us make sense of their consolidation and evolution, both in the past and into the future.

I have approached this task through the study of particular regions within China and India, but my point is not to suggest that these two countries are somehow representative of the rest of the world. It would be equally valuable to ask similar questions about capitalism's history in other postcolonial sites, such as the Americas, Central and Southeast Asia, Africa, and Central Europe. The tea districts of China and colonial India were but two constituents of a global story. But because these two regions have so often been viewed together as objects of Orientalist fantasy—as an antithesis to Euro-American civilization, whether positive or negative—they also, I believe, serve as useful entry points into the continual task of retheorizing the complex global histories of capital and economic life as they have unfolded over the most recent centuries. However one approaches this colossal undertaking, it is clear that any analysis will remain limited insofar as it relies upon ahistorical speculation about individual behavior, evolutionary stages, or nation-bound cultural difference. Globally informed historical analysis is at its best when it proceeds from a comparative and synthetic study of specific times, people, places, and ideas, in order to ascend upward.

Notes

ACA	Assam Company Archives, London Metropolitan Archives.
CCJ	*Chen Chi Ji.* Edited by Zhao Shugui and Zeng Liya. Beijing: Zhonghua Shuju, 1997.
FHA	First Historical Archives, Beijing.
INR	Indian Newspaper Reports. Full run is located in IOR/L/R/5/1 to 208, India Office Records, British Library, London.
IOR	India Office Records, British Library, London.
ITA Report (Year)	Indian Tea Association, *Detailed Report of The General Committee.* Full run of annual reports located in Mss Eur F174/584 to 670, India Office Records, British Library, London.
JFA	James Finlay & Co. Archives, University of Glasgow.
JMA	Jardine Matheson & Co. Archives, Cambridge University.
JSA	Jardine Skinner & Co. Archives, Cambridge University.
NAI	National Archives of India, New Delhi.
RALEC	*Report of the Assam Labour Enquiry Committee, 1906.* Kolkata: Office of the Superintendent of Government Printing, 1906.
WBSA	West Bengal State Archives, Kolkata.
WJX	*Wu Juenong Xuanji.* Edited by Zhongguo Chaye Xuehui. Shanghai: Shanghai Kexue Jishu Chubanshe, 1987.
ZCWJ	*Zhongguo Cha Wenhua Jingdian.* Edited by Chen Binfan, Yu Yue, and Guan Bowen. Beijing: Guangming Ribao Chubanshe, 1999.

INTRODUCTION

1. Wu, "Chashu Yuanchandi Kao" (1922), WJX, 1–3. Students of modern Chinese history may recognize parallels between Wu Juenong's experiences and those of his friend, the great fiction writer Lu Xun (1881–1936), who in the same year, 1922, published his own account of heightened national self-awareness while

studying overseas. For Lu Xun, it was the humiliation of viewing slides of Chinese soldiers executed during the Russo-Japanese War (1904–1905) inside a classroom full of patriotic Japanese students that pushed him to leave medicine for literature, convinced that the Chinese people required not just bodily but also "spiritual" (*jingshen*) healing. Likewise, Wu Juenong's lifelong efforts to revive the collapsed Chinese tea trade were sparked by the realization that overseas consumers could question whether or not tea was grown in "China, too." The Chinese people demanded not only spiritual remedies, he concluded, but also economic ones.

2. Crole, *Tea*, 18, 42–43.

3. Pomeranz, *Great Divergence*, 1.

4. Ho, "Inter-Asian Concepts"; Subrahmanyam, "Connected Histories."

5. Crole, *Tea*, 39–40.

6. For a review of the current literature, see Ghosh, "Before 1962," 700–704.

7. Shaikh, *Capitalism*, 259.

8. The terms "coolie" and "comprador" are archaic ones. They carried specific ideological meanings when voiced by different actors, from European colonial officials to Indian and Chinese nationalists, and I explore these issues near the end of this book. Although I have minimized putting quotation marks around them for the sake of readability, I have used these terms to refer to contested political categories as much as in reference to empirical individuals and groups.

9. Schivelbusch, *Tastes of Paradise*, 17; Pomeranz and Topik, *World That Trade Created*, 71–96; Rappaport, *Thirst for Empire*, ch. 1; Mintz, *Sweetness and Power*, 121–22; Sahlins, "Cosmologies of Capitalism," 455; D. Davies, quoted in Mintz, *Sweetness and Power*, 116.

10. House of Commons, "Papers Relating to Measures for Introducing Cultivation of Tea Plant in British Possessions in India," *19th Century House of Commons Sessional Papers*, vol. 39, paper 63, 12. Hereafter referred to as "Papers Relating (63)."

11. Sen, "Questions of Consent," 231; *Industrial Census of India, 1911*, in Chapman, "Agency Houses," 248; Bagchi, *Private Investment*, 177. The railroads were actually the number one investment in colonial India, but they were considered the "public" sector; Gardella, *Harvesting Mountains*, 154; Royal Commission on Labour, 6, 350. These figures reflect "average daily working strength" in Assam.

12. Smith, *Consumption and the Making*, 121; Wakeman, "Canton Trade," 171; Du Bois, *Black Reconstruction*, 15–16.

13. Pomeranz, *Great Divergence*, "Introduction."

14. Wong, *China Transformed*, 21; Pomeranz, "East-West Binary," 554, 573; Parthasarathi, *Why Europe*, 7–14.

15. Beckert, "American Capitalism," 314–15; Levy, "Capital as Process," 484.

16. Rappaport, *Thirst for Empire*; Gardella, *Harvesting Mountains*; Chen, *Jindai Zhongguo Chaye*; Guha, "Big Push"; Behal and Mohapatra, "Tea and Money"; Beckert, *Empire of Cotton*, ch. 3; I have elaborated upon the broader historiographies of capitalism for Chinese and South Asian history elsewhere. Liu, "Production, Circulation, Accumulation."

17. Berg, "Industrial Organisation," 123; O'Brien, "Deconstructing," 32, 36; de Vries, *Industrious Revolution*, 73–92; Harvey, *Postmodernity*. See also Eley,

"Historicizing the Global," 164–66; e.g., on slavery, see Beckert, *Empire of Cotton*, xv–xviii, and Mintz, *Sweetness and Power*, 46–52; on informality, see Breman, *Footloose Labour*; on gendered labor, Lee, *South China Miracle*; on household and labor-intensive production, see Hsiung, *Living Rooms,* and Hamilton and Kao, *Making Money*; Banaji, "Merchant Capitalism," 424.

18. The term "mature critique" here refers to the roughly three versions of *Capital* Marx drafted from 1857 until his death. Equally significant with the economic crises of the 1970s was the English publication of Marx's first draft, known as the *Grundrisse* (1973), which clarified Marx's ultimate method of presentation in the final draft. Central to this reevaluation of Marx has been the reintegration of Hegelian categories and their role in the dense presentation of *Capital*. Influential scholars in this tradition include: Jairus Banaji, Diane Elson, David Harvey, György Lukács, Moishe Postone, and the feminist school of social reproduction theory; Banaji, "Materialist Conception of History," 58–61.

19. Karl, *Magic of Concepts*, 46; cf. Marx, *Grundrisse*, 489; Marx and Engels, "Manifesto," 473–83; Sewell, "Temporalities," 533.

20. Marx, *Capital*, 1:876n, 949–53; Marx, *Grundrisse*, 103. One must be clear here that Marx's concept of "general" (*allgemeine*)—often translated as "universal"—did not mean each and every person worked for wages; rather it suggested a process in which wage labor has become so predominant in society that even non-waged production assumed its basic patterns, as we see below. Thus, the first forms of wage-labor-based production predated its "generalization" by several centuries. Marx's strongest pronouncement on the concept of "general" comes from the 1857 introduction, where he wrote: "In all forms of society there is one specific kind of production which predominates over the rest, whose relations thus assign rank and influence to the others. It is a general illumination which bathes all the other colours and modifies their particularity." Marx, *Grundrisse*, 106–17. This was a view shaped by Hegel, who wrote of the same concept: "What is universal [*das Allgemeine*] about the Concept is indeed not just something common against which the particular stands on its own; instead the universal is what particularises (specifies) itself, remaining at home with itself in its other, in unclouded clarity." Hegel, *Encyclopaedia Logic*, 240, § 163, add. 1.

21. Marx, *Grundrisse*, 246.

22. Marx, *Capital*, 1:142; Weber, "Protestant Ethic," 9.

23. Elson, "Value Theory," 150; Marx, *Capital*, 1:436–37.

24. Marx, *Grundrisse*, 651.

25. On existing Marxist interpretations, see Brenner, "Capitalist Development"; Huang, *Peasant Economy* and *Peasant Family*; Brenner and Isett, "England's Divergence." As Pomeranz has suggested, these arguments also shared a curious agreement with the neoclassical school of New Institutional Economics popularized by Douglass North. Pomeranz, *Great Divergence*, 15. On the canonization of England as the model for industrial revolution worldwide, see Cannadine, "English Industrial Revolution." On global labor history, see Amin and van der Linden, "Introduction," 3; Banaji, "Fictions"; Banaji, "Merchant Capitalism," 425; Marx, *Capital*, 1:274, 949–53. This interpretation of labor under capitalism followed from political economy's definition of "productive labor," in which workers produce

value for capitalist employers in the form of commodities: "capital-positing, capital-producing labour." Marx, *Grundrisse*, 463; Banaji, "Synthesis," 356–58. Marx himself located the origins of capitalist production along the Mediterranean region of the fourteenth century, geographically and temporally far from nineteenth-century Britain. Marx, *Capital*, 1:876; n.b., within Brenner's social property framework, the category "market dependency" also helps to explain how non-proletarian producers could still be capitalist. Post, "Laws of Motion," 80–81.

26. Marx, *Capital*, 1:345, 645; on the new histories of capitalism, see Baptist, *Never Been Told*; Beckert, *Empire of Cotton*; on the literature on industrious revolutions, see de Vries, *Industrious Revolution*, 101–113; Sugihara, "Global History"; cf. Marx and Engels, *Collected Works*, 34:102.

27. Marx, *Capital*, 1:645, 1021. Emphases in original; for a further exploration of the persistence of earlier modes of economic life in Marx's work, see Harootunian, *Marx after Marx*, ch. 1.

28. The term "classical" was first coined by Marx, who dated the tradition back to William Petty (1623–1687), but today it conventionally begins with Smith's *The Wealth of Nations*. Marx, *Capital*, 1:174–75, n34. For other definitions, see Schumpeter, *History of Economic Analysis*, 51; Ambirajan, *Classical Political Economy*, 9–10; Polanyi, *Great Transformation*, ch. 10; Berg, *Machinery Question*, 17.

29. Sartori, "Political Economy," 123–24.

CHAPTER ONE. THE TWO TEA COUNTRIES

1. Hoh and Mair, *True History*, 28; Huang, *Fermentations and Food Science*, 506.

2. Perdue, *China Marches West*, 553–55.

3. Fortune, *Journey to the Tea Countries*, 20, 208, 272; *Two Visits*, 20 and 208.

4. Benn, *Tea in China*, chs. 2, 3, and 6; Hoh and Mair, *True History*, ch. 5

5. Chen, *Anhui Cha Jing*, 35; Wu Shi quoted in Chen and Zhu, *Zhongguo Chaye*, 336; Zou, *Huizhou Chaye*, 60–65.

6. Wu Zhenchen quoted in Chen and Zhu, *Zhongguo Chaye*, 360–61.

7. Benn, *Tea in China*, 174–76; Jiang Heng quoted in Peng, ed., *Shougong Shiliao*, 304.

8. Quoted in Huang, *Fermentations and Food Science*, 540.

9. Liu, *Dutch East India Company*, 141–46, emphases added; Strickland quoted in Mintz, *Sweetness and Power*, 110; Robins, *Corporation*, 53; MacGregor, *Commercial Statistics*, 58; Ukers, *All About Tea*, 67.

10. Mui and Mui, "'Trends,'" 165; Bowen, *Business of Empire*, 241.

11. Flynn and Giráldez, "Born with a 'Silver Spoon'," 202; Frank, *ReOrient*, 147–49; Chung, "Trade Triangle," 415–16; Bowen, "Tea, Tribute," 163.

12. Farooqui, "Bombay"; Banaji, "Self-Delusion," 6–13; Sugihara, "Intra-Asian Trade," 149–50. N.b., Sugihara also stresses that although the Anglo-Indian-Chinese triangular trade was certainly a major economic force, the historiographical emphasis on this circuit has come at the expense of examining other routes with

which it was interlinked, including those across southern India (Madras), Southeast Asia (Java, Singapore, Sumatra, Siam, Burma, Penang), and the North Atlantic.

13. Ward, "Industrial Revolution," 52; E. H. Pritchard, quoted in Sahlins, "Cosmologies," 424.

14. Smith, *Consumption and the Making*, ch. 6, 121–22; McCants, "Poor Consumer," 174, 179; Mintz, *Sweetness and Power*, 114, ch. 6; Rappaport, *Thirst for Empire*, ch. 2; Bowen, "Tea, Tribute," 159.

15. Greenberg, *British Trade*, 3, 14–15; Richards, "Opium Industry," 159–61, 180; Trocki, *Opium and Empire*, xiii.

16. Eyles, "Abolition," chs. 5–7; Greenberg, *British Trade*, 99–103; Sahlins, "Cosmologies," 420.

17. Van Schendel, *History of Bangladesh*, 50–56; Roy, *World Economy*, 78–122.

18. Rappaport, *Thirst for Empire*, 87–88; Johnson quoted in Perelman, *Invention of Capitalism*, 65; Pomeranz and Topik, *World That Trade Created*, ch. 4; Sell, *Capital through Slavery*; "Papers Relating (63)," 19.

19. Ukers, *All About Tea*, 134–35; "Papers Relating (63)," 32; Cornwallis, quoted in Banerjee, "East-India Company," 301.

20. Scott, *Not Being Governed*, 16–18; cf. Barpujari, *Days of the Company*, 2.

21. Guha, *Early Colonial Assam*, ch. 4, 86–87; Barpujari, *Days of the Company*, 24–27.

22. Guha, *Early Colonial Assam*, chs. 6–7; Barpujari, *Days of the Company*, 1–12.

23. Richards, "Indian Empire," 72; Richards, "Opium Industry," 174; Mintz, *Sweetness and Power*, 52–54; Beckert, *Empire of Cotton*, 104, 188–90.

24. O'Rourke and Williamson, "Globalisation Begin?" 26–27.

25. Ibid., 34; Chung, "Trade Triangle," 415; Gardella, *Harvesting Mountains*, 133; Pritchard, *Anglo-Chinese Relations*, 216.

26. Arrighi, *Twentieth Century*, 235–37; Wallerstein, *World-System III*, 129–38; on the British EIC's falling ratio of bullion to commodity exports in the eighteenth century, see Pritchard, *Anglo-Chinese Relations*, 204. On the dynamic of falling prices encouraging industrial capital, see Marx, *Capital*, 3:444, 447.

27. On the debate over globalization and Eurocentrism, see Flynn and Giráldez, "Path Dependence"; O'Rourke and Williamson, "Once More."

CHAPTER TWO. INCENSE AND INDUSTRY

1. E.g., Wu, "Zhongguo Chaye Gaige Fangzhun" (1922), WJX, 43; Gardella, *Harvesting Mountains*, 7, 170–74; Huang, *Peasant Family*, 236–41. See also Elvin, *Pattern of Chinese Past*, ch. 17.

2. Brenner, "Capitalist Development," 33–41; Huang, *Peasant Family*, 311–12; Banaji, "Merchant Capitalism," 425; Perlin, "Proto-Industrialization and Pre-Colonial South Asia," 91; Sugihara, "Labour-Intensive Industrialisation"; de Vries, *Industrious Revolution*, ch. 3. Although Sugihara uses the phrase "labor-intensive industrialization," I prefer the idea of "accumulation," which better accounts for

capitalist expansion in both its early commercial, labor-intensive and its later capital-intensive forms.

3. Pomeranz has recently argued for this distinction in conceptualizing labor intensification, one archaic and one modern. Pomeranz, "Yangzi Delta," 122–26. See also Peng, *Ban Gongyehua*, 134. Further, the question of labor intensification as traditional versus modern becomes less vexing once we remind ourselves that the concepts in question are relative rather than absolute. For both the Marxian tradition and an economist such as Sugihara, extensive growth (relative surplus-value) is defined based on what intensive growth looks like (absolute surplus-value) at a given moment and vice versa. Rather than attempting to pin down the exact contours of where different forms of growth begin and end, the more interesting question for intermediary processes such as labor-intensive accumulation is their long-run historical significance. The implication of this new literature is that labor intensification, formerly seen as a type of extensive growth, can also be seen as a form of intensive growth, or, in Marxian terms, as part of the repertoire of relative surplus-value creation. See Marx, *Capital*, 1:646, 1022; Sugihara, "Labour-Intensive Industrialisation," 135–36.

4. Weber, "Protestant Ethic," 14; Thompson, "Time, Work-Discipline," 79–81.

5. On central China, see Ding, "Yangloudong." This region was the main source of commercial tea that flowed through Hankou, as described in Rowe, *Hankow*, 122–57; *Zhongguo Shiye Zhi* quoted in Wang and Zhang, *Huishang Yanjiu*, 232–33.

6. Lin, *Wuyi Chaye*, 8–9—My great thanks to professors Xiao Kunbing and Shui Haigang for helping me obtain a copy of this work and to Lin Yangfeng for giving me permission to quote from it; Fortune, *Journey to Tea Countries*, 259.

7. Lin, *Wuyi Chaye*, 9; Hu, "People of Hui-Chou," 5.

8. Guo, *Ritual Opera*, 51; Wang and Zhang, *Huishang Yanjiu*, 7, 582.

9. Shigeta, *Shindai Shakai*, 311–12.

10. Ibid., 315.

11. "Proclamation of Min County Magistrate," May 1853, Papers re: Fukien tea business, JM/H5/4/1, JMA; Ling, *Zhongguo Chashui*, 119; Hao, *Commercial Revolution*, 177; Gardella, *Harvesting Mountains*, 50; Lin, *Wuyi Chaye*, 9.

12. September 1854, Private Letters: Foochow and River Min, JM/B2/9, JMA; F. B. Johnson, quoted in Hao, *Commercial Revolution*, 98; cf. 173.

13. October 1860; 14 May 1866; 6 June 1868, Private Letters: Foochow and River Min, JM/B2/9, JMA.

14. Fortune, *Three Years' Wandering*, 211, emphasis in original. On the production of export *hongcha*, see 217; Fortune, *Journey to the Tea Countries*, 263; *Guangze County Gazetteer*, quoted in Shui, "Jindai Minjiang," 59; "Letter from Ahee," May 1853, Papers re: Fukien tea business, JM/H1/57/2, JMA; Bruce, *Account of Manufacture*, 9.

15. Jiang Heng quoted in Peng, ed., *Shougong Shiliao* 1:430–31; Bian, *Bian Zhijun*, 11:9; Fortune, *Journey to the Tea Countries*, 260–61; Tang and Wei, *Fujian zhi Cha*, 60, 70.

16. Tang and Wei, *Fujian zhi Cha*, 64–65; Lin, *Wuyi Chaye*, 13, 18.

17. Shigeta, *Shindai Shakai*, 316–17.

18. Wang and Zhang, *Huishang Yanjiu*, 584.

19. Ibid., 585, 579.

20. Ibid., 584–86.

21. Bell, *One Industry*, 46–64; Li, *Silk Trade*, 51–58, ch. 5; Walker, *Chinese Modernity*, ch. 4.

22. Shigeta, *Shindai Shakai*, 318.

23. Tang and Wei, *Fujian zhi Cha*, 99.

24. Tōa Dōbunkai, *Shina Shōbetsu*, 9:536; 12:432–33; 14:481.

25. Lu, "Beyond the Paradigm," 34; Li, "Cong 'Fufu Bingzuo,'" 99–100; Bray, *Technology and Gender*, 236.

26. Reeves quoted in Ball, *Manufacture of Tea*, 377; Lu, "Beyond the Paradigm," 26–35.

27. Yu Lianyuan, "Zou qing zhi chi xia chu Cha Sheng fen Dufu Yanjin Jianchang Guyong Nügong shi," Guangxu 14 (ca. 1888), 03–5513–042, FHA; cf. Jiang in Hu, *Huizhou Cha Jing*, 163.

28. Li, *Agricultural Development*, 154.

29. Jiang Wenzuan quoted in Wang and Zhang, *Huishang Yanjiu*, 584.

30. Tang Yaoqing quoted in ibid., 592, 597–98.

31. Letter to Jiang Yaohua quoted in ibid., 587, 598.

32. Jiang Yaohua, *An Outline for Making Tea*, quoted in Hu, *Huizhou Cha Jing*, 152–53.

33. Yu Jianwu quoted in Bedini, *Trail of Time*, 54.

34. Ball, *Manufacture of Tea*, 220. Cf. 225, 229, 238. I am unsure what the word "Che" refers to, but one possibility is the measure term *zhi*, used for objects such as incense that are thin and stick-like; Hommel, *China at Work*, 4.

35. Thompson, "Time, Work-Discipline," 60.

36. Needham, *Science in Traditional China*, 131.

37. Ibid.; Landes, *Revolution in Time*, 23–25.

38. Postone, *Time, Labor*, 201–2.

39. Ball, *Manufacture of Tea*, 233.

40. Jiang in Hu, *Huizhou Cha Jing*, 166; Fan, "Tunxi Chaye," 121; Postone, *Time, Labor*, 214–15.

41. Fan, "Tunxi Chaye," 121.

42. Thompson, "Time, Work-Discipline," 75, 92; Marx called the "piece-wage" the "form of wage most appropriate to the capitalist mode of production." Marx, *Capital*, 1:694, 698–99.

43. Fan, "Tunxi Chaye," 121–22.

44. Ibid.

45. Jiang Yaohua quoted in Hu, *Huizhou Cha Jing*, 199–203. Quoted with the permission of Hu Wulin. My thanks to Professor Kang Jian for helping me with this material.

46. Lin, *Wuyi Chaye*, 18.

47. Ibid., 13–17, 40; Tang and Wei, *Fujian zhi Cha*, 70–71; baotou are mentioned in Li, *Silk Trade*, 48, 61, 186 and for 1990s Hong Kong in Leung, "Local Lives," 184. On the etymological history of *bao* and *baogong*, see Yang 1987, 15–18.

48. Lin, *Wuyi Chaye*, 47, 40.

49. Ibid., 42.

50. Ibid., 46–47, 62.

51. Ibid., 47.

52. Ibid.

53. Ibid., 83. Quoted with the permission of Lin Yangfeng.

54. Ibid., 47.

55. Ibid., 59, 82.

56. Elvin, *Chinese Past*, chs. 9–13; Dirlik, "Marxist Concept of Capitalism"; Hartwell, "Social Transformations."

57. Wong, *China Transformed*, ch. 2; Perlin, "Proto-Industrialization," 34–51; Peng, *Ban Gongyehua*, 125–37. I thank Margherita Zanasi for this recommendation.

CHAPTER THREE. A CRISIS OF CLASSICAL POLITICAL ECONOMY IN ASSAM

1. James Matheson, quoted in Greenberg, *British Trade*, 232.

2. The following Bentinck and Walker quotes come from "Papers Relating (63)."

3. M'Cosh quoted in Barpujari, *Days of the Company*, 11; Greenberg, *British Trade*, 183; "Minute by the Right Honble the Governor General," 22 February 1840, p. 266; "Minute by the Honble HT Prinsep Esqre," 25 February 1840, pp. 293–95; "Papers Regarding the Promotion of Tea Cultivation in Assam, Vol. 2," IOR/F/4/1882/79965, IOR.

4. RALEC, 135.

5. Behal, *One Hundred Years*, 9, 141; Bagchi, *Private Investment*, 161–63; Guha, "Big Push," 202–4; Bhattacharya and Chaudhuri, "Eastern India," 270–331, 325.

6. I thank Julia Stephens for suggestions that pushed me to look into this direction.

7. Bracken quoted in Stokes, *English Utilitarians*, 39.

8. This trend may be seen as part of a "historicist counter-revolution against the system of what came to be known as Smithianism" during the nineteenth century. Rothschild, "Political Economy," 751; comparatively, this history shares parallels with Ritu Birla's legal history of economic life, wherein the standardization of economic laws based on the principle of free and public "economic" practice simultaneously produced categories of private, archaic "culture," on which the continued practices of coercion were justified. Birla, *Stages of Capital*.

9. Barpujari, *Days of the Company*, 23–29; 49–51; 81–83; Guha, *Early Colonial Assam*, 142–43; Scott quoted in Guha, 148.

10. Stokes, *English Utilitarians*, 1; Marshall, *East Indian Fortunes*, 104–36; Stokes, *English Utilitarians*, 81; Metcalf, *Ideologies of the Raj*, 18–23; Ambirajan, *Classical Political Economy*, 11; Webb quoted in Ambirajan, 15.

11. Smith, *Wealth of Nations*, 12; 456–80; 718–46; 14; Ambirajan, *Classical Political Economy*, 214, 221; Stokes, *English Utilitarians*, 58–59. Smith was not the first to articulate a labor-premised theory of value, but he was perhaps its most forceful and articulate proponent. Meek, *Labour Theory of Value*, 11–81.

12. Sen, *Empire of Free Trade*; Ambirajan, *Classical Political Economy*, 221.

13. Ambirajan, *Classical Political Economy*, 25, 221–22.

14. Kolsky, *Colonial Justice*, 42; Bentinck quoted in Ambirajan, *Classical Political Economy*, 47; Bhattacharya, "Indigo Planters," 56–61.

15. Metcalf, *Ideologies of the Raj*, 29; Bentinck in Stokes, *English Utilitarians*, 51.

16. Walker quoted in "Papers Relating (63)," 11–12; Jenkins, *Report on the North-East*, 35–36; Jenkins quoted in Barpujari, *Political History*, 52; cf. Guha, *Early Colonial Assam*, 148–55.

17. Jenkins quoted in "Papers Relating (63)," 30–34; cf. Griffiths, *Indian Tea Industry*, 36–41.

18. Guha, *Early Colonial Assam*, 172; cf. Bhattacharya, "Laissez Faire," and Behal, *One Hundred Years*, 141–86.

19. Bruce, *Report on the Manufacture*, 3, 7; Griffiths, *Indian Tea Industry*, ch. 4; "Papers Relating (63)," 70, 86, 92; Brown quoted in Sharma, *Empire's Garden*, 44.

20. *Friend of India*, quoted in Griffiths, *Indian Tea Industry*, 64; J. Berry White, quoted in Griffiths, 50; "Resolution from the Government of India," "Transfer of the Tea Plantations Established in Assam to Private Enterprise," 15 June 1839, Nos. 1–10, p. 73, Revenue Agriculture Branch, Home Department, NAI; for a more detailed analysis of these ventures, see Liu, "Noble Tea Country."

21. "Employment Contracts," 1839–1840, JM/F11/2–13, JMA; cf. "Original Consultations," 1840, Tea Department, Board of Revenue—Agriculture, WBSA and "Papers Regarding the Promotion of Tea Cultivation in Assam, Vol. 2," pp. 541–86, IOR/F/4/1882/79965, IOR.

22. Letter from the Revd C. Gutzlaff to Wallich, 13 December 1839, pp. 559–61, emphases added; Letter from Grant to Wallich, 27 January 1840, 562–563, "Papers Regarding the Promotion of Tea Cultivation in Assam, Vol. 2," IOR/F/4/1882/79965, IOR.

23. Letter from Wallich to Maddock, 17 February 1840, "Papers Regarding the Promotion of Tea Cultivation in Assam, Vol. 2," p. 577, IOR/F/4/1882/79965, IOR.

24. "Papers Relating (63)," 44–45; Letter from Wallich to Grant, 18 July 1839, "Papers Regarding the Promotion of Tea Cultivation in Assam, Vol. 2," pp. 399–400, IOR/F/4/1882/79965, IOR.

25. Metcalf, *Ideologies of the Raj*, 34; Bentinck in "Papers Relating (63)," 5; Arrighi, *Adam Smith*, 57–58.

26. "Resolution from the Government of India," "Transfer of the Tea Plantations Established in Assam to Private Enterprise," 15 June 1839, Nos. 1–10, p. 72, Revenue Agriculture Branch, Home Department, NAI; Minute by the Governor-General Eden, 22 February 1840, pp. 268–69; Minute by Prinsep, 25 February 1840, pp. 293–94, "Papers Regarding the Promotion of Tea Cultivation in Assam, Vol. 2," pp. 293–94, IOR/F/4/1882/79965, IOR.

27. Antrobus, *Assam Company*, 45–47; Sharma, *Empire's Garden*, 71; Letter from Jenkins to Grant, 19 January 1849, "Sanctions the Deputation of Lum Ping Yung to Promote Resort of Chinese Merchants into Assam," 19 May 1849, Nos. 15–17, p. 7, Home Department, NAI; on the fate of the Chinese workers, see

entries from 4 May 1848 and 9 June 1854, "India (Calcutta) Committee Minute Books," MS 9925, vol. 5, 128; vol. 7, 144, ACA.

28. Entries from 1845 to 1848, "India (Calcutta) Committee Minute Books," MS 9925, vol. 1, 871, 1014–15, 1136, 1190; vol. 5, 111; vol. 11, 276–78, ACA. Emphasis in original.

29. Sen, "Commercial Recruiting and Informal Intermediation," 6; Behal, *One Hundred Years*, 236–37, 255; Bernstein and Brass, "Introduction," 17, 31n38.

30. Entries from 1850 and 1852, "India (Calcutta) Committee Minute Books," MS 9925, vol. 5, 143; vol. 6, 134, ACA; Burkinyoung quoted in Antrobus, *Assam Company*, 477–78.

31. G. Williamson, quoted in Antrobus, *Assam Company*, 485; Entry from 18 September 1854, "India (Calcutta) Committee Minute Books," MS 9925, vol. 7, 204–5, ACA; Antrobus, *Assam Company*, 99, 67; Guha, "Colonisation of Assam," 305.

32. Guha, *Planter Raj*, 3–4.

33. Mantena, *Alibis of Empire*, 1–2. Emphasis in original.

34. E.g., Cohn, *Colonialism and Its Forms*; Mantena, *Alibis of Empire*, 179–88; Sartori, *Liberalism*, chs. 2–3.

35. Lees, *Tea Cultivation*, 211; Lees, *Land and Labour*, iv, 84–85; Lees, *Memorandum Written*, 1–2; Lees, ed., *Resolutions, Regulations, Despatches*, 1–2; Edgar "Tea Cultivation," 17, 13; Money, *Cultivation & Manufacture*, 2–3.

36. *The Englishman* quoted in Beckert, *Empire of Cotton*, 251; Lees, *Tea Cultivation*, 93, 2, 97. Emphasis in original.

37. Lees, *Tea Cultivation*, 105, 130, 95, 108. Italics in original.

38. Mantena, *Alibis of Empire*, 3, 49–50, 119–21; Lees, *Tea Cultivation*, 261–62.

39. Lees, *Tea Cultivation*, 113–16, 320; Lees, *Memorandum Written*, 7; Maine quoted in Mantena, *Alibis of Empire*, 147; Mantena, *Alibis of Empire*, 2; Metcalf, *Ideologies of the Raj*, 68.

40. Lees, *Tea Cultivation*, 299–305, 314–21.

41. Ibid., 354–55, 29, 345–46.

42. Lees approved of Wakefield's plan elsewhere in his text. Lees, *Tea Cultivation*, 349; on the reception of Wakefield's theories in India, see Ambirajan, *Classical Political Economy*, 45; Wakefield, "England and America," 500–503, 515, 517; Letter from Jenkins to Halliday, 20 April 1840, "Grant of Lands for the Cultivation of Tea in Assam," 8 June 1840, Nos. 1–6, p. 53, Revenue Branch, Home Department, NAI.

43. Lees, *Tea Cultivation*, 323, 326, 348, 331–32, emphases added, 337–44; Lees, *Memorandum Written*, 6–7.

44. Lees, *Tea Cultivation*, 359, 349, app. iv–v.

45. *The Economist* cited in Beckert, *Empire of Cotton*, 254.

46. Lees, *Tea Cultivation*, 110–12.

47. Smith, *Wealth of Nations*, 300; Marx, *Capital*, 1:873.

48. Marx, *Capital*, 1:932.

49. Devine, "Scotland," 394–401; Muller, *Adam Smith*, 16–20, 23; Smith, *Lectures on Jurisprudence*, 351; Meek, *Labour Theory of Value*, 54; Smith, *Wealth of Nations*, 75.

50. Perelman, "Adam Smith's Pin Factory," 22–24.

51. Marx, *Grundrisse*, 104.

52. Sartori, *Global Concept History*, 61.

CHAPTER FOUR. AFTER THE GREAT SMASH

1. Blechynden quoted in ITA Report (1897), 218; the details of the ITA's ad campaign in America can be found in Griffiths, *Indian Tea,* 579–91.

2. Rappaport, *Thirst for Empire,* 162; Crole, *Tea,* 6, 42; Bernstein and Brass, "Introduction," 9, 26. My analysis on this point is indebted to Jairus Banaji's appraisal of the category "freedom" in Brass's other works. Banaji, "Fictions."

3. Crole, *Tea,* 39.

4. Banaji, "Fictions," 137–39; Steinfeld, *Coercion, Contract,* 234; see also Baptist, *Never Been Told,* 111–44; Beckert, *Empire of Cotton,* 98–136; Mintz, *Sweetness and Power,* 19–73.

5. "For a tea garden is in a less favourable position, when trade prospects are bad, than any ordinary manufacturing concern. A mill or a factory can reduce its staff, or go on short time, or if need be close down temporarily, and wait for better times. But a tea garden must carry on, and the extent to which it can restrict its operations or reduce its working costs is necessarily small. To close down altogether means the abandonment of the capital sunk in the enterprise; and tea garden labour is so costly to recruit that any material reduction in the labour strength represents a partial loss of capital." ITA Report (1920), 3.

6. Money, *Cultivation & Manufacture,* 2–3, 8; Griffiths, *Indian Tea Industry,* 96; Edgar, "Tea Cultivation," 16, 34, 18; Rungta, *Business Corporations,* 98; *Report of the Commissioners Appointed to Enquire into the State and Prospects of Tea Cultivation in Assam, Cachar and Sylhet* (1868), 1869, p. 18, Home Department, NAI.

7. Money, *Cultivation & Manufacture,* 3, 178, 2; Edgar, "Tea Cultivation," 14; Rungta, *Business Corporations,* 95.

8. Rungta, *Business Corporations,* 71; *Friend of India* quoted in Rungta, *Business Corporations,* 94; cf. Memorandum from Charlu, "Bill to Amend the Law of Partnership in India," February 1866, no. 20, pp. 64–66, Legislative Branch, Home Department, NAI; Letter from Ghosh, n.d., and letter from Mullick, 17 November 1881, "The Bill for Incorporation, Regulations, and Winding-Up of Trading Companies," February 1882, File 794, pp. 303, 307, Judicial Department, WBSA; Letter from Hopkinson to Government of Bengal, "Eastern Bengal Railway Communication with Assam," November 1873, File 12, nos. 20–21, General Department, NAI; Crole, *Tea,* 37.

9. Rungta, *Business Corporations,* 101–4; Money, *Cultivation & Manufacture,* 178–79.

10. Campbell quoted in Edgar, "Tea Cultivation," 34–35. Cf. Rungta, *Business Corporations,* 100.

11. For a history of this legislation, see RALEC, 135–47; Hay and Craven, "Introduction," 1–2; "The Report of the Commission on the Labour Districts Emigration Act," August 1881, Progs. 1–9, A, p. 4, NAI.

12. Letter from J. Crerar to Government of India, June 1922, "Workman's Breach of Contract Act 1859," IOR/L/E/7/1339, File 1142, IOR; Hay, quoted in Steinberg, "Marx, Formal Subsumption," 201.

13. Edgar, "Tea Cultivation," 36, 15; Rungta, *Business Corporations,* 116; "Resolution," "Annual Report on the Province of Assam for 1872–1873," 8 September 1873, File 1, no. 81, p. 2, General Department, NAI.

14. Greenberg, *British Trade,* 145–48; Chapman, "Agency Houses," 240–43; Bayly and Subrahmanyam, "Portfolio Capitalists," 422.

15. Antrobus, *Assam Company,* 126, 152–54.

16. On managing agencies that moved in from other sectors, see Bagchi, *Private Investment,* 124, 162, 177; Money, *Cultivation & Manufacture,* 180; C. B. Skinner to C. H. Brown, 9 October 1863, JS/10/6, JSA; cf. entries from 30 December 1862 into 1863, "India (Calcutta) Committee Minute Books," MS 9925, vol. 13, 18, 26, ACA.

17. C. B. Skinner to C. H. Brown, 26 February 1863, and C. B. Skinner to C. H. Brown, 9 September 1863, Extracts from Letters to Calcutta, JS/10/6, JSA; see also letters from 10 June 1863 and 17 July 1863. In April 1866, memos began to appear that outlined the inventory of shipments from "your tea gardens" and "tea companies." The next year, 1867, the agency also bought two more tea companies. See letters from 26 April and 19 December 1866, Letters to Calcutta, JS/1/112; and 11 February 1867, JS/1/113, JSA.

18. Guha, *Early Colonial Assam,* 189; Stone, *Global Export of Capital,* 4–6, 82–91, 381. Stone documented "capital calls," which were pledged by investors with only a fraction paid up front. Cain and Hopkins, *British Imperialism,* 171–72; Bagchi, *Private Investment,* 161–71, 182–83; Chapman, "Agency Houses," 248–50.

19. Jeffrey, "Merchant Capital," 242; *James Finlay,* 102–4; "Retrospective typescript History of Calcutta branch Finlay Muir & Co, Calcutta 1870–1900," UGD91/11/6/1, JFA.

20. *James Finlay,* 104; "Office notes on Upper Assam Tea company Limited," 28 August 1953, "Correspondence, notes, drafts and other papers concerning Sir Percival Griffiths' History of the Indian Tea Industry," p. 2, MSS EUR/F174/2073, London archives of the Indian Tea Association, IOR; Jeffrey, "Merchant Capital," 242–43.

21. Steinfeld, *Coercion, Contract,* 9–10; Baptist, *Never Been Told,* ch. 7.

22. "Memorial from the Indian Tea Districts Association, London, Representing the Present State and Prospects of the Tea Industry in India," March 1880, Progs. 20–23, p. 3, Emigration Branch, Home, Revenue, and Agricultural Department, NAI.

23. "Papers Relating (63)," 11; Griffiths, *Indian Tea Industry,* 487; Gardella, *Harvesting Mountains,* 128, 54; Buckingham, *Indian Tea,* 25; Crole, *Tea,* 39–40.

24. Edgerton, "Innovation, Technology, or History," 689–93; Edgerton, *Shock of the Old,* xi; "Memorial from the Indian Tea Districts Association, London, Representing the Present State and Prospects of the Tea Industry in India," March 1880, Progs. 20–23, p. 3, Emigration Branch, Home, Revenue, and Agricultural Department, NAI; Barker, *Tea Planter's Life,* 238; Crole, *Tea,* 50.

25. Griffiths, *Indian Tea Industry,* 493–94; Ukers, *All About Tea,* 474–79; Barker, *Tea Planter's Life,* 238; Crole, *Tea,* 126–27, 59, 149.

26. Money, *Cultivation & Manufacture,* 171; Gardella, *Harvesting Mountains,* 118; Behal, *One Hundred Years,* 353–58; cf. productivity rates in Antrobus, *History of Jorehaut Tea Company,* 47–48; Antrobus, *Assam Company,* 408–11.

27. Money, *Cultivation & Manufacture,* 170. According to Berry White, tea in London dropped from one shilling and nine pence in 1878 to one shilling in 1886. White, "Indian Tea Industry," 741. Crole claimed that prices in 1893 were 45 percent lower than in 1881. Crole, *Tea,* 39, 40, 108; Barker, *Tea Planter's Life,* 117–18, 231–32, 237.

28. Barker, *Tea Planter's Life,* 119–21.

29. Allen, *Global Perspective,* 25–57; Beckert, *Empire of Cotton,* 65; Baildon, *Tea Industry,* 141; "Report on Labour Immigration into Assam for the Year 1900," p. 10, IOR/L/PJ/6/584, File 2118, IOR, hereafter cited as the "Cotton Report"; Behal, *One Hundred Years,* 199–226; Dowding, *Tea-Garden Coolies,* 33–34. That labor was the largest expense was a truism within the industry. See, for instance, ITA Report (1916), ii–iii; ITA Report (1920), iii.

30. Behal, *One Hundred Years,* 356–57; 82–87.

31. Burawoy, *Politics of Production,* 88–102; 97–98.

32. Sen, "Commercial Recruiting and Informal Intermediation," 3–4; Quanguo Jingji, *Yindu Xilan,* 56; cf. Barker, *Tea Planter's Life,* 136, 171, 154; cf. Baildon, *Tea Industry,* 162; Crole, *Tea,* 7.

33. "Report on Inland Emigration, Bengal/into Assam, 1881," February 1883, Progs. 22–26, p. 364, Revenue and Agricultural Department, NAI; Behal, *One Hundred Years,* 124; Edgar, "Tea Cultivation," 23.

34. Edgar "Tea Cultivation," 23; Dowding, *Tea-Garden Coolies,* 9; RALEC, 99; cf. Baildon, *Tea Industry,* 169–70; Barker, *Tea Planter's Life,* 171; "Report on Labour Immigration into Assam for the Year 1890," December 1891, Prog. no. 4, A, pp. 70–71, Emigration Branch, Revenue and Agricultural Department, NAI.

35. Edgar, "Tea Cultivation," 23, 49–52; Behal, *One Hundred Years,* 112; cf. Vidyāratna, *Kuli Kāhinī,* 26, 36; Ganguli, *Slavery in British Dominion,* 10, 33.

36. "Cotton Report," 23; cf. Behal, *One Hundred Years,* 167; Kolsky, *Colonial Justice,* 158.

37. Barker, *Tea Planter's Life,* 131; Crole, *Tea,* 49.

38. Barker, *Tea Planter's Life,* 134–35; cf. Crole, *Tea,* 60.

39. Vidyāratna, *Kuli Kāhinī,* 33.

40. Behal, *One Hundred Years,* 64–65; Ogle, "Whose Time," 1383–90.

41. Griffiths, *Indian Tea Industry,* 298–99; Behal, *One Hundred Years,* 65–66.

42. Postone, *Time, Labor,* 289; White, "Indian Tea Industry," 742; Ganguli, *Slavery in British Dominion,* 11; cf. Crole, *Tea,* 63.

43. Vidyāratna, *Kuli Kāhinī,* 75–76; cf. Barker, *Tea Planter's Life,* 132. Henry Cotton also denounced "the odious practice of allowing only quarter haziris" as "the sweating of labour." "Cotton Report," 10, 17–19.

44. Barker, *Tea Planter's Life,* 126–28, 146–47.

45. Behal, *One Hundred Years,* 269; RALEC, 14; Ghosh, "Market for Aboriginality," 31; Crole, *Tea,* 191.

46. Jenkins to Tea Committee, 20 February 1837, "Papers Relating (63)," 92; Ghosh, "Market for Aboriginality," 21–28.

47. Barker, *Tea Planter's Life*, 131; Baildon, *Tea Industry*, 153–54; Crole, *Tea*, 194; Ghosh, "Market for Aboriginality," 32. For instance, Barbara Fields locates much of the original ideological force of American-style scientific racism in the struggles between planter-capitalists and African labor in the United States South. Fields, "Slavery, Race, and Ideology."

48. Sen, "Questions of Consent," 231; Letter from Jenkins to Halliday, "Tea, Assam in, Cultivation of, Reports on and Measures to Improve," IOR/Z/E/4/15/T48, IOR, 703–5; RALEC, 37; Sen, *Women and Labour*, 7.

49. RALEC, 86; Crole, *Tea*, 201–5.

50. As a more recent comparison, Nancy Fraser has argued that twentieth-century Euro-American feminism's promotion of waged women's work under the banner of equality and emancipation has also abetted, unintentionally, the rise of a new form of capital accumulation friendly to markets and hostile to workers. Fraser, *Fortunes of Feminism*, ch. 9; Sen, "Questions of Consent," 232; RALEC, 82–86; Sen, *Women and Labour*, chs. 2–3.

51. Barker, *Tea Planter's Life*, 131–48; Crole, *Tea*, 56–68; Chatterjee, *Time for Tea*, 2–4.

52. Crole, *Tea*, 61; Behal, *One Hundred Years*, 365. Several times Kaushik Ghosh uses the term "fetishism" to describe the naturalization of Dhangars as particularly suited for manual labor. Here is how I interpret Ghosh's argument: For Marx, commodity fetishism arises from the confusion between (1) the price or value of a commodity as determined by its relation to other commodities on the market and (2) the appearance of value as a result of the inherent, natural qualities of that commodity. The latter then takes on a "magical" and "supra-sensible" quality. For Ghosh, the high prices of Dhangar recruits were the result of social market dynamics but appeared to observers as the result of their inherent qualities as a "race" perfectly suited to the type of labor to which they were assigned. Similarly, a woman seen as a good worker would be highly valued and in demand by planters (and male workers seeking a spouse). This value, determined by the dynamic relations of the labor market and expressed in commercial terms, could appear as the result of her natural gift for womanly labor, reinforcing the link between femininity and the act of plucking. In these formulations, modern ideas about gender and race likewise assume magical and metaphysical qualities as a result of their commodification. Ghosh, "Market for Aboriginality," 28, 31, 34; Marx, *Capital*, 1:163–77.

53. Braverman, *Monopoly Capital*, 127; Griffiths, *Indian Tea Industry*, 493; Berg, *Machinery Question*, 83–86.

54. Crole, *Tea*, 142, 154.

55. Saito, "Proto-Industrialization," 93–95; Braverman, *Monopoly Capital*, 125; Ukers, *All About Tea*, 468–70; Crole, *Tea*, 149; Barker, *Tea Planter's Life*, 142.

56. Barker, *Tea Planter's Life*, 135.

57. Berg, *Machinery Question*, 94; Kang, *Sublime Dreams of Living Machines*, 231–35; Ure quoted in Marx, *Grundrisse*, 690.

58. Marx, *Capital*, 1:457.

59. Baildon, *Tea Industry*, 155 (emphasis in original), 177; Dowding, *Tea-Garden Coolies*, 14.

60. Smith, *Wealth of Nations*, 840; Barker, *Tea Planter's Life*, 143.

61. Lin, *Wuyi Chaye*, 57.

62. "The Tea Trade," 8 June 1914, ITA Report (1914), 297.

63. *Home and Colonial Mail* (1880), quoted in Rappaport, *Thirst for Empire*, 160; Rappaport, *Thirst for Empire*, 165; Baildon, *Tea Industry*, 120; Crole, *Tea*, 41.

64. Baildon, *Tea Industry*, 122–23.

65. Ibid., 117–19; cf. Barker, *Tea Planter's Life*, 234–35; Rappaport, *Thirst for Empire*, 158.

66. Smith, *Uneven Development*, 196–202.

CHAPTER FIVE. NO SYMPATHY FOR THE MERCHANT?

1. E. Faragó quoted in Imperial Maritime Customs (IMC), *Decennial Reports*, 423; Ye Yaoyuan, "Wanguo Huozhi Lun," 520.

2. IMC, *Tea, 1888*, 130, 80; IMC, *Decennial*, 408–9; 422–23; Rowe, *Hankow*, 153; "Lun Hankou Chawu," ZCWJ, 624; "Lun Baoquan Chaye," ZCWJ, 622; Bian, *Bian Zhijun*, 16:1–4.

3. For the first generation of historians, see Wright, *Last Stand of Chinese Conservatism*, and Feuerwerker, *China's Early Industrialization*; for recent studies, the now-classic articulation of this view is Elman, "Naval Warfare."

4. Pomeranz, *Making of Hinterland*, 274.

5. The memorial was submitted on 13 January 1896, and the translations of Fawcett began to be published on 25 December 1896. CCJ, 393–95. Fawcett's work has been seen as a simpler version of Mill's *Principles*, which itself had carried forward many of the basic assumptions of Ricardo. Schumpeter, *History of Economic Analysis*, 530–33.

6. Liu Kunyi, "Wannan Xuzeng Chajuan Yaoqing Chongjian Pian," ZCWJ, 574. There was an official request to lower taxes in 1891. Ling, *Chashui Jianshi*, 123–24, 141–44.

7. Kleinwächter in IMC, *Tea, 1888*, 84–85. In the 1930s, reformers wrote that the entire history of the administration of tea until then had been a series of adjustments to taxation. Wu and Hu, *Fuxing Jihua*, 178.

8. Liu Kunyi, "Wannan Xuzeng Chajuan Yaoqing Chongjian Pian," ZCWJ, 574; Rowe, *Saving the World*, 198.

9. Lin, *China Upside Down*, 83, 141–42, 267; Yeh, *Shanghai Splendor*, 13–14, 222; Hankow Tea Guild in IMC, *Tea, 1888*, 48–49.

10. This section draws comparisons between late Qing economic thought and the well-known doctrines of mercantilism and Physiocracy in European history. The goal is not to assert some metaphysical stageism of ideas but to suggest that the history of economic thought around the world was actively engaged with material transformations in global economic practice; for examples of comparisons between the Physiocrats and Chinese economic thought, see Dunstan, *State or Merchant?*, 145; Perdue, *Exhausting the Earth*, 1–8; Rowe, *Saving the World*,

187–89, 213–14; Chao, *Development of Cotton Textile Production*, 38–40; Berg, *Machinery Question*, 38; Quesnay, "Despotism in China," 205–6; Meek, *Economics of Physiocracy*, 18–27; Perdue, *China Marches West*, 541. Cf. Wright, *Chinese Conservatism*, 153.

11. Hu, *Jingji Sixiang Shi*, 706; Twitchett, "Merchant, Trade, and Government," 64–65.

12. Lufrano, *Honorable Merchants*, 1–50; Pincus, "Machiavellian Moment," 707, 722; Morris-Suzuki, *Japanese Economic Thought*, 26–30.

13. Rowe, *Saving the World*, 159–60, 198–99, 176; Dunstan, *State or Merchant?*, 145, 468n3.

14. Meek, *Economics of Physiocracy*, 163–65, 27; Rowe, *Saving the World*, 161–64, 217, 187–89, 286; cf. Perdue, *Exhausting the Earth*.

15. Morris-Suzuki, *Japanese Economic Thought*, 17–20; Ermis, *Ottoman Economic Thought*, 50–51; Dasgupta, *Indian Economic Thought*, 49; Guha, *Rule of Property*, 11–57; Meek, *Economics of Physiocracy*, 362.

16. Hu, *Concise History*, 524; Hu, *Jingji Sixiang Shi*, 674.

17. Wang Tao, "Li Cai" (1861), 2:5–6; Wang Tao, "Xing Li" (ca. 1882), 2:16, both in Zhao and Yi, eds., *Ziliao Xuanji*.

18. Bian Baodi was the Hunan provincial governor (*xunfu*) from 1882 to 1888, with a stint as the Hubei-Hunan governor-general (*zongdu*) in the middle. His memorials on Hankou tea were quoted throughout Rowe, *Hankow*, 122–58.

19. Bian, *Bian Zhijun*, 12:39–41; 11:45–48; 15:1–3; 16:1–4.

20. Schumpeter, quoted in Shaikh, *Capitalism*, 350; Marx, *Capital*, 3:361–62; Shaikh, *Capitalism*, 261.

21. Pong, "Vocabulary of Change," 43; Zheng, *Shengshi Weiyan*, 238; Rowe, *Saving the World*, 204.

22. Zheng, *Shengshi Weiyan*, 238. The original phrase was "in one hundred battles you will not face danger" (*baizhan budai*).

23. Ibid., 240.

24. IMC, *Tea, 1888*, 65, 42, 73; Zhang Zhidong, "Zha Jiang-Han Guandao Quanyu Huashang Gouji Zhicha" (23 May 1899), ZCWJ, 603; "Lun Chawu," ZCWJ, 619.

25. "Cha Shi," ZCWJ, 621.

26. "Zhenxing Chaye Chuyan," ZCWJ, 623.

27. "Lun Baoquan Chaye," ZCWJ, 622; "Lun Chashi," ZCWJ, 619.

28. Marx, *Grundrisse*, 650–51; Marx, *Capital*, 3:1020; Elson, "Value Theory," 154; Baildon, *Tea Industry*, 137; White quoted in IMC, *Tea, 1888*, 124, emphasis in original.

29. Yeh, *Shanghai Splendor*, 9–10; Zhang, *Qiufu*, ch. 3; Hu, *Jingji Sixiang Shi*, 530.

30. Zhang, *Xunqiu Jindai Fuguo*, 316–17; 320–21; cf. Chen, "Xu Fuguo Ce" (1896), CCJ, 221–22.

31. Zhang, *Xunqiu Jindai Fuguo*, 68–69; Li and Li, "Shengchan Guan," 38; Cohen, *Tradition and Modernity*, 180.

32. Chen, "Chawu Tiaochen" (31 January 1896), CCJ; cf. Zheng, *Shengshi Weiyan*, 241–42; Ma, "Fumin Shuo" (1890), in Zhao and Yi, eds., *Ziliao Xuanji*, 2:32; "Hubu Yi Fu Zou Zhengdun Chawu Zhe," ZCWJ, 633.

33. The quotes from Chen's memorial come from Chen, "Chawu Tiaochen," CCJ, 346–50.

34. Zhang, *Xunqiu Jindai Fuguo*, 208–9.

35. Chen, "Xu Fuguo Ce," CCJ, 148.

36. Cohen, *Tradition and Modernity*, 180.

37. Chen, "Xu Fuguo Ce," CCJ, 149.

38. Ibid. Compare this to Marx, *Capital*, 1:325: The worker "creates surplus-value which, for the capitalist, has all the charms of something created out of nothing."

39. Although Smith did not view merchants as "productive," he also could not fully condemn them as unproductive, as the Physiocrats had. This was a logical inconsistency in his work that would disappear with future iterations of the theory of value by Ricardo et al. Cf. Boss, *Surplus and Transfer*, 55–56.

40. Chen, "Xu Fuguo Ce," CCJ, 232. Here, Chen also established a developmental trajectory for organizing different productive sectors, from primary production to "manufacturing arts" (*gongyi*), or, from low-value to high-value types of labor.

41. Zhao and Shi, *Sixiang Tongshi*, 286–87; Li and Li, "Shengchan Guan," 39; Hu, *Concise History*, 3:80–82; Rowe, *Saving the World*, 286–87.

42. Chen, "Chongyi Fuguo Ce" (1896), CCJ, 276.

43. Chen, "Xu Fuguo Ce," CCJ, 148–49.

44. Chen, "Chongyi Fuguo Ce," CCJ, 280.

45. Huang, *Peasant Economy*, 79–81; Huang, *Peasant Family*, 59; Walker, *Chinese Modernity*, 188.

46. Walker, *Chinese Modernity*, 74; Pan, "Ming-Qing Jiangnan," 96–110.

47. Chen, "Xu Fuguo Ce," CCJ, 171, 158, 164–66.

48. "Description of the Tea Plant" quoted in IMC, *Tea, 1888*, 143–48; Thomson quoted in Gardella, *Harvesting Mountains*, 67; IMC, *Tea, 1888*, 15–16. Marx described similar dynamics with the "independent peasant" who exists in a society in which capitalist production "predominates." The result is that the peasant becomes "cut into two," as both employer and employee, with the former appropriating value from the latter. Marx and Engels, *Collected Works*, 34:141–43.

49. Chen, "Xu Fuguo Ce," CCJ, 172.

50. Chen, "Xu Fuguo Ce," CCJ, 168; "Chawu Tiaochen," CCJ, 348.

51. Chen, "Xu Fuguo Ce," CCJ, 228–29.

52. Ibid., 158, 162, 169–73.

53. Ibid., 230–31, 202.

54. Zhao and Shi, *Jingji Sixiang Tongshi*, 273.

55. Zhang, *Xunqiu Jindai Fuguo*, 24.

56. He Runsheng, "Huishu Chawu Wuchen," ZCWJ, 625.

57. "Cha Shi," ZCWJ, 621.

58. Fu Run, "Zaizhun Hubu Ziyi Lü Zhongshu Liu Duo Yuan Wailang Chen Chi Dengtiao," 16 Second Month Guangxu 23 (18 March 1897), 03–6507–012, FHA.

59. De Shou, "Zhuoyi Chazheng Shiyi You," 8 Fourth Month Guangxu 22 (20 May 1896), 03–6507–023, FHA.

60. Chen Chi, "Chawu Tiaochen," CCJ, 350; cf. Yu Lu, a general of Fuzhou, who used the phrase "express personal empathy for the merchants' hardships"

(*tixu shangjian*). Yu Lu, "Yu Lu Deng Qing Jian Chajuan Siqian You," 21 Eleventh
Month Guangxu 23 (14 December 1897), 03–131–6509–014, FHA.
 61. He Runsheng, "Huishu Chawu Wuchen," ZCWJ, 625.

PART II. COOLIES AND COMPRADORS

 1. Van der Meer, "Colonial to Patriotic Drink."
 2. Hellyer, "1874."
 3. Chen, *Taibei Xian*, chs. 1–2.
 4. Peebles, *Plantation Tamils*, ch. 2; Wenzlhuemer, *From Coffee to Tea*, 53–89.

CHAPTER SIX. COOLIE NATIONALISM

 1. Ghosh, "Swāmī Rāmānanda," 158; Vidyāratna, "Āsām Bhramaṇ," 9, 16.
 2. Vidyāratna, "Āsām Bhramaṇ," 11–12.
 3. Vidyāratna, *Kuli Kāhinī*, 66–67.
 4. Behal and Mohapatra, "Tea and Money," 169–71; Behal, *One Hundred Years*, 244–45; speech by R. P. Karandikar in "Extract from the Legislative Assembly Debates," 5 February 1925, "File 1142 Workman's Breach of Contract Act 1859," IOR/L/E/7/1339, File 1142, IOR.
 5. Breman and Daniel, "Making of a Coolie," 270.
 6. Letter from Mackenzie, 19 September 1873, "Free Recruiting in Assam, Cachar and Sylhet," October 1873, File 11A, Progs. 4–6, General Department, NAI.
 7. "General Administration Report of the Province of Assam for the Year 1872–1873," 1874, File 1, Progs. 78–80, p. 18, General Department, NAI; Letter from Hopkinson, 18 October 1873, File 29, November 1873, nos. 44–45, General Department, NAI, emphasis added; Smith, *Wealth of Nations*, 24, emphasis added.
 8. Letter from Lyall (Secretary for Bayley), 11 August 1880, Prog. 55, p. 10, "Appointment of a Commission to Investigate and Report upon the Working and Amendment of Act VII (BC) of 1873," November 1880, Progs. 53–57, Emigration Branch, Home, Revenue, and Agriculture Department, NAI; Letter from Lyall, 28 October 1880, Prog. 71, "Appointment of a Commission to Investigate and Report upon the Working and Amendment of Act VII (BC) of 1873," December 1880, Progs. 68–72, p. 4, Emigration A, Home, Revenue, and Agriculture Department, NAI.
 9. Letter from Lyall (Secretary for Bayley), 11 August 1880, Prog. 55, p. 9; Letter from C. Grant, 25 August 1880, Prog. 57, p. 28, "Appointment of a Commission to Investigate and Report upon the Working and Amendment of Act VII (BC) of 1873," November 1880, Progs. 53–57, Emigration Branch, Home, Revenue, and Agriculture Department, NAI.
 10. Letter from Lyall, 28 October 1880, Prog. 71, "Appointment of a Commission to Investigate and Report upon the Working and Amendment of Act VII (BC) of 1873," December 1880, Progs. 68-72, p. 3, Emigration A, Home, Revenue, and Agriculture Department, NAI; Calcutta firm quoted in McKeown, *Melancholy*

Order, 72; Alexander Miller, member of the Legislative Council of India, quoted in ITA Report (1893), 208.

11. Polanyi, *Great Transformation*, 72–73.

12. Letter from MacDonnell, 9 December 1885, "Working of the Inland Emigration Act I of 1882," Prog. no 15, August 1886, Emigration Branch, Revenue and Agricultural Department, NAI.

13. RALEC, 23, 45; Sen, "Commercial Recruiting and Informal Intermediation," 11.

14. Sen, "Commercial Recruiting and Informal Intermediation," 19–22.

15. For a detailed history of the various associations, see Seal, *Indian Nationalism*, ch. 5.

16. Chandra, *Economic Nationalism*, 360–70; Sarkar, *Swadeshi Movement*, 109–10. Dowding was also a shareholder in a tea garden. Dowding, *Tea-Garden Coolies*, iv; Kopf, *Brahmo Samaj*, 133–45. For a quantitative analysis of the occupations of these organization's members, see McGuire, *Colonial Mind*, Appendices.

17. Sartori, *Global Concept History*, ch. 3; Goswami, *Producing India*, 212; Dutt, *Economic History of India*, xvi–xvii; Ganguli, *Slavery in British Dominion*, 1.

18. The "mirror" in the title was fashioned after the famous play *The Mirror of the Indigo Planter* (*Nīl Darpan*), which inspired others to use "mirror" in their titles. The term suggested the play was holding up a mirror to the actual conditions of British rule in India. Bhatia, *Acts of Authority*, 38; Chattopādhyāy, *Chā-Kar Darpan*, 230—I thank Subir Sarkar, Mandira Sen, and Samita Sen for helping me locate different versions of this text; "Report on Native Papers" in Biswās, *Hujur Darpan*, 134; Chattopādhyāy, "Introduction," vii–viii; "Treatment of Tea Garden Labourers in Assam; Report from Aborigines Protection Society," 17 January 1887, IOR/L/PJ/6/193, File 112, IOR; on the Indian Association's activities regarding tea labor, see Bagal, *Indian Association*, xx, 88–89.

19. Pal, *Memories of My Life and Times*, 414–15; cf. Chandra, *Economic Nationalism*, 363.

20. Vidyāratna, *Kuli Kāhinī*, 22.

21. Ibid., 27, 23.

22. Ganguli, *Slavery in British Dominion*, 1.

23. Holt, *Problem of Freedom*, 26; Vidyāratna, *Kuli Kāhinī*, 24.

24. Dowding, *Tea-Garden Coolies*, 32.

25. Vidyāratna, *Kuli Kāhinī*, 63, 110. I thank Meghna Chaudhuri and Rishad Choudhury for help with this and other Bengali translations.

26. Ibid., 141–44.

27. Holt, *Problem of Freedom*, 21–24, 3–4.

28. Ibid., 25.

29. Ibid., 50; 25–26; Atiyah, *Freedom of Contract*, 300–301.

30. McKeown, "How the Box," 22; Holt, *Problem of Freedom*, 25–26; Kale, *Fragments of Empire*, 87.

31. Carter, *Servants, Sirdars*, 18, Prinsep quoted on 21; Kale, *Fragments of Empire*, 16–20.

32. Kale, *Fragments of Empire*, 36, 147–174, 28–29; Lees, *Tea Cultivation*, 366; RALEC, 135.

33. Breman and Daniel, "Making of a Coolie," 276; Sen, "Gender and Class," 79–87; Banerjee, *Politics of Time*, 103; Chatterjee, *Nation and Fragments*, 6–7, 74–75, 116–34.

34. 10 January 1888, *Hindu Ranjiká*, reel 10; cf. 14 January 1888, *Sanjivani*, reel 10, INR; Chattopādhyāy, *Chā-Kar Darpan*, 248; Vidyāratna, *Kuli Kāhinī*, 173, 224; Sarkar, *Hindu Wife*, 41, 45–46.

35. Vidyāratna, *Kuli Kāhinī*, 169.

36. Ibid.; 8 June 1888, *Sanjivani*, reel 10; 1 July 1889, *Navavibhákar Sádhárani*, reel 11, INR.

37. Sarkar, *Hindu Wife*, 259.

38. Vidyāratna, *Kuli Kāhinī*, 11.

39. Ibid., 48.

40. Chattopādhyāy, *Chā-Kulīr Ātmakāhinī*, 1–2.

41. Bose, *Agrarian Bengal*, 20, 5, 29–30; Chaudhuri, "Agrarian Relations," 134–42; Chandra, *Economic Nationalism*, 323.

42. Bose, *Agrarian Bengal*, 74; Vidyāratna, *Kuli Kāhinī*, 41.

43. Chattopādhyāy, *Chā-Kar Darpan*, 233.

44. Ibid., 236; Chattopādhyāy, *Chā-Kulīr Ātmakāhinī*, 6.

45. Ganguli, *Slavery in British Dominion*, 1; Dutt, *Economic History of India*, 351–52.

46. Vidyāratna, *Kuli Kāhinī*, 92–93; Pal, *Memories of My Life and Times*, 414.

47. Vidyāratna, *Kuli Kāhinī*, 110–11.

48. Bagal, "Tea Garden Labour in Assam," in *Indian Association*, xxxvi; Dutt, *Economic History*, 352, 522.

49. Marx, *Capital*, 1:1064. Italics in original.

50. 9 January 1887, *Paridarshak*, reel 9, INR; speech by R. P. Karandikar, "Extract from the Legislative Assembly Debates," 5 February 1925, "File 1142 Workman's Breach of Contract Act 1859," IOR/L/E/7/1339, File 1142, IOR; Marx, *Capital*, 1:719.

51. Sir Charles Rivaz quoted in RALEC, 22.

52. McKeown, "How the Box," 33.

53. RALEC, 16–20, 27, 112.

54. Das, *Plantation Labour*, 35–36; RALEC, 105; "Note," "The Workman's Breach of Contract Act of 1859 and Its Repeal (1936)," IOR/L/E/8/884, IOR; ITA Report (1917), 12.

55. Speeches by Malaviya in "Extract from Proceedings of the Indian Legislative Council," 17 September 1919, and quoting Srinivasa Iyengar on 4 February 1920; Letter from Chamber of Commerce, 10 November 1919, "File 1142 Workman's Breach of Contract Act 1859," IOR/L/E/7/1339, File 1142, IOR.

56. ITA Report (1920), 77; Guha, *Planter Raj*, 105.

57. ITA Report (1922), 75, 89; "Note," "The Workman's Breach of Contract Act of 1859 and Its Repeal (1936)," IOR/L/E/8/884, IOR.

58. M. Krishna, "Assam Labour," 6 June 1925, "File 3296 Coolie Labour in Assam Tea Gardens—Conditions and Exodus of Labourers from Assam," IOR/L/E/7/1354, File 3296, IOR.

59. Speeches by William Vincent and B. S. Kamat in "Resolution re: Repeal of Workmen's Breach of Contact Act," 10 September 1921; Letter from L. S. White,

5 June 1922, "File 1142 Workman's Breach of Contract Act 1859," IOR/L/E/7/1339, File 1142, IOR.

60. Speeches by Malaviya in "Extract from Proceedings of the Indian Legislative Council," 17 September 1919, "File 1142 Workman's Breach of Contract Act 1859," IOR/L/E/7/1339, File 1142, IOR; M. Krishna, "Assam Labour," 6 June 1925, "File 3296 Coolie Labour in Assam Tea Gardens—Conditions and Exodus of Labourers from Assam," IOR/L/E/7/1354, File 3296, IOR.

61. Kling, *Partner in Empire*, 1, 198–229; Sarkar, *Swadeshi Movement*, 109, 96; Dutt, *Economic History of India*, vii–ix, 351.

62. Dasgupta, *Indian Economic Thought*, 74, for background on the drain theory see 74–86; Goswami, *Producing India*, 227, 243.

63. ITA Report (1920), 65–66; Behal, *One Hundred Years*, 309–10; Sarkar, *Modern India*, 209–26; Guha, *Planter Raj*, 108–14.

64. Pal quoted in *Report of the Seventeenth Indian National Congress*, 167–68.

65. Quoted in Chatterjee, *Time for Tea*, 106.

CHAPTER SEVEN. FROM COHONG TO COMPRADOR

1. Ichiko, "Institutional Reform," 382–89.

2. Lu, "Yisinian Diaocha," 52–56.

3. Karl, *Staging the World*, ch. 6.

4. Bright and Geyer, "Global Condition," 296–97; Lu, "Yisinian Diaocha," 133–34; Lu, "Wo de Zishu," 133; Lu, "Woguo Chaye," 868; cf. Wu, "Zhongguo Chaye Yanjiu Gaijin Shi" (1943), WJX, 262.

5. Wu and Fan, *Chaye Wenti*, 167.

6. Wu, "Zhanshi Chaye Tongzhi Zhengce zhi Jiantao" (1945), WJX, 306–8; Wu, "Gaijin Shi," WJX, 261.

7. E.g., Ghosh, *Big Bourgeoisie*; Sheriff, *Spices & Ivory*; Vitalis, "Theory and Practice," 291, 309; Astourian, "Testing World-System Theory," 479. Thanks to Owen Miller and Mari Webel for these recommendations; a similar argument can be found in Karl, "Compradors," 237–238; notably, Ma Yinchu, a famed Chinese economist, in 1923 compared the Chinese comprador to the Japanese "Banto" and the Indian "Banian." Ma, "Maiban Zhi," 129.

8. Wu and Fan, *Chaye Wenti*, 237–38. Chinese speakers at first began to refer to this same employee as the *maiban zhi ren*, or, "the one who makes purchases and manages business," later shortened to simply *maiban*. The term dates back to at least the Ming Dynasty. Bell, *One Industry*, 50–54.

9. Dyce, *Personal Reminiscences*, 233; Rowe, *Saving the World*, 248–49; Hao, *Comprador*, 110–34; Yeh, *Shanghai Splendor*, 9–29.

10. Nie, *Zhongguo Maiban*, 136–37; Li, *Silk Trade*, 155–62. Similar "warehouses" (*zhan*) existed in the sugar and opium trades (Nie, *Zhongguo Maiban*, 59). The first documented usage of the term "warehouse" can be traced to the Fuzhou trade of the 1850s, with the advent of the up-country trade. By the 1860s, records from Jardine Matheson & Co. began to use the term "tea hotels," an alternative translation of the term *zhan*, whose meaning I believe is better conveyed as "godown" or "warehouse" (Hao, *Commercial Revolution*, 140–53); for instance,

in the treaty port Jiujiang, no tea warehouses existed in 1861, but by the next year, about sixteen had emerged, followed by over three hundred more by the 1880s (Nie, *Zhongguo Maiban*, 137).

Commentaries from the Republican period (1912–1949) suggested that although the tea warehouses existed long before the Guangxu Era began (1875), the modern Shanghai business model could only be traced back to 1884 ("Shanghai Chazhan zhi Qiyuan," *Zhejiang Nongye*, 1939, [7/8], 21). In 1889, the Shanghai paper *Shen Bao* recorded a story of a Hankou comprador who left his employer in order to start his own warehouse, crushing foreign competition (Nie, *Zhongguo Maiban*, 120). Records from pre-1895 Taiwan indicated it was also during the 1880s that American and British export tea trade there began to rely on Cantonese and Fujianese firms known as "tea warehouses" (Chen, *Taibei Xian Chaye*, 16–21). The warehouses were a highly fluid institution, with many firms starting up and shutting down from year to year. In 1931, when the first systematic surveys were conducted, the Shanghai market was dominated by eighteen tea warehouses, none older than 1901, and most created after the 1911 Revolution (Shanghai, *Cha?*, 102–4).

11. Wu and Fan, *Chaye Wenti*, 237–38; Wu, "Kangzhan yu Chaye Gaizao" (1939), WJX, 218; Wu and Hu, *Zhongguo Chaye Fuxing*, 62; Nie, *Zhongguo Maiban*, 87; Xu Run, *Xu Yuzhai*, 26–27.

12. Sha, *Maiban Zhi*, 27–39; Hao, *Comprador*, 102; Mao, *Midnight*; Wu Shan, "Guai Maiban," *Minzhong wenxue* 8:4 (1924), 1–12; Mao, "Classes in Chinese Society," 13–14.

13. For instance: "Pipan Hu Shi Maiban Zichan Jieji de Shijie Zhuyi Wenhuaguan," *Sichuan Daxue Xuebao*, no. 1 (1956); "Shenru Pipan Deng Xiaoping Yangnu Maiban de Zichan Jieji Jingji Sixiang," *Liaoning Ribao*, August 31, 1976; Tao Dayong, "Liang Shuming Shehui Zhengzhi Guandian de Fengjianxing yu Maibanxing," *Beijing Shifan Daxue Xuebao* (1956); "Lin Biao Fengkuang Gongji Wuchan Jieji Zhuanzheng jiushi Wangtu Jianli Fengjian Maiban Faxisi Wangchao," *Jilin Ribao*, September 5, 1973; Zhang Jingui, Shi Shuming, "Pipan Li Hongzhang zai Zhongguo Jindaishi Jiaoxuezhong de Fengjian Maiban Guandian," *Yangzhou Shiyuan Xuebao*.

14. Bergère, "Golden Age," 49; cf. Coble, *Shanghai Capitalists*, 266.

15. Tsai, "Comprador Ideologists," 192; Hao, *Comprador*, 10–11; Zanasi, *Saving the Nation*, 230, 51, 4. For Japanese perspectives, see Tsuchiya, *Baiben Seido*; for American perspectives, see George Sokolsky, "How Business is Conducted," 18 March 1920, *Manufacturers' News*, pp. 11–12, and "Passing of the Compradore Order in Shanghai," 1 March 1930, *China Weekly Review*, p. 4.

16. Lu, "Woguo Chaye," 868–70, 74; Zhuang Wanfang, *Cha Shi Sanlun*, ch. 13; Lu, "Zishu," 133–34; further historical inquiry into the peculiar origin stories of Qimen black tea can be found in Liu, *Two Tea Countries*, appendix.

17. Wu, "Wo zai Shanghai Shangjianju Gao Chaye Gongzuo de Huiyi" (1983), WJX, 434; Wang, *Cha zhe Sheng*, 15; Wu, "Nongmin Wenti," 20.

18. Fitzgerald, *Awakening China*, 3–4; Liu, "Woman Question"; Wang, *Cha zhe Sheng*, 33–34.

19. Wu, "Shanghai Shangjianju," WJX, 440; Wu, "Gaijin Shi," WJX, 257–59.

20. Zanasi, *Saving the Nation*, 98–99, 104–5; Wu, "Shanghai Shangjianju," WJX, 437, 440; on the history of "economic control," see Zheng, "'Tongzhi Jingji,'" 93–98.

21. Wu and Hu, *Fuxing Jihua*, 142.

22. Chiang, *Social Engineering*, 201–10.

23. Wu and Hu, *Fuxing Jihua*, 29–37; Wu, "Zhongguo Chaye de Fazhan yu Hezuo Yundong" (1944), WJX, 271; Sun, Liu, and Wang, *Qimen*, 22.

24. Wu and Hu, *Fuxing Jihua*, 49–51; for specific numbers, see Sun, Liu, and Wang, *Qimen*, 27–35, and Sun, Liu, and Wang, *Tunxi*, 7–14; Fu, "Wan-Zhe Xin'an," 123; Wu, "Qihong Tongzhi de Xian Jieduan" (1937), WJX, 201.

25. Wu and Hu, *Fuxing Jihua*, 53; Wu, "Qihong Tongzhi," WJX, 202; Sun, Liu, and Wang, *Qimen*, 55; Jiang, "Qimen Hongcha," 99; Shanghai, *Cha?*, 60–61.

26. Wu and Hu, *Fuxing Jihua*, 32; Wu and Hu, "Qihong Chaye," 43; cf. Shanghai, *Cha?*, 47; Wu and Fan, *Chaye Wenti*, 204.

27. Wu, "Qihong Tongzhi," WJX, 203; Sun, Liu, and Wang, *Tunxi*, 38

28. Shanghai, *Cha?*, 59.

29. Shanghai, *Cha?*, 48–49, 59–60; Wu and Fan, *Chaye Wenti*, 239–40; 211–12.

30. Wu and Hu, *Fuxing Jihua*, 61–65; Fu, "Wan-Zhe Xin'an," 117.

31. Wu and Hu, *Fuxing Jihua*, 187; Shanghai, *Cha?*, 60; Fan, "Tunxi Chaye," 115.

32. Jaynes, *Branches without Roots*, 33–53. Thanks to David Weiman for this reference. Cf. Marx, *Capital*, 1:278; Fu, "Wan-Zhe Xin'an," 146.

33. Sun, Liu, and Wang, *Tunxi*, 32, 7.

34. Wu, "Qihong Tongzhi," WJX, 201.

35. Banaji, "Capitalist Domination"; Walker, *Chinese Modernity*, ch. 8; Wu, "Shanghai Shangjianju," WJX, 439.

36. Wu and Hu, *Fuxing Jihua*, 65–66.

37. Chiang, *Social Engineering*, 202–3; Wu and Fan, *Chaye Wenti*, 187; Wu and Hu, *Fuxing Jihua*, 61–62.

38. Wu and Hu, *Fuxing Jihua*, 65, 169; Tsuchiya, *Baiben Seido*, 4. He later refers to the "theory of the comprador's uselessness" (*baiben muyōron*), 88.

39. Wu, "Chaye Gaizao," WJX, 226.

40. Xiao Qiu, "Huiyi he Ganchu," *Chasheng Banyuekan*, no. 3 (1939), 9–10.

41. Sha, *Maiban Zhi*, 41–42, 55; Zhang, "Pingli Hezuoshe," 23.

42. Boss, *Surplus and Transfer*, 2–3, 78, emphasis in original; for Smith's original definition, see Smith, *Wealth of Nations*, 360–81; Maoyi Weiyuanhui, "Wannan Chagong," *Chasheng Banyuekan*, no. 12 (1939), 127.

43. Rubin, *Theory of Value*, 267–68. N.b., Marx criticizes the concept of "productive capital" for mystifying the role of labor. Marx, *Capital*, 1:1052–58.

44. Postone, "Anti-Semitism," 110; Goswami, *Producing India*, 225–26.

45. Beckert, *Empire of Cotton*, xv–xvi; Marx, *Capital*, 3:441–54.

46. Braudel, *Wheels of Commerce*, 25–26; Banaji, "Islam, the Mediterranean"; Banaji, "Merchant Capitalism"; Bell, *One Industry*, 46–64.

47. Wang, *Cha zhe Sheng*, 77–79; see discussion of Wu Juenong's overseas expedition in the conclusion.

48. "Only after returning from India and Ceylon, where I accumulated several years of experience, did I understand that reform did not have to be limited to existing tools, like old baking baskets, but that new methods can be taught, such as employing machines for rolling, sifting, and cutting leaves." Lu, *Guonei Chawu*, 34.

49. Lu, *Woguo Chaye*, 868.

50. Wu and Hu, *Fuxing Jihua*, 5.

51. By comparison, earlier, when Chen Chi and Lu Ying first described the vertical integration of tea, they used the colloquial expressions "in one breath of air" (*yiqi hecheng*) or "strung together as one" (*yiyiguanzhi*). As men of the late Qing, Chen Chi and Lu Ying aimed to redeploy old phrasings in order to describe modern phenomena such as vertical integration. By contrast, Wu Juenong, a member of the May Fourth generation, was well-versed in the assortment of European and Japanese loanwords, such as "enterprise," circulating throughout Shanghai and Tokyo.

52. Wu and Hu, *Fuxing Jihua*, 143–47.

53. Ibid., 179.

54. Chan, *Modern Enterprise*, 33–34, romanization modified. The reference to "ghosts" by Wu Juenong is an apt metaphor insofar as Marx frequently described capital-intensive improvements as the application of prior, "dead labor" that confronts still-living labor. Marx, *Capital*, 1:342, 548.

55. Marx, *Grundrisse*, 87.

56. Wu and Fan, *Chaye Wenti*, 244–45.

57. Chen, "Cooperatives as Panacea," 71–73; Liu, "Woman Question," 42–43.

58. Zhang, "Pingli Hezuoshe," 23.

59. Wu and Hu, *Fuxing Jihua*, 169, 2–3, 130.

60. Wang Ruiqi, "Qimen Chaye Gailiang Chang Lishi Gaikuang," in Anhui Yanjiusuo, *Qishi Zhounian*, 44–45; Anhui Gailiangchang, *Pingli Chaye*, 1–2.

61. Wang Ruiqi, "Qimen Chaye Gailiangchan Lishi Gaikuang," in Anhui Yanjiusuo, *Qishi Zhounian*, 45.

62. Qian Liang, "Qimen Chaye Gailiang Chang: Woguo Chaye Keji Renyuan de Yaolan," in Anhui Yanjiusuo, *Qishi Zhounian*, 39–40; Feng Shaoqiu, "Qihong de Chuzhi he Jizhi Shiyan," in Anhui Yanjiusuo, *Qishi Zhounian*, 35–36.

63. Anhui Gailiangchang, *Pingli Chaye*, 1.

64. Wu, "Gaijin Shi," WJX, 261.

65. Wu and Fan, *Chaye Wenti*, 245.

66. "Shanghai Tea Hongs Strike in Protest Move," 24 April 1936; and "Tea Districts in Furor over Credit Refusal," 26 April 1936, *China Press* (Shanghai); "Yangzhuang Chaye Shisi Jia Zuo Tingdui hou Fendian Qingyuan," 24 April 1936; and "Wan-Gan Hongcha Yunxiao Dengji Erbaishu Shi Jia Daikuan Bai Liushi Wan Yuan," 28 April 1936, *Shen Bao*.

67. The following quotes from the *Rural China* essay come from Wu Juenong, "Fandi Fanfengjian de Banmu Ju" (1936), WJX, 176–82.

68. H. H. Kung quoted in "Yangzhuang Chazhan Tingdui hou Chaye Jiaoyi Biantai," 25 April 1936, *Shen Bao*.

69. Shanghai Chamber of Commerce quoted in "Shi Shanghui Dian Qing Che Xiao Qicha Tongzhi," 11 April 1936, *Shen Bao*.

70. Rather than the standard term *maiban*, the author described the warehouses with the old-fashioned colloquial phrases *jiaofan* (in-house translators for foreign firms) and *paolou* (runners who take orders from foreigners). The effect was to underscore the anachronistic elements of the Chinese export trade in a rapidly changing global economy.

71. Merkel-Hess, *Rural Modern*, ch. 4; Chen, "Cooperative Movement," 134–40, 184–92; Zanasi, *Saving the Nation*, chs. 4–5; Wu, "Muqian Chaye Chanxiao Qushi he Women de Renwu" (1950), WJX, 319.

72. Quoted in Wang, *Cha zhe Sheng*, 132.

73. Wang, *Cha zhe Sheng*, 119, 154, 157–59.

74. Zanasi, *Saving the Nation*, conclusion; Merkel-Hess, *Rural Modern*, 9–10.

75. Mao, "Democratic Dictatorship," 421.

76. Wang, *Cha zhe Sheng*, ch. 15; Wu, "Muqian Chaye," WJX, 320.

CONCLUSION

1. Quanguo, *Yindu Xilan*, 1–3, 56, 58; personal correspondence with Wu Ning.

2. Mintz, *Sweetness and Power*, 46–55; Fu, "Chinese Agriculture," 312–14.

3. Quanguo, *Yindu Xilan*, 58–59.

4. Davidson, "Multiple Nation-States," 237.

5. Rappaport, *Thirst for Empire*, 342–45.

6. Chatterjee, *Time for Tea*, 104–7; Banerjee, *Tea Plantation Industry*, chs. 6–8; Wickizer in Banerjee, 180.

7. Rappaport, *Thirst for Empire*, 345–47; Lutgendorf, "Making Tea," 17–24.

8. Wang, *Cha zhe Sheng*, 180.

9. Forster, "Strange Tale"; Eisenman, *Green Revolution*; Schmalzer, *Red Revolution*.

10. FAO, "Current Market"; Besky, "Tea as Hero Crop"; Pramod Giri, "Indian Tea Industry Has a Lot to Learn from Its Chinese Counterpart, Say Traders and Growers," 22 April 2017, *Hindustan Times*.

Bibliography

Allen, Robert C. *The British Industrial Revolution in Global Perspective.* Cambridge: Cambridge University Press, 2009.

Ambirajan, S. *Classical Political Economy and British Policy in India.* Cambridge: Cambridge University Press, 1978.

Amin, Shahid, and Marcel van der Linden, eds. "Introduction." In *"Peripheral" Labour?: Studies in the History of Partial Proletarianization,* 1–8. Cambridge: Cambridge University Press, 1997.

Anhui Sheng Nongye Kexueyuan Qimen Chaye Yanjiusuo. *Qishi Zhounian Suoqing Jinian.* Qimen: Anhui Sheng Nongye Kexueyuan Qimen Chaye Yanjiusuo, 1985.

Anhui Shengli Chaye Gailiangchang. *Pingli Chaye Yunxiao Xinyong Hezuo Baogao.* Qimen: Dawen Yinshuasuo, 1934.

Antrobus, H. A. *A History of the Assam Company, 1839–1953.* Edinburgh: T. and A. Constable, 1957.

———. *A History of the Jorehaut Tea Company Ltd., 1859–1946.* London: Tea and Rubber Mail, 1948.

Arrighi, Giovanni. *Adam Smith in Beijing: Lineages of the Twenty-First Century.* London: Verso, 2007.

———. *The Long Twentieth Century: Money, Power, and the Origins of Our Times.* London: Verso, 1994.

Assam Labour Enquiry Committee. *Proceedings of the Assam Labour Enquiry Committee in the Recruiting and Labour Districts.* Kolkata: Office of the Superintendent of Government Printing, 1906.

———. *Report of the Assam Labour Enquiry Committee, 1906.* Kolkata: Office of the Superintendent of Government Printing, 1906.

———. *Report of the Assam Labour Enquiry Committee, 1921–1922.* Shillong: Government Press, 1922.

Astourian, Stephen. "Testing World-System Theory, Cilicia, 1830s–1890s: Armenian-Turkish Polarization and the Ideology of Modern Ottoman Historiography." PhD diss.: University of California, Los Angeles, 1996.

Atiyah, P. S. *The Rise and Fall of Freedom of Contract*. Oxford: Clarendon Press, 1985.

Bagal, Jogesh Chandra. *History of the Indian Association, 1876–1951* (1953). 3rd ed. Kolkata: Indian Association, 2002.

Bagchi, Amiya Kumar. *Private Investment in India, 1900–1939*. Cambridge: Cambridge University Press, 1972.

Baildon, Samuel. *Tea in Assam: A Pamphlet on the Origin, Culture, and Manufacture of Tea in Assam*. Kolkata: W. Newman, 1877.

———. *The Tea Industry in India: A Review of Finance and Labour, and a Guide for Capitalists and Assistants*. London: W. H. Allen, 1882.

Ball, Samuel. *An Account of the Cultivation and Manufacture of Tea in China*. London: Longman, Brown, Green, and Longmans, 1848.

Banaji, Jairus. "Capitalist Domination and the Small Peasantry: The Deccan Districts in the Late Nineteenth Century." In *Theory as History: Essays on Modes of Production and Exploitation*, 277–332. Chicago: Haymarket Books, 2011.

———. "The Fictions of Free Labour: Contract, Coercion, and So-Called Unfree Labour." In *Theory as History: Essays on Modes of Production and Exploitation*, 131–54. Chicago: Haymarket Books, 2011.

———. "Islam, the Mediterranean and the Rise of Capitalism." In *Theory as History: Essays on Modes of Production and Exploitation*, 251–76. Chicago: Haymarket Books, 2011.

———. "Merchant Capitalism, Peasant Households and Industrial Accumulation: Integration of a Model." *Journal of Agrarian Change* 16, no. 3 (2016): 410–31.

———. "Modes of Production in a Materialist Conception of History." In *Theory as History: Essays on Modes of Production and Exploitation*, 45–102. Chicago: Haymarket Books, 2011.

———. "Modes of Production: A Synthesis." In *Theory as History: Essays on Modes of Production and Exploitation*, 349–360. Chicago: Haymarket Books, 2011.

———. "Seasons of Self-Delusion: Opium, Capitalism and the Financial Markets." *Historical Materialism* 21, no. 2 (2013): 3–19.

Banerjee, Gangadhar. *Tea Plantation Industry, between 1850 and 1992: Structural Changes*. Gauhati: Lawyer's Book Stall, 1996.

Banerjee, Prathama. *The Politics of Time: "Primitives" and the Writing of History in Colonial Bengal*. New Delhi: Oxford University Press, 1998.

Baptist, Edward E. *The Half Has Never Been Told: Slavery and the Making of American Capitalism*. New York: Basic Books, 2014.

Barker, George M. *A Tea Planter's Life in Assam.* Kolkata: Thacker, Spink, 1884.

Barpujari, H. K. *Assam in the Days of the Company, 1826–1858.* 2nd ed. Gauhati: Spectrum Publications, 1980.

———. *Political History of Assam: 1920–1939.* Gauhati: Government of Assam, 1978.

Bayly, C. A., and Sanjay Subrahmanyam. "Portfolio Capitalists and the Political Economy of Early Modern India." *Indian Economic & Social History Review* 25, no. 4 (1988): 401–24.

Beckert, Sven. *Empire of Cotton: A Global History.* New York: Knopf, 2014.

———. "History of American Capitalism." In *American History Now,* edited by Eric Foner and Lisa McGirr, 314–35. Philadelphia: Temple University Press, 2011.

Bedini, Silvio A. "The Scent of Time: A Study of the Use of Fire and Incense for Time Measurement in Oriental Countries." *Transactions of the American Philosophical Society* 53, no. 5 (1963): 1–51.

———. *The Trail of Time: Time Measurement with Incense in East Asia.* Cambridge: Cambridge University Press, 1994.

Behal, Rana Partap. *One Hundred Years of Servitude: Political Economy of Tea Plantations in Colonial Assam.* New Delhi: Tulika Books, 2014.

Behal, Rana, and Prabhu Mohapatra. "'Tea and Money versus Human Life': The Rise and Fall of the Indenture System in the Assam Tea Plantations, 1840–1908." *Journal of Peasant Studies* 19, no. 3 (1992): 142–72.

Bell, Lynda S. *One Industry, Two Chinas: Silk Filatures and Peasant-Family Production in Wuxi County, 1865–1937.* Stanford: Stanford University Press, 1999.

Benn, James A. *Tea in China: A Religious and Cultural History.* Honolulu: University of Hawai'i Press, 2015.

Berg, Maxine. "Factories, Workshops and Industrial Organisation." In *The Economic History of Britain since 1700: 1700–1860,* edited by Roderick Floud and Deirdre N. McCloskey, 123–50. Cambridge: Cambridge University Press, 1994.

———. *The Machinery Question and the Making of Political Economy, 1815–1848.* Cambridge: Cambridge University Press, 1982.

Bergère, Marie-Claire. *The Golden Age of the Chinese Bourgeoisie, 1911–1937.* Translated by Janet Lloyd. Cambridge: Cambridge University Press, 1989.

Bernstein, Henry, and Tom Brass. "Introduction: Proletarianisation and Deproletarianisation on the Colonial Plantation." *Journal of Peasant Studies* 19, no. 3–4 (1992): 1–40.

Besky, Sarah. "Tea as Hero Crop? Embodied Algorithms and Industrial Reform in India." *Science as Culture* 26, no. 1 (2017): 11–31.

Bhatia, Nandi. *Acts of Authority, Acts of Resistance: Theater and Politics in Colonial and Postcolonial India.* Ann Arbor: University of Michigan Press, 2004.

Bhattacharya, Sabyasachi. "Laissez Faire in India." *Indian Economic & Social History Review* 2, no. 1 (1965): 1–22.

Bhattacharya, Sabyasachi, and B. Chaudhuri. "Eastern India." In *The Cambridge Economic History of India*, vol. 2, edited by Dharma Kumar and Meghnad Desai, 270–331. Cambridge: Cambridge University Press, 1983.

Bhattacharya, Subhas. "Indigo Planters, Ram Mohan Roy and the 1833 Charter Act." *Social Scientist* 4, no. 3 (1975): 56–65.

Bian Baodi. *Bian Zhijun Zouyi*. 1900.

Birla, Ritu. *Stages of Capital: Law, Culture, and Market Governance in Late Colonial India.* Durham: Duke University Press, 2009.

Biswās, Pratibhā, ed. *Hujur Darpan: Kam Ālocita Nātake Ūnis Satker Bānglā.* Kolkata: Pharma K.L.M. Private, 1983.

Bose, Sugata. *Agrarian Bengal: Economy, Social Structure, and Politics, 1919–1947.* Cambridge: Cambridge University Press, 1986.

Boss, Helen. *Theories of Surplus and Transfer: Parasites and Producers in Economic Thought.* Boston: Unwin Hyman, 1990.

Bowen, H. V. *The Business of Empire: The East India Company and Imperial Britain, 1756–1833.* Cambridge: Cambridge University Press, 2005.

———. "Tea, Tribute and the East India Company, c. 1750–c. 1775." In *Hanoverian Britain and Empire: Essays in Memory of Philip Lawson*, edited by Stephen Taylor, Richard Connors, and Clyve Jones, 158–76. Rochester: Boydell Press, 1998.

Braudel, Fernand. *The Wheels of Commerce.* Translated by Siân Reynolds. New York: Harper & Row, 1982.

Braverman, Harry. *Labor and Monopoly Capital: The Degradation of Work in the Twentieth Century.* 25th anniv. ed. New York: Monthly Review Press, 1998.

Bray, Francesca. *Technology and Gender: Fabrics of Power in Late Imperial China.* Berkeley: University of California Press, 1997.

Breman, Jan. *Footloose Labour: Working in India's Informal Economy.* Cambridge: Cambridge University Press, 1996.

Breman, Jan, and E. Valentine Daniel. "Conclusion: The Making of a Coolie." *Journal of Peasant Studies* 19, no. 3–4 (1992): 268–95.

Brenner, Robert. "The Origins of Capitalist Development: A Critique of Neo-Smithian Marxism." *New Left Review* I, no. 104 (1977): 25–92.

Brenner, Robert, and Christopher Isett. "England's Divergence from China's

Yangzi Delta: Property Relations, Microeconomics, and Patterns of Development." *Journal of Asian Studies* 61, no. 2 (2002): 609–62.

Bright, Charles, and Michael Geyer. "Benchmarks of Globalization: The Global Condition, 1850–2010." In *A Companion to World History*, edited by Douglas Northrop, 285–300. Chichester: Wiley-Blackwell, 2012.

Bruce, C. A. *An Account of the Manufacture of the Black Tea, as Now Practised at Suddeya in Upper Assam.* Kolkata: G. H. Huttman, Bengal Military Orphan Press, 1838.

———. *Report on the Manufacture of Tea, and on the Extent and Produce of the Tea Plantations in Assam.* Kolkata: Bishop's College Press, 1839.

Buckingham, Sir James. *A Few Facts about Indian Tea.* London: Indian Tea Association, 1910.

Burawoy, Michael. *The Politics of Production: Factory Regimes under Capitalism and Socialism.* London: Verso, 1985.

Cain, P. J., and A. G. Hopkins. *British Imperialism, 1688–2015.* 3rd ed. London: Routledge, 2016.

Cannadine, David. "The Present and the Past in the English Industrial Revolution, 1880–1980." *Past & Present*, no. 103 (1984): 131–72.

Carter, Marina. *Servants, Sirdars and Settlers: Indians in Mauritius, 1834–1874.* New Delhi: Oxford University Press, 1995.

Chan, Wellington K. K. *Merchants, Mandarins, and Modern Enterprise in Late Ch'ing China.* Cambridge: East Asian Research Center, Harvard University Press, 1977.

Chandra, Bipan. *The Rise and Growth of Economic Nationalism in India: Economic Policies of Indian National Leadership, 1880–1905.* New Delhi: People's Publishing House, 1966.

Chao, Kang. *The Development of Cotton Textile Production in China.* Cambridge: East Asian Research Center, Harvard University, 1977.

Chapman, S. D. "The Agency Houses: British Mercantile Enterprise in the Far East, c.1780–1920." *Textile History* 19, no. 2 (1988): 239–54.

Chatterjee, Partha. *The Nation and Its Fragments: Colonial and Postcolonial Histories.* Princeton: Princeton University Press, 1993.

Chatterjee, Piya. *A Time for Tea: Women, Labor and Post-Colonial Politics on an India Plantation.* Durham: Duke University Press, 2001.

Chattopādhyāy, Dakshinācharan. *Chā-Kar Darpan Nātak* (1874). In *Bānglā Nātya Sankalan*, edited by Ajitkumār Ghosh, Bishnu Basu, and Nripendra Sāhā, 1:229–53. Kolkata: Paschimbanga Nātya Ākādemi, 2001.

Chattopādhyāy, Jogendranāth. *Chā-Kulīr Ātmakāhinī.* Kolkata: Hindu Dharma Press, 1901.

Chattopādhyāy, Kānāilāl, ed. *Āsāme Chā-Kuli Āndolan O Rāmkumār Vidyāratna.* Kolkata: Papyrus, 1989.

———. "Introduction." In *Slavery in British Dominion*, edited by Sris Kumar Kunda and K. L Chattopadhyay. Kolkata: Jijnasa, 1972.

Chaudhuri, B. "Agrarian Relations: Eastern India." In *The Cambridge Economic History of India,* vol. 2, edited by Dharma Kumar and Meghnad Desai, 86–177. Cambridge: Cambridge University Press, 1983.

Chen Binfan, Yu Yue, and Guan Bowen, eds. *Zhongguo Cha Wenhua Jingdian*. Beijing: Guangming Ribao Chubanshe, 1999.

Chen Chi. *Chen Chi Ji*. Edited by Zhao Shugui and Zeng Liya. Beijing: Zhonghua Shuju, 1997.

Chen Chuan. *Anhui Cha Jing*. Hefei, Anhui: Anhui Kexue Jishu Chubanshe, 1984.

Chen Ciyu. *Jindai Zhongguo Chaye de Fazhan yu Shijie Shichang*. Nangang: Zhongyang Yanjiuyuan Jingji Yanjiusuo, 1982.

———. *Taibei Xian Chaye Fazhanshi*. Taipei: Daoxiang Chuabanshe, 1994.

Chen, Han-Seng. "Cooperatives as a Panacea for China's Ills." *Far Eastern Survey* 6, no. 7 (1937): 71–77.

Chen, Yixin. "The Guomindang's Approach to Rural Socioeconomic Problems: China's Rural Cooperative Movement, 1918–1949." PhD diss.: Washington University, 1995.

Chen Zugui and Zhu Zizhen, eds. *Zhongguo Chaye Lishi Ziliao Xuanji*. Beijing: Nongye Chubanshe, 1981.

Chiang, Yung-chen. *Social Engineering and the Social Sciences in China, 1919–1949*. Cambridge: Cambridge University Press, 2001.

Chung, Tan. "The Britain-China-India Trade Triangle, 1771–1840." *Indian Economic & Social History Review* 11, no. 4 (1974): 411–31.

Coble, Parks M. *The Shanghai Capitalists and the Nationalist Government, 1927–1937*. Cambridge: Council on East Asian Studies, Harvard University Press, 1980.

Cohen, Paul A. *Between Tradition and Modernity: Wang T'ao and Reform in Late Ch'ing China*. Cambridge: Harvard University Press, 1974.

Cohn, Bernard S. *Colonialism and Its Forms of Knowledge*. Princeton: Princeton University Press, 1996.

Crole, David. *Tea: A Text Book of Tea Planting and Manufacture*. London: Crosby Lockwood, 1897.

Das, Rajani Kanta. *Plantation Labour in India*. Kolkata: R. Chatterjee, 1931.

Dasgupta, Ajit K. *A History of Indian Economic Thought*. London: Routledge, 1993.

Davidson, Neil. "The Necessity of Multiple Nation-States for Capital." In *Nation-States: Consciousness and Competition*, 187–246. Chicago: Haymarket Books, 2016.

de Vries, Jan. *The Industrious Revolution: Consumer Behavior and the Household Economy, 1650 to the Present.* Cambridge: Cambridge University Press, 2008.

Devine, T. M. "Scotland." In *The Cambridge Economic History of Modern Britain,* vol. 1, edited by Roderick Floud and Paul Johnson, 388–416. Cambridge: Cambridge University Press, 2004.

Ding Guangping. "Yangloudong Chaqu Jindai Xiangcun Gongyehua yu Difang Shehui Jingji Bianqian." MA thesis: Huazhong Daxue, 2004.

Dirlik, Arif. "Chinese Historians and the Marxist Concept of Capitalism: A Critical Examination." *Modern China* 8, no. 1 (1982): 105–32.

Dowding, Charles. *Tea-Garden Coolies in Assam.* Kolkata: Thacker, Spink, 1894.

Du Bois, W. E. B. *Black Reconstruction in America: 1860–1880* (1935). New York: Free Press, 1998.

Dunstan, Helen. *State or Merchant?: Political Economy and Political Process in 1740s China.* Cambridge: Harvard University Asia Center, 2006.

Dutt, Romesh. *The Economic History of India: In the Victorian Age,* vol. 2. London: Kegan Paul, Trench, Trubner, 1904.

Dyce, Charles M. *Personal Reminiscences of Thirty Years' Residence in the Model Settlement Shanghai, 1870–1900.* London: Chapman & Hall, 1906.

Edgar, J. W. "Report on Tea Cultivation." In *East India (Products). Part I. Reports on the Tea and Tobacco Industries in India,* 9–27. London: George Edward Eyre and William Spottiswoode, 1874.

Edgerton, David. "Innovation, Technology, or History: What Is the Historiography of Technology About?" *Technology and Culture* 51, no. 3 (2010): 680–97.

———. *The Shock of the Old: Technology and Global History since 1900.* New York: Oxford University Press, 2007.

Eisenman, Joshua. *Red China's Green Revolution: Technological Innovation, Institutional Change, and Economic Development under the Commune.* New York: Columbia University Press, 2018.

Eley, Geoff. "Historicizing the Global, Politicizing Capital: Giving the Present a Name." *History Workshop Journal* 63, no. 1 (2007): 154–88.

Elman, Benjamin A. "Naval Warfare and the Refraction of China's Self-Strengthening Reforms into Scientific and Technological Failure, 1865–1895." *Modern Asian Studies* 38, no. 2 (2004): 283–326.

Elson, Diane. "The Value Theory of Labour." In *Value: The Representation of Labour in Capitalism,* 115–80. Reprint. London: Verso Books, 2015.

Elvin, Mark. *The Pattern of the Chinese Past.* Stanford: Stanford University Press, 1973.

Ermiş, Fatih. *A History of Ottoman Economic Thought*. London: Routledge, 2014.

Eyles, Douglas. "The Abolition of the East India Company's Monopoly, 1833." PhD diss.: University of Edinburgh, 1956.

Fan Hejun. "Tunxi Chaye Diaocha." *Guoji Maoyi Daobao* 9, no. 4 (1937): 113-35.

FAO (Food and Agriculture Organization of the United Nations). "Current Market Situation and Medium-Term Outlook, CCP:TE 18/CRS1," 17 May 2018. www.fao.org/3/BU642en/bu642en.pdf.

Farooqui, Amar. "Bombay and the Trade in Malwa Opium." In *Opium City: The Making of Early Victorian Bombay*, 17-49. Gurgaon: Three Essays Collective, 2006.

Feuerwerker, Albert. *China's Early Industrialization: Sheng Hsuan-Huai (1844–1916) and Mandarin Enterprise*. New York: Atheneum, 1970.

Fields, Barbara Jeanne. "Slavery, Race and Ideology in the United States of America." *New Left Review* I, no. 181 (1990): 95–118.

Fitzgerald, John. *Awakening China: Politics, Culture, and Class in the Nationalist Revolution*. Stanford: Stanford University Press, 1998.

Flynn, Dennis O., and Arturo Giráldez. "Born with a 'Silver Spoon': The Origin of World Trade in 1571." *Journal of World History* 6, no. 2 (1995): 201–21.

———. "Path Dependence, Time Lags and the Birth of Globalisation: A Critique of O'Rourke and Williamson." *European Review of Economic History* 8, no. 1 (2004): 81–108.

Forster, Keith. "The Strange Tale of China's Tea Industry during the Cultural Revolution." *China Heritage Quarterly*, no. 29 (2012). http://www.chinaheritagequarterly.org/features.php?searchterm=029_forster.inc&issue=029.

Fortune, Robert. *A Journey to the Tea Countries of China: Including Sung-Lo and the Bohea Hills*. London: John Murray, 1852.

———. *Three Years' Wanderings in the Northern Provinces of China*. London: John Murray, 1847.

Frank, André Gunder. *ReOrient: Global Economy in the Asian Age*. Berkeley: University of California Press, 1998.

Fraser, Nancy. *Fortunes of Feminism: From State-Managed Capitalism to Neoliberal Crisis*. London: Verso, 2013.

Fu Hongzhen. "Wan-Zhe Xin'an Jiangliuyu zhi Chaye." *Guoji Maoyi Daobao* 6, no. 7 (1934): 113–80.

Fu Yiling. "Capitalism in Chinese Agriculture: On the Laws Governing Its Development." *Modern China* 6, no. 3 (1980): 311–16.

Ganguli, Dwarkanath. *Slavery in British Dominion*. Edited by K. L. Chattopadhyay and Sris Kumar Kunda. Kolkata: Jijnasa, 1972.

Gardella, Robert. *Harvesting Mountains: Fujian and the China Tea Trade, 1757–1937*. Berkeley: University of California Press, 1994.

Ghosh, Arunabh. "Before 1962: The Case for 1950s China-India History." *Journal of Asian Studies* 76, no. 3 (2017): 697-727.

Ghosh, Durgānāth. "Paribrājakācārya Swāmī Rāmānanda" (1927). In *Āsāme Chā-Kuli Āndolan O Rāmkumār Vidyāratna*, edited by Kānāilāl Chattopādhyāy, 109–238. Kolkata: Papyrus, 1989.

Ghosh, Kaushik. "A Market for Aboriginality: Primitivism and Race Classification in the Indentured Labour Market of Colonial India." In *Subaltern Studies X: Writings on South Asian History and Society*, edited by Susie Tharu, Gautam Bhadra, and Gyan Prakash, 8–48. New Delhi: Oxford University Press, 1999.

Ghosh, Suniti Kumar. *The Indian Big Bourgeoisie: Its Genesis, Growth and Character*. Kolkata: Subarnarekha, 1985.

Goswami, Manu. *Producing India: From Colonial Economy to National Space*. Chicago: University of Chicago Press, 2004.

Greenberg, Michael. *British Trade and the Opening of China, 1800–1842*. Reprint. New York: Monthly Review Press, 1979.

Griffiths, Sir Percival Joseph. *The History of the Indian Tea Industry*. London: Weidenfeld & Nicolson, 1967.

Guha, Amalendu. "A Big Push without a Take-off: A Case Study of Assam, 1871–1901." *Indian Economic & Social History Review* 5, no. 3 (1968): 199–221.

———. "Colonisation of Assam: Second Phase 1840–1859." *Indian Economic & Social History Review* 4, no. 4 (1967): 289–317.

———. *Medieval and Early Colonial Assam: Society, Polity, Economy*. Kolkata: Published for Centre for Studies in Social Sciences, Calcutta, by K. P. Bagchi, 1991.

———. *Planter Raj to Swaraj: Freedom Struggle and Electoral Politics in Assam, 1826–1947*. Rev. ed. New Delhi: Tulika Books, 2006.

Guha, Ranajit. *A Rule of Property for Bengal: An Essay on the Idea of Permanent Settlement*. Reprint. Durham: Duke University Press, 1996.

Guo, Qitao. *Ritual Opera and Mercantile Lineage: The Confucian Transformation of Popular Culture in Late Imperial Huizhou*. Stanford: Stanford University Press, 2005.

Hamilton, Gary G., and Kao Cheng-shu. *Making Money: How Taiwanese Industrialists Embraced the Global Economy*. Stanford: Stanford University Press, 2017.

Hao, Yen-p'ing. *The Commercial Revolution in Nineteenth-Century China: The Rise of Sino-Western Mercantile Capitalism*. Berkeley: University of California Press, 1986.

———. *The Comprador in Nineteenth Century China: Bridge between East and West*. Cambridge: Harvard University Press, 1970.

Harootunian, Harry. *Marx after Marx: History and Time in the Expansion of Capitalism.* New York: Columbia University Press, 2015.

Hartwell, Robert. "Demographic, Political, and Social Transformations of China, 750–1550." *Harvard Journal of Asiatic Studies* 42, no. 2 (1982): 365–442.

Harvey, David. *The Condition of Postmodernity: An Enquiry into the Origins of Cultural Change.* Cambridge: Blackwell, 1990.

Hay, Douglas, and Paul Craven. "Introduction." In *Masters, Servants, and Magistrates in Britain and the Empire, 1562–1955,* edited by Douglas Hay and Paul Craven, 1–58. Chapel Hill: University of North Carolina Press, 2005.

Hegel, G. W. F. *The Encyclopaedia Logic* (1830). Translated by T. F. Geraets, W. A. Suchting, and H. S. Harris. Indianapolis: Hackett Publishing Company, 1991.

Hellyer, Robert. "1874: Tea and Japan's New Trading Regime." In *Asia Inside Out: Changing Times,* edited by Eric Tagliacozzo, Helen F. Siu, and Peter C. Perdue, 186–206. Cambridge: Harvard University Press, 2015.

Ho, Engseng. "Inter-Asian Concepts for Mobile Societies." *Journal of Asian Studies* 76, no. 4 (2017): 907–28.

Hoh, Erling, and Victor H. Mair. *The True History of Tea.* New York: Thames & Hudson, 2009.

Holt, Thomas C. *The Problem of Freedom: Race, Labor, and Politics in Jamaica and Britain, 1832–1938.* Baltimore: Johns Hopkins University Press, 1992.

Hommel, Rudolf P. *China at Work: An Illustrated Record of the Primitive Industries of China's Masses, Whose Life Is Toil, and Thus an Account of Chinese Civilization.* New York: John Day, 1937.

Hsiao Liang-lin. *China's Foreign Trade Statistics, 1864–1949.* Cambridge: East Asian Research Center, Harvard University Press, 1974.

Hsiung, Ping-Chun. *Living Rooms as Factories: Class, Gender, and the Satellite Factory System in Taiwan.* Philadelphia: Temple University Press, 1996.

Hu Jichuang. *A Concise History of Chinese Economic Thought.* Beijing: Foreign Languages Press, 1988.

———. *Zhongguo Jingji Sixiang Shi.* Shanghai: Shanghai Caijing Daxue Chubanshe, 1998.

Hu Shih. "The People of Hui-Chou" (1959). *Chinese Studies in History* 14, no. 4 (1981): 4–7.

Hu Wulin. *Huizhou Cha Jing.* Beijing: Dangdai Zhongguo Chubanshe, 2003.

Huang, H. T. *Fermentations and Food Science,* vol. 6, part 5 of *Science and Civilisation in China.* Edited by Joseph Needham. Cambridge: Cambridge University Press, 2000.

Huang, Philip C. C. *The Peasant Economy and Social Change in North China.* Stanford: Stanford University Press, 1985.

———. *The Peasant Family and Rural Development in the Yangzi Delta, 1350–1988.* Stanford: Stanford University Press, 1990.

Ichiko Chūzō. "Political and Institutional Reform 1901–11." In *Cambridge History of China,* vol. 11, edited by John K. Fairbank and Kwang-Ching Liu, 375–415. Cambridge: Cambridge University Press, 1980.

Imperial Maritime Customs (IMC). *Decennial Reports on the Trade, Industries, Etc. of the Ports Open to Foreign Commerce, and on Conditions and Development of the Treaty Port Provinces, 1882–1891.* Shanghai: Statistical Department of the Inspectorate General of Customs, 1893.

———. *Tea, 1888.* China. Shanghai: Statistical Department of the Inspectorate General of Customs, 1889.

James Finlay & Company Limited: Manufacturers and East India Merchants, 1750–1950. Glasgow: Jackson Son, 1951.

Jaynes, Gerald David. *Branches without Roots: Genesis of the Black Working Class in the American South, 1862–1882.* New York: Oxford University Press, 1986.

Jeffery, Roger. "Merchant Capital and the End of Empire: James Finlay, Merchant Adventurers." *Economic and Political Weekly* 17, no. 7 (1982): 241–48.

Jenkins, Francis. *Report on the North-East Frontier of India: A Documentary Study.* Edited by H. K. Barpujari. Gauhati: Spectrum Publications, 1995.

Jiang Xuekai. "Qimen Hongcha." *Nongcun Hezuo* 2, no. 3 (1937): 93–101.

Kale, Madhavi. *Fragments of Empire: Capital, Slavery, and Indian Indentured Labor Migration to the British Caribbean.* Philadelphia: University of Pennsylvania Press, 1998.

Kang, Minsoo. *Sublime Dreams of Living Machines: The Automaton in the European Imagination.* Cambridge: Harvard University Press, 2011.

Karl, Rebecca E. "Compradors: The Mediating Middle of Capitalism in Twentieth-Century China and the World." In *East-Asian Marxisms and Their Trajectories,* edited by Joyce C. H. Liu and Viren Murthy, 119–36. London: Routledge, 2017.

———. *The Magic of Concepts: History and the Economic in Twentieth-Century China.* Durham: Duke University Press, 2017.

———. *Staging the World: Chinese Nationalism at the Turn of the Twentieth Century.* Durham: Duke University Press, 2002.

Kling, Blair B. *Partner in Empire: Dwarkanath Tagore and the Age of Enterprise in Eastern India.* Berkeley: University of California Press, 1977.

Kolsky, Elizabeth. *Colonial Justice in British India.* Cambridge: Cambridge University Press, 2010.

Kopf, David. *The Brahmo Samaj and the Shaping of the Modern Indian Mind*. Princeton: Princeton University Press, 1979.

Landes, David S. *Revolution in Time: Clocks and the Making of the Modern World*. Cambridge: Belknap Press of Harvard University Press, 1983.

Lee, Ching Kwan. *Gender and the South China Miracle: Two Worlds of Factory Women*. Berkeley: University of California Press, 1998.

Lees, William Nassau. *The Land and Labour of India: A Review*. London: Williams and Norgate, 1867.

———. *A Memorandum Written after a Tour through the Tea Districts of Eastern Bengal in 1864–65*. Kolkata: Bengal Secretariat Press, 1866.

———, ed. *The Resolutions, Regulations, Despatches and Laws Relating to the Sale of Waste Lands and the Immigration of Labor in India*. Kolkata: Military Orphan Press, 1863.

———. *Tea Cultivation, Cotton and Other Agricultural Experiments in India: A Review*. London: W. H. Allen, 1863.

Leung, Hon-Chu. "Local Lives and Global Commodity Chains: Timing, Networking and the Hong Kong-Based Garment Industry, 1953–1993." PhD diss.: Duke University, 1997.

Levy, Jonathan. "Capital as Process and the History of Capitalism." *Business History Review* 91, no. 3 (2017): 483–510.

Li Bozhong. *Agricultural Development in Jiangnan, 1620–1850*. New York: St. Martin's Press, 1998.

———. "Cong 'Fufu Bingzuo' dao 'Nangeng Nüzhi': Ming-Qing Jiangnan Nongjia Funü Laodong Wenti Tantao zhi Yi." *Zhongguo Jingjishi Yanjiu*, no. 3 (1996): 99–107.

Li Jiangmin, and Li Zimao. "Lun Chen Chi de Shengchan Guan." *Jiangxi Jiaoyu Xueyuan Xuebao* 19, no. 5 (1998): 38–40.

Li, Lillian M. *China's Silk Trade: Traditional Industry in the Modern World, 1842–1937*. Cambridge: Council on East Asian Studies, Harvard University Press, 1981.

Lin Fuquan. *Wuyi Chaye zhi Shengchan Zhizhao ji Yunxiao*. Yongan: Fujian Sheng Nonglin Chu Nongye Jingji Yanjiushi, 1943.

Lin Man-houng. *China Upside Down: Currency, Society, and Ideologies, 1808–1856*. Cambridge: Harvard University Asia Center, 2006.

Ling Dating. *Zhongguo Chashui Jianshi*. Beijing: Zhongguo Caizheng Jingji Chubanshe, 1986.

Liu, Andrew B. "The Birth of a Noble Tea Country: On the Geography of Colonial Capital and the Origins of Indian Tea." *Journal of Historical Sociology* 23, no. 1 (2010): 73–100.

———. "Production, Circulation, and Accumulation: The Historiographies of Capitalism in China and South Asia." *Journal of Asian Studies*. Forthcoming.

———. "The Two Tea Countries: Competition, Labor, and Economic Thought in Coastal China and Eastern India, 1834–1942." PhD diss.: Columbia University, 2014.

———. "The Woman Question and the Agrarian Question: The Feminist and Political-Economic Writings of Wu Juenong, 1921–1927." *Twentieth-Century China* 43, no. 1 (2018): 24–44.

Liu Yong. *The Dutch East India Company's Tea Trade with China, 1757–1781*. Leiden: Brill, 2007.

Lu Chengxi. "Wo de Zishu" (1951). In *Jiangsu Wenshi Ziliao Xuanji*, 18:124–51. Nanjing: Jiangsu Renmin Chubanshe, 1986.

———. See Lu Ying.

Lu, Weijing. "Beyond the Paradigm: Tea-Picking Women in Imperial China." *Journal of Women's History* 15, no. 4 (2004): 19–46.

Lu Ying. *Diaocha Guonei Chawu Baogaoshu*. 1910.

———. "Lu Ying jiu Woguo Chaye Shuaibai Qingxing zhi Shiyebu Cheng" (1931). In *Zhonghua Minguoshi Dang'an Ziliao*, edited by Zhongguo Di'er Lishi Dang'anguan, 5.1, Caizheng Jingji no. 8:867–74. Nanjing: Jiangsu Guji Chubanshe, 1994. See Lu Chengxi.

———. "Yisinian Diaocha Yin-Xi Chawu Riji" (1909). In *Tang-Song-Yuan-Ming-Qing Cangshi Shiliao Huibian*, edited by Zhang Yuxin and Zhang Shuangzhi, vol. 69. Beijing: Xueyuan Chubanshe, 2009.

———. See Lu Chengxi.

Lufrano, Richard John. *Honorable Merchants: Commerce and Self-Cultivation in Late Imperial China*. Honolulu: University of Hawai'i Press, 1997.

Lukács, György. "Reification and the Consciousness of the Proletariat" (1923). In *History and Class Consciousness: Studies in Marxist Dialectics*, translated by Rodney Livingstone. Cambridge: MIT Press, 1971.

Lutgendorf, Philip. "Making Tea in India: Chai, Capitalism, Culture." *Thesis Eleven* 113, no. 1 (2012): 11–31.

Lyons, Thomas P. *China Maritime Customs and China's Trade Statistics, 1859–1948*. Trumansburg: Willow Creek, 2003.

Ma Yinchu. "Zhongguo zhi Maiban Zhi." *Dongfang Zazhi* 20, no. 6 (1923): 129–32.

MacGregor, John. *Commercial Statistics: A Digest of the Productive Resources, Commercial Legislation, Customs Tariffs . . . of All Nations*, vol. 5. London: Whittaker, 1850.

Mantena, Karuna. *Alibis of Empire: Henry Maine and the Ends of Liberal Imperialism*. Princeton: Princeton University Press, 2010.

Mao Tun. *Midnight* (1933). Translated by Hsu Meng-hsiung. 2nd ed. Beijing: Foreign Languages Press, 1979.

Mao Zedong. "Analysis of the Classes in Chinese Society" (1926). In

Selected Works of Mao Tse-Tung, vol. 1, 13–21. Oxford: Pergamon Press, 1965.

———. "On the People's Democratic Dictatorship" (1949). In *Selected Works of Mao Tse-Tung*, vol. 4, 411–24. Oxford: Pergamon Press, 1961.

Marshall, P. J. *East Indian Fortunes: The British in Bengal in the Eighteenth Century*. Oxford: Clarendon Press, 1976.

Marx, Karl. *Capital: A Critique of Political Economy*, vol. 1 (1867). Translated by Ben Fowkes. Reprint. New York: Penguin Classics, 1990.

———. *Capital: A Critique of Political Economy*, vol. 3 (1894). Translated by David Fernbach. Reprint. New York: Penguin Classics, 1991.

———. *Grundrisse: Foundations of the Critique of Political Economy* (1859). Translated by Martin Nicolaus. Reprint. New York: Penguin Books, 1993.

Marx, Karl, and Friedrich Engels. *Collected Works*. Vol. 34. New York: International Publishers, 1994.

———. "Manifesto of the Communist Party" (1848). In *The Marx-Engels Reader*, edited by Robert Tucker, 469–501. 2nd ed. New York: W. W. Norton, 1978.

McCants, Anne E. C. "Poor Consumers as Global Consumers: The Diffusion of Tea and Coffee Drinking in the Eighteenth Century." *Economic History Review* 61, no. 1 (2008): 172–200.

McGuire, John. *The Making of a Colonial Mind: A Quantitative Study of the Bhadralok in Calcutta, 1857–1885*. Canberra: Australian National University, 1983.

McKeown, Adam. "How the Box Became Black: Brokers and the Creation of the Free Migrant." *Pacific Affairs* 85, no. 1 (2012): 21–45.

———. *Melancholy Order: Asian Migration and the Globalization of Borders*. New York: Columbia University Press, 2011.

Meek, Ronald L. *The Economics of Physiocracy: Essays and Translations*. Reprint. London: Routledge, 2003.

———. *Studies in the Labour Theory of Value*. 2nd ed. New York: Monthly Review Press, 1975.

Merkel-Hess, Kate. *The Rural Modern: Reconstructing the Self and State in Republican China*. Chicago: University of Chicago Press, 2016.

Metcalf, Thomas R. *Ideologies of the Raj*. Cambridge: Cambridge University Press, 1995.

Mintz, Sidney W. *Sweetness and Power: The Place of Sugar in Modern History*. New York: Viking, 1985.

Money, Edward. *The Cultivation & Manufacture of Tea*. 4th ed. London: W. B. Whittingham, 1883.

Morris-Suzuki, Tessa. *A History of Japanese Economic Thought*. London: Routledge, 1989.

Mui, Hoh-cheung, and Lorna H. Mui. *The Management of Monopoly: A Study of the English East India Company's Conduct of Its Tea Trade, 1784–1833*. Vancouver: University of British Columbia Press, 1984.

———. "'Trends in Eighteenth-Century Smuggling' Reconsidered." *Economic History Review* 28, no. 1 (1975): 28–43.

Muller, Jerry Z. *Adam Smith in His Time and Ours: Designing the Decent Society*. New York: Free Press, 1993.

Needham, Joseph. *Science in Traditional China: A Comparative Perspective*. Cambridge: Harvard University Press, 1981.

Nie Baozhang. *Zhongguo Maiban Zichan Jieji de Fasheng*. Beijing: Zhongguo Shehui Kexue Chubanshe, 1979.

O'Brien, Patrick K. "Deconstructing the British Industrial Revolution as a Conjuncture and Paradigm for Global Economic History." In *Reconceptualizing the Industrial Revolution*, edited by Jeff Horn, Leonard N. Rosenband, and Merritt Roe Smith, 21–46. Cambridge: MIT Press, 2010.

Ogle, Vanessa. "Whose Time Is It? The Pluralization of Time and the Global Condition, 1870s–1940s." *American Historical Review* 118, no. 5 (2013): 1376–1402.

O'Rourke, Kevin H., and Jeffrey Williamson. "Once More: When Did Globalisation Begin?" *European Review of Economic History* 8, no. 1 (2004): 109–17.

———. "When Did Globalisation Begin?" *European Review of Economic History* 6, no. 1 (2002): 23–50.

Pal, Bipin Chandra. *Memories of My Life and Times* (1932). New Delhi: UBSPD, 2004.

Pan Ming-te. "Rural Credit in Ming-Qing Jiangnan and the Concept of Peasant Petty Commodity Production." *Journal of Asian Studies* 55, no. 1 (1996): 94–117.

Parthasarathi, Prasannan. *Why Europe Grew Rich and Asia Did Not: Global Economic Divergence, 1600–1850*. Cambridge: Cambridge University Press, 2011.

Peebles, Patrick. *The Plantation Tamils of Ceylon*. London: Leicester University Press, 2001.

Peng Nansheng. *Ban Gongyehua: Jindai Zhongguo Xiangcun Shougongye de Fazhan yu Shehui Bianqian*. Beijing: Zhonghua Shuju, 2007.

Peng Zeyi, ed. *Zhongguo Jindai Shougongye Shi Ziliao, 1840–1949*, vol. 1. Beijing: Sanlian Shudian, 1957.

Perdue, Peter C. *China Marches West: The Qing Conquest of Central Eurasia*. Cambridge: Belknap Press of Harvard University Press, 2005.

———. *Exhausting the Earth: State and Peasant in Hunan, 1500–1850*. Cambridge: Council on East Asian Studies, Harvard University Press, 1987.

Perelman, Michael. "The Curious Case of Adam Smith's Pin Factory: Another Look at Smith's Famous Pin Factory," lecture, 2014. https://michaelperelman.files.wordpress.com/2014/06/smith.docx.

———. *The Invention of Capitalism: Classical Political Economy and the Secret History of Primitive Accumulation*. Durham: Duke University Press, 2000.

Perlin, Frank. "Proto-Industrialization and Pre-Colonial South Asia." *Past & Present*, no. 98 (1983): 30–95.

Pincus, Steve. "Neither Machiavellian Moment nor Possessive Individualism: Commercial Society and the Defenders of the English Commonwealth." *American Historical Review* 103, no. 3 (1998): 705–36.

Polanyi, Karl. *The Great Transformation: The Political and Economic Origins of Our Time*. Reprint. Boston: Beacon Press, 1957.

Pomeranz, Kenneth. "Beyond the East-West Binary: Resituating Development Paths in the Eighteenth-Century World." *Journal of Asian Studies* 61, no. 2 (2002): 539–90.

———. *The Great Divergence: China, Europe, and the Making of the Modern World Economy*. Princeton: Princeton University Press, 2000.

———. "Labour-Intensive Industrialization in the Rural Yangzi Delta: Late Imperial Patterns and Their Modern Fates." In *Labour-Intensive Industrialization in Global History*, edited by Gareth Austin and Kaoru Sugihara, 122–43. London: Routledge, 2013.

———. *The Making of a Hinterland: State, Society, and Economy in Inland North China, 1853–1937*. Berkeley: University of California Press, 1993.

Pomeranz, Kenneth, and Steven Topik. *The World That Trade Created: Society, Culture, and the World Economy, 1400 to Present*. 2nd ed. Armonk, N.Y.: M. E. Sharpe, 2006.

Pong, David. "The Vocabulary of Change: Reformist Ideas of the 1860s and 1870s." In *Ideal and Reality: Social and Political Change in Modern China, 1860–1949*, edited by David Pong and Edmund S. K. Fung, 25–62. Lanham, Md.: University Press of America, 1985.

Post, Charles. "Capitalism, Laws of Motion and Social Relations of Production." *Historical Materialism* 21, no. 4 (2013): 71–91.

Postone, Moishe. "Anti-Semitism and National Socialism: Notes on the German Reaction to 'Holocaust.'" *New German Critique*, no. 19 (1980): 97–115.

———. *Time, Labor, and Social Domination: A Reinterpretation of Marx's Critical Theory*. Cambridge: Cambridge University Press, 1993.

Pritchard, Earl Hampton. *Anglo-Chinese Relations during the Seventeenth and Eighteenth Centuries*. Reprint. New York: Octagon Books, 1970.

Quanguo Jingji Weiyuanhui Nongyechu, ed. *Yindu Xilan zhi Chaye*. Nanjing: Quanguo Jingji Weiyuanhui, 1936.

Quesnay, François. "Despotism in China" (1767). In *China, a Model for Europe*, edited and translated by Lewis A. Maverick, 139–304. San Antonio, Tex.: Paul Anderson, 1946.

Rappaport, Erika. *A Thirst for Empire: How Tea Shaped the Modern World*. Princeton: Princeton University Press, 2017.

Report of the Seventeenth Indian National Congress Held at Calcutta, on the 26th, 27th & 28th December, 1901. Kolkata: W. C. Nundi at the Wellington Printing Works, 1902.

Richards, John F. "The Indian Empire and Peasant Production of Opium in the Nineteenth Century." *Modern Asian Studies* 15, no. 1 (1981): 59–82.

———. "The Opium Industry in British India." *Indian Economic & Social History Review* 39, no. 2–3 (2002): 149–80.

Robins, Nick. *The Corporation That Changed the World: How the East India Company Shaped the Modern Multinational*. London: Pluto Press, 2006.

Rothschild, Emma. "Political Economy." In *The Cambridge History of Nineteenth-Century Political Thought*, edited by Gareth Stedman Jones and Gregory Claeys, 748–79. Cambridge: Cambridge University Press, 2011.

Rowe, William T. *Hankow: Commerce and Society in a Chinese City, 1796–1889*. Stanford: Stanford University Press, 1984.

———. *Saving the World: Chen Hongmou and Elite Consciousness in Eighteenth-Century China*. Stanford: Stanford University Press, 2001.

Roy, Tirthankar. *India in the World Economy: From Antiquity to the Present*. Cambridge: Cambridge University Press, 2012.

Royal Commission on Labour in India. *Report of the Royal Commission on Labour in India*. London: His Majesty's Stationery Office, 1931.

Rubin, Isaak Illich. *Essays on Marx's Theory of Value* (1928). Translated by Miloš Samardžija and Fredy Perlman. Reprint. Montreal: Black Rose Books, 1976.

Rungta, Shyam. *The Rise of Business Corporations in India, 1851–1900*. London: Cambridge University Press, 1970.

Sahlins, Marshall David. "Cosmologies of Capitalism: The Trans-Pacific Sector of 'The World System.'" In *Culture in Practice: Selected Essays*, 415–70. New York: Zone Books, 2000.

Saito, Osamu. "Proto-Industrialization and Labour-Intensive Industrialization: Reflections on Smithian Growth and the Role of Skill Intensity." In *Labour-Intensive Industrialization in Global History*, edited by Gareth Austin and Kaoru Sugihara, 85–106. London: Routledge, 2013.

Sarkar, Sumit. *Modern India, 1885–1947*. New Delhi: Macmillan, 1983.

———. *The Swadeshi Movement in Bengal, 1903–1908*. New Delhi: People's Publishing House, 1973.

Sarkar, Tanika. *Hindu Wife, Hindu Nation: Community, Religion, and Cultural Nationalism*. New Delhi: Permanent Black, 2001.

Sartori, Andrew. *Bengal in Global Concept History: Culturalism in the Age of Capital*. Chicago: University of Chicago Press, 2008.

———. "Global Intellectual History and the History of Political Economy." In *Global Intellectual History*, edited by Samuel Moyn and Andrew Sartori. New York: Columbia University Press, 2013.

———. *Liberalism in Empire: An Alternative History*. Berkeley: University of California Press, 2014.

Schivelbusch, Wolfgang. *Tastes of Paradise: A Social History of Spices, Stimulants, and Intoxicants*. Translated by David Jacobson. New York: Vintage Books, 1993.

Schmalzer, Sigrid. *Red Revolution, Green Revolution: Scientific Farming in Socialist China*. Chicago: University of Chicago Press, 2016.

Schumpeter, Joseph A. *History of Economic Analysis*. Edited by Elizabeth Boody Schumpeter. New York: Oxford University Press, 1954.

Scott, James C. *The Art of Not Being Governed: An Anarchist History of Upland Southeast Asia*. New Haven: Yale University Press, 2009.

Seal, Anil. *The Emergence of Indian Nationalism: Competition and Collaboration in the Later Nineteenth Century*. London: Cambridge University Press, 1968.

Sell, Zachary. *Capital through Slavery: U.S. Settler Slavery and the British Imperial World*. Chapel Hill: University of North Carolina Press. Forthcoming.

Sen, Samita. "Commercial Recruiting and Informal Intermediation: Debate over the Sardari System in Assam Tea Plantations, 1860–1900." *Modern Asian Studies* 44, no. 1 (2010): 3–28.

———. "Gender and Class: Women in Indian Industry, 1890–1990." *Modern Asian Studies* 42, no. 1 (2008): 75–116.

———. "Questions of Consent: Women's Recruitment for Assam Tea Gardens, 1859–1900." *Studies in History* 18, no. 2 (2002): 231–60.

———. *Women and Labour in Late Colonial India: The Bengal Jute Industry*. Cambridge: Cambridge University Press, 1999.

Sen, Sudipta. *Empire of Free Trade: The East India Company and the Making of the Colonial Marketplace*. Philadelphia: University of Pennsylvania Press, 1998.

Sewell, William H. "The Temporalities of Capitalism." *Socio-Economic Review* 6, no. 3 (2008): 517–37.

Sha Weikai. *Zhongguo Maiban Zhi*. Shanghai: Shangwu Yinshuguan, 1927.

Shaikh, Anwar. *Capitalism: Competition, Conflict, Crises*. New York: Oxford University Press, 2016.

Shanghai Shangye Chuxu Yinhang Diaochabu, ed. *Cha?* Shanghai: Shanghai Shangye Chuxu Yinhang Xintuobu, 1931.

Sharma, Jayeeta. *Empire's Garden: Assam and the Making of India*. Durham: Duke University Press, 2011.

Sheriff, Abdul. *Slaves, Spices, & Ivory in Zanzibar: Integration of an East African Commercial Empire into the World Economy, 1770–1873*. Athens: Ohio University Press, 1987.

Shigeta Atsushi. *Shindai Shakai Keizaishi Kenkyū*. Tokyo: Iwanami Shoten, 1975.

Shui Haigang. "Jindai Minjiang Liuyu Jingji yu Shehui Yanjiu (1861–1937)." PhD diss.: Xiamen Daxue, 2006.

Smith, Adam. *An Inquiry into the Nature and Causes of the Wealth of Nations* (1776). Edited by Edwin Cannan. New York: Modern Library, 1994.

———. *Lectures on Jurisprudence* (1762–1766). Edited by R. L. Meek, D. D. Raphael, and P. G. Stein. Oxford: Clarendon Press, 1978.

Smith, Neil. *Uneven Development: Nature, Capital, and the Production of Space*. 3rd ed. Athens: University of Georgia Press, 2010.

Smith, Woodruff D. *Consumption and the Making of Respectability, 1600–1800*. New York: Routledge, 2002.

Steinberg, Marc W. "Marx, Formal Subsumption and the Law." *Theory and Society* 39, no. 2 (2010): 173–202.

Steinfeld, Robert. *Coercion, Contract, and Free Labor in the Nineteenth Century*. Cambridge: Cambridge University Press, 2001.

Stokes, Eric. *The English Utilitarians and India*. Oxford: Clarendon Press, 1959.

Stone, Irving. *The Global Export of Capital from Great Britain, 1865–1914: A Statistical Survey*. New York: St. Martin's Press, 1999.

Subrahmanyam, Sanjay. "Connected Histories: Notes towards a Reconfiguration of Early Modern Eurasia." *Modern Asian Studies* 31, no. 3 (1997): 735–62.

Sugihara, Kaoru. "The Resurgence of Intra-Asian Trade, 1800–1850." In *How India Clothed the World: The World of South Asian Textiles, 1500–1850*, edited by Giorgio Riello and Tirthankar Roy, 139–69. Leiden: Brill, 2009.

———. "The Second Noel Butlin Lecture: Labour-Intensive Industrialisation in Global History." *Australian Economic History Review* 47, no. 2 (2007): 121–54.

Sun Wenyu, Liu Runtao, and Wang Fuchou, eds. *Qimen Hongcha zhi Shengchan Zhizao ji Yunxiao*. Nanjing: Jinling Daxue Nongye Jingji Xi Yinhang, 1936.

———, eds. *Tunxi Lücha zhi Shengchan Zhizao ji Yunxiao*. Nanjing: Jinling Daxue Nongye Jingji Xi Yinhang, 1936.

Tang Yongji and Wei Deduan. *Fujian zhi Cha*, vol. 1. Yongan: Fujian Sheng Zhengfu Tongjichu, 1941.

Thompson, E. P. "Time, Work-Discipline, and Industrial Capitalism." *Past & Present*, no. 38 (1967): 56–97.

Tōa Dōbunkai. *Shina Shōbetsu Zenshi*. 18 vols. Tokyo: Tōa Dōbunkai, 1917–1922.

Trocki, Carl A. *Opium and Empire: Chinese Society in Colonial Singapore, 1800–1910*. Ithaca: Cornell University Press, 1990.

Tsai, Jung-fang. "The Predicament of the Comprador Ideologists." *Modern China* 7, no. 2 (1981): 191–225.

Tsuchiya Keizō. *Baiben Seido*. Tokyo: Shina Keizai Kenkyūjo, 1940.

Ukers, William H. *All about Tea*, vol. 1. New York: Tea and Coffee Trade Journal Company, 1935.

van der Meer, Arnout. "From a Colonial to a Patriotic Drink: Tea and National Identity in Late Colonial Indonesia." Paper presented at the conference "Tea High and Low: Elixir, Exploitation and Ecology," Cornell University, 2018.

Van Schendel, Willem. *A History of Bangladesh*. Cambridge: Cambridge University Press, 2009.

Vidyāratna, Rāmkumār. *Kuli Kāhinī* (1888). *Sketches of Coolie Life*. Kolkata: Yogamāyā Prakāsanī, 1982.

———. "Udāsīn Satyasrabār Āsām Bhraman" (1881). In *Āsāme Chā-Kuli Āndolan O Rāmkumār Vidyāratna*, edited by Kānāilāl Chattopādhyāy, 3–106. Kolkata: Papyrus, 1989.

Vitalis, Robert. "On the Theory and Practice of Compradors: The Role of Abbud Pasha in the Egyptian Political Economy." *International Journal of Middle East Studies* 22, no. 3 (1990): 291–315.

Wakefield, Edward Gibbon. "England and America: A Comparison of the Social and Political State of Both Nations" (1833). In *The Collected Works of Edward Gibbon Wakefield*, edited by M. F. Lloyd Prichard, 311–636. London: Collins, 1968.

Wakeman, Fredric, Jr. "The Canton Trade and the Opium War." In *The Cambridge History of China*, vol. 10, edited by John K. Fairbank, 163–212. Cambridge: Cambridge University Press, 1978.

Walker, Kathy Le Mons. *Chinese Modernity and the Peasant Path: Semicolonialism in the Northern Yangzi Delta*. Stanford: Stanford University Press, 1999.

Wallerstein, Immanuel. *The Modern World-System III: The Second Era of Great Expansion of the Capitalist World-Economy, 1730s–1840s*. Reprint. Berkeley: University of California Press, 2011.

Wang Tingyuan, and Zhang Haipeng. *Huishang Yanjiu*. New ed. Beijing: Renmin Chubanshe, 2010.

Wang Xufeng. *Cha zhe Sheng: Wu Juenong Zhuan*. Hangzhou: Zhejiang Renmin Chubanshe, 2003.

Ward, J. R. "The Industrial Revolution and British Imperialism, 1750–1850." *Economic History Review* 47, no. 1 (1994): 44–65.

Weber, Max. "The Protestant Ethic and the 'Spirit' of Capitalism (1905)." In *The Protestant Ethic and the "Spirit" of Capitalism and Other Writings*, translated by Peter Baehr and Gordon C. Wells, 1–202. New York: Penguin Books, 2002.

Wenzlhuemer, Roland. *From Coffee to Tea Cultivation in Ceylon, 1880–1900: An Economic and Social History*. Leiden: Brill, 2008.

White, J. Berry. "The Indian Tea Industry: Its Rise, Progress during Fifty Years, and Prospects Considered from a Commercial Point of View." *Journal of the Society of Arts* (10 June 1887): 734–51.

Wong, R. Bin. *China Transformed: Historical Change and the Limits of European Experience*. Ithaca: Cornell University Press, 1997.

Wright, Mary Clabaugh. *The Last Stand of Chinese Conservatism: The T'ung-Chih Restoration, 1862–1874*. 2nd ed. Stanford: Stanford University Press, 1962.

Wu Juenong. *Wu Juenong Xuanji*, edited by Zhongguo Chaye Xuehui. Shanghai: Shanghai Kexue Jishu Chubanshe, 1987.

———. "Zhongguo de Nongmin Wenti." *Dongfang Zazhi* 19, no. 16 (1922): 2–20.

Wu Juenong and Fan Hejun. *Zhongguo Chaye Wenti*. Shanghai: Shangwu Yinshuguan, 1937.

Wu Juenong and Hu Haochuan. "Qihong Chaye Fuxing Jihua." *Guoji Maoyi Daobao* 5, no. 11 (1933): 37–54.

———. *Zhongguo Chaye Fuxing Jihua*. Shanghai: Shangwu Yinshuguan, 1935.

Wu Shan. "Guai Maiban." *Minzhong Wenxue* 8, no. 4 (1924): 1–12.

Yang Liansheng. *Zhongguo Wenhua zhong "Bao," "Bao," "Bao" zhi Yiyi*. Hong Kong: Zhongwen Daxue Chubanshe, 1987.

———. See Yang, Lien-sheng.

Yang, Lien-sheng. "Schedules of Work and Rest in Imperial China." *Harvard Journal of Asiatic Studies* 18, no. 3/4 (1955): 301–25.

———. See Yang Liansheng.

Ye Yaoyuan. "Wanguo Huozhi Lun." In *Huangchao Jingshi Wen Xinbian* (1898), edited by Mai Zhonghua, 2:515–25. Reprint. Taipei: Wenhai Chubanshe, 1972.

Yeh, Wen-hsin. *Shanghai Splendor: Economic Sentiments and the Making of Modern China, 1843–1949*. Berkeley: University of California Press, 2007.

Zanasi, Margherita. *Saving the Nation: Economic Modernity in Republican China*. Chicago: University of Chicago Press, 2006.

Zhang Dengde. *Qiufu yu Jindai Jingjixue Zhongguo Jiedu de Zuichu Shijiao: "Fuguo Ce" de Yikan yu Chuanbo.* Hefei: Huangshan Shushe, 2009.

———. *Xunqiu Jindai Fuguo zhi Dao de Sixiang Xianqu: Chen Chi Yanjiu.* Ji'nan: Qi-Lu Shushe, 2005.

Zhang Wei. "Guanyu Pingli Hezuoshe." In *Pingli Chaye Yunxiao Xinyong Hezuo Baogao,* edited by Anhui Shengli Chaye Gailiangchang, 23–26. Qimen: Dawen Yinshuasuo, 1934.

Zhao Jing and Shi Shiqi, eds. *Zhongguo Jingji Sixiang Tongshi Xuji: Zhongguo Jindai Jingji Sixiangshi.* Beijing: Beijing Daxue Chubanshe, 2004.

Zhao Jing and Yi Menghong, eds. *Zhongguo Jindai Jingji Sixiang Ziliao Xuanji,* vol. 2. Beijing: Zhonghua Shuju, 1982.

Zheng Guanying. *Shengshi Weiyan* (1894), edited by Chen Zhiliang. Shenyang: Liaoning Renmin Chubanshe, 1994.

Zheng Huixin. "Zhanqian 'Tongzhi Jingji' Xueshuo de Taolun jiqi Shijian." *Nanjing Daxue Xuebao,* no. 1 (2006): 86–100.

Zhuang Wanfang. *Zhongguo Cha Shi Sanlun.* Beijing: Kexue Chubanshe, 1988.

Zou Yi. *Ming-Qing yilai de Huizhou Chaye yu Difang Shehui (1368–1949).* Shanghai: Fudan Daxue Chubanshe, 2012.

Index

Page numbers followed by "f" and "n" indicate figures and notes, respectively.